RAISE YOUR GLASSES

A Celebration of 50 Years of KISS Songs by Celebrities, Musicians & Fans.

Published by Shout It Out Loudcast & Satta Entertainment.
Written by Tom Gigliotti, George Piandes & Joey Cassata.
Book design by Joey Cassata.
Cover design by Jeff Trott.
Edited by Nige Savage.

Editor's Note:
The editing of the interviews in this work has been carefully designed to
preserve as far as possible the original intent and "voice" of the interviewees,
even at the (occasional) expense of correct grammar.

Tom would like to thank...

First, I want to thank KISS for being a part of my life for over 40 years and for giving me such joy and happiness over that time. Because of them, I have been blessed to have started Shout It Out Loudcast.

I need to thank the one and only Zeus. He is not only my co-host, but also my KISS brother and my friend. We have shared so much over the years, both personally and in the world of our podcast. Without him, there is no Shout It Out Loudcast, nor this book you're holding. His tireless efforts editing each episode, scheduling interviews and always picking the right soundbite to make our shows even better is what separates us from everyone else.

I also want to thank my friend, Joey Cassata. His enormous efforts to get this book organized and into print proves that he can do more than just play drums and take care of his beautiful hair. It's been an honor to be his friend and to share this experience with him.

I also need to thank my friends and the entire Loudcaster family. Without their never-ending support and encouragement, Shout It Out Loudcast would not be the same, and neither would this book. And my gratitude towards all of them during the worst time of my life in 2022 can never be put into words. I want to specifically mention John "Murph" Murphy for being the very first guest to ever appear on SIOL, and our biggest supporter. He's the brother I never had in so many ways.

I also want to thank each and every contributor to this book. The relationships we've fostered over the years because of this podcast and KISS have allowed us to create this incredible book you're holding right now. Special thanks to: longtime friend and supporter, Jeff Trott, for his amazing artwork and design, especially the front and back covers. Our friend and supporter overseas, Nige Savage,

for his editorial skills. And fellow author, friend and supporter, James Campion, a huge KISS fan himself who spent so much time helping us get the book off the ground and answered every question we had.

Lastly and most importantly, I need to thank my family. My son Michael for always thinking it was "cool" that I had this podcast and this book, and for making him a little more interested in KISS. And also for making it all come full circle as he joined me for a few KISS concerts over the years. My mom for actually becoming quite a big KISS fan – even to the point of seeing a KISS tribute band in her retirement years! I also want to thank my late dad, who always indulged my KISS fandom from day one and got a kick out of how much I loved them, even as an adult.

And finally, my late wife, Bridget. This book is dedicated to her. Her encouragement and support when this podcast took off years ago is one of the main reasons I am still here today talking KISS and having fun with it. I know she would've been so proud of what we've accomplished.

"EVERYBODY'S GOT A REASON TO LIVE. EVERYBODY'S GOT A DREAM AND A HUNGER INSIDE"

Zeus would like to thank...

I dedicate this book to my hero, my dad Teddy.

First and foremost, I would like to thank my family. To my daughter Natalia, who is my favorite person in the whole world. Thank you for being supportive of my KISS fandom and of Shout It Out Loudcast, and for listening to my KISS stories and music in the car. To my Greek parents for allowing me to listen to KISS and letting me become a fan at the tender age of about 4, despite never understanding what KISS was all about. To my older brother Kerry, along with many cousins who initially helped me discover KISS – especially my cousin Mike, who reintroduced me to the then non-makeup KISS while visiting Detroit and seeing *Animalize Live Uncensored* for the first time.

Thanks to my college friend, KISS brother, and Shout It Out Loudcast co-host, Tom. It was fate that brought us together that day as Freshmen at Stonehill College in Pitts South at O'Hara Hall. I can't imagine life, with or without SIOL, without you in it. Nobody is on the same page as much as me and Tom are. We share the same sense of humor, passion and philosophy on life and KISS. Tom may be the straight man to my crazy act, but he is the funniest person I know. My whole goal on Shout It Out Loudcast has always been to make Tom laugh. If I can make that happen, then I can help make SIOL a fun show. Thank you for being the rock of SIOL and my best friend.

Thanks to Joey Cassata. We love to bust balls with each other, but meeting Joey has been one of the best parts of SIOL. This book would not be possible without Joey. Thank you for your invaluable contributions, knowledge, and work ethic. You are truly a SIOL Hall Of Famer!

Thanks to Murph, Jeff Trott, Nige Savage and James Campion for all your help on *Raise Your Glasses*. Thank you for the advice, input and work that you each put into the book. I can't thank you enough.

Thanks to all the contributors to *Raise Your Glasses*. To all the people that emailed their songs, did Zoom calls, voice memos and just took the time out of their schedule to help with our KISS project. This book is OUR testament to the power of KISS music.

Thanks to our Loudcaster family, especially our Patreons. Your support is why SIOL is the #1-ranked KISS podcast, and why we work so hard to give you the type of content YOU deserve. Your support means everything to Tom and me, and we will always do our best to keep you listening and laughing.

Finally, thank you to KISS. Thank you for 50 years of entertainment and being there for us… the fans.

"RAISE YOUR GLASSES!!"

Joey would like to thank…

I want to send a loving thank you to my family, starting with my beautiful wife, Madalyn, whose support and encouragement have been the backbone of my journey. Her support through every crazy project and endeavor means everything. My family's presence is my greatest source of strength. To them, I say, "Without you, I am nothing."

I also want to express my deep gratitude to my fans, who are always there to embrace my next thing. Your dedication has fueled my passion and driven me to push boundaries and pursue my dreams.

A special thank you to every person who contributed to this book. This seemed like a massive undertaking when we started it, but you are the ones who really made it possible.

And of course, the one and only Tom & Zeus. We may love to rag on each other, but these two have really become like brothers to me. Working on this book with them has been a real honor. This has really been a labor of love by the three of us. Tom & Zeus may be idiots, but they are MY idiots, goddammit!!

This book is dedicated to my children, Angelina and Joe. I encourage you to remember that you hold the power to achieve anything you set your minds to. As you journey through life, I want you to always believe in the magic of your dreams and to reach for the stars with unwavering determination and resilience. Papa loves you always.

"THEY SAID I DIDN'T STAND A CHANCE, I WOULDN'T WIN, NO WAY. BUT I'VE GOT NEWS FOR YOU, THERE'S NOTHING I CAN'T DO"

BruceKulick

Foreword By:

BRUCE KULICK
of
KISS

When I got the opportunity to become the new guitarist in KISS, my life transformed. Those years touch my life every day. I didn't realize then what an impact the music I helped create and perform would make upon so many fans. Defining what KISS means to a fan is nearly impossible. For so many of them, it is a part of their everyday life. I am forever grateful for my relationship to the band, and its fans. In Raise Your Glasses, Tom and Zeus, along with Joey Cassata have presented stories, insights and reflections of every song from KISS spanning 5 decades. From iconic classics that have stood the test of time to the lesser-known gems waiting to be discovered, this book offers a comprehensive journey through the band's unparalleled discography. To the devoted members of the KISS Army who have stood by the band through fifty years of highs and lows, this book is a tribute to their unwavering dedication and passion. Raise Your Glasses serves as a fitting celebration of the band's remarkable journey and the enduring legacy of their music. As I reflect upon my own experiences with KISS and the profound influence their music has had on my life and career, I am reminded of the power of the band. How it unites, inspires, and transcends boundaries. KISS's music has always been more than just songs. It's a celebration of freedom, individuality, and the unbreakable spirit of rock and roll.

Let's raise our glasses to fifty years of KISS songs, and remember that "God Gave Rock 'N' Roll to You".

- Bruce Kulick

INTRODUCTION

The story goes that when KISS was formed, they wanted to be the band that they wanted to see.

In 2019, two best friends set out to create the podcast that they wanted to hear. Not just *any* podcast – a KISS podcast. KISS has probably the most podcasts of any band out there, so why did the KISS world need another one?

From the introduction, Shout It Out Loudcast (Tom came up with the name) immediately told their listeners they were lifelong KISS fans, but that they weren't in the business of giving KISS foot rubs. This KISS podcast was going to have strong opinions. It would be honest.

However, the real uniqueness of the podcast comes from the undeniable chemistry between Tom and Zeus, and their shared sense of humor. They figure that KISS is all about fun, and should never be boring or too academic. They've been proved right. Within a few years, these two working professionals, with no music background, industry connections or podcasting experience have risen to become the world's #1-ranked KISS podcast on Apple Podcasts.

While KISS is known for their incredible live shows, the makeup, the costumes and more, in the end none of their success would have been possible without their MUSIC. On the 50th anniversary of their debut album, Shout It Out Loudcast wanted to commemorate the occasion by focusing on KISS's incredible music. Therefore, they decided on a

KISS book that would break down KISS songs as Shout It Out Loudcast does on their KISS album review episodes.

But why stop at just two podcasters' opinions? What about the opinions of some of the amazing guests who've appeared on Shout It Out Loudcast – the musicians, actors, TV and radio presenters, comedians, wrestlers, podcasters and more? Tom and Zeus enlisted the help of their favorite New Yorker, Joey Cassata, to join in this endeavor. Joey has the same work ethic, sense of humor, love of KISS and no-holds-barred strong opinions as Tom and Zeus.

The result is this book, *Raise Your Glasses* (Tom again coming up with the name). *Raise Your Glasses* boasts well over 1,500 comments, covering every KISS song, from over 100 contributors, including three members of KISS – Gene Simmons, Ace Frehley, and Bruce Kulick – nine KISS songwriters, and so much more. This book has been a labor of love, with constant interviews, transcriptions, brainstorming sessions and more.

Raise Your Glasses is the kind of KISS book that Tom, Zeus and Joey would want to read – a testament to the undeniable greatness of KISS and their music. So, let's celebrate KISS on their 50th anniversary, and Raise Your Glasses!

TABLE OF CONTENTS

RAISE YOUR GLASSES:
A Celebration of 50 Years of KISS Songs
by Celebrities, Musicians & Fans.

CHAPTER I

"KISS"

Released: February 18, 1974

KISS's self-titled debut album marked the birth of one of the most iconic rock bands in history. This self-produced record introduced audiences to the larger-than-life personas and explosive live performances that would become the band's signature. With its raw energy, catchy riffs, and anthemic choruses, *KISS* laid the foundation for the band's enduring career and established them as pioneers of glam and hard rock.

In an era dominated by disco, soft rock, and progressive rock, KISS emerged as a thunderous force with their eponymous debut album. Released on February 18, 1974, KISS brought a shot of adrenaline to the music scene. The album featured a striking cover, showcasing the band's iconic face-painted personas: The Demon (Gene Simmons), The Starchild (Paul Stanley), The Spaceman (Ace Frehley), and The Catman (Peter Criss).

From the opening track, "Strutter," it was clear that KISS meant business. The song's heavy guitar riffs and catchy melodies set the tone for the album. Songs like "Nothin' to Lose" and "Firehouse" blended hard rock with a glam rock sensibility, boasting memorable hooks and sing-along choruses. These tracks established KISS as masters of creating anthems designed to be played loud and enjoyed with a rebellious spirit.

KISS was a relatively straightforward record compared to some of the band's later, more elaborate works. Still, it captured the essence of KISS's early years, which was all about unapologetic rock 'n' roll, larger-than-life personas, and a commitment to delivering an unforgettable live experience.

While the album didn't immediately catapult KISS to superstardom, it laid a solid foundation for their future success. It showcased their potential and garnered a dedicated fan base that would grow exponentially in the years to come. KISS's self-titled debut album is a testament to the power of rock 'n' roll and the enduring appeal of a band that would go on to become rock legends.

STRUTTER

EDDIE TRUNK *(RADIO DJ & TV PERSONALITY)* – It's the first song on the first record and it's still a song that I love. Something about the song that totally conjures up the 1970s 42nd Street New York City. There's so much of a swagger and an attitude, and a very '70s seedy NYC vibe.

BRYCE MILETO *(SISTERS DOLL)* – Killer iconic drum intro! People always get the drumbeat wrong… It's a straight 4x4 beat in the verses and throughout. Listen to the drums carefully on the first KISS record, you'll know what I mean. Peter taught me this himself.

BOBBY ROCK *(VINNIE VINCENT INVASION, LITA FORD)* – Back in the '70s, the corner market in my neighborhood had a modest display of albums for sale near the register. One day, I walked in and saw the infamous debut KISS record, with those four painted faces jumping off that stark black background. *"What the fuck?"* I thought. I suppose my reaction, at 11 years old, was precisely what the Casablanca crew was going for. I snagged a copy for $4.95, then fifteen minutes later, the opening track, "Strutter," became my indoctrination to the band. I dug the album, but was initially underwhelmed by its lack of heaviness, given the vibe of the cover, as well as my being such a huge Sabbath fan at the time (of course, this would be rectified with *Alive!* in due time). Cut to a few years later: as a freshman, I was asked to play at the high school talent show with a group of seniors who had a band called… you guessed it, Strutter. Our short set featured my first public drum solo for the school, and a rendition of… you guessed it, "Strutter." This performance was a game-changer in my life, so this tune will always hold a good deal of sentiment for me. Great song!

RAISE YOUR GLASSES:
A Celebration of 50 Years of KISS Songs
by Celebrities, Musicians & Fans.

CHARLIE BENANTE *(ANTHRAX)* – It's such a signature song, such a Paul song.

AHMET ZAPPA *(MUSICIAN)* – The fucking groove and jam to me, it's classic KISS. This first record came out the year I was born. I feel like the moment I saw those action figures and saw their faces it was just all encompassing, my superior love for this band. But as the years have gone by, when seeing them live, I was impressed every single time they played "Strutter". Everyone gets up on their feet. It's an undeniable groove. I think it's a prototypical melody and a great example of Paul crushing the verses. And then band coming in on the choruses and you know, just a classic KISS song. If you don't like "Strutter", then you don't like KISS. (I don't know if this is true or not, but I would think that the song "Firehouse" inspired Ian Astbury from the Cult to write "Fire Woman", and then he started wearing fire helmets with skulls on them, which are so bad ass.)

MISTRESS CARRIE *(RADIO DJ)* – Drop the needle on side A and this is what you hear first. I've always said rock 'n' roll wouldn't exist if women weren't bitches, and right out of the gate KISS wanted to put women front and center. If you took away all of the songs written about women, the KISS catalog would be a LOT smaller than it is!

RICHIE RANNO *(STARZ)* – Great opening riff, great lyrics & catchy chorus.

RAISE YOUR GLASSES:
A Celebration of 50 Years of KISS Songs
by Celebrities, Musicians & Fans.

NOTHIN' TO LOSE

BILL STARKEY *(FOUNDER, KISS ARMY)* – What a proposition. At first you want to join in on this "sing-along song" with its cheesy, well-placed piano in the backdrop. (Yes, a KISS song with a piano). Everything is fine 'till you hear something about "the backdoor" and you realize it has nothing to do with being locked out of your home. Gene has written many books. I only wish his penis would write one too!

WES BEECH *(THE PLASMATICS)* – I had seen pictures of KISS in *Rock Scene* magazine when it first came out and they were lumped in with bands on the NY punk rock scene at the time. I was intrigued and bought their debut album when it came out, and as a fledgling guitarist I loved the rhythmic guitar interplay between Paul and Ace; this is something not talked about as most reviews emphasize Ace's solos, but his rhythm work really stood out to me. I like the whole record but the song that stands out to me is the one where the Ringo of the group, Peter, takes over on vocals, "Nothin' to Lose". From the cowbell-powered intro to the fiery Ace solo, this song just sizzles and was always a crowd pleaser live. Not until years later did I learn it was about backdoor love, which has only heightened my appreciation of it!

RICHIE RANNO *(STARZ)* – My favorite song on the debut album. "You got, you got, you got nothin' to lose." More catchy choruses and guitar licks and riffs.

JASON BAKKEN *(COBRAS & FIRE PODCAST)* – I'm not sure if I should be impressed or repulsed that as a 7-year-old KISS had me singing a song about butt sex. Great riff. Great early, raw vocal from Gene. In many ways the perfect KISS song.

ZEUS *(SHOUT IT OUT LOUDCAST)* – This song was the first single from KISS, the first duet and the first to feature a non-KISS member (Bruce Foster on piano). The only song that Gene and Peter share vocals. The chorus was so catchy I thought it had to be a cover. Peter's vocals make this song. Hearing him passionately wail during the chorus is just one of the reasons he's my favorite KISS member. The studio, *Alive!* and *MTV Unplugged* versions are all incredible. Plus, it's about the "back door."

FIREHOUSE

TOM GIGLIOTTI *(SHOUT IT OUT LOUDCAST)* – Many people gravitate towards the *Alive!* version, and rightfully so. But for me, I love the slow and sleazy groove of the studio version. Paul's vocals and the separation of the bass, drums and guitars sounds amazing. People complain about the thin production on this album, but I love these versions because you can feel the youth and the rawness of the band.

AHMET ZAPPA *(MUSICIAN)* – This song is interesting to me. When I hear it, Gene's bass line sticks out and I'm so locked in. That's one of the things about KISS; unique characters playing their instruments in a unique way. You really can identify each member's playing style. Also, "Firehouse" is such a seminal part of their early theatrics on stage. When that siren came on and the red lights flashed, smoke covering the stage... then Gene stepped out and

blew fire. Holy shit, it felt dangerous. It felt like rock 'n' roll panic
– without any real disasters onstage.

Zeus with his brother Kerry, Halloween 1978

KEITH ROTH *(SIRIUS XM, THE DICTATORS)* – The first record
will always be my favorite, the birth of KISStory! Seeing KISS live
and you heard the opening riff to "Firehouse", you know what's
coming. Gene breathing fire, sirens, red lights… YES!!! Watching

them doing this on *The Mike Douglas Show* had such a profound impact on me!!

BRITT LIGHTNING *(VIXEN)* – When I started my first band, Jaded, we rehearsed all the time at a studio in Boston. I'd always hear this band jamming KISS songs down the hall, they sounded great. One night after rehearsal I heard "Firehouse" and decided to follow the sound. I found the studio where these KISS songs were coming from and when the song was over, I popped my head inside. To my surprise, the whole studio was a shrine to KISS. That song led me to make some lifelong friends that I could always count on to jam some KISS with!

NEIL DAVIS *(CREATURES FEST, KISS AMERICA)* – For me, the version of this song on the original debut KISS album was low energy and lethargic. But that all changed with *Alive!* Over the years, "Firehouse" has been performed countless times and includes Gene's fire breathing. A real historic moment for this song was when KISS performed for the first time on national TV, appearing on *The Mike Douglas Show*. The now famous interview features Gene looking very nervous while answering questions about the band while also being ridiculed by comedian Totie Fields. After the interview and commercial break, Mike Douglas introduces the entire band and they perform "Firehouse".

COLD GIN

STEVE VAI *(SOLO ARTIST, DAVID LEE ROTH, WHITESNAKE)* – One of my favorites, I liked playing everything off of *Alive!* That was the era I was a teenager and really exploring that stuff and I've been a fan ever since. It was great music, the melodies and the chords worked. The music is good music, it's got melody, it's got attitude.

JOEL HOEKSTRA *(WHITESNAKE, TRANS-SIBERIAN ORCHESTRA)* – Fast forward to around 2013. I had been playing with Night Ranger for about 5-6 years at this point. We were asked to perform at a Rock N Roll Memorabilia Museum. Part of the deal was at various points we would be joined by Bun E. Carlos, George Lynch and Ace Frehley!!! So, this event was actually held in a pretty small room that was all wood. Ace straight-up dimed his Marshall (that's slang for putting everything on 10) and asked for it even louder in the monitors before we finally rocked this epic song. It's the loudest I've ever heard a guitar in my life. As it should be. What better way to lose some of your hearing than jamming this? I'm just a kid from suburban Chicago and here I am, one of 4 guitarists onstage... the other 3 are Brad Gillis, George Lynch and Ace Frehley. I might add that Ace was so nice to me. We'd never met and he initiated a conversation with me backstage and even complimented me after. So, this anthem will forever hold a special place in my heart.

RAISE YOUR GLASSES:
A Celebration of 50 Years of KISS Songs by Celebrities, Musicians & Fans.

Joel Hoekstra with Paul Stanley

BRIAN TICHY *(THE DEAD DAISIES, GENE SIMMONS BAND)* – One of their best riffs! The middle jam riff is also killer! The live arrangement is awesome. Why is Peter's snare strainer off on the *Alive!* version? Maybe it broke but the take was good.

MARTIN POPOFF *(AUTHOR)* – This undeniable KISS classic was the first song ever written for the band by Ace, and that narrative has stuck ever since, to the point of many a KISS fan forgetting that it's actually Gene that sings it. That mental slip is exacerbated by the fact that Gene sounds kinda like Ace in terms of vocal phrasing and melody, and that he's singing about booze. Let's take a moment to notice that Ace, Peter and Gene all had cool voices and that each sung with a fair degree of vocal fry, all more than Paul, who wasn't averse to vocal fry either, but who had more of a clean and technical singer's voice. Still, Gene was every bit the pro-shot singer that Paul was, even if our track at hand finds him actually slumming it a bit.

GREG PRATO *(AUTHOR, Take It Off: KISS Truly Unmasked* **and** *The Eric Carr Story)* – A rock song about the enjoyment of alcohol sung by a gentleman who has been a teetotaler all his life? It turns out that although it's Gene Simmons providing lead vocals, its composer was a few albums away from finding the confidence to sing his own compositions – Ace Frehley.

JAMES CAMPION *(AUTHOR, Shout It Out Loud – The Story of KISS's Destroyer and the Making of an American Icon)* – Is this the best pure riff in a KISS song? Yes, it is. And it keeps coming. It has about four different riffs and they all work. Ace's contribution to my list – everyone has to have an Ace song and it doesn't get much better than this. But it's Gene who is the MVP here. His mid-verse descending bass line is a tasty surprise, but when he sings "the cheapest stuff is all I need" I believe him, even now, understanding he has never sipped gin and probably never will. His loss. Gin rules. And this song rules right beside it. I heard Ace recently give Gene credit for that outstanding breakdown change, which vaults it into this Top Ten list. The *Alive!* version again is simply sublime. The band is revving on all cylinders, a tight, ballsy tour de force assault with titanic fills from Peter and one of Ace's great leads. When I saw them on the comeback tour in 1996 at Madison Square Garden, "Cold Gin" was the highlight.

LET ME KNOW

TODD KERNS *(BRUCE KULICK, SLASH)* – It is my feeling after many years that the 1ˢᵗ album may be my favorite KISS album and in fact may be one of the best debut albums of all time, up there with *Appetite for Destruction*, *Led Zeppelin 1* or Boston's debut. 99% of the songs on the first album could be played live today and we'd be thrilled: "Deuce", "Strutter", "Firehouse", "Nothin' to Lose", "Cold Gin", "100,000 Years" and "Black Diamond" are all straight up mainstays. In fact, "Kissin' Time", "Love Theme From KISS" and "Let Me Know" are the only songs that didn't cycle through the set list on a regular basis. "Let Me Know" has always been special to me as it is, by all accounts, one of the first songs Gene and Paul ever put together, if not THE first, under the title "Sunday Driver". Paul wrote it but Gene sings it, which is not the norm. "God Of Thunder" is a similar story. I have always loved the big *a cappella* vocal at the end that seems to be multiple layers of Paul's voice before launching into the guitar solo outro that was later attached to the end of "She" on *Alive!* I think I love it because it Is a bit of a lost stepchild from a powerhouse of an album. Although the mix on the album lacks a bit, the first album is still a monster collection of songs.

JOE McGINNESS *(KUARANTINE, KLASSIK '78)* – Love how Paul and Gene trade off lines. Just basic meat and potatoes rock 'n' roll and just great vocal harmonies together – and of course the ending is untouchable.

RAISE YOUR GLASSES:
A Celebration of 50 Years of KISS Songs
by Celebrities, Musicians & Fans.

Joe McGinness, age 12

$TEVE WRIGHT *(PODDER THAN HELL PODCAST)* – The KISStorical significance of this song can't be understated. It started out as "Sunday Driver", Paul played it for Gene and the partnership was struck. I've always loved the head-bobbing feel to this and the fact that Gene and Paul both take lead vocals in different verses was always one of my favorite elements of the band. Ace plays a really laid-back solo and it's actually one of the longest on the album. And we can't forget the coda that just jams and would be used on the end of "She" that we know from *Alive!*

ZACH THRONE *(COREY TAYLOR, BRUCE KULICK)* – Great trade-off vocal between Paul and Gene. Cool gospel *a capella* ending, and then Ace's great outro riff jam.

BILL STARKEY *(FOUNDER, KISS ARMY)* – A hidden gem revealed to us decades later when played unplugged for us! Like "Got To Choose", the guy is asking his lady to "decide and let me know." Anytime Simmons and Stanley share vocals, "it's gold, Jerry."

Bill Starkey with Paul Stanley

TOM HIGGINS *(KLASSIK '78)* – The first time I heard this wasn't until 1982. My girlfriend's brother had the first album on cassette. She let me borrow it (without telling her brother). I was blown away hearing this. Love this song! Makes me think of NYC and how Paul and Gene were a team.

KISSIN' TIME

BRYCE MILETO *(SISTERS DOLL)* – I'm a sucker for the first KISS record. Love this tune and the 3rd verse is the best, hearing Peter belt it!!!

JOE McGINNESS *(KUARANTINE, KLASSIK '78)* – A super-underrated track. It truly shows the raw energy of the original four. The way that they can take a basic bubblegum pop song and make it kick major ass proves their greatness.

ROBERT CONTE *(AUTHOR)* – Casablanca Records founder Neal Bogart had KISS cover this song for promotion and later added it to their first album. Co-producers Kenny Kerner and Richie Wise's effort to ensure the production of this track remained consistent on the LP's overall sound is exceptional. Its slower-tempo, heavier rendition of Bobby Rydell's pop original was fresh by having Gene Simmons, Paul Stanley, and Peter Criss sing each verse individually. This song feels like a true team effort. I once asked Gene if he knew how the song's composers, Karl Mann and Bernie Lowe, felt about KISS's cover, and he replied: "Very good. They get songwriting royalty checks." I laughed.

COURTNEY CRONIN DOLD *(COMEDIAN)* – Isn't it always? KISS's badass version of this Bobby Rydell song is like "Dancing in the Street" meets the Bay City Rollers. I love KISS's covers of the oldies and this song does its job. Best part? Peter's vocals in the middle, that's where this song really becomes KISS to me. "Let's all do it in Detroit..." – a little foreshadowing?

SHANDON SAHM *(MEAT PUPPETS)* – It was my very first introduction to KISS. Dad brought it home after Neil Bogart gave him a copy. I just remember rocking out on bed doing air guitar. I was like four or five maybe? I remember the heavy riff and double-time backbeat, and what stuck with me at an early age was the band was KISS and the lyrics said KISS. They truly had such a brilliant swing and swagger. Early hungry KISS is the best.

ZEUS *(SHOUT IT OUT LOUDCAST)* – I love KISS songs where two or more members share vocals. Yes, I know they didn't want this on the album, but I am glad it made it. I love the guys naming cities throughout the country on this Bobby Rydell cover. As usual for me, Peter steals this one. Catchy as all hell.

DEUCE

ACE FREHLEY – My favorite KISS song? Off the top of my head, "Deuce". It's the first KISS song I actually heard; it's got a soft spot in my heart. They kept playing the solo section over like ten times and I just kept riffing and riffing and riffing. Paul said to me at the end of session, "We'll get back to you in 2 weeks," but he told me not that long ago, they knew right away that I was the guy, but they just said that I think because they had a lot of other people that were going to audition for the band and they didn't want to snub them.

RAISE YOUR GLASSES:
A Celebration of 50 Years of KISS Songs
by Celebrities, Musicians & Fans.

CHARLIE BENANTE *(ANTHRAX)* – A show starter. In the '70s, a lot of these bands were using what I call "Rolling Stones" chords and KISS used it in pretty much every song.

Charlie Benante with Gene Simmons

CHRIS CAFFERY *(TRANS-SIBERIAN-ORCHESTRA, SAVATAGE)* – Three words. Changed my life... The first two records I purchased with my own money were Boston and KISS *Alive!* The same day, way back in the year *Alive!* came out. I had heard of KISS but as a very young child I didn't know much about them. I heard that first song and it made me inspired enough to make sure my life and career came out exactly the way they did. Just raw power and energy that excited me to a new level!

PJ FARLEY *(TRIXTER, FOZZY)* – What got me right away was the opening line. "Get up and get your grandma outta here" – that just jumps out and grabs your attention, plus live it has the signature choreography!

RAISE YOUR GLASSES:
A Celebration of 50 Years of KISS Songs
by Celebrities, Musicians & Fans.

MISTRESS CARRIE *(RADIO DJ)* – I have mentioned my love of Peter Criss already, and this song put the drums on display. I love the fills, and spent so much time playing air drums to it growing up, it had to be mentioned.

BILL STARKEY *(FOUNDER, KISS ARMY)* – What classic rock song mentions your granny then hits you between the eyes? When we would bring fresh recruits to see KISS for the first time, it was this song that made EVERYONE stand up and pledge allegiance to the KISS Army. The studio version never had the same effect. You had to SEE and HEAR this live. It will always have a special place for me as a fan.

Bill Starkey

JEFF PLATE *(TRANS-SIBERIAN ORCHESTRA, SAVATAGE)* – July 11, 1975 was the night my life changed. KISS performed on *The Midnight Special* and they opened the performance with "Deuce", and I was in orbit from there on. I was too young to really understand what had hit me, but the sound of the band, the look of the band, and the attitude of the band won me over. Regardless of what Gene is singing about – does anyone really know? – it was the perfect opener.

MARTIN POPOFF *(AUTHOR)* – It's heavy BTO-ish songs like "Deuce" that did much of the heavy lifting in terms of KISS garnering respect from budding metalheads back in 1974, and Gene increases the excitement already there from the riff with a thespian, committed vocal. It all culminates in the "You know your man is working hard/He's worth a deuce!" punctuated refrain, and then we're back to that curious geometric riff.

LOVE THEME FROM KISS

ZEUS *(SHOUT IT OUT LOUDCAST)* – It evolved from a song called "Acrobat", where they would sing "You're much too young." But on this album, it comes across like '70s porn music. One of the few tracks where all four members get a writing credit.

GARY "ACTION" JACKSON *(UGLY AMERICAN WEREWOLF IN LONDON PODCAST)* – Sandwiched between two hard rockers, "Deuce" and "100,000 Years" on the debut record, it gives the listener a chance to take a break and groove. I can't help but think that this one could easily have been used for a mid-'70s adult film intro.

PETER DANKELSON *(PETE'S DIARY)* – A rocking instrumental track that everyone has a moment to shine on. I love how Paul and

Ace harmonize over the riff and how there are breaks that Gene gets to fill in with the bass. Some of the fills that Peter does are tasteful and sound really cool.

COURTNEY CRONIN DOLD *(COMEDIAN)* – Who needs words with two guitars more "N Sync" than Justin Timberlake and Joey Fatone. It feels like a scene from a '70s cop movie. You know, the one where the cop is getting ready to go to a disco, then runs into some bad guys on the way? So he kicks some ass, shows up at the club with a little blood on his tie, then gets funky with the ladies. Has someone said this already?

CHRIS "THE WALLET" HAICK *(GENE SIMMONS MONEYBAG SODA)* – Although "Love Theme From KISS" is traditionally not my favorite track from the debut album, I've learned to love it after hearing it as the intro to "Acrobat" (Live at the Daisy) from the 2001 Box Set. The heavier sound and feel takes it up a few notches and makes it much more likable.

TOM GIGLIOTTI *(SHOUT IT OUT LOUDCAST)* – I'm a fan of instrumentals and although this one may seem boring to some people, I find it fascinating, especially when you consider the connection it has to early KISS and the performance of "Acrobat" at their early shows. It's groovy and something you don't really see again from the band. In that sense, I enjoy its uniqueness.

Tom, Zeus and Murph, Stonehill College, 1994

100,000 YEARS

BRIAN TICHY *(THE DEAD DAISIES, GENE SIMMONS BAND)* – Another unique KISS song. Most don't say much about it, but KISS had a nice selection of shuffle grooves! This, "Detroit Rock City", "Love Gun", etc… Gene and Peter are swinging hard, and once again Ace delivers super-memorable solos! And Paul's vocal is outstanding. It's a unique arrangement, and live, this turned into the ultimate rock 'n' roll sermon! This became unique to KISS and is still as powerful today as it was back then in all its crowd-rallying excitement!

RAISE YOUR GLASSES:
A Celebration of 50 Years of KISS Songs by Celebrities, Musicians & Fans.

Brian Tichy with Peter Criss

JEREMY ASBROCK *(ACE FREHLEY)* – To me, this song destroys the narrative that KISS can't play and isn't creative musically. Every member is bringing something to the table in this song. The bass line is one of the first things I play if I ever pick up a bass. The beat, with the ghost notes on the snare isn't your average, basic drum beat. Ace's solo is very unorthodox, particularly after the section with the bends. Even his rhythm parts are smoking, with the little lead bit over the title tag. The fact that a 22-year-old kid came up with that is pretty unreal. Paul's counterpart on guitar is very complementary, if not the driver. Even lyrically, it runs a little deeper than your average "Room Service" or "Love Gun". The song is like a showcase of every member's strengths.

RAISE YOUR GLASSES:
A Celebration of 50 Years of KISS Songs
by Celebrities, Musicians & Fans.

BOBBY ROCK *(VINNIE VINCENT INVASION, LITA FORD)* – It was nearly impossible to be a young drummer in the mid-'70s and not be influenced by the Catman's memorable drum solo on this track. There was no video to see back then, but as you connected the dots between those gleaming silver Pearl drums, stationed just under that massive KISS logo, and the "flanged cannon" sound of those toms... it all seemed otherworldly—like the motherfucker just stepped off a spaceship and started pounding. A year later, "the professor" would permanently disrupt the drumming world with his *All The World's a Stage* solo with Rush. But Neil's shit, at that time, seemed too out of reach to play. Peter's solo stuff was a bit more relatable and, certainly, idiom-appropriate for the kind of arena rock KISS was doing. But between Criss and Peart, my fate was sealed for my first brand new kit: a chrome, 13-piece Pearl Octaplus. Hell, yes!

PAUL JANIK *(GENE SIMMONS MONEYBAG SODA)* – This song has everything. The menacing opening bass, screaming guitars, badass drum solo and Paul's energetic rant that tells everybody to "Stand up for what you believe in!!!". This song simply can't be beat.

RUSSELL PETERS *(COMEDIAN)* – Live version because as a kid I always wanted to be a drummer, my parents got me a practice pad and I would do the drum solo with that. I would rock out in my basement to that.

AUSTIN MILETO *(SISTERS DOLL)* – I love how this song shows the incredible musicianship between all 4 original members. You really hear the chemistry they had together, they were untouchable. Ace Frehley's guitar work was on another level!

BLACK DIAMOND

MIKE PORTNOY *(DREAM THEATER, WINERY DOGS)* – As far as I'm concerned, it is the quintessential KISS song. Of course, it was always the show closer with Peter Criss' drum riser going up in the air. Probably one of Peter's best vocal performances. My favorite song off the first album and definitely one of my all-time favorites.

Mike Portnoy with Peter Criss

RAISE YOUR GLASSES:
A Celebration of 50 Years of KISS Songs
by Celebrities, Musicians & Fans.

EDDIE TRUNK *(RADIO DJ & TV PERSONALITY)* – It's the ultimate set closer. I remember hearing the studio version first and that droning end. You've got the dual vocals with Paul singing the beginning and Peter singing the bulk of the song. The soft intro going into the explosiveness of the song. I really used to love it when they played it live when I would see them. It's got the sound and the attitude.

ACE VON JOHNSON *(FASTER PUSSYCAT, L.A. GUNS)* – Again, a masterfully crafted piece of music that paints a picture while drawing us in before giving you a kick in the chest. Their debut LP holds so many classics but for me, this is the standout track. Paul screaming "Hit it!" is as cool as it gets. An absolute tour de force from a band who had already set the bar pretty damn high for a debut LP. Definitely one of my favorite songs in their catalog.

CHRIS "THE WALLET" HAICK *(GENE SIMMONS MONEYBAG SODA)* – This song has it all! Paul's opening riff, Peter's raspy voice, Ace's killer guitar solo and Gene's constant bass slides are just off the charts! There's so much feeling and passion in this song. You really see and feel it in the 1975 *Midnight Special* video. It gives me chills every time I watch it and see Ace drop to his knees during his passionate solo. By far my favorite KISS song. God only knows that if I had a time machine, I'd go back to '75 and see KISS perform.

MISTRESS CARRIE *(RADIO DJ)* – I remember a band at my high school covering this song at a Battle of the Bands. It has everything, Oooohs, cowbell, and is a time capsule of the early '70s sound. Just when you think it's over... it's not! I thought it was a weird song for a band to cover, especially the last minute, but it's epic!

RAISE YOUR GLASSES:
A Celebration of 50 Years of KISS Songs by Celebrities, Musicians & Fans.

BRYCE MILETO *(SISTERS DOLL)* – Such a hard-hitting track that touches my soul in every way.

JEFF PLATE *(TRANS-SIBERIAN ORCHESTRA, SAVATAGE)* – Recorded the same night as "Deuce", April 1,1975, "Black Diamond" was not aired until later that year, on November 28. I had impatiently waited for months to see KISS again on *The Midnight Special* and this did not disappoint. Probably my all-time favorite KISS song, the intro with Paul on vocals, and then the band exploding into the verse with Peter on vocals was, and is still, amazing. The best part being the end of the song, with the drum set rising into the air, the explosions, and then Peter destroying his kit. I had recorded both of these performances on a General Electric cassette recorder and listened to them over and over until I purchased *Alive!*

JAMES CAMPION *(AUTHOR, Shout It Out Loud – The Story of KISS's Destroyer and the Making of an American Icon)* – "Black Diamond" defines early KISS. The damn title alone is worth the price of admission. And while the studio version from the first album is less dynamic than *Alive!* – and what isn't?? – this is, again, a perfectly structured KISS composition. Its soft opening of street laments eases us into a false state of inertia until "Hit it!" and the daunting hammer chords, killer drum fills, double-harmony leads, and Peter Criss doing his bluesy, smoky vocal thing elevates this baby to greater heights. Give me his "Black diamond!" scream at the end and I am one satisfied customer. The gothic breakdown that inspired the famous Ace on his knees wailing out those brain-bending lead notes while Gene and Paul swing their instruments toward him conjures the coolest images in a KISS song. And the bombastic ending? It just cries K-I-S-S. Magnificent. If I have any reason to drag a fence-sitter into KISS-land I just show them the *Midnight Special* performance of "Black Diamond" from 1975. A hungry, wild, unrepentant American rock band stomping the terra.

RAISE YOUR GLASSES:
A Celebration of 50 Years of KISS Songs
by Celebrities, Musicians & Fans.

CHAPTER 2

"HOTTER THAN HELL"

Released: October 22, 1974

Hotter Than Hell, the second studio album, brought another dose of high-octane, in-your-face rock 'n' roll. Building on the success of their self-titled debut, this album pushed the boundaries of their signature sound, delivering heavier riffs and darker themes.

The album erupts with "Got To Choose," an anthem that grabs the listener by the throat. It's a statement of intent, setting the tone for the rest of the album. "Parasite" follows, showcasing Gene Simmons' growling vocals and driving bass line, epitomizing KISS's edgier, hard-rocking side.

But *Hotter Than Hell* isn't just about high-energy rockers. "Goin' Blind" reveals the band's willingness to explore darker, more introspective themes. Gene Simmons' haunting vocals add depth to the album, showcasing the band's versatility.

As with their debut album, *Hotter Than Hell* wasn't an instant commercial hit. But it cemented KISS's reputation as a formidable live act and a band unafraid to push the boundaries of rock 'n' roll. Their theatrical stage presence, face-painted personas, and unforgettable live shows started to define them as much as their music did.

Hotter Than Hell remains an essential part of KISS's catalog, capturing a band in the midst of their ascent to rock stardom.

GOT TO CHOOSE

JEREMY ASBROCK *(ACE FREHLEY)* – "Got To Choose" is an overlooked great. After backing Gene and Ace, Ryan Cook, Phil Shouse, and myself were getting booked to play lots of KISS-related events. This was one of our standards because there is a lot of three-part harmony through the song. You don't realize what an amazing, melodic, memorable guitar solo it has until you put it under a microscope. Then when you really check out what Peter is playing on the chorus, you can hear that he was a very creative drummer and made KISS a little different than your average rock band. The song is very strong, and when you realize it was written by a 22-year-old, you can see there's a little more to KISS than makeup, smoke, and flash pots.

BRENNEN MILETO *(SISTERS DOLL)* – I've always loved this song, probably one of my favorite KISS songs. From the storyline of the lyrics, to the amazing minor guitar intro, and Ace's melodically cool simple solo make this song amazing. The studio version is a little slow in my opinion, but the live versions are all amazing.

CHARLIE BENANTE *(ANTHRAX)* – Such a great song and when it got the *Alive!* treatment, it became another animal.

RAISE YOUR GLASSES:
A Celebration of 50 Years of KISS Songs
by Celebrities, Musicians & Fans.

Sisters Doll at a KISS concert

BILL STARKEY *(FOUNDER, KISS ARMY)* – "I know you need a change of pace. But I ain't gonna run no race." Not a typical KISS song due to the way it is paced. But still a problem most couples become faced with. I always liked it live when they sung "Who's your baby?" and pointed to certain people in the crowd.

HAL SPARKS *(COMEDIAN)* – One of the greatest early examples of KISS as a band. Harmony parts and lead vox interacting so organically you don't even notice the work that went into it. This is the song that defines "making it look easy" when it clearly took dedication and lots of rehearsal. Also, this song more than any other introduced the world to Ace's vibrato.

Bill Starkey with Gene Simmons and Paul Stanley

ZACH THRONE *(COREY TAYLOR, BRUCE KULICK)* – My all-time favorite KISS song. Just a great power pop song. Very catchy. Clever call and response vocals in the verses and I love the falsetto choruses. Paul sounds so great. Great poppy solo by Ace. Cool ending too. I prefer the *Alive!* version, but this is its first appearance. 10/10.

PARASITE

MATT STARR *(ACE FREHLEY)* – Such a peculiar-sounding riff. I love how the vocal follows the guitar chords. Some of Peter's finest drumming. He has a way of playing drum rolls that are musical while supporting the guitar and vocal. My favorite song to play with Ace.

JEREMY ASBROCK *(ACE FREHLEY)* – Energy. KICK-ASS riff. More proof that Peter Criss is a great drummer. What he chooses to play in the verses is unlike what most drummers would play. Lots of ghost notes happening on the beat during the riff. This is one of Peter's stand-out KISS songs to me. So good, in fact, that KISS still does this Ace Frehley classic to this day. Playing this song with Gene was an amazing life highlight. Playing the riff with a great band is one thing, but hearing that voice come in… holy shit! And then getting to play that great solo right next to him is the cherry on top. Having the opportunity to play it with Ace also, is the stuff KISS dreams are made of.

BELLA PERRON *(PLUSH)* – "Parasite" is another song that always reminds me why KISS is the reason I started playing guitar. The riff is so catchy, and paired with Gene's vocals it has a darker heavier sound that I love. Going into the solo you hear all of the trademarks that make Ace's style so iconic – the big bends, the repeating licks, and the best vibrato ever!

BRIAN TICHY *(THE DEAD DAISIES, GENE SIMMONS BAND)* – I just love the riff! It's perfect! So catchy! The chorus is such a great place to go after the verse. Gene kills the vox! Ace's solo is great! And this is a great example of Peter NOT playing like a hard rock, metal drummer. He gives us this "boogaloo swing" that gives KISS its unique groove and swagger, setting them apart from most heavy rock bands. Peter's drumming enhances KISS's music and it just adds a nice "party" flavor to it all! It's an intangible thing that Peter deserves way more credit for!

RAISE YOUR GLASSES:
A Celebration of 50 Years of KISS Songs
by Celebrities, Musicians & Fans.

ROXY PETRUCCI *(VIXEN)* – I jammed this tune with Ty Tabor from King's X and his feel and groove was so infectious it took on a whole new life for me.

CHARLIE BENANTE *(ANTHRAX)* – Such a heavy song that Ace comes up with.

DALE TORBORG *(THE DEMON WCW)* – One of my all-time favorite songs to this day. That groove is absolutely amazing. Every time I hear that it gets my juices flowing. It was one of the hardest songs in their catalog.

MARTIN POPOFF *(AUTHOR)* – Seems fitting that the evilest bat-winged creature in the band would howl away on the heaviest KISS song across the first three albums. But "Parasite" is another Ace Frehley-penned track, with the Space Ace still reticent to sing a lead vocal of his own. So, it's up to the resident Viking marauder to do the dirty deed, which he does with aplomb, abdicating the job of vocal melody and just banging heads directly with Ace's rocky riff, whether we're dealing with the verse or the more expansive and grooving chorus.

JASON HOOK *(FIVE FINGER DEATH PUNCH)* – I'm sure a lot of people picked this song. The guitar riff is just heavy and awesome. I believe this was an Ace Frehley composition. In the early days Ace was too insecure to sing it hence the Gene Simmons lead vocal.

GOIN' BLIND

MATT STARR *(ACE FREHLEY)* – The only melancholy KISS song ever. This is pure Gene. As a kid I was so confused by this lyric, but as I get older, I really like it. I hear the Cream influence in this one. I love Paul's harmony vocal too.

AHMET ZAPPA *(MUSICIAN)* – I don't quite know what the song is about. I'm 93 and you're 16. I mean, is it about an old man talking to his 16-year-old nephew or something? I don't know. But I think it's just about jacking off constantly and going blind. And that's why I think I originally liked the song. I was like, wow, the God of Thunder is singing about this story I made up in my mind. It's him cranking his Thunder Dong to *Penthouse* magazine or *Playboy* or whatever. And this became one of those like, "Oh yeah, they really write about sex a lot" moments for me. And that's cool. Really, it's pure rock 'n' roll.

HAL SPARKS *(COMEDIAN)* – Literalists will wince at the lyrics to this Gene classic, but that's because they're morons. The whole song is a cry of heartbreak and distance. While Paul was trying to find ways to cut the crap and get to the point, Gene was using every poetic allegory and analogy he could find. Ironically they would swap styles just a few years later. "Goin' Blind" is a cathartic puzzle, never to be solved.

NEIL DAVIS *(CREATURES FEST, KISS AMERICA)* – As an early KISS fan in the '70s, this song initially never resonated with me. This was likely due to my youth, which drove me more towards harder-toned songs. It really wasn't until *MTV Unplugged* in 1996 that I came to appreciate this gem of a song. Yes, some of the lyrics are a bit odd but Gene's melodic bass playing and the harmonies make this a powerful song that became a staple on all of the KISS Kruise sail-away shows.

LISA LANE KULICK *(BRUCE KULICK'S WIFE)* – When I first started investigating the KISS makeup-era catalog, I discovered this touching song. Gene's vocals are tender, yet tragic, as the lyrics tell the story of a relationship that can't be. The meandering walking bass line accentuates the sadness of this heartbreaking melody. I was sixteen when I first heard "Goin' Blind" and yes, I would imagine Gene was singing it to me.

ROBERT CONTE *(AUTHOR)* – The first KISS song where I understood its story. "I'm 93, you're 16," says it all; an elderly man's inappropriate lust for a teenage girl can be interpreted as either his dying fantasy or an unattainable mutual connection. The instrumental part of this track's chorus ties into *Hotter Than Hell*'s Japanese-inspired cover design and motif by photographer/designer Norman Seef. Like "Christine Sixteen," "Goin' Blind" crosses the current cultural boundary of what some once considered "cool" (older men seducing underage girls) versus what many now deem "creepy." Its legacy is further diminished as Gene Simmons' co-writer on this song, Steven Coronel, would later be arrested and convicted of sexually exploiting a minor.

HOTTER THAN HELL

CHRIS JERICHO *(FOZZY, WRESTLER)* – *Alive!* came out where the songs are all kind of sped up a bit and more energetic, and "Hotter Than Hell" was one of my favorites. "She looked good, she looked hotter than hell." I must have used that phrase in my own life a hundred times. Great tune, midtempo tune but I love the end where it kind of kicks in and gets a little bit faster. I love that tune, but it has to be from *Alive!*

Chris Jericho with Gene Simmons

DAVID LAGRECA *(BUSTED OPEN RADIO)* – First song I ever heard from KISS. I still remember my older brother Don blasting it from his bedroom. Changed my life.

RAISE YOUR GLASSES:
A Celebration of 50 Years of KISS Songs by Celebrities, Musicians & Fans.

AHMET ZAPPA *(MUSICIAN)* – The title track of a fucking awesome record. Killer track. I love how Paul's vocals just jump right out at you. He's just right in your face. You hear the groove of the track, the chunk of the guitar. And what I LOVE is when you want that fucking power chorus, Gene's vocal is just so on point. I say this all the time. Paul Stanley is known as the lead singer and the frontman for KISS but I think that if you go track by track on all the records, you'll be hard-pressed if you really ask yourself, do you like more of the Paul songs, or do you like more of the Gene songs? Just vocally. I like all the songs and I'm not trying to discount Paul. I just find myself appreciating Gene's voice. Another reason why I love KISS is that everyone has these great moments to shine with their vocal performances.

PETER DANKELSON *(PETE'S DIARY)* – This is such a killer guitar riff! I love the tone of the guitars on this song and the gaps that the guitar leaves during the vocals really allow the vocals to shine through and the melody choice in general is super-catchy.

BRITT LIGHTNING *(VIXEN)* – My first personal encounter meeting the band KISS was in a hotel elevator during Mardi Gras. The band invited me to come see the show, but I couldn't make it. Later that night at the engagement I was scheduled to attend, the DJ cranked "Hotter Than Hell", and I felt like he was rubbing it in. How did he know?!

TOM GIGLIOTTI *(SHOUT IT OUT LOUDCAST)* – Now here is a great example of a song that had new life breathed into it during *Alive!* Everything on this album is muddy and even the good songs like this suffer from it. It's classic Paul and his tone is so cool. You know a song is that good when it can fight its way through this terrible studio production.

LET ME GO. ROCK 'N' ROLL

BRYCE MILETO *(SISTERS DOLL)* – Balls to the wall. Love this tune. I feel like this tune resembles what KISS is all about.

Bryce Mileto with KISS

RAISE YOUR GLASSES:
A Celebration of 50 Years of KISS Songs
by Celebrities, Musicians & Fans.

WES BEECH *(THE PLASMATICS)* – When I saw the cover of *Hotter Than Hell* in the record store it just leaped out at me and I couldn't wait to get it home. Muddy production aside there were some great songs on it, but the standout track for me was their glam-era stomper "Let Me Go, Rock 'n' Roll". Starting off with Ace's lone guitar and Gene's shout of "Rock and roll" to start it off it kicks into high gear with an infectious rhythm delivering Ace's modern take on Chuck Berry's signature guitar licks. Gene's powerful vocal delivery and plea to his current object of affection leads into some truly spectacular drum fills courtesy of Peter before Ace shreds again, delivering more of what would become his signature guitar leads. Peter plays his ass off throughout and the guitar interplay of Paul and Ace lays down a great groove.

ZEUS *(SHOUT IT OUT LOUDCAST)* – Another track that I thought had to be a cover. So old-school rock 'n' roll. Very different from what we usually hear from KISS. The only single from *Hotter Than Hell*. That breakdown in the middle with just Peter on the drums and then Ace comes blazing in, is just magic. The live version of this song is an easy metric of what type of KISS show you are seeing because when KISS is on, this song is electric!

TOMMY LONDON *(OZZY'S BONEYARD, SIRIUS XM)* – I grew up with '50s/'60s music all my life. My father played it constantly in the house when I was a kid. I'm pretty sure that's why this has always been one of my favorite KISS songs. It doesn't sound like a '50s/'60s song per se but it has that vibe, musically and lyrically.

BILL STARKEY *(FOUNDER, KISS ARMY)* – Not the smartest lyrics ever but neither was Doo Wah Diddy. What counts is the melody that gets you off your ass. No wonder it was often one the encores because it doesn't let you catch your breath. "Baby's got the feelin' baby wants a show." And KISS provided one for sure!

ALL THE WAY

MIKE PORTNOY *(DREAM THEATER, WINERY DOGS)* – It's one of those deep cuts that I've always loved. It's one of the songs that I think of when I think of songs that weren't on *Alive!* and *Alive II*. It's really cool and I love Gene's vocal on it. But the mix and the production on the album is horrible. Snare drum sounds like paper bag.

PJ FARLEY – *(TRIXTER, FOZZY)* – This song struck me right away before I was even a bass player, I was a kid but playing drums. Gene's wind-ups or "slides" on the bass in that song is something I'd never heard before and has probably been Gene's biggest influence on me.

CHARLIE BENANTE *(ANTHRAX)* – It's just such a great Gene song. One of my favorite songs. I wish it was on *Alive!* so it got that treatment. Those songs took on a new life on *Alive!*

MARTIN POPOFF *(AUTHOR)* – Guilty pleasure time here. I'd put this quite forgotten side two-opener from *Hotter Than Hell* in my top five tracks across the trio of records that make up the pre-*Alive!* canon. And much of the glory goes to Gene, who places a simple but effective vocal and vocal melody across chunky guitars that occupy a curious place between riff and chord structure. The Kerner and Wise production job is just batty, but that contributes to the BTO heft of the thing, once again, Gene playing the Fred Turner role, although here he's comparatively calm of voice, almost reflective.

JASON BAKKEN *(COBRAS & FIRE PODCAST)* – For a single guy who lived at home, Gene sure had a lot to say about naggy women. *Hotter Than Hell* is pretty locked in as my fave KISS album. The transition from the open riff verses to the upbeat chorus is killer. This is my favorite era of Gene and KISS.

ZACH THRONE *(COREY TAYLOR, BRUCE KULICK)* – Crunchy Gene song. Great riff, catchy chorus.

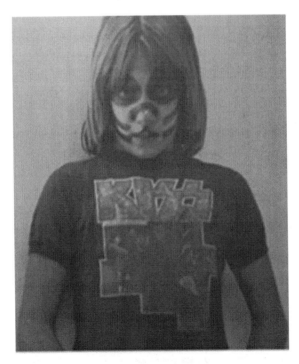

Zach Throne, age 10

WATCHIN' YOU

TOM HIGGINS *(KLASSIC '78)* – The riffs, the sinister vibe, the solo & the outstanding drumming. Anyone who says "KISS can't play" needs to hear this song. Memories of staring at the *Alive!* booklet for hours come to mind when I hear this.

JAMES CAMPION *(AUTHOR, Shout It Out Loud – The Story of KISS's Destroyer and the Making of an American Icon)* – Did I say there was no better riff than "Cold Gin"? That was so four songs ago. We may have a new contender; "Watchin' You" sports a whiz-bang kick-ass riff. That opening boogie alone slays the weak. And oh, those harmony guitars, so brutal and threatening. If a song was the essence of that giant spider-creature from the climax to Stephen King's *It*, this is it. The vocals are creepy weird, a sordid testimony to Gene's dogishness. He is at his hissing best here, and that *Alive!* version… oof. More cowbell, please, Mr. Criss. And once again a classic KISS breakdown, bridge, change, whatever. Ace leading his wobbly ass off to beat every other band on the circuit. There was some inner debate about whether I should put "Deuce" here, but this is plainly a better song. One of the finest ad hoc arrangements in the early KISS canon, considering the sound-fart that is *Hotter Than Hell* and the fifteen minutes the band had to write, record, and mix it. I wish it was on *Destroyer*, so I could have further waxed poetic on its attributes. Not sure you get something as funky as AC/DC's "Back in Black" without this beauty.

BRENNAN MILETO *(SISTERS DOLL)* – This riff and dual vocal parts throughout make this song a KISS classic. Peter's drumming to Ace's guitar work, it's just a great track. I loved how heavy it was when they brought it back to the set for *Alive III*.

ROXY PETRUCCI *(VIXEN)* – I love the guitar riff and the cowbell of course. This might seem crazy but I hear a taste of Jethro Tull in the guitar riffs, accents and chord changes. It's refreshing to hear the drums without all the samples being used in today's mixes. Drummers add to the signature sound of a band and in my opinion when they start programming and replacing the drum sounds with processed drums it loses the human feel that's so important to the song.

MARTIN POPOFF *(AUTHOR)* – Me and my 11-year-old buds always considered this somewhat algebraic early metal rocker to be the creepy follow-up to the first album's "Deuce," a thought reinforced by both of them making the smash *Alive!* album of 1975. It's all clumpy and bashy, which makes it a perfect off-road vehicle for Gene's hurly-burly Fred Turner/Dusty Hill vocal.

MAINLINE

ZEUS *(SHOUT IT OUT LOUDCAST)* – The first Peter Criss solo lead vocal on a KISS album. Peter demanding to sing this Paul Stanley-penned song is an early sign of trouble ahead. There's just something about Peter singing Paul songs. As much as there's tension between the two, I believe the music they create is fantastic and "Mainline" is a great example. What a great catchy number and straightforward Peter raspy vocals. A deep cut gem.

RAISE YOUR GLASSES:
A Celebration of 50 Years of KISS Songs
by Celebrities, Musicians & Fans.

TOM GIGLIOTTI *(SHOUT IT OUT LOUDCAST)* – Peter's vocals are so incredible and beloved and this song is such a highlight for me in that regard. It's early power pop with an undeniable chorus and hooks throughout. And who doesn't love some cowbell during the intro? Great stuff here from the Catman.

BRYCE MILETO *(SISTERS DOLL)* – What a belting vocal! Killer chorus, one of my all-time faves by the Catman.

PETER DANKELSON *(PETE'S DIARY)* – I love the vibe of this track, always fun hearing some more cowbell on a track and Peter's vocals sound great.

Tom and Zeus with Peter Criss

KEITH ROTH *(SIRIUS XM, THE DICTATORS)* – I was talking to Richie Wise years ago (he's the guy that produced the debut and

Hotter Than Hell). He said he finds this record (*Hotter Than Hell*) unlistenable compared to the first one, said he would love to remix it but apparently the masters don't exist anymore. I was thinking if he did, I'm sure it wouldn't be as good no matter how much it got brightened, tweaked, etc. The original is what's embedded in me. "Mainline", one of my faves off *Hotter Than Hell*. Peter, great vocal. The cowbell, the infectious chorus!!

COMIN' HOME

TODD KERNS *(BRUCE KULICK, SLASH)* – Most of the songs I'm choosing are in part due to my viewing them through the lens of my initial exposure to them. Most of us first came across the early KISS records as children. We had only been exposed to our parents' music or whatever was randomly playing on AM radio in the car. KISS, in many cases, was the first time we'd discovered OUR music. *Hotter Than Hell* gets a lot of varied reactions due to its mix, but I think that has always added to the experience for me. A lot of the darker and heavier songs on the record take on more depth due to the cavernous mix. Songs like "Parasite", "Strange Ways", "Watchin' You" seemed way heavier at the time than they do from our current vantage point. I've selected "Comin' Home" as it represents the other side of that coin. It is a bright and sunny, cheerful number about being on the road and missing your girl. I always love that the guys were so productive in these early days. Songs were just falling out of them. This song has all the British rock-isms that Gene and Paul always talk about as their early influences. The fact that I never heard a live version of "Comin' Home" until it opened the *MTV Unplugged* set years later makes it all the more special.

RAISE YOUR GLASSES:
A Celebration of 50 Years of KISS Songs
by Celebrities, Musicians & Fans.

SONNY POONI *(PODCAST ROCK CITY)* – When the whole *MTV Unplugged* happened, I remember hearing this song and thinking that it was a new unreleased song that we were hearing for the first time. I was excited because I loved the song immediately upon first listen. When one of my friends told me that it was an older song from the *Hotter Than Hell* record, I realized that I didn't even own that record. I bought a copy of *Hotter Than Hell* the very next day.

JAY SCOTT *(THE HOOK ROCKS PODCAST)* – The best song on *Hotter Than Hell*. A song they should've played live outside of the *MTV Unplugged* show.

MIKE BRUNN *(THE ROCK EXPERIENCE)* – If you would have asked me in 1985 what my favorite KISS song was, I probably would have said "Comin' Home". At that time that answer would get me blank stares since many KISS fans were not familiar with this deep cut from a decade earlier. Fast forward to 1995 and I was stunned when I found out that the band tried to play the song acoustic while in Australia. I'm so happy that over the past 30 years this has become a staple of their unplugged performances and that it led off the great *MTV Unplugged* album. To this day it's still one of my all-time favorite KISS songs!

JASON HOOK *(FIVE FINGER DEATH PUNCH)* – Great simple tune. I really liked it when they re-envisioned it on acoustic guitar for the *MTV Unplugged* album. *Hotter Than Hell* has the weirdest drum sound I think I have ever heard on an album.

STRANGE WAYS

ROXY PETRUCCI *(VIXEN)* – Simple but not. Peter's opening tom-tom fills and his cool ghost snare accents in the verse made this song even more interesting, not to mention his voice is sexy and strong. The song is short but the heaviness is right up my alley.

CHRIS CAFFERY *(TRANS-SIBERIAN ORCHESTRA, SAVATAGE)* – This is probably one of my favorite KISS songs. It is also probably my favorite Ace solo ever. It is definitely one of those solos that inspired me to be "that guy" when I grew up. I love the fact that it features in its high points Peter on vocals and that Ace solo. It shows just how great that original 4 was together. Can't say it enough… "That solo!"

ZACH THRONE *(COREY TAYLOR, BRUCE KULICK)* – One of their heaviest early songs with a vocal and guitar solo that can't be replicated. When I played with Ace, we had "Strange Ways" in the set. Jeremy sang it every night, but myself and Matt gave it our best shots too. None of us could match the intensity and whisky-soaked passion of Peter's vocal here. I wish he sang more heavy songs with his heavy metal Wilson Pickett voice. I always thought that Peter had one of the scariest rock 'n' roll screams I had ever heard. Very under-rated singer. And that solo! A one-take wonder. Total freak of nature. NOBODY can replicate it... not even Ace. Every note Ace plays here just says "Fuck you". Pure attitude. Playing with him made me realize why Gene and Paul chose him over the others back in the day.

RAISE YOUR GLASSES:
A Celebration of 50 Years of KISS Songs
by Celebrities, Musicians & Fans.

GREG PRATO *(AUTHOR, Take It Off: KISS Truly Unmasked and The Eric Carr Story)* – KISS does Sabbath? I'd be comfortable with that musical description of this delightfully plodding *Hotter Than Hell* album closer. Features one of my favorite Ace guitar solos, and I've always thought that Peter Criss had an underrated/great "rock 'n' roll voice," which he showcases here.

HAL SPARKS *(COMEDIAN)* – In the '70s shuffle of songwriting where members of the band would write a defining song for someone else, "Strange Ways" represented the best of Peter Criss to me. Written by Ace, you can hear the bridge from Sabbath to Alice In Chains in this underrated gem.

CHAPTER 3

"DRESSED TO KILL"

Released: March 19, 1975

Dressed to Kill, the third studio album by KISS, saw the band at a pivotal moment in their career. Featuring a blend of anthemic rockers and catchy pop-infused tracks, this album displayed KISS's ability to craft radio-friendly hits while maintaining their signature hard rock edge. With iconic songs like "Rock And Roll All Nite" and "C'mon and Love Me," *Dressed to Kill* marked a turning point in KISS's journey to becoming rock legends.

In 1975, KISS was a band on the brink of superstardom, and *Dressed to Kill* was the album that thrust them into the spotlight. Released on March 19, it showcased the band's evolving sound and their knack for creating memorable, infectious rock anthems.

The album opens with "Room Service," a catchy and energetic track that sets the tone for what's to come. Paul Stanley's charismatic vocals and Ace Frehley's distinctive guitar work shine throughout the record, starting with this opener.

"C'mon and Love Me" is a standout track with a chorus that's impossible to forget. This song perfectly exemplifies KISS's ability to blend pop sensibilities with their hard rock roots, making it an instant classic.

The album also includes "Rock And Roll All Nite," arguably KISS's most iconic song. With its anthemic chorus and infectious energy, it became an anthem for generations of rock fans and remained a staple in the band's live shows.

Dressed to Kill is notable for its concise and focused approach, with most songs clocking in at under four minutes. This brevity allowed KISS to deliver a tight, cohesive album filled with memorable hooks and sing-along choruses.

While KISS had already established their larger-than-life personas, *Dressed to Kill* was an important step in refining their image. The album cover featuring the band in suits added to their mystique.

RAISE YOUR GLASSES:
A Celebration of 50 Years of KISS Songs
by Celebrities, Musicians & Fans.

Though *Dressed to Kill* didn't achieve the commercial success of some of their later albums, it played a pivotal role in KISS's ascent to rock 'n' roll royalty. It solidified their reputation as a band that could craft catchy, radio-friendly hits while maintaining their hard rock edge.

In retrospect, *Dressed to Kill* stands as a crucial chapter in KISS's storied career. It's an album that captures the band in transition, poised on the cusp of worldwide fame, and showcases their ability to craft memorable rock anthems that have stood the test of time. With its mix of infectious hooks and unapologetic rock 'n' roll attitude, *Dressed to Kill* is a testament to KISS's enduring influence on the world of music.

ROOM SERVICE

JOEY CASSATA *(ZO2, Z ROCK)* – "Room Service" is undoubtedly one of the most under-appreciated and under-utilized gems in the band's catalog. How this song isn't a staple in their live set is a mystery to me. What a fantastic way to kick off one of the most overlooked albums in KISS's history. Everyone always talks about *Destroyer* or *Rock and Roll Over* being the best classic KISS album, but *Dressed to Kill* is just as good, if not better!!

AHMET ZAPPA *(MUSICIAN)* – Now, here's where I don't want to insult anybody, but I love this song because I think it's so bad. And I'm okay with that. When you have lyrics that say "I'm a lucky guy, I hardly ever cry" I don't know how much time they spent on it. It seems like they just needed to quickly write something.

It's laughable to me. But here's why I think the song is magical to people who want to be in a rock 'n' roll band; it's still a banger because everyone comes in on that chorus and it crushes. The lyrical content is not their strongest work, but I feel like it gives hope to musicians like, "Shit, I could fucking write a song like "Room Service" and be like KISS!" So that's why I think it's an inspirational song. At least that's what I tell myself.

Joey Cassata as Peter Criss, age 12

RAISE YOUR GLASSES:
A Celebration of 50 Years of KISS Songs
by Celebrities, Musicians & Fans.

KEITH ROTH *(SIRIUS XM, THE DICTATORS)* – Paul, giving us a snapshot to rock star life. I played this as he was walking into an interview with me, and him humming the intro and playing air drums was the best!!

SONNY POONI *(PODCAST ROCK CITY)* – This song gets lost in the mix because of all the other classic songs on *Dressed to Kill*. The deceptively dirty lyrics that move from the hotel… to the flight… to his hometown… are written well and the song has an amazingly memorable vocal melody. A great deep cut that no one ever mentions but it's one of my favorite songs in the KISS catalog.

Tom, Zeus and Murph with Loudcaster Tally Fochler,
Dressed to Kill subway, December 1, 2023

TOM GIGLIOTTI *(SHOUT IT OUT LOUDCAST)* – The leadoff track from the spectacular *Dressed to Kill*. Paul is in full Starchild mode here and the layered vocals of him and Gene during the chorus are amazing. Peter is a madman on the drums here and the band is on fire. Ace crushes it with a fantastic solo as always. A song that I wish was a live staple.

TWO TIMER

ZEUS *(SHOUT IT OUT LOUDCAST)* – An early Gene plodding song that gets better and better every time that you listen to it. Maybe its Gene's vocal delivery, the extremely underrated production by Casablanca President, Neil Bogart, Peter's awesome drumming or Ace's solo. By the way, I am not sure there is any other song where Gene is singing about being a loser. He's always the conqueror, demon or winner.

BRAD RUSTOVEN *(SLAMFEST PODCAST)* – I was not a fan of this song when I first heard it on 8-track in the late '70s. Over the years it has grown on me. Cool riff and groove – the pre-chorus harmonies are awesome, and I love when they bring the intro riff back into what I'll call a post-chorus… so good.

COURTNEY CRONIN DOLD *(COMEDIAN)* – Love this doo-wop hard rock ditty where Gene puts his woman on blast. There's no guessing when it comes to the title of this song. They repeat it 17 times, more if you count the fade out. I think any woman dating Gene around this time would have to be a two-timer just to keep things even.

NICHOLAS BUCKLAND *(AUTHOR, Hottest Brand in the Land)* –
A great Gene song, and despite his protestations, some great
basslines in the verse that prove the guy could actually write some
melodic parts. This song also featured his voice moving closer and
closer to the 'Cookie Monster' voice that would be his style in the
late '70s. And talking about himself being a "three-time loser"
because of his lady's two-timing ways is actually a cool lyric.

ROBERT CONTE *(AUTHOR)* – *Dressed to Kill* was the album that
helped me learn which band members sang lead on each song. This
deep, groovy cut written and sung by Gene Simmons has a simple
story: "Call me a three-time loser, 'cause my baby is a two-timer..."
I often felt that this track was inspired by a personal experience
where Gene, in his younger years, may have loved a woman he was
involved with who wanted or needed to have her fun, too. For me,
"Two Timer" validated that only men could be sexual scoundrels.
Neal Bogart co-producing with KISS resulted in a hard-rock sound,
coupled with a pop edge.

SHANDON SAHM *(MEAT PUPPETS)* – Hard rock Charlie Watts
drum beat – ba ba boom bap bap ba ba boom – then the drum lick
into the verses is just fantastic. Solid pocket drumming from Peter.
Gene's vocal delivery and the brash lyrics all make this song stand
out, not to mention the killer walking bass lines. So tasty and
yummy.

LADIES IN WAITING

MARTIN POPOFF *(AUTHOR)* – KISS's third record, *Dressed to Kill*, was considered a little clean an' neat after the sludgefest that was *Hotter Than Hell*. But it's ribboned with quietly good songs, "Ladies In Waiting" being one of the backroom classics here. Gene gets a sole writing credit here (as he does on the comparatively insipid "Two Timer") and he fills the song up with sexual tension, walking us through some imagined action-packed disco ballroom across an up-tempo track that's over and out in 2:33.

CHRIS CZYNSZAK *(DECIBEL GEEK PODCAST)* – Absolute two-chord trash. KISS would write plenty of sophomoric stuff in the '70s but there would always a bit of cleverness in the lyrics or a great riff or solo. This song has none of that. I'd be shocked if they spent more than 30 minutes writing it.

SHANDON SAHM *(MEAT PUPPETS)* – Again pocket drumming boom bap bap boom boom. Another hard rock Charlie Watts-type drumming. Great feel and swing. Lyrics "been to market and the meat sure looks good tonight." Oh boy so brash and sexually charged. Stellar walking bass line. Simple but effective guitar solo with that extra echo or delay. Just wonderful. This song just swings. Ace and Peter were the reason I was drawn to them. It's truly like Beatles on steroids. You would have your favorite but after a few weeks your favorite member would switch.

MURPH *(SHOUT IT OUT LOUDCAST)* – I have always been a fan of this song mainly because the opening riff pulls me in every time. Gene's voice during the early years had such a rawness but I mean that as a compliment. His voice seemed to become more polished as time went on, but it is perfect for this song.

ROBERT CONTE *(AUTHOR)* – My favorite Gene song on *Dressed to Kill*. My teenage self could vividly picture the Demon, possibly during medieval times or inside a 1970s sex club like The Vault, being escorted down a long hall covered with scantily clad women for his choosing either individually or several at a time to enjoy multiple sexual excursions as he pleased. While working on 1996's *You Wanted the Best, You Got the Best*, a live soundcheck of this song was discovered on analog tape and submitted to the band (with several others) for inclusion on the album but didn't make the final cut.

Tom, Zeus and Murph, *End of the Road*, TD Garden, March 26, 2019

GETAWAY

TOM GIGLIOTTI *(SHOUT IT OUT LOUDCAST)* – *Dressed to Kill* is the height of Peter's drumming. The band is so tight, and they kick ass on every track. Peter's vocals on this are incredible and the band is hitting on all cylinders. Ace rips a great little solo and the outro, as Peter is wailing, make this a classic for me although it would be considered a deep cut on the album.

JASON HOOK *(FIVE FINGER DEATH PUNCH)* – I love Peter's voice on this one. Good tune and great guitar solo (over a completely unique section of music). I like the fact that the outro gets more aggressive and screamy.

CLAUDIO SPERA *(KISS ARMY NATION PODCAST)* – Out of the first three records, I have no doubt that *Dressed to Kill* is the most 'rocky' one. I love Peter's singing and Gene's bass line is quite unique. The song transmits a party atmosphere. Ace's solo is a signature one and it fits perfectly in the song. The last part of the song with Peter screaming his lungs out is the perfect ending for a great forgotten tune.

JEFF TROTT *(ART DIRECTOR)* – Kicking off with a killer riff, "Getaway" is the standout track on *Dressed to Kill*, solely written by Ace Frehley and featuring Peter Criss on lead vocals. This song delivers a pure rock 'n' roll sound with stellar riffs, powerful vocals, and compelling lyrics. The gang vocals from Gene and Paul add the perfect finishing touch. An awesome song and a fantastic listen from start to finish.

IZZY PREJLEY *(MUSICIAN, COMIC)* – Monster Peter vocal on this tune, highlighted by one of Ace's shining solos and the ending that turned out to be the live classic ending of "Rock 'n' Roll All Nite". 2:44 of unadulterated KISS pleasure.

KEITH ROTH *(SIRIUS XM, THE DICTATORS)* – Always loved Peter's voice, this is my favorite from him. *Dressed to Kill,* such a solid record. Straight-up production, it's like Rod Stewart singing in a hard rock band!!!

ROCK BOTTOM

TODD KERNJ *(BRUCE KULICK, SLASH)* – There are two kinds of people in this world: Those who think of either UFO or KISS when you mention the title "Rock Bottom". I'm in the KISS category. I love me some UFO but "Rock Bottom" by KISS casts a long shadow for me. The intro alone deserves its own chapter. Ace and Paul on acoustic guitars, at least one a 12-string, is the pinnacle of '70s epicness. Exploding into the full-on song is such a delight. The arrangement is of great interest to me. Rather than going into a second verse after the first chorus, Mr. Frehley steps up and steals the spotlight with one of his all-time classic solos. I love how on *Alive!* they double the length of this solo. Ace is the most underrated solo composer in rock. You cannot play KISS songs without knowing the solo because they are as much a part of the songs as any lyric, melody or riff. There is something powerful about the last chorus when Paul removes the in-between lines "girl, you know you gotta treat me good" and "you never treat me like you should" allowing the repetition of the "ROCK BOTTOM" chorus to carry its own weight. Peter Criss' tight kick drum carrying the space in between is masterful. *Dressed to Kill* is another treasure trove of classic songs.

MATT STARR *(ACE FREHLEY)* – Another song where the vocal and the guitar chords are synchronized. A pure rocker. The version on *Alive!* is amazing. A great example of how the band sounded so different live than on studio albums. Paul's vocals are amazing and Gene's backing vocals and bass playing are killer.

CHARLIE BENANTE *(ANTHRAX)* – It's a little ditty by Paul. When you hear it on *Alive!*, it's a fucking whole new monster.

TOM HIGGINS *(KLASSIC '78)* – Always loved this one. Paul Stanley attitude all over it. Heard it on my friend's *Alive!* album first. I was bummed when my mom bought me *Double Platinum* and it only had the intro and not the whole song.

BRIAN TICHY *(THE DEAD DAISIES, GENE SIMMONS BAND)* – I've always loved this! A really cool, mellow, melodic intro, straight into a power verse with Paul just owning the vocal! The chorus is also killer! And Ace's solo is classic Ace! This is just so "KISS" to me! Melodic and tough!

LISA LANE KULICK *(BRUCE KULICK'S WIFE)* – The song's picking guitar intro, especially on the studio version, is emotionally moving. What makes "Rock Bottom" so special is how it quickly switches gears into a hard-hitting, gritty and glittery '70s sound. The lyrics scream enough is enough and by the time the song ends, you're ready to climb out of depression and make life happen. I love this song!

JAMES CAMPION (*AUTHOR, Shout It Out Loud – The Story of KISS's Destroyer and the Making of an American Icon*) – It took all the restraint I could muster not to move this further up the list. I absolutely LOVE "Rock Bottom." Everything about it; the melancholy open, the nuisance of silence, the funky groove, the fist-cracking chorus, and that deliciously concussive ending. I know I'm going into sacrilege territory here, but the *Alive!* version is just not as good as the studio one. Granted, it has an extra measure of Ace's solo, and when it kicks into the second verse buttressed by Gene's bass swoosh plowing under the drums it gives me chills, but they rush the cool twelve-string, acoustic section, and I'm a sucker for that. I'm especially fond of its modulating on the third turnaround and easing back into the core melody for the final run. Did Ace write this? If he did, he needed to do more of it. He missed his calling as a soft rocker. And as for the ram-jamming part, well, come on. Paul spitting out those first lines is sensational rock phrasing. When they do the final chant chorus and it just lays out with the drums carrying the day, all three electric stringed instruments diving in... so damn cool. It also possesses that signature KISS opaque motif – is this song about love, sex, money, fear? What? Has me thinking they went title first again and let it go where it will. Of course, none of this matters. "Rock Bottom" is a beast.

HAL SPARKS (*COMEDIAN*) – You can see the seeds of songs like "I Want You" in the intro to "Rock Bottom" and the absolute shame of the riff and vocals coming in. It's as though the band is trying to lure you in and then pow! The lyrics are a complex mix of thoughts from a disgruntled lover, and you can almost smell the apartment this couple lives in.

C'MON AND LOVE ME

COURTNEY CRONIN DOLD *(COMEDIAN)* – This is my absolute favorite KISS song. It's sexy, it has fun lyrics that rhyme like dancer, romancer, and cancer! Don't forget mirror, and nearer. I do prefer the *Alive!* version to the *Dressed to Kill* version. It's faster, louder, and Paul screams the song title which I always love.

MATT STARR *(ACE FREHLEY)* – One of my favorite lyrics. So innocent and pure. "She's a dancer, a romancer. I'm a Capricorn and she's a cancer." Come on! The quintessential lyric about being an up-and-coming rock star.

TODD KERNS *(BRUCE KULICK, SLASH)* – One of my favorite things about listening to the Beatles is being able to pick out the band members' individual voices within a song. The same could be said about the experience of listening to KISS. Though Paul carries the verses, Gene comes in loud and proud in the pre-chorus. This song represents all of my favorite things about KISS. The opening riff is a banger. The lyric "she's a dancer, a romancer, I'm a Capricorn and she's a cancer" is one of the most quotable of the entire KISS catalog. I love on *Alive!* the way Paul augments the melody a bit, but the delivery on *Dressed to Kill* is all swagger and attitude in its perfection. If aliens from a far-off galaxy landed tomorrow and asked what rock and roll was, I'd play them this song as the perfect example.

MISTRESS CARRIE *(RADIO DJ)* – *Dressed to Kill* is my favorite KISS album cover, and this song was always a standout for me. For no reason in particular, I just always loved it.

RUSSELL PETERS *(COMEDIAN)* – I like the live version of this. The first time I heard it was on *Alive!* That's how it stuck with me. They just really rock on that one and all in synch. The lyrics on this one now is like happy Pride Month.

JAMES CAMPION *(AUTHOR, Shout It Out Loud – The Story of KISS's Destroyer and the Making of an American Icon)* – Once again, KISS's pop master, Paul Stanley, pens a snappy confection worthy of a better chart fate. Verse to chorus, this is a hook machine masquerading as a hard rocker – Stanley snapping off the melody with nary a care, almost willing its earworm to penetrate the frontal cortex. When the band halts and he shouts the song's title, I can only conjure the Beatles at their most seductive.

ANYTHING FOR MY BABY

WES BEECH *(THE PLASMATICS)* – I was never a big fan of *Dressed to Kill* and it was the last KISS album I listened to until coming back to them with *Love Gun*, but this track always stood out to me and was my favorite on the album. It bears more than a passing resemblance to "Strutter" and the rhythm guitar stands out. Peter's propulsive drumming drives it and Paul pours his heart out to his latest girl that we can all relate to – and who wouldn't do anything for their baby? Gene's bass playing is a bit reserved but provides a nice foundation for the guitars. Short, sweet, and neat with no guitar solo – a good poppier tune.

RAISE YOUR GLASSES:
A Celebration of 50 Years of KISS Songs
by Celebrities, Musicians & Fans.

JAY SCOTT *(THE HOOK ROCKS PODCAST)* – Another underrated gem. Great vibe and groove. This is KISS doing the Stones.

MURPH *(SHOUT IT OUT LOUDCAST)* – For every "Plaster Caster", there is a song like this where the band demonstrates they can write a track with heartfelt lyrics and still have an incredible sound. This song would always be at the top of my list for a deep cut/most underrated tune in their catalog.

BRAD RUSTOVEN *(SLAMFEST PODCAST)* – While this song tends to get some shit, it's my favorite on the album. The drum intro mirrors the drum intro to RARAN, which can be confusing. The verse vocal is one of Paul's best recorded vocals of all time. And the call and response chorus is so damn catchy. Only negative: no guitar solo.

TOM GIGLIOTTI *(SHOUT IT OUT LOUDCAST)* – Detractors of this song point to the chorus, which, admittedly is not great. But don't sleep on the rest of this song. Paul once again showing why he is the absolute Starchild. Gene's bass line and Peter's rolling drum fills make this a deep cut that needs to be given a chance.

RAISE YOUR GLASSES:
A Celebration of 50 Years of KISS Songs
by Celebrities, Musicians & Fans.

Tom, Zeus and Murph with Loudcaster Tally Fochler, *Dressed to Kill* corner, West 23rd St. & 8th Avenue, December 1, 2023

ΣHE

ΣTEVE VAI *(SOLO ARTIST, DAVID LEE ROTH, WHITESNAKE)* – I really like the hard rockers, I love Gene's voice, so guttural, menacing and nefarious. KISS created their vision and they just stuck to it no matter what. When I was young KISS represented a freedom that nothing else was offering.

RAISE YOUR GLASSES:
A Celebration of 50 Years of KISS Songs
by Celebrities, Musicians & Fans.

MIKE PORTNOY *(DREAM THEATER, WINERY DOGS)* – Definitely one of my favorite tracks on *Dressed to Kill* but the live version goes to a whole new level. The whole middle section with Ace's solo, and those extra jams and bits and pieces. I just love the live version, even down to the drum fills at the intro. An all-time favorite.

CHARLIE BENANTE *(ANTHRAX)* – Such a great riff. I think this is one of the more funkier KISS songs. Great groove and Peter uses cowbell in it. Gene has that breakdown section with Peter. It's a drummer and bass player's dream. We (Anthrax on *KISS My Ass*) had so much fun doing it because they (KISS) were there.

Mike Portnoy with Gene Simmons

RAISE YOUR GLASSES:
A Celebration of 50 Years of KISS Songs
by Celebrities, Musicians & Fans.

CHARLIE PARRA *(KUARANTINE)* – Even though the studio version is cool, the live version of "She" on *The Midnight Special* is by far the best. Peter doing those high-pitched screams while hitting the drums and Ace's guitar solo (featuring a double hand-tapping section before Van Halen 1 was released) is pure fire. That closing solo in particular made me even forget that he kinda does the same lick Robby Krieger does in "Five to One" by the Doors.

GREG PRATO *(AUTHOR, Take It Off: KISS Truly Unmasked* **and** *The Eric Carr Story)* – KISS does Sabbath? This tune is probably the closest KISS ever got to being "groovy" and "funky." Would soon become a jam-heavy highlight at KISS concerts (as heard in the extended version on *Alive!*). Also, don't forget that Mike McCready nicked the beginning of Ace's solo here for Pearl Jam's "Alive" (and that Ace might have borrowed *his* bit from Robby Krieger in the Doors' "Five to One").

AHMET ZAPPA *(MUSICIAN)* – This is another prime example of 'if you do not like this song then there's something seriously wrong with you'. While other bands like Black Sabbath are singing about the supernatural and warlocks, "She" is this awesome track about a magical sexy lady. That's what it feels like to me, like banging the magic lady. Sweet.

LOVE HER ALL I CAN

MIKE PORTNOY *(DREAM THEATER, WINERY DOGS)* – Absolutely love this song, another one not on *Alive!* A sleeper and an underrated and forgotten song. I love Peter's drum fills on it and the tight harmonies are amazing. One of KISS's more intricate or sophisticated harmonies.

JEFF PLATE *(TRANS-SIBERIAN ORCHESTRA, SAVATAGE)* – *Dressed to Kill* was my first KISS album. As the band has stated many times, their early studio albums did not represent the power of the live performances, and even at that age I noticed that, and was a bit confused as why my GE cassette recording had more energy than this record. But "Love Her All I Can" stood out. It was different than the other songs and has such a great groove. The cowbell, the drum break at 2:08, followed by one of my favorite Ace solos... great tune.

CHARLIE BENANTE *(ANTHRAX)* – It's not even 3 minutes long (like a lot of songs on *Dressed to Kill*). It's got a great drum beat from Peter, it's classic Peter Criss.

JAMES CAMPION *(AUTHOR, Shout It Out Loud – The Story of KISS's Destroyer and the Making of an American Icon)* – If you can get past the gory fact that the opening of this song is a note-for-note doppelganger of a Nazz song, it is one of, if not the most fun KISS song. This sounds so off-the-cuff, yet also meticulously arranged. It is also the one song I often point to in which every member is bringing something special to the table. Peter's drumming is funky, Paul and Gene are tight as a frog's posterior, and Ace's power-chord asides crackling into the double-down solo is superb studio performance.

RAISE YOUR GLASSES:
A Celebration of 50 Years of KISS Songs by Celebrities, Musicians & Fans.

Charlie Benante with Paul Stanley

GREG PRATO *(AUTHOR, Take It Off: KISS Truly Unmasked and The Eric Carr Story)* – An oft-overlooked Paul rocker (like "She," a holdover from the Wicked Lester days), whose riff was supposedly inspired by a Nazz tune, "Open My Eyes" – a '60s band that included a young Todd Rundgren.

BRIAN TICHY *(THE DEAD DAISIES, GENE SIMMONS BAND)* – This song drives! It's relentless! The cowbell and little ghost notes on the snare in the chorus also give it a little more hookiness thanks to the Catman! The verse is totally rowdy and it drives straight into the chorus with a great hook and killer, funky riff!

ZACH THRONE *(COREY TAYLOR, BRUCE KULICK)* – Super-funky song. Great vocal from Paul. Great solos from Ace and Peter. One of the most appealing songs ever from KISS. I don't know anybody that doesn't like this song.

ROCK AND ROLL ALL NITE

RUDY SARZO *(QUIET RIOT, OZZY)* – I've been doing Rock And Roll Fantasy Camp for 15 years and in the past Paul Stanley and Gene Simmons have been guests and now Bruce Kulick is a counselor there with me too. We get to perform KISS songs together and Bruce is meticulous. He would send me the link to a show from Brazil and we would perform it just like KISS did it that night. Bruce showed me the correct bass line to "Rock And Roll All Nite". Gene doesn't get enough credit. He is a real good bass player.

JOEL HOEKSTRA *(WHITESNAKE, TRANS-SIBERIAN ORCHESTRA)* – So, now I'm going to go REALLY obvious on you. But, hey this is the ultimate anthem...the ultimate CLOSER. What else can I close with here? The first time I performed this onstage was when I joined Night Ranger. We were touring Japan with Firehouse and both bands jammed it onstage together at the end of the night. THEN, when I briefly played with Dee Snider's solo band, Tom Kiefer, Dee and Bret Michaels had a show together. At the end of the night, Tom and Dee joined Bret onstage to sing this and, much to my surprise, I was invited to be a part of that as well. SO, at one point I got to jam this with 3 legendary rock frontmen. How big does a song have to be for all 3 guys with huge hits to say "yes, that's our anthem!"? This was also included in the Night Ranger jam with Ace and George Lynch. I'm proud to say I played the ultimate anthem with the Spaceman himself!!

CHRIS CAFFERY *(TRANS-SIBERIAN ORCHESTRA, SAVATAGE)* – Many generations have had anthems. This was and is the anthem from my generation. One of the greatest live songs ever written. I took it as far to play and sing it with 18-time Grammy Award Winner Jimmy Sturr and his Orchestra. Of course I kinda rewrote the words and said I want to rock and roll all night…but Jimmy Sturr he polkas every day. It was always a fan favorite at every show, just like it is at every KISS concert. It also has another one of those Ace solos that if you play it differently than Ace it changes the song! Priceless.

PJ FARLEY *(TRIXTER, FOZZY)* – Not much to say here that isn't said already. The first REAL rock anthem in my life.

PJ Farley onstage with Ace Frehley

RAISE YOUR GLASSES:
A Celebration of 50 Years of KISS Songs
by Celebrities, Musicians & Fans.

HOLLY KNIGHT *(SONGWRITER)* – It's their most anthemic song. It's a real meat and potatoes rock tune. They may not have reinvented the wheel, but it's a great memorable song.

BULLY RAY *(WRESTLER)* – Greatest way to end a rock 'n' roll show. End of story. Because of the world I live in, with wrestling. That's it. That's the be all and end all to me. There is no better opening ("Detroit Rock City") and closing. No other two songs mean more to any other concert.

Bully Ray, Tom, Dave LaGreca and Zeus

RAISE YOUR GLASSES:
A Celebration of 50 Years of KISS Songs
by Celebrities, Musicians & Fans.

MARTIN POPOFF *(AUTHOR)* – Well, it's pretty cool that the birthday boy is the singer on what is essentially the heart and soul of the KISS catalog, one of the great rock 'n' roll anthems for the ages, and one of those hummable, boogie woogie-pulsed KISS songs that Gene does so well. And it's also fitting that it's the band's unrelenting salesman that gets to express the KISS credo, as laid out in this cheerfully boasting lyric. "I Was Made for Loving You," by some measures, might be a bigger KISS song, but "Rock And Roll All Nite" is the whole crazy, impressive career all balled-up in a scant 2:49 of yummy old-school pop metal goodness.

GRAHAM BONNET *(RAINBOW, MICHAEL SCHENKER)* – I have heard this song a million times, but originally, I didn't know it was KISS, because I was in England. Then one day I was sitting with Cozy Powell and we saw some young kids with makeup on and I said what the fuck is this? Cozy said it's KISS. It is an undeniably catchy song.

JAMES CAMPION *(AUTHOR, Shout It Out Loud – The Story of KISS's Destroyer and the Making of an American Icon)* – That opening floor-tom-fest by Peter Criss is prologue perfection, a tingling omen to all that rock 'n' roll offers – a celebration of feral delights and hedonistic rights adorned by loud guitars and requisite chanting. "Rock And Roll All Nite" is pure unfettered joy. By all rights, it should always be #1 on any KISS list. It is their (our) anthem. I even love the less lauded studio version. It's got that thick, crunchy New Yawk grit. The *Alive!* one, of course, kicks major ass with Ace acing all over the joint. And let's give it up for Gene for his "Drive Me Wild" part and that rumbling bass line. (maybe his best effort?) But let's talk about that chorus, shall we? Excellence in leather and high-heeled boots. The best element of "I-I-I wanna rock and roll allll nite and pawty ev-er-y day!" is its singular proclamation. They could have gone the Slade route, something KISS did often (they loved Slade), but "I" evidently works better than "we" when put in the mouths of thousands of concertgoers screaming it with unfettered glee. Let's face it, if this was the one-hit-wonder portion of our story, then what a hit! I know true KISS fanatics find it rote to gush on this tune – over-played, over-hyped, sick-of-it – but there is a reason clichés exist and classic rock songs keep on with the classic, and this is one of them. It must be in the conversation as a signature rock song of the period, and the one that will haunt KISS long after we exit the mortal coil.

Graham Bonnet and Beth-Ami Heavenstone with Gene Simmons

RAISE YOUR GLASSES:
A Celebration of 50 Years of KISS Songs
by Celebrities, Musicians & Fans.

MISTRESS CARRIE *(RADIO DJ)* – I had to put this song in because any band would sell their soul to Satan himself to have one song that changed rock forever. A song that is heard on every rock radio station, in every pool hall, played by every cover band, covered by every touring band, and referenced in popular culture. A career-defining anthem, just one song... KISS could have just written this song and be HUGE, but they have way more than this.

RAISE YOUR GLASSES:
A Celebration of 50 Years of KISS Songs
by Celebrities, Musicians & Fans.

CHAPTER 4

"DESTROYER"

Released: March 15, 1976

Destroyer, the fourth studio album by KISS, unleashed a sonic explosion. With its grandiose production, diverse songwriting, and iconic tracks like "Detroit Rock City" and "Beth," this album elevated KISS to new heights of rock stardom.

Destroyer is a masterclass in the fusion of hard rock and theatricality, solidifying the band's status as rock legends.

In 1976, KISS was a band at the peak of their powers, and *Destroyer* stands as a testament to their creative and commercial zenith. This album was a monumental step forward, both in terms of sound and storytelling.

Destroyer opens with a cinematic flourish in "Detroit Rock City," a song that would become one of KISS's defining anthems. The track's thundering guitar riffs and dramatic narrative set the stage for an album that was as much about storytelling as it was about rock 'n' roll.

"God of Thunder," featuring the ominous vocals of Gene Simmons, continue the album's theatrical themes.

But it's with "Beth" that *Destroyer* reveals its softer, more introspective side. This ballad, sung by drummer Peter Criss, became one of the band's biggest hits and demonstrated their versatility beyond the bombast of their rock anthems.

"Shout It Out Loud" and "Do You Love Me" provide the album with the energetic, anthemic rockers that KISS was known for. These tracks, with their catchy choruses and powerful guitar work, are quintessential examples of the band's enduring appeal.

One of the defining features of *Destroyer* is its lush production, overseen by producer Bob Ezrin. The album featured orchestral arrangements, choirs, and various sound effects, giving it a cinematic quality that set it apart from KISS's earlier works.

The album's cover art, depicting the band against a post-apocalyptic backdrop, further solidified KISS's image as larger-than-life rock gods. This visual element, combined with the album's thematic storytelling, added an extra layer of intrigue to *Destroyer*.

In retrospect, *Destroyer* remains one of KISS's most iconic albums. It showcased the band's ability to evolve and experiment with their sound while staying true to their hard rock roots. With its mix of grandiose production, memorable anthems, and theatricality, *Destroyer* solidified KISS's status as rock royalty and left an indelible mark on the world of music. It remains a classic in the rock genre and a testament to KISS's enduring influence.

DETROIT ROCK CITY

EDDIE TRUNK *(RADIO DJ & TV PERSONALITY)* – It's really one of the quintessential KISS songs. It was technically the first KISS song I ever heard because my first KISS record was *Destroyer*. When the needle dropped, it pretty much changed my life that minute. The next day I got every KISS record my parents would buy me. That's how it all started for me so it had to be on my list and one of the band's biggest songs to this day.

DON JAMIESON *(COMEDIAN)* – *Destroyer* is the first KISS album I ever bought so naturally DRC was the first KISS song that I ever heard. And to this day, if I had to pick my favorite KISS song, it would be yep you guessed it… still "Detroit Rock City". It totally captures the excitement of going to see a KISS concert (bummer ending notwithstanding) and is the perfect live concert opener. The whole build-up with the radio changing channels, the big riff coming in and the thunder of the drums blew my 12-year-old mind out. And I guess it still does! *Destroyer* is also still my favorite KISS album.

The cast of *That Metal Show* with Peter Criss

BRIAN TICHY *(THE DEAD DAISIES, GENE SIMMONS BAND)* – Top to bottom excitement! Another shuffle! Relentless / anthemic / melodic / bombastic... classic Paul vocals! Let's give it up for how powerful and huge Paul's vocals are! That is a tall order and he kept it up for decades! He really built up a thick set of lungs! I don't think he gets enough credit for how solid and powerful his vocals are!!!

PAULIE Z *(ZO2, Z ROCK)* – *Live in Sydney 1980* is by far my favorite version of "DRC", and I feel it's worth adding to the list on its own merits. The two main elements that stand out here are Paul's varied vocal melody for the verses and Eric's thunderous groove. To me this version trumps the original and has a life of its own. There is so much energy and vitality to it, which I assume stemmed from them having a new member in the band at the time and trying to prove that they can still rock – and they did!

ZO2 with Ace Frehley

BLA⁊ ELIA⁊ *(SLAUGHTER)* – If I had to choose one KISS song to play for someone from outer space who's never heard KISS it would be this one. Great combination of guitar riffs and lyrics and one of my favorite of Peter's drum grooves. There is so much nuance and cool funk in the drum and bass parts and it's probably my favorite KISS song to play. Gotta be played with a good bass player!

RAISE YOUR GLASSES:
A Celebration of 50 Years of KISS Songs
by Celebrities, Musicians & Fans.

Bully Ray, Loudcaster Tally Fochler, Tom, Dave LaGreca and Zeus,
final KISS show, December 2, 2023

DAVID LAGRECA *(BUSTED OPEN RADIO)* – I remember being at Sears in November 1977 and my mom giving me $10 dollars to buy anything I wanted. I went straight to the record department and bought this gem (I still have the original vinyl I bought that day). The opener will always be the greatest opener to any album. EVER!

RAISE YOUR GLASSES:
A Celebration of 50 Years of KISS Songs by Celebrities, Musicians & Fans.

ZACH THRONE *(COREY TAYLOR, BRUCE KULICK)* – First KISS song I ever heard. Heaviest song I had heard from a band at that point. I was hooked.

BELLA PERRON *(PLUSH)* – "Detroit Rock City" always makes me think of the anticipation of going to see a KISS show. You hear the powerful opening riff as the curtain drops and the show begins. One of my favorite qualities of KISS is that every song is filled with attitude, energy and catchy hooks that stay stuck in your head. "Detroit Rock City" is no exception, with a high-energy shuffle groove, huge chords and lyrics that take the listener on an adventure.

MISTRESS CARRIE *(RADIO DJ)* – I had never been to a concert when *Alive II* came out, I was just a kid. When I heard "Detroit Rock City" on the album, I was fascinated by the fact that it was recorded 'live' at a concert. Hearing all the screaming people set my imagination on fire. I loved the epic band intro too. It isn't easy to capture a band's essence on a live album, many have tried, few have truly succeeded. This song starts one of the BEST live rock albums ever released.

JAMES CAMPION *(AUTHOR, Shout It Out Loud – The Story of KISS's Destroyer and the Making of an American Icon)* – The best KISS song featuring the best KISS lyrics realized by the best KISS performance that makes up the best KISS studio recording. The irrefutable brilliance of "Detroit Rock City" was the inspiration for my writing *Shout It Out Loud*. From its opening radio vignette (yes, I love this) to the screeching car crash that ends our epic young anti-hero's journey, "Detroit Rock City" is not just *the* KISS klassic, it is one of the greatest songs of the seminal rock era, *and* it appears on *Destroyer*, the band's finest album. Structured beautifully from the ostinato guitar intro that builds in momentum until the "Get up! Everybody's gonna leave their feet (seat)!" refrains, and then into the gorgeous melodic guitar aria portending a dangerous road ahead, "Detroit Rock City" joins the distinct tradition of American car songs. It also doubles as a tribute to the city that heralded KISS from the start. Paul Stanley never sang better, hitting those high notes with grit, Peter Criss (and he will tell you) never drummed better, shuffling that relentless beat, Gene Simmons "punching above his weight," as famed producer and co-songwriter, Bob Ezrin put it in my book, drove hard with funk bass descants, and Ace Frehley's sweet harmonies on the solos are pure bliss. The damn thing sounds like a tank regiment crushing all comers with the sonic tremors of a Godzilla bender. Close the books, this one wins.

BULLY RAY *(WRESTLER)* – Greatest way to kick off a rock 'n' roll show. Other than "For Those About To Rock", I don't think there's a better opening and closing song ("Rock And Roll All Nite"). You may say open with "Live Wire", close with "Kickstart My Heart". Okay it's great, but it's still not "Detroit Rock City" and "Rock And Roll All Nite". I don't know any two other songs by any other band that mean more to any other concert.

KING OF THE NIGHT TIME WORLD

AUSTIN MILETO *(SISTERS DOLL)* – Such a killer opening with that guitar feedback. The chorus of this song is so melodic and gets me hyped, and those guitar harmonies in the solo are too good!

DAVID JULIAN *(SONGWRITER)* – After I started band number two, my friend and drummer Rod Ryan, who is a great musician (now a big morning DJ in Houston), would give me a hard time at band practice because I wanted to play newer KISS songs. He said, "you have to listen to old KISS… it's better!" We would debate it even though I hadn't heard much. I picked up *Alive II* (always doing things backwards) and heard "King of the Night Time World". My friend was onto something. I started going back and listening to older KISS because of not only the songs but because I loved Ace's guitar playing. The fact I got to be involved in the writing of two songs on Ace's *10,000 Volts* record still blows my mind.

PJ FARLEY *(TRIXTER, FOZZY)* – "King Of The Night Time World" – I was about 5 years old when *Alive II* came out and this song being 2nd in the setlist, and this really being my introduction into a live concert and hearing how songs segued into another, for some reason I am always transported back to being a 5-year-old when I hear it, and I always wanted it in the setlist because of that.

ZEUS *(SHOUT IT OUT LOUDCAST)* – Is there an album that has a better three opening songs than *Destroyer*, with "Detroit Rock City", this and "God Of Thunder"? Can't hear this without "DRC" preceding this or a car crash. Although somewhat of a cover, this is all Paul Stanley and KISS. Just a fun and energetic song. Peter is killing it on this song. Paul screaming "I'm the King!" eight times after the solo and then Ace coming in gives me goose bumps. Just a kick-ass song. KISS and Bob Ezrin at their best!

NEIL DAVIS *(CREATURES FEST, KISS AMERICA)* – A lot of vivid memories around this song. First impression was hearing it on *Destroyer* and how it transitioned into this song a couple of years later on June 15, 1979, when I attended my first KISS concert during the *Dynasty* tour in Lakeland, Fl. KISS opened with "King of the

Night Time World". The band coming up through the stage and then starting with this song is still etched in my memory. Final strong memory was the *Reunion* tour on July 14, 1996 at the Rosemont in Chicago. "KNW" was the second song and had the speakers that rose from the ground and the ceiling. I see it in my mind like it was yesterday.

KEITH ROTH *(SIRIUS XM, THE DICTATORS)* – The winter of '78, it seemed like it was never going to stop snowing. School was cancelled for what seemed like a month. So, we would bundle up and walk around at night, delinquent kids with our 8-track player. *Destroyer* was playing on a loop thru the blizzards of '78. When I hear this song particularly, it just brings me back to that time!

Keith Roth with Ace Frehley

GOD OF THUNDER

DON JAMIESON *(COMEDIAN)* – Although it was written by Paul Stanley it has Gene Simmons written all over it. Thank God (Of Thunder!) that Bob Ezrin knew that too. As we all know, Gene thinks of himself as a God of sorts and this song feeds his bombastic ego. It's a dark, moody song... kind of sounds like the soundtrack on the road to Hell. Plus, when you're 12 years old and you hear the word "virgin" in a song it's pretty exciting.

FRANKIE KAZARIAN *(WRESTLER)* – On this one from *Destroyer*, the intro to this song always gets me. Then the epic chorus that I love with Gene singing, "the god of thunder, and rock 'n' ro- a-woll". So cool! Ace is absolutely on fire all throughout, and as a kid I always thought this song was about Thor from *Marvel* comics, so it scored extra cool points for me.

ACE VON JOHNSON *(FASTER PUSSYCAT, L.A. GUNS)* – My favorite KISS song, full stop. This is what I think of when someone mentions the band; Gene spitting blood and pyro and smoke and this riff. I've probably played it at soundcheck with every band I've ever been in. Insert Gene "Ooh-Yeah!" here.

CHRIS "THE WALLET" HAICK *(GENE SIMMONS MONEYBAG SODA)* – I would crank this song as loud as I could! Gene's voice was so evil: "I am the Lord of the Wasteland!........". I got this crazy idea one day as I blasted this song while staring at the picture of Gene's bloody face on the gatefold of the record. I was going to spit blood in my bedroom!!! I filled my mouth with ketchup and instead of spewing blood, I vomited all over! My younger brother still hammers me for that.

DALE TORBORG *(THE DEMON WCW)* – That's a special song for me. That was my walk-out music when I came out to the wrestling ring in WCW. As soon as the drumbeat would start, I'd be laying in that coffin that would tilt up and the doors would open and let me out, my heart started bumping and I thought about that when I saw them in the last show at MSG. I tried to soak that in. A special moment for me.

Dale Torborg as The Demon

GREG PRATO *(AUTHOR, Take It Off: KISS Truly Unmasked* **and** *The Eric Carr Story)* – The Demon at his most demonic? Interesting that such a "trademark Gene tune" was penned entirely by Stanley. In my younger days, I was always a bit bothered by the odd children's voices (supposedly Bob Ezrin's children)… but have since learned to accept it. By the way, Eagles of Death Metal do a dandy cover of this.

JAMES CAMPION *(AUTHOR, Shout It Out Loud – The Story of KISS's Destroyer and the Making of an American Icon)* – *Destroyer* is a masterpiece. Did I mention this yet? Perhaps my nearly 400-page homage to it didn't quite drive that home. "God of Thunder" is its gory centerpiece, a sound-collage worthy of a young boy's imagination: all fiery cherubs and bestial growling, the Demon's serenade rising from the depths to headphones near you. This never ages; its studio version (and I am not counted among those who espouse that it is better being galloped at twice the speed live) is terra-stomping perfection. All those years Bob Ezrin guided Alice Cooper is distilled here. Stanley told me once, as he tells everyone, that this may be his proudest moment – to compose Gene's signature song – but truth is he bitched about its abduction but then had to realize there is no human who could capture this mayhem and then spend the next nearly half century performing it. Also, props to Peter's elevator shaft tom-tom assault.

PJ FARLEY *(TRIXTER, FOZZY)* – I was almost afraid of this song when I was a kid, yet I could not turn it off. Talk about a song that stops you dead in your tracks. Thank GOD Paul gave it to Gene!!

GREAT EXPECTATIONS

AHMET ZAPPA *(MUSICIAN)* – I don't know why people give me such shit for loving this song. It is actually one of my all-time favorite KISS songs. I love Gene's performance. I love the melody. I love that it's a song about, well, fucking. And I guess they never hid the fact that they were into playing the sold-out mega shows and getting pussy. I know people are going to rip what I'm saying to shreds, but I think that's pretty much the rock star fantasy. I think for some people, one big reason why they want to be in a band is to say something musically and express themselves politically or whatever. And then maybe some other bands are writing about getting laid. And here's a super-awesome track about the special time that you spend with a lady, and the Great Expectations of what you want to accomplish with her.

NEIL DAVIS *(CREATURES FEST, KISS AMERICA)* – A very divisive song amongst KISS fans. I am in the small minority that I have always loved this song. I was happy to see it included in *Alive IV* but then it fell back into obscurity.

JAMES CAMPION *(AUTHOR, Shout It Out Loud – The Story of KISS's Destroyer and the Making of an American Icon)* – Try and remember for a moment the spring of 1976 and how music was being consumed. The album was king. And one thing producer Bob Ezrin knew was how to present his artists in this format. He told me several times he saw the album as a play with acts and how the final song on side one was as important as the album's opener and closer. *Destroyer* has all of those and its anchor is "Great Expectations." Choir, lush strings, and balefully strummed acoustic guitars, Gene again spreads his creative wings telling tales of his lofty position in the firmament with a croon worthy of Dean Martin's booziest. Besides "Beth," which this song helped to get on the album as Simmons alerted Peter Criss to how far Ezrin was willing to go with this collection of songs, "Great Expectations" is the initial sonic departure of KISSdom, allowing the band to avoid a "sound" in place of an ethos beyond rock and forge new paths into the types of musical left-turns they would infamously try and sometimes fail to achieve, but remains creatively noteworthy for not repeating themselves.

IZZY PRESLEY *(MUSICIAN, COMIC)* – For many this song is considered a "WHAT THE FUCK?!?" moment in KISStory, yet to an impressionable 4-year-old Tommy Elwell… yes, that's my real name… I loved it from the first time I heard it even though I had no clue what it was. Still do. He said breast. That was cool.

MURPH *(SHOUT IT OUT LOUDCAST)* – Since this is on *Destroyer*, I have heard this track more than I would like to admit. Each time it is played, I am still trying to determine why a song with such suggestive lyrics is played at such a slow/operatic pace. Play it at a faster/harder clip and maybe it fits in a little better with the rest of the album.

FLAMING YOUTH

TODD KERNS *(BRUCE KULICK, SLASH)* – In retrospect I look at *Destroyer* as the great experiment within the KISS universe. A very successful one but not necessarily what I would call the quintessential KISS sound. Obviously, it is a classic and carries the weight of great success to prove it. "Flaming Youth" is another easily overlooked gem in my opinion. It is lost in a collection of straight-up classics, making it a classic in its own right. As kids my brother and I wanted to name our eventual band "Flaming Youth" (long before either of us played instruments), which wouldn't have really worked due to the connotations later attached to the word 'flaming'. Its grandiosity in the lyric about the very audience it's being sung to makes it all the more palatable. Ezrin's production, complete with pipe organ, is perfectly over the top. The Aerosmith-type riff that carries the post-choruses is almost uncharacteristic, especially when it breaks into odd time signatures during the solo. Not something KISS usually did. Definitely a hallmark of Bob Ezrin's influence.

STEVE WRIGHT *(PODDER THAN HELL PODCAST)* – From the bombastic beginning to the first lines in the verse, "My parents think I'm crazy and they hate the things do. I'm stupid and I'm lazy and if they only knew…" How can that not resonate on an impressionable 8-year-old just getting into "his" new music? This song seems to get a lot of crap for the calliope on it. I don't mind it; it adds some substance to the song and Gene's bass lines are fantastic! Apparently, Dick Wagner played the leads on this song, but back then we had no idea. And I don't really care now. Brings back some awesome memories of sitting listening and studying EVERYTHING on the album!

TOM HIGGINS *(KLASSIC '78)* – The first KISS song I ever heard at age 6 in 1976. The way the song kicks in and with Paul's "Whoah yeah" vocal intro. It gets me every time. It's like KISS meets The Who. This song should have been in the 1979 movies *Over The Edge* or *The Warriors*.

BRAD RUSTOVEN *(SLAMFEST PODCAST)* – "I'm stupid and I'm lazy, man, if they only knew" – my brother used to make fun of me for liking KISS and used this lyric as ammo – see, they're stupid and lazy! I always loved the effect on Paul's vocal during the higher,

higher and higher part, and I never minded the calliope that was included in the song.

JASON BAKKEN *(COBRAS & FIRE PODCAST)* – Vocally one of Paul's best. He was at his peak during 75-77. I still remember the first time I heard the line, "My parents think I'm crazy. And they hate the things I do". I would try to tell my mom that's how she feels. And she would say something like, "Well Jason. You are a little crazy, but I don't hate anything about you". She just wouldn't let me rebel. This in one of many songs that didn't work as well live as it did in the studio. Too bad because it rips.

TOM GIGLIOTTI *(SHOUT IT OUT LOUDCAST)* – About as anthemic as it gets for a deep cut. A sing-along, fist-pumping chorus and Paul is cheering us on as we listen like teenagers to this song about rebellion and music. The calliope music near the outro may not be what KISS fans are used to hearing, but Bob Ezrin tried so many different things, it's hard to complain about anything from *Destroyer*.

SWEET PAIN

TODD KERNS *(BRUCE KULICK, SLASH)* – I realize this is my first Gene selection, but it should be noted that I'm trying to steer off the beaten path for my choices so as to not repeat too much of others' selections. There are many in Gene's collection of songs that in my opinion are quintessential to the KISS sound and aesthetic. Gene always had a way of introducing themes way beyond the comprehension of the single-digit-aged audience discovering them. Like me! "Plaster Caster" comes to mind. A song about S&M was as easily understood as advanced calculus for my age group. All we knew was that it rocked. Gene's groan off the top of the song was always a big hit for me and my friends. We'd all bellow it in unison. Ezrin's use of female backup singers took it pretty close to R&B town yet still remains very KISS. Gene is one of the most underrated vocalists in rock. His range and pitch are spot on. His tone is the most unique in the genre. The fact that he committed to sing 'in character' is such a statement of his conviction to a much bigger goal that on the odd occasion when he'd step away from that voice he was like a whole new guy. Interesting to imagine if he'd never found 'The Demon' persona what voice Gene would have committed to.

Tom and Zeus at Creatures Fest

RAISE YOUR GLASSES:
A Celebration of 50 Years of KISS Songs
by Celebrities, Musicians & Fans.

NEIL DAVIS *(CREATURES FEST, KISS AMERICA)* – "My leather fits tight around me". What a great opening line from Gene! In my opinion, this is one of the best KISS songs that was never included in a KISS tour. When they did play it on KISS Kruise VII, the crowd went crazy. I still watch the YouTube video of this song regularly.

STEVEN MICHAEL *(GROWIN' UP ROCK PODCAST)* – This a song that comes a little later in the record that I think many discount because of the front-loaded classics that are on this record, but I dig the poppy riff and the somewhat darker, sexy lyrics. I like that phrasing in the chorus as well. It's a short basic pop/rock tune that covers up the overall darker theme.

JASON HERNDON *(KISS MY WAX PODCAST)* – My introduction to KISS. It's tough for me to only choose one song to write about from the album. I don't know what my life would be like today without this record and every song on it. I gravitated to "Sweet Pain" for some reason. The push and pull in the tempo makes the song incredibly exciting to listen to. There is so much going on in the instrumentation. And Gene's vocal is just perfect. Everything on *Destroyer* was layered with so much. I spent hours and hours listening intently while staring at the cover. Life-changing.

JAMES CAMPION *(AUTHOR, Shout It Out Loud – The Story of KISS's Destroyer and the Making of an American Icon)* – Gene has always touted his Beatles obsession, from being awakened by them on *The Ed Sullivan Show* appearing as more gang than band, and his occasional songwriting hat tips, but *Destroyer* was the album where he revealed his funky side. In addition to his Curtis Mayfield pilfering of "Freddy's Dead" for the rolling bass line in "Detroit

Rock City," he offered up his most soulful tune in "Sweet Pain." Passing over the S&M elements, which are sublime, this is a major departure for the band three years before their "disco" turn. From the soul-singer background vocals to the effervescent keyboards, this is the album's secret weapon. Maybe it's the least liked song on the beloved *Destroyer* precisely because it stands out, and more importantly shows Simmons to be a far more elastic composer than anyone else in the band. And having spent the final years of his life in a pen-pal friendship with Dick Wagner after giving him his last nickname that he adored, The Invisible Maestro, and lent a blurb to his insightful memoir, *Not Only Women Bleed* – I really dig this guitar solo.

SHOUT IT OUT LOUD

RUDY SARZO *(QUIET RIOT, OZZY)* – I really like this song. It's hooky, KISS has a great musical element. If you can hum it or whistle it, you've got a hit. KISS has a lot of those. Definitely.

JEREMY ASBROCK *(ACE FREHLEY)* – I bought sides 3 and 4 of *Alive II* in my backyard when I was 4 years old for 50 cents. My brother told me to get that one because it had "Shout It Out Loud". Dropped the needle. Crowd on STUN. Band kicks in. Cocaine speed. Paul screams. Bombs go off. My path was immediately set and my fate was sealed. I didn't even know what being a guitarist in a band was, but I knew I wanted it. The song itself is fantastic. Straight-up '60s Motown filtered through '70s guitar rock. Brilliant, economic solo by Ace. I will always credit this song with my life path, and if you single out playing in both Gene and Ace's bands only, it's been worth the blood, sweat, and many tears.

RAISE YOUR GLASSES:
A Celebration of 50 Years of KISS Songs
by Celebrities, Musicians & Fans.

JAMES CAMPION *(AUTHOR, Shout It Out Loud – The Story of KISS's Destroyer and the Making of an American Icon)* – I know this one gets shit for being "Rock And Roll All Nite"-light, but it ain't. "Shout It Out Loud" stands on its own. A wonderful call-and-response duet by Paul and Gene, the two vocal brands of KISS, preaching above a rollicking Motown-esque piano-bass motif cooks, jack. And here we have another chant-addled chorus, but this time a tad more melodic. I hear this song and I am back in 8th grade diving into a pool with it cranking from speakers somewhere. The summer of *Destroyer*, the bringer of good tidings and anarchic suburban dreams. Again, like everything on that album it sounds so fucking good. The needle could hardly contain the vinyl back in the '70s when this captured our rapturous rebellion, "they're too old to understand" wrapped in pep talk "time for you to make a stand." Gene *does* demand that "you got to have a party," and who is arguing with the Demon? And again, since I am not only presenting my Top Ten favorite KISS songs I cannot forget to deconstruct this baby – a banger from the opening "Oh, yeah!" to the tumbling cold out. Short. Sweet. Rocking. As a lifelong bigmouth, shouting it out loud always made sense to me. And although the "message song" does not fall under the KISS *raison dêtre*, this rings many a bell.

BETH-AMI HEAVENSTONE *(GRAHAM BONNET BAND)* – It's one of those songs when you hear it once you absolutely love it. I was in a band and we covered this song and I used to love singing it.

TOMMY LONDON *(OZZY'S BONEYARD, SIRIUS XM)* – The song where I became a proud member of the KISS Army. I was a little kid. My parents were members of the Columbia House Music Club and that month they got *Destroyer* on 8-track (yes, 8-track!). My brother and I were captivated by the cover. We saw four superheroes! We couldn't wait to hear it. My mom popped it in and my brother and I just stared at the stereo like we were watching a movie. I remember it was "Shout It Out Loud" that got us jumping on the furniture.

Tommy London with Paul Stanley

BETH

BLAS ELIAS *(SLAUGHTER)* – Another one of my all-time favorites. I love everything about this song, the vocals, the lyrics, the musical arrangement and the orchestration. Captures the essence of the working and touring musician's life so perfectly.

RICHIE RANNO *(STARZ)* – An absolute gem of a ballad. When KISS were recording the song I was a member of Starz and both bands were at the Record Plant recording at the same time. We were both managed by Bill Aucoin and had become pretty good friends.

RAISE YOUR GLASSES:
A Celebration of 50 Years of KISS Songs
by Celebrities, Musicians & Fans.

I would be hanging around in the hallway & lounge on breaks then would wander into their studio while they were recording. I had the pleasure of meeting the great Bob Ezrin.

CRAIG GASS *(COMEDIAN)* – Their most popular song for a reason: it's a legendary song that comes WAAYYY out of left field for the music that they're known for, and has lyrics that show actual sensitivity from a band that also put out lyrics like "I wanna put my log in your fireplace", which I have found to not be helpful in convincing women to have sex with you, because it sounds like your crotch is on fire, which apparently women don't like hearing. But they sure do like "Beth".

BRYCE MILETO *(SISTERS DOLL)* – I've sang this live a few times and it always hits my heartstrings like no other KISS song.

JAMES CAMPION *(AUTHOR, Shout It Out Loud – The Story of KISS's Destroyer and the Making of an American Icon)* – Bring those eyes back from staring at the ceiling and keep that sigh to yourself. At the risk of losing credibility for my list thus far, "Beth" is a great ballad by a band that wouldn't know a ballad if it kicked it in the collective balls. Should I also mention. it is arguably one of the first "power ballads" in rock history? By the way, like it or not, it is still the highest charting KISS single, topping out at #7 on the *Billboard* Top 100. So, sue me; I love *Destroyer*, and this is that album's little engine that could. Beyond the rocket fuel terror of "Detroit Rock City" to the fist-pumping mania of "Shout It Out Loud," there is always Peter sitting on a stool singing to those sweeping piano trills from Mr. Ezrin and the scintillating orchestral bridge composed/arranged by Master Bob and his mentor, Allan Macmillan. It is tear-inducing stuff, the softer side of KISS. Love that story of the inimitable Scott Shannon pushing it to all his radio buddies, the grass roots ascent of a song nobody really wanted, the runt of the litter (Catman pun), making good. I always think of the underdog film *Rocky* taking best picture just a few months after KISS won its only award, the People's Choice. Indeed.

Bryce Mileto with Peter Criss

MISTRESS CARRIE *(RADIO DJ)* – Growing up, Peter Criss was the KISS member that I loved the most. I was a little girl, and he was the Catman. My twin aunts, who were 10 years older than I was, used to sing this song when I was in the car and it came on the radio and when I found out that the Catman sang it, it was my 'favorite'. It's the perfect love song.

SHANDON SAHM *(MEAT PUPPETS)* – To me this is just so great. One of the best ballads ever and Peter's voice at this time had that perfect cigarette-smoked voice and scratch. The fact that Peter brought this in at all is a win for KISS regardless of if he wrote anything other than just. "I hear you calling." Peter wins just for mentioning the tune and it doesn't matter how much he had to do with the final tune.

PJ FARLEY *(TRIXTER, FOZZY)* – Obviously something completely different from KISS at this time. It showed a human side to the band from a lyrical standpoint, and to me they were always super-human.

DO YOU LOVE ME

MIKE PORTNOY *(DREAM THEATER, WINERY DOGS)* Another track that didn't make it on to *Alive II*. One of my favorite Paul songs. It's just such a badass song. The lyrics are great, it's just a great rock 'n' roll song, one of their heavier ones. One of my favorites on *Destroyer*.

BLAS ELIAS *(SLAUGHTER)* – Great song musically and lyrically. I love how it starts with just the drums and vocals before the full band comes in. When I was a kid I'd listen to the lyrics and imagine what it would be like to be a "Rock Star." After I got in the music biz it took on a whole other meaning to me as I could relate to it from the other side.

RAISE YOUR GLASSES:
A Celebration of 50 Years of KISS Songs by Celebrities, Musicians & Fans.

Mike Portnoy with Eric Singer

NEIL DAVIS *(CREATURES FEST, KISS AMERICA)* – A glorious song that has aged well. Furthermore, the changes they made to the live version have made this song even better. The harmonic guitar part at the end of the song is so high energy. I remember Ace and Paul playing the ending notes on the *Reunion* tour and it made the song sound so good. This melodic ending evolved since that time with Paul and Tommy Thayer enhancing it even more.

BILL STARKEY *(FOUNDER, KISS ARMY)* – Critics resented the band's popularity and always claimed it was due to gimmicks. They never gave them a fair chance. This was one of my faves because *Destroyer* really shook up KISS fans who were weaned on *Alive!* Some left. Some stayed. Some left and then came back. To me this was Paul just getting accustomed to his fame and fortune and asking ANY girl... do you love ME... or is it all the other things like the makeup and the limos?

AHMET ZAPPA *(MUSICIAN)* – It's that chanty anthemic, staccato vocal performance. And that easy-to-sing chorus that that Paul gives you. He's telling this classic little groupie story, about the band's success and the people that are hanging on. And then when the chorus comes in, this is the moment when he's trying to find out whether or not someone really likes him for him, or just likes him for all the stuff that he has. This is one of the first times I heard a song that told that story. People go hamburger in the audience when the song comes on. The chorus is just so big and so rad, and to me it's a taste of what's to come: "Love Gun". I think "Do You Love Me" is the is the redheaded stepchild of "Love Gun".

RAISE YOUR GLASSES:
A Celebration of 50 Years of KISS Songs
by Celebrities, Musicians & Fans.

CHAPTER 5

"ROCK AND ROLL OVER"

Released: November 11, 1976

Rock and Roll Over, the fifth studio album, marked a return to the band's hard rock roots. It's an explosive record that captures the raw energy and essence of KISS at their prime. With classic tracks like "Calling Dr. Love" and "Ladies Room," this album demonstrated KISS's ability to create infectious, no-nonsense rock 'n' roll while maintaining their iconic stage personas.

In the mid-1970s, KISS was at the height of their fame, and *Rock and Roll Over*, released on November 11, 1976, captured them at their most electrifying. This album was a deliberate return to the band's hard rock roots after the ambitious production of *Destroyer*.

Rock and Roll Over wastes no time in delivering a punch with the opening track, "I Want You." Paul Stanley's gritty vocals and Ace Frehley's fiery guitar work set the stage for an album that's all about the raw power of rock 'n' roll.

One of the album's standout tracks is "Calling Dr. Love," featuring Gene Simmons on lead vocals. With its infectious chorus and Simmons' swaggering performance, it became a live favorite and remains a classic KISS song.

Rock and Roll Over marked a return to basics for KISS, emphasizing their musical prowess and the chemistry that made them such a formidable live act. It proved that KISS could produce an album that was both musically satisfying and commercially successful without the elaborate production of their previous record.

In retrospect, *Rock and Roll Over* remains a pivotal album in KISS's discography. With its mix of hard-hitting rockers and melodic ballads, it showcased the band's ability to keep evolving while staying true to their core sound. It's a reminder of the band's timeless ability to deliver the electrifying spirit of rock 'n' roll.

I WANT YOU

STEVE BROWN *(TRIXTER)* – *Rock and Roll Over* was the record that completely changed my life forever. This was the first KISS song I ever heard. I remember I was an 8-year-old kid and I borrowed this record from my sister-in-law's brother. I took it home and put it on the turntable and I remember listening to it with the intro with the acoustic guitar. I remember thinking 'wow this kind of reminds me of the Beatles, kind of sounds like Rod Stewart. Then all of a sudden the power chords come in and then Paul's voice and literally, that moment when I heard the band kick in, it was like being at a KISS concert in my mind. The sound of the guitars, the sound of Paul's voice, the sound of the drums. The sound of Gene's bass. I'd never heard anything heard like that and it was mesmerizing for an 8-year-old kid. I remember just being completely spellbound.

CHARLIE BENANTE *(ANTHRAX)* – Is there a better opener? I don't know. It's just a great fucking song. Paul has some great songs on this record. It fits him so well and there's a great Ace Frehley lead.

JOE McGINNESS *(KUARANTINE, KLASSIC '78)* – The 12-string/vocal intro is like its own kick-ass mini-song within itself, would have loved to hear this on the *End of the Road* tour, might be some of Paul's greatest songwriting overall, also love the fact that Paul throws in the first half of the solo.

RAISE YOUR GLASSES:
A Celebration of 50 Years of KISS Songs by Celebrities, Musicians & Fans.

Joey Cassata and Joe McGinness

AUSTIN MILETO *(SISTERS DOLL)* – Love the soft gentle start with the acoustic and Paul's voice, and then that killer riff hits you right in the face. Plus, the trade-off of solos between Paul and Ace is mad!!

HAL SPARKS *(COMEDIAN)* – Paul's jab at '70s singer/ songwriters sitting on a stool trying to use chump poetry to get a woman in bed. Why not just get to the point? This was my first experience of true satire in a song. And the main riff is like a huge middle finger at those guys and for those girls.

LISA LANE KULICK *(BRUCE KULICK'S WIFE)* – I first saw KISS in 1983 during the *Creatures of the Night* tour in Dubuque, Iowa. I wasn't very familiar with many of their songs but when I heard Paul

Stanley sing "I Want You" I fell in love with the song immediately. As time goes by, I've come to admire this Led Zeppelin-style, riff-heavy tune. It's a great representation of KISS's impressive songwriting style.

Sisters Doll with Tommy Thayer

TAKE ME

JEFF TROTT *(ART DIRECTOR)* – Take me any way you want me! Put your hand in my pocket grab onto my rocket. Is there anything more cock rock than "Take Me"? "Take Me" embodies the essence of rock 'n' roll sleaze, with its raw energy and infectious hook and slamming groove.

MIKE PORTNOY *(DREAM THEATER, WINERY DOGS)* – Another one not on the live album and another favorite of Paul's songs. One of my favorites on *Rock and Roll Over* and a great rocker. It's a great forgotten track.

Mike Portnoy with Tommy Thayer

TODD KERNS *(BRUCE KULICK, SLASH)* – It is my opinion that *Dressed to Kill* and *Rock and Roll Over* are the perfect representations of the perfect OG KISS sound. *Love Gun* is not far behind. Just straight-up guitar/drums rock 'n' roll. *RARO* is the last OG KISS record I acquired as a kid because I only had enough allowance money for what I could find. By 1978, when my brother and I discovered the band, there were already eight KISS records to convince our parents were worthwhile investments. We acquired them out of sequence on a week-to-week onslaught of KISS nirvana until we caught up to *Dynasty* in real time by 1979. That said, I definitely heard the *Alive II* versions of the *RARO* songs before actually owning *RARO*. Once I finally got my hands on the record it was obvious to me, even then, that this was the band making a statement about who they truly were. I think that statement still rings true to this day. "Take Me" is another just straight-up rock 'n' roll song by Mr. Stanley, albeit with the very adult opening line about the rocket in his pocket. As kids we would have found this endlessly entertaining. The sixteenths on the high hats in the chorus is such an interesting choice. Peter was underrated. I love his swing. Great in your face ROCK 'N' ROLL.

CHRIS L. *(POD OF THUNDER)* – The second KISS song I ever heard at age 10, this one grabbed me by my rocket and made me an instant fan of the band in 1977. The sound, the attitude, the aggression, the lyrical subject matter that I didn't fully understand but knew I wanted to understand – it was a perfect storm that led me away from the Beatles, Simon & Garfunkel, and other music my parents liked in favor of stuff that was more rebellious and dangerous.

KEITH ROTH *(SIRIUS XM, THE DICTATORS)* – Me and Tom Morello got to host KISS at The Whisky a Go Go, it was so surreal!!! Before the gig, Tom was at their hotel and questioned them about their career when we did the post-show. Tom asked me the same questions; something along the lines of my most memorable KISS lyrics. What jumped out was put your hand in my pocket and grab onto my rocket!!

Keith Roth with Paul Stanley

TOM GIGLIOTTI *(SHOUT IT OUT LOUDCAST)* – Arguably the greatest opening line in any KISS song (or any song for that matter). Paul is so sexed up in this song and that infectious riff along with that pumped up chorus make this song a must-listen on the legendary *Rock and Roll Over* album. And Ace burns it up as usual with a killer solo.

CALLING DR. LOVE

HOLLY KNIGHT *(SONGWRITER)* – I love this song. It's so quintessentially KISS, like the songs in *This is Spinal Tap*… which I happen to like immensely.

RAISE YOUR GLASSES:
A Celebration of 50 Years of KISS Songs
by Celebrities, Musicians & Fans.

BRIAN TICHY *(THE DEAD DAISIES, GENE SIMMONS BAND)* – Great groove! Great riff! And the cowbell rules! Gene's vocal is classic! Great chorus and solo! Classic KISS!

JAMES CAMPION *(AUTHOR, Shout It Out Loud – The Story of KISS's Destroyer and the Making of an American Icon)* – There might be better Gene Simmons songs, but this one hits home for me every time. It is stupidly brilliant, knuckle-dragging double-entendre fun. Give it up for shifting "Call me" into "Calling." It sounds like a bass player wrote this on guitar, so he could snap off those downbeats. "Calling Doctor Love" plods and seduces, but never seems to cut loose, yet it burrows deep into my subconscious for no reason and abducts me out of nowhere more times than I'd like to admit. I think that says less about Gene and more about whatever chips are missing in my skull. There is also a menacing guitar solo from Ace, and you just know Paul always loves singing those background vocals; "Calling Doctor Love!" Three cheers for the *Double Platinum* version and whatever corner of Hades the Demon crawls out of to begin proceedings. I also dig the *Alive II* version, because it rushes just enough to *never* be boring.

CHARLIE BENANTE *(ANTHRAX)* – Gene's vocal approach on this song, it's so awesome and it just fits the persona of the Demon.

MISTRESS CARRIE *(RADIO DJ)* – The song that spawned 1,000 Halloween costumes. This song is so fun for a fan at a show, cowbell, great solo, and every sexual innuendo you can cram into a song under 4 minutes. This song alone had groupies lining up after the show!

SHANDON SAHM *(MEAT PUPPETS)* – To me it's the "I Want To Hold Your Hand" type song. It just sums up KISS really well. The cowbell – OMG! Just thick and in your face and again the pocket is so wonderful. The tom-tom fills in this tune are amazing, you can hear that they sound like concert tom-toms with no bottom heads, kind of dry but very present. The background vocals sound far away and spacey. I absolutely love it. The lyrics are brash and just fit. KISS always had this great sexually charged energy about them.

MARTIN POPOFF *(AUTHOR)* – Sure, we're at that fine line between clever and stupid, but "Calling Dr. Love" is probably the most famed song from a well-regarded KISS album from the golden era. What makes it, besides Peter's cowbell and Eddie Kramer's simple but effective production (never sounded good on vinyl, but on my computer, weirdly joyful), is Gene's vocal melody, which does more of the heavy lifting than the song's caveman chords.

ZACH THRONE *(COREY TAYLOR, BRUCE KULICK)* – The 45 had "Calling Dr. Love" on the A-side and "Take Me" on the B-side. My very first KISS purchase. It would not be my last...

LADIES ROOM

STEVE BROWN *(TRIXTER)* – One of the most powerful KISS songs for me as a little kid. To me, this is almost like KISS's "Brown Sugar". One of the first KISS songs I learned when I was taking guitar lessons.

TOM HIGGINS *(KLASSIC '78)* – This is so catchy and so Gene. On the choruses, I always imagined Gene & Paul singing into the same microphone doing those backup vocals. Lots of hooks in this and great cowbell. Many hours looking at the *RNR Over* album cover while listening to this.

Ryan Spencer Cook, age 10

PETER DANKELSON *(PETE'S DIARY)* – Could you imagine if this song was written today?! Gene's vocals are fun and mischievous. The chord choices in the intro have that cool Rolling Stones kind of voicing! Ace's guitar tone really jumps out at you on this song. Love how Peter uses the cowbell to lead into the chorus.

ZEUS *(SHOUT IT OUT LOUDCAST)* – Love the cool opening guitar riff followed by the Gene bass line and of course that Peter signature cowbell. Based on a previous Gene demo, "I Don't Want No Romance," which is on the *Destroyer* Deluxe Box Set. The song is an underrated gem from KISS's most consistent album, *Rock and Roll Over*. Fun and catchy as all hell. Bonus points for Paul's classic intro on *Alive II*!

Tom and Zeus on the KISS Kruise

MARTIN POPOFF *(AUTHOR)* – Hey, I'm as surprised as you are seeing three songs here from *Rock and Roll Over*, an album I'm kinda tepid on. But it looks like Gene is the record's star, or at least star seducer, whipping out his Dr. Love character again and continuing to build and then embed a mini-rock opera concept album within the album, the band's second of 1976. I'm a sucker for these Stonesy, in-the-pocket boogie rockers from the band, and Gene's got the perfect bluesman's voice to fit the bill.

BABY DRIVER

AUSTIN MILETO *(SISTERS DOLL)* – Such a killer groove, always been a massive favorite of mine. I love Peter Criss's vocals in this, what a tone, can't beat that raspiness he has!! Still hoping to perform this with him one day haha!

CHARLIE BENANTE *(ANTHRAX)* – The end of that song, the way he (Peter) kind of ad libs and he's screaming. Peter had that great raspy voice.

STEVE WRIGHT *(PODDER THAN HELL PODCAST)* – This song just stomps in, and Peter's raspy vocals are perfect here. Lots of great guitar work throughout the song in and between the lines in the verses, and the very memorable Ace wailing leads during the chorus. No real solo per se in the song, but you do get some great leads as the song fades out from Ace. Just a fun song that does give you the feeling of cruising down the road.

CLAUDIO SPERA *(KISS ARMY NATION PODCAST)* – I like this song. It shows, once more, Peter's roots back when he was in Lips. His soul voice makes the chorus shine. Peter is not well known for very strong and profound lyrics, but I find this tune fits very well into the whole *Rock and Roll Over* scheme. Sonically, it shows how capable Eddie Kramer was in getting the real KISS sound on this record.

IZZY PRESLEY *(MUSICIAN, COMIC)* – One could quickly point to Peter's vocals on this tune, but the shining light is Ace. Killer filler licks, which is something you don't hear in very many KISS tunes. Gives it a little jammy element.

LOVE 'EM AND LEAVE 'EM

JEREMY ASBROCK *(ACE FREHLEY)* – I didn't pay much attention to this song when I was younger. But it grabbed me when I was older. Maybe not so much lyrically, but musically, it's trickier that it seems, with an absolutely killer solo from Ace. One of my jobs in the Gene Simmons Band was to make Gene's extremely oversized lyric sheets. I always had lyrics to this song ready to go. We asked and asked and asked and asked. He always poo-pooed this one. We did a snippet maybe once. Maybe next time?

Jeremy Asbrock, age 19

RAISE YOUR GLASSES:
A Celebration of 50 Years of KISS Songs
by Celebrities, Musicians & Fans.

TODD KERNS *(BRUCE KULICK, SLASH)* – Another great example of Gene at the peak of his straight-up rockness. The riff is relentless, with Gene singing about being Gene. Paul's voice in the chorus blends so well with Gene's – it's the magic sauce that unites the entire catalog. Peter is in drum solo mode in the pre-chorus, which creates a wild abandon hoping he'll be able to get things back on track. Which he always does. Eddie Kramer loves loud guitar solos. Me too!

NEIL DAVIS *(CREATURES FEST, KISS AMERICA)* – Anybody that knows me is aware of my love for the *Rock and Roll Over* album. It is the number #1 album from my youth and the single biggest reason why I continue to be a KISS fanatic to this day. I remember learning that KISS would be on the *Don Kirschner Rock Concert* show in the spring of 1977. "Love 'Em and Leave 'Em" was one of three songs on the show that night. The performance was choreographed and lip-synced to album. But it did not matter as it was a powerful performance, with the band coming down the stairs and Gene leaping in the air. Many years later when I was put on KISSmas Masquerade in Sarasota, Fl in December 2020, I had the Talismen (Ryan Spencer Cook, Jeremy Asbrock, Philip Shouse) plus Ken Trapp from KISS America perform the *Rock and Roll Over* album in its entirety. The four guys performed the record flawlessly and Jeremy sang lead vocals on Love 'Em and Leave 'Em.

NICHOLAS BUCKLAND *(AUTHOR, Hottest Brand in the Land)* – One of the most underrated songs by '70s KISS. The bass line will have your groin thrusting in syncopated agreement as though it shared a symbiotic relationship with Gene's codpiece. Our Demon runs through a stunning amount of sex clichés with absolute delight: "Well, make a reservation, between the hours of ten and two", "I've got a stiff proposition" are pure odes to horizontal refreshment. The

RAISE YOUR GLASSES:
A Celebration of 50 Years of KISS Songs
by Celebrities, Musicians & Fans.

MVP award goes to Peter Criss here, who eschews all traditional time-keeping in the bridge to turn it into one long drum solo to take you into the bravado of the chorus!

Nicholas Buckland with Gene Simmons and Tommy Thayer

PETER DANKELSON *(PETE'S DIARY)* – I love Peter's drums on this song; the driving rhythm with the chords in the intro make you want to head bang! The chorus is simple but super-catchy! Ace's guitar tone during the solo is awesome.

ROBERT CONTE *(AUTHOR)* – My absolute favorite Gene track on *Rock and Roll Over*. Its tempo is just right, and the lyrics represent the quintessential "rock-star-getting-the-groupies" lifestyle before we knew of such things as AIDS and other long-term consequences of raw, random sex with people who you would likely never see again. To me, it's the hardest-sounding Gene track on the album and represents the true grit of rock 'n' roll; a great road story translated into song. Ace Frehley's solo is my favorite on the album, too. I wished the original band had played it live during the late 1970s.

MR. SPEED

BRUCE KULICK *(KISS)* – My brother Bob kills it on that (demo) track. Now we can imagine what those vintage KISS songs would sound like if Bob was in the band then. He's doing his best Leslie West (from Mountain). There's no way all those riffs would've wound up on the original.

EDDIE TRUNK *(RADIO DJ & TV PERSONALITY)* – I love the song, and it's different from anything else KISS had done. Some people say its KISS meets Lynyrd Skynyrd or even the Rolling Stones. You can hear some "Can't You Hear Me Knocking". *Rock and Roll Over* top to bottom is probably my all-time favorite KISS studio record. This song is just a little bit different because there's a little southern-y sort of lick to it. Paul's vocals are spot on for why he's one of my favorite singers. The attitude, the grit, the power.

CHARLIE BENANTE *(ANTHRAX)* – It's one of those songs that gets overlooked and it's a great Paul song.

DAVID LAGRECA *(BUSTED OPEN RADIO)* – Catchy song. Instantly puts me in a good mood. Don't agree? Go f**k yourself.

GREG PRATO (*AUTHOR, **Take It Off: KISS Truly Unmasked** and **The Eric Carr Story**) – Might be KISS's most underrated song – as it sounds like they're replicating a "Stones-y swagger" kinda vibe. And I'm shocked it was never given a good honest try to be performed live way back in '76/'77 (whereas a tune like "Take Me," which I don't find nearly as strong, was included in the setlist instead).

ZEUS (*SHOUT IT OUT LOUDCAST*) – Everyone's favorite KISS deep cut. How this was not on every KISS compilation or a live staple I will never understand. Perhaps, the lyric, "I'm so fast, that's why the ladies call me Mr. Speed"? Who knows. Strangely it did make it to the movie *Speed* soundtrack. But for me, this is the best KISS demo of all time, which is on the 2001 KISS Box Set, disc 2. Bob Kulick's guitar absolutely kills it on the demo version. His fills and lead work make it even better than the already incredible album version. Give it a listen and you will see.

SEE YOU IN YOUR DREAMS

JOE McGINNESS (*KUARANTINE, KLASSIK '78*) – This is a really catchy tune that I feel is always overlooked. Paul's back-up vocals at the end of the song really make the production very climactic. I've always loved to hear Paul and Gene harmonizing, especially in the early days.

COURTNEY CRONIN DOLD (*COMEDIAN*) – Who needs a third verse when you have a catchy-ass chorus like this! It's a fun song but easily the weakest tune on this almost perfect album. It's hard to be the meat in a "Mr. Speed" and "Hard Luck Woman" sandwich. But I love it so much I ever HEAR it in my dreams.

TOM HIGGINS *(KLASSIK '78)* – This is another song where some love it and some hate it. I've always liked it. Again, the personality of it overrides any "filler song" labels. Gene's vocals are great and hearing Paul's vocals so prominently on the choruses is awesome. They made a point to make sure the songs showed some sort of unity on them back in the day.

MARTIN POPOFF *(AUTHOR)* – It's back to 1976's *Rock and Roll Over* for this happy, humpy rocker, old-school boogie at the verse but then modestly dramatic with those hanging chords at the chorus, basically the strongest chorus on the album. Lyrically, Gene's up to his usual Dr. Love tricks, but this is just a snappy pop-metal rocker, one with a bit of a *Dressed to Kill* vibe.

TOM GIGLIOTTI *(SHOUT IT OUT LOUDCAST)* – *Rock and Roll Over* is loaded with classics so it's easy to forget about this one. I think the chorus where the guitar chugs along and breathes is so cool and unique. Gene was in his prime during this era and he reminds everyone of that during each verse. Ace absolutely smokes during another insane solo. We would get a different version of this a few years later on Gene's 1978 solo album (which I admittedly enjoy also).

HARD LUCK WOMAN

RYAN SPENCER COOK *(ACE FREHLEY)* – The 2022 Ace Frehley tour stopped in Nashville, TN to perform at a KISS-inspired event called *Creatures Fest*. Whenever Ace mentions Peter Criss, I immediately picture Lois from the animated TV series *Family Guy*. Both Lois and Ace pronounce "Peter" with a thick, East Coast accent... "Pee-tah". "Pee-tah's gonna join us on stage in Nashville", said Ace. "We'll do a few songs, some full band with Pee-tah on drums and another stripped down, acoustic numbah". I was thrilled to learn that the 'numbah' was "Hard Luck Woman". Not only is this my favorite Peter Criss vocal ever, it's also one of my all-time fave Paul Stanley compositions; top five, no doubt. Not only because it's a great song, but also because of its origin. I've read that Paul initially approached this song as a lesson... maybe even a self-imposed assignment. He once stated in an interview that he challenged himself to see if he could write a song similar to Rod Stewart's "Maggie May" or "You Wear It Well". I'd say he hit a direct bullseye. The beautiful arrangement combined with the lavish twelve-string guitar fit with Peter's voice like hand in glove.

Peter couldn't have been nicer to us at soundcheck. He cheerfully greeted each of us by name, with a big bear hug. A very kind and humbling gesture on his part. We actually spent a great deal of time with him that afternoon, just getting to know one another and mutually enjoy our time together, playing music. The soundcheck was not open to the public, so it was just the band and Peter... Ace was not scheduled show up until later so it was just us guys with the Catman. Here's the truth bomb... as much as I enjoyed the show later that evening, my fondest memory of that day will remain the time we spent alone, talking to our hero, playing music. It was a moment in time for us, and no one else. *"PETER CRISS ON THE DRUMS!!"* Meeting your heroes is joyous, performing with them is a gift and receiving recognition from them as a peer is a dream come true. My heart is full.

Philip Shouse and Ryan Spencer Cook onstage with Gene Simmons

JORDAN CANNATA *(SLAUGHTER)* – This song blew my mind. I had no clue that it was KISS. It doesn't sound like them at all. When I first heard it, I thought it was an old Rod Stewart or Faces song. Not only did it have that feel musically, but Peter Criss even sang like him. The song highlighted another side of KISS that I had never heard before. Also, let's not forget how rare it is for a drummer to sing lead vocals. As a drummer, that's a skill I have always admired.

BRYCE MILETO *(SISTERS DOLL)* – Very sentimental to me. I performed this at a local talent comp at 5 years old. Talk about a dream coming true at 22 years of age performing this alongside Peter Criss himself in New York City.

RAISE YOUR GLASSES:
A Celebration of 50 Years of KISS Songs by Celebrities, Musicians & Fans.

Bryce Mileto as Peter Criss

JEFF PLATE *(TRANS-SIBERIAN ORCHESTRA, SAVATAGE)* – I grew up listening to my parents' country music and this song brought me right back to that. The music, the lyrics, the vocals, it's such a great tune. And again, it was different, I was not expecting this when I first heard it. *Rock and Roll Over* is one of my favorite KISS albums.

BLAS ELIAS *(SLAUGHTER)* – Peter Criss was my first favorite member so I love the songs he sings on. This has such a cool Rod Stewart vibe and I love his voice on it.

ACE VON JOHNSON *(FASTER PUSSYCAT, L.A. GUNS)* – Unpopular opinion; Peter was my favorite singer in the band. I love this song so much. I heard it as a kid on the radio (that was the thing we had in our cars, kids) and was certain it was a Faces/Rod Stewart tune. But better. Who was "Rags", anyhow? Like "Beth", this song showcases the band's ability to function way beyond just your average hard rock outfit. Would have loved to have seen this performed live, back in the day.

ALLISON HAGENDORF *(MUSIC JOURNALIST, TV HOST & PRODUCER)* – What a timeless great song, heartfelt and bluesy. Great road trip song.

JAMES CAMPION *(AUTHOR, Shout It Out Loud – The Story of KISS's Destroyer and the Making of an American Icon)* – This possesses all the greatest attributes of KISS for me – a poppy song written by Paul Stanley and one of the few of his sung by Peter Criss, whose voice I adore. I know Paul likely went there because he envisioned Rod Stewart's signature rasp telling this tale of the lonely sailor's daughter and it seemed like a cynically planned follow-up to the beseeching "Beth", a hit when they were recording this song, but, man, this one suits the Catman perfectly. He sounds genuinely broken up by his macho dickishness, a rare trait of self-awareness from a vain rocker. Another excellent chorus, one of Paul's best – and that's saying something – and a fantastic use of acoustic guitars, which I think is an underrated attribute of *Rock and Roll Over*. Props to the *Double Platinum* version that doesn't bring the drums in until the second verse and punched-up harmonies that add to the lyrical solemnity. Peter's scatting at the end is a highlight.

MAKIN' LOVE

JASON HOOK *(FIVE FINGER DEATH PUNCH)* – Mean guitar riff, and I like the plucked acoustic part in the pre-chorus. Notable moments come when Paul Stanley plays with his vocal double on the word LOVE in the chorus, to emulate some kind of delay effect.

SHANDON SAHM *(MEAT PUPPETS)* – Just a brilliant, blistering guitar solo from Ace. Once again Peter really shines on this. The back beat drums sound amazing, like you can tell there's no bottom heads on the tom-toms like concert tom-toms.

ZACH THRONE *(COREY TAYLOR, BRUCE KULICK)* – Heavy, fast song. "Thick like oatmeal" solo from Ace, great drumming from Peter and amazing, loud vocal from Paul.

Zach Throne, Todd Kerns, Bruce Kulick and Brent Fitz

RAISE YOUR GLASSES:
A Celebration of 50 Years of KISS Songs by Celebrities, Musicians & Fans.

HAL SPARKS *(COMEDIAN)* – This song is a New York serenade. You get the feeling the tempo was set by Paul's dance steps onstage. Other bands might have played it way slower or faster, but KISS fans can see Paul onstage when they listen to this song. Though it came out when I was in elementary school, this song was the defining song of my teenage years.

BRENNAN MILETO *(SISTERS DOLL)* – Just a KISS classic. I love playing this song live; this song just screams '70s and it's just balls-to-the-wall, classic KISS which we all know and love.

RUSSELL PETERS *(COMEDIAN)* – I like the live version, it sounds harder. The album version is cool, but it sounds too clean, and I need that grit on it. It sounded too polished in the studio, and it didn't match what they were doing.

Ad for Russell Peters show

RAISE YOUR GLASSES:
A Celebration of 50 Years of KISS Songs
by Celebrities, Musicians & Fans.

CHAPTER 6

"LOVE GUN"

Released: June 30, 1977

Love Gun, the sixth studio album, captured the band at the pinnacle of their fame. This record is a raucous celebration of rock 'n' roll excess, featuring anthems like the title track, "Shock Me," and "Christine Sixteen." With its signature hard-hitting sound, *Love Gun* further solidified KISS's status as rock icons and provided a fitting soundtrack to their extravagant live shows.

In the late 1970s, KISS was at the height of their superpowers. This album marked another high point in the band's career, blending hard-hitting rock anthems with memorable hooks and lyrics that resonated with fans worldwide.

The title track, "Love Gun," is one of KISS's most iconic songs. Paul Stanley's infectious riff and soaring vocals made this anthem an instant classic. The song embodies KISS's trademark blend of catchy melodies, raw energy, and over-the-top charisma.

"Christine Sixteen" is a cheeky, tongue-in-cheek track with Gene Simmons delivering his characteristic swagger. It's a playful nod to the band's indulgence and the rock star lifestyle.

Ace Frehley takes the lead vocals on "Shock Me," a track that showcases his guitar prowess with a blistering solo. This song demonstrated that each member of KISS could take center stage and shine in their own right.

The album cover, featuring the band members in their iconic costumes and makeup, reinforces KISS's image as larger-than-life rock gods. It's an image that helped define the band's brand and contribute to their status as rock 'n' roll legends.

In retrospect, *Love Gun* exemplifies the band's ability to combine their bombastic stage personas with a tight, musically satisfying record. With its mix of anthemic rockers, memorable ballads, and catchy hooks, *Love Gun* is a testament to KISS's enduring appeal and their status as one of the most iconic rock bands in history. It's a snapshot of an era when rock 'n' roll was bigger, louder, and more spectacular than ever before.

I STOLE YOUR LOVE

MIKE PORTNOY *(DREAM THEATER, WINERY DOGS)* – I have a personal attraction to this song because it's what they opened with the first time I saw them live on December 14, 1977 at MSG. I remember getting goosebumps and the hair on the back of my neck standing up. I remember smelling the pot smoke in the air. It was such a life-changing experience. Them opening up with this is just something I'll always remember.

Mike Portnoy with KISS

RAISE YOUR GLASSES:
A Celebration of 50 Years of KISS Songs by Celebrities, Musicians & Fans.

JORDAN CANNATA *(SLAUGHTER)* – What can you say about this song other than it is THE quintessential KISS song. This tune highlights everything that makes KISS... KISS. The riffs, the arrangement, the lyrics... just awesome. This song truly captured their over-the-top attitude and persona. I would say this may also be my favorite vocal performance from Paul Stanley. It really highlights who they were and is another song that just gets stuck in your head all day long.

TODD KERNS *(BRUCE KULICK, SLASH)* – Another example of Paul's rock and roll might. That opening riff is a monster. When Paul screams "ALL RIGHT!" It's like your speakers are going to explode. Then all hell breaks loose. The fact that the band opened their accompanying tour with this song says it all. The rare example of Paul and Ace trading off solos. Paul's tasty slow hand before Ace lights it all on fire. This same magic was also utilized in the "I Want You" solos from *Rock and Roll Over*.

RYAN SPENCER COOK *(ACE FREHLEY)* – Big Rock Show had been become a staple on the annual KISS Kruises. Our '80s metal-inspired set lists were quite popular with the fans, allowing us to garner encore performances, year after year. On this particular cruise, BRS were asked to perform at the Sail Away show. This was a coveted spot as it was the exact moment the ship actually set sail, officially proclaiming the beginning of the week-long trip with our favorite band. The stage was set amidst the ship's lido deck amongst thousands of KISS fans from around the world... Japan, Australia, France, Mexico, Sweden and of course, the U.S.A... For this particular sail-away show, we were asked to perform a set of KISS klassiks, a task both easy AND difficult. Easy, because we were able to perform any KISS tune upon command, it was in our DNA.

RAISE YOUR GLASSES:
A Celebration of 50 Years of KISS Songs
by Celebrities, Musicians & Fans.

Difficult, because we needed to put together a set that did not include any songs that KISS themselves would perform on said cruise.

Amongst our set of deep cuts was "I Stole Your Love". The song's immediately recognizable intro was so well received that it took me aback for a moment; an almost out-of-body experience (NOTE: unbeknownst to me, it would be a feeling that I would experience over and over again in my future). I actually remembered my first time hearing this song in 1977 as I sat at the end of my bed listening to *Love Gun*, then again as I dissected *Alive II*. As the band played on, the crowd's reaction became stronger and stronger... by the time we reached the end of the first chorus, we were one with our audience. "We're really killing it!!" I thought to myself. Then, just as I approached the mic to sing the next verse, there was a swell... a HUGE swell... I could see the crowd's excitement rise exponentially and their decibel level increased ten-fold. What I didn't realize was that Paul had come up behind me from stage left. The only person on the entire cruise that didn't know he had done so was ME. As he took over lead vocals for the rest of the song, he and I stood shoulder to shoulder, sharing the mic... once we got to the lyric "How does it feel / To find out you're failing your......
TEST?!?!", Paul immediately picked up on the fact that the FOH engineer hadn't engaged the delay effect, so he did it himself... "TEST, TEST, TEST, TEST!! HOW DOES IT FEEL?!?!" This was a dream realized... an unplanned, once-in-a-lifetime moment. A moment that didn't take place at just any random music festival. Make no mistake, this was an event created by KISS, exclusively for KISS fans. *"WHAT JUST HAPPENED?!?...........*

RAISE YOUR GLASSES:
A Celebration of 50 Years of KISS Songs
by Celebrities, Musicians & Fans.

Ryan Spencer Cook onstage with Gene Simmons

JOE McGINNESS *(KUARANTINE, KLASSIC '78)* – Should be an opener for every KISS song over "Deuce" and "Detroit Rock City". Great groove, great riff, tempo gets my blood pumping instantly. Gene's bass slide before the chorus is so epic, the studio version is way better than *Alive II*, so energetic.

DAVID PEA *(KISS REPLICAS)* – This is the very first KISS song I ever heard. I was 8 years old in 1977 and remember staring at the album cover and being totally in awe of the artwork and how epic the band members looked. Weeks went by before I even thought of asking my mom to play the record, and when she did: BAM! The music resonated with me instantly and a KISS fan was born. "Love Gun" may be my favorite song from the album, but "I Stole Your Love" is what started it all for me and is a very close second. This is a perfect song from a perfect album. Paul's voice became a staple and benchmark for all other singers to live up to.

RUSSELL PETERS *(COMEDIAN)* – That was the first song I had ever put on headphones and listened to, and it would startle me every single time. That has a lot of great memories. KISS had a lot of funk to them, the bass line.

CHRISTINE SIXTEEN

CHRIS JERICHO *(WRESTLER, FOZZY)* – Part of Gene's trilogy (singing about young girls) with "Goin' Blind" and "Domino". On *Alive II*, it's so much better. I don't like the piano in the back on the studio recording. I think on *Alive II*, it does (no pun intended), come alive. It had the potential to be a hit.

SHANDON SAHM *(MEAT PUPPETS)* – I love the bap bap bap of the Pearl snare drum sound and the vocal delivery and walking bass lines. Pocket drumming again, which is on the whole *Love Gun* album. Thick bass tones. The Pearl snare drum. Simple but effective and right to the point. Solo is simply effective but it's the overall feel, and had the production been crappy none of those songs on *Love Gun* would have stood out.

TOM GIGLIOTTI *(SHOUT IT OUT LOUDCAST)* – Who cares if the lyrics haven't aged well, the song rocks! The studio version is incredible with the piano during the verses, and who doesn't love a creepy Demon breakdown as he hunts down Christine? Have some fun, people! The song is over 45 years old and it's harmless KISS fun. Just try not to sing along with the chorus!

BRITT LIGHTNING *(VIXEN)* – This is the first KISS song I remember ever hearing. I remember I was in the car, riding with my mom, and I immediately started singing along to the chorus. After that day, I discovered the rest of KISS's catalog and became a proud member of the KISS Army!

MURPH *(SHOUT IT OUT LOUDCAST)* – Yes, the lyrics are creepy, but the song is still awesome. Musically, I think this is one of their best-sounding tracks. When Tone Loc is sampling Ace Frehley's riff in "Funky Cold Medina", it is clear that the sound of KISS expanded well beyond the traditional rock audience.

GOT LOVE FOR SALE

RUSSELL PETERS *(COMEDIAN)* – I love that song and it's another song I've never heard live, which is weird because it's from their prime album and you would think they would have done every song from *Love Gun* on that tour and *Alive II*, which sucks because it's a great song.

KENT SLUCHER *(LUKE BRYAN, KUARANTINE)* – Love the guitar riff and I'm a sucker for a great melody. I love the call and answer vocals on the outro with Ace playing guitar fills. Overall, a KISS gem with a great Gene vocal.

RAISE YOUR GLASSES:
A Celebration of 50 Years of KISS Songs
by Celebrities, Musicians & Fans.

Matt Starr, Troy Luccketta, Kent Slucher, Brent Fitz and Joey Cassata

MIKE BRUNN *(THE ROCK EXPERIENCE)* – For many decades this song was a throwaway for me. In my opinion there were so many better songs on the album. However, over the past decade I've grown to love this song and was so happy that Gene performed this with his solo band in 2018. Now it's one of my favorites on the album.

STEVE WRIGHT *(PODDER THAN HELL PODCAST)* – This track just bangs right in, and then the band really gets chugging as Gene starts to sing. And just listen to the bass lines under the verses. The acoustic guitar laying underneath the tracks really chunks up the sound as well. The song was formerly known as "Have Love Will Travel", famously recorded with the brothers Van Halen. Peter has some great drum fills in between the verses and chorus. Ace just rips on the solo while the band kills it underneath. This song is hands-down my favorite KISS song! And how can we forget the title being sung softly as Ace rips it up as the song fades out! Absolutely LOVE IT.

TOM GIGLIOTTI *(SHOUT IT OUT LOUDCAST)* – *Love Gun* is my album and this song is absolutely one of the reasons. The deepest of deep cuts. The layered acoustic guitar over certain sections, along with the greatest version of the Demon growl vocals, make this song one of my all-time favorites. The chorus is so cool with Paul jumping in to harmonize. Ace is in his glory during this era, and he doesn't disappoint with another solo. Peter is killing it on the ride cymbals during that infectious chorus. Classic KISS that I wish was a bigger hit. But that's ok, I consider this "my song".

SHOCK ME

STEVE BROWN *(TRIXTER)* – *Alive II* was the second KISS record I ever got. The sound of *Alive II*, I love. The performance and recording of "Shock Me", Ace's guitar tone completely captivated me. And his voice as well. And of course, the centerpiece of it is the guitar solo. I think it's the best solo he's ever played. He even does some pick tapping at the end.

PJ FARLEY *(TRIXTER, FOZZY)* – The first we hear of Ace on lead vocals and it added a new dimension to the band. As a kid at that time, it was great to hear Ace have a voice in the band.

RAISE YOUR GLASSES:
A Celebration of 50 Years of KISS Songs by Celebrities, Musicians & Fans.

RYAN SPENCER COOK *(ACE FREHLEY)* – CHS Field Stadium, St. Paul, MN, September 21, 2017. The Gene Simmons Band tour was well underway at this point. As one can imagine, it was a tour that picked up steam quickly, not only generating more tour dates, but also creating a buzz within the industry. Every major music media outlet was covering us and the chatter amongst our peers was overwhelming... all eyes and ears were upon us.

We were asked to headline an event at a baseball stadium in St. Paul, MN... CHS Field Stadium, home of the St. Paul Saints. This would be the largest show we'd done up to this point. We were particularly excited for this show as the promoter added two very special guests to the bill... Cheap Trick and one Ace Frehley. "Ace is gonna sit in with us for this show" explained Gene. "Let's do our set and then bring him out at the end". We were flabbergasted. This would be the first time Gene and Ace had performed together in 13 years. Our ever-changing set list seemed extra special that night, knowing that Ace would be joining us...

"Back in 1973 in New York City, this guy and I and two other guys put together the band that we never saw on stage... LET'S HEAR IT FOR ACE FREHLEY!!!" We kicked into "Parasite", "Cold Gin", and then... "SHOCK ME". Cue out-of-body-experience... here I am in the year 2017 playing the Spaceman's signature song, a song that I listened to over and over throughout my childhood into adulthood. I reflected on how often I'd stare at his photo whilst listening to this very track, and now here I was playing it with the man himself, not to mention with The Demon as well. There are several photos of this exact moment; we stood elbow to elbow in one solid line across the stage, three guys, two heroes... "ACE FREHLEY! LEAD GUITAR! SHOCK ME! *"AM I DREAMING?!?"*

NOTE: Little did I know that this very moment would spearhead our future with Ace Frehley. He was so pleased with our performance at this show that he would ask us to support him again in Australia, ultimately hiring us as his full-time band.

EDDIE TRUNK *(RADIO DJ & TV PERSONALITY)* – It's got to be there because if you grew up in the '70s, *Love Gun* was the pinnacle. The idea of hearing Ace Frehley sing a lead vocal just blew everyone's mind. Up to that point, he was the guy we knew the least about. Just another real landmark in KISS history. There was such a whole different layer of KISS then that isn't there now.

Eddie Trunk with Ace Frehley

BELLA PERRON *(PLUSH)* – One of my absolute favorite KISS songs. I remember watching videos of "Shock Me" as a kid and thinking that Ace is the coolest person to ever exist. Everything about the song – the opening riff, the amazing solo, the creative lyrics, the catchy melodies, not to mention the live version going into the solo with the infamous smoking guitar. The solo on the recording is one of my favorites. I love how Ace seamlessly combines melodic lines and repetition with his faster licks, taking the song to an entirely new place.

Ryan Spencer Cook onstage with Ace Frehley

TOMORROW AND TONIGHT

JOEY CASSATA *(ZO2, Z ROCK)* – This is a song that the band gave up on too early! I know they included it on *Alive II*, but they never really played this song live. This is a very catchy pop song with so many hooks it's immediately singable upon first listen!

TOM GIGLIOTTI *(SHOUT IT OUT LOUDCAST)* – KISS tried to capture the vibe of "Rock And Roll All Nite" and "Shout It Out Loud", and to some extent, I really think they did it here. It gets buried among the classics on *Love Gun* and fans may have been fatigued at this point with the attempts at anthems, but the hook is catchy as hell and the version on *Alive II* is absolutely awesome.

ZEUS *(SHOUT IT OUT LOUDCAST)* – That intro howl is just so fun and so Paul. Yes, it's another attempt at "Rock And Roll All Nite" Part 2, but it works. A kind of old-school rock 'n' roll song. A "You can do it Waterboy!"-type of KISS lyric. Paul's vocal delivery and New York accent and annunciation is so underrated in lines like, "Take it in the cellar, let me be your fella." What a fun and catchy song. Classic Paul Stanley chorus and hook. Should have been a live staple.

Tom and Zeus with Kuarantine

MAC *(UGLY AMERICAN WEREWOLF IN LONDON PODCAST)* – Another song that is much better on *Alive II* than it was on the studio version, "T&T" mixes some great pop vocals with

KISS riffs and a swinging beat from Peter makes this a fun one. I know the lyrics of the chorus may be a little basic but they're fun and you know it was fun to play live. The studio version does contain a boogie-woogie piano bit that makes it different. But the breakdown where Paul sings *a capella* is so much better live, it makes the song a live classic and crowd favorite.

JAY SCOTT *(THE HOOK ROCKS PODCAST)* – This is a great tune... the sequel to "Mr. Speed". It gets elevated with an incredible performance on *Alive II*.

LOVE GUN

PJ FARLEY – *(TRIXTER, FOZZY)* – My favorite KISS song of all time. It's arguably their best song. From Gene's bass line to the guitar solo and everything in between this song always stood out as my favorite.

CHARLIE PARRA *(KUARANTINE)* – Gotta admit that the first time I ever listened to this one was during the intro of 1999 movie *Detroit Rock City* when I was 14 years old. That intro was mind-blowing: a resumé of the '70s, pop culture, music icons and footage of when KISS ruled the world. Besides, that guitar solo was some kind of a pentatonic scale lesson with a pyrotechnical plot twist. I became a Spaceman fan instantly.

PETER DANKELSON *(PETE'S DIARY)* – Such a killer and classic KISS tune! The whole band is on fire. I love the harmonies that Paul is doing in the chorus, and Ace's guitar solo is killer! I loved hearing this song when I saw KISS for the first time on their *End of the Road* tour. My dad and I were close to the platform that Paul flew out to, and to see Paul up close and hear him singing that song live was such a cool moment I'll never forget!

BRITT LIGHTNING *(VIXEN)* – This is always my favorite part of a KISS show – when Paul Stanley flies over everyone's head to a stage in the center of the arena to sing this song. Absolutely epic! No one puts on a show like the hottest band in the world. No one!

AHMET ZAPPA *(MUSICIAN)* – When I heard it as a kid, I just thought it was something like *Flash Gordon* or *Star Wars*. Like singing about a laser, but it's just talking about, you know... your Johnson. This is disgusting, but when I was younger, any time I would pee in a public restroom, if there was anything on the toilet, I would use it like target practice and try to shoot it off the toilet while singing "Love Gun". Am I the only one? *Barbarella* was often on in my house, around the same time I was listening to this album a lot. You know how you can replace the audio track of *The Wizard of Oz* with *Dark Side of the Moon*? I think you could replace the audio track of *Barbarella* with *Love Gun*.

ALLISON HAGENDORF *(MUSIC JOURNALIST, TV HOST & PRODUCER)* – "Love Gun" is my favorite KISS song. It's a straight-up banger and I listen to it often. I will forever have the image of Paul zip-lining across Madison Square Garden for the final show. It was a perfect moment that encapsulated rock KISStory for me, and I cherished every second of it.

RAISE YOUR GLASSES:
A Celebration of 50 Years of KISS Songs by Celebrities, Musicians & Fans.

Allison Hagendorf with Paul Stanley

CHRISTIAN SWAIN *(CEO, PANTHEON PODCASTS)* – I used to despise KISS. I thought I was above it. Instead, I was prog, or I was punk, or I was glam, or, well you get the picture. What I was, was a snobby Anglophile when it came to rock 'n' roll and KISS was crass, over-the-top, fake Kabuki theater, staged by sludgy and cartoonish Americans for children, at least in my extremely nerdy teenage brain... That is until I joined my first rock 'n' roll band in 1977 and the other guys wanted to play a KISS song. Ugh, I thought. But KISS had recently released a new album, so I figured I had to learn a KISS song. The album was *Love Gun* and for me, the song was the title track. And for some reason, they finally spoke to me. Why? Well, because it was something achievable. Even I could sing and play "Love Gun"! And it was fresh that the other kids would love to hear it! Damn you, logic!

Of course, over the years, I dove into the rest of their catalog and in the end, begrudgingly accepted the greatness that is KISS. Once I dropped my own pretentions and realized they are more than anything just about fun and making sure everyone is having fun through their over-the-top and crass spectaculars in song and show, then I became a fan. I mean how can you not. Over the years, so many of their indelible anthems made it to various personal playlists, but I still remember fondly how "Love Gun" was one of my earliest attempts at actually playing rock '' roll, and for that I will be eternally grateful to the band.

HOOLIGAN

JOEY CASSATA *(ZO2, Z ROCK)* – God I love Peter's voice!! He's got that rasp and soul that is impossible to duplicate. *Love Gun* is my favorite classic KISS album, and this is one of the reasons why. I definitely hated school as a kid and I would always sing "I'm a hooligan… I won't go to school again, won't go no"!!

TOM GIGLIOTTI *(SHOUT IT OUT LOUDCAST)* – May sound strange to some but this has always been my favorite Peter lead vocal. *Love Gun* is my favorite album and I think the vibe of this track is so cool for Peter. We don't have to get into the silliness of the lyrics because after all, it's a KISS song!

RAISE YOUR GLASSES:
A Celebration of 50 Years of KISS Songs
by Celebrities, Musicians & Fans.

Joey Cassata making Peter Criss crack up

NICHOLAS BUCKLAND *(AUTHOR, Hottest Brand in the Land)* – Extra points go to Criss and Penridge for rhyming "hooligan" with "school again" in this straight-ahead rocker that seemed to suit Peter's voice infinitely better than a "Beth" or "I Can't Stop The Rain" ever did.

CHRIS L. *(POD OF THUNDER)* – What's not to like about a glimpse into the rough-and-tumble past of the Catman? "Beth" was great and all, but on the heels of "Baby Driver," "Hooligan" continued the welcome return of Peter the rocker. I also have a soft spot for this song because of the misheard lyric "chicken salad and roast beef" that inspired a delicious sandwich for me in real life.

RAISE YOUR GLASSES:
A Celebration of 50 Years of KISS Songs
by Celebrities, Musicians & Fans.

Nicholas Buckland with Paul Stanley

COURTNEY CRONIN DOLD *(COMEDIAN)* – Peter's vocals on this are sexy, sultry, and fierce. I think "Hooligan" could have been a hit song. It's catchy, the lyrics are fun, and they rhyme "hooligan" with "school-agin". Pretty sure that's a musical first.

JOE POLO *(PODCAST ROCK CITY)* – I always loved this song – the riff is cool, the lyrics are cool, and I think Peter sounds great! I really enjoy it live on some of the bootlegs.

TOM HIGGINS *(KLASSIK '78)* – Part of the charm of KISS albums was the different vocalists. This is a rock 'n' roll song. Who cares if it's not a "hit"? What does "hit" even mean? What a voice on Peter! This is KISS music. Every member's personality is present on this. Paul's & Gene's backing vocals, Ace's guitar solo and Peter's vocals & drumming. When I buy an album, I want to hear the personalities of the band members. This does that.

ALMOST HUMAN

TODD KERNS *(BRUCE KULICK, SLASH)* – Another great Gene song as sung in the character of "The Demon". Gene is channeling his inner Bela Lugosi/Lon Chaney. It almost has shades of future disco musings with the percussion adding an almost dancey quality. The falsetto voice in the chorus creates an almost creepy effect. This is an example of the many voices of Gene Simmons. Gene's bass tone on this is fierce. Ace's solo lays waste to eardrums. Underrated banger.

SHANDON SAHM *(MEAT PUPPETS)* – Right out of the gate with the gong in the beginning and the Demon going "Ahhhhrgghh and saying, "HOT." The guitars riffs are off the hook. The space-y guitar solo is out of this world. It just hits you square in the face. Killer production on this tune and the whole *Love Gun* album. It's just fantastic. The Gene songs are some of his best. This is absolutely the KISS that I love.

CLAUDIO SPERA *(KISS ARMY NATION PODCAST)* – This is KISS at its pinnacle. Typical KISS sound. And to me, this is not

Gene Simmons singing, this is the Demon singing. It is a fascinating kind of Jekyll and Hyde idea. With lyrics like "I'm almost human, can't help feeling strange, the moon is out, I think I'm gonna change", I cannot avoid thinking of Gene getting ready to hit the stage. Ace's intricated solo is perfect, and I love those demoniac voices in the back.

JEFF TROTT *(ART DIRECTOR)* – "Almost Human" is a deep cut that complements the hits from *Love Gun* well. The intro scared the shit out of me as a kid because all I could do is picture Gene breaking through the wall from *Phantom of the Park*. Gene's growl in the beginning of the song is fantastic and very memorable. "Almost Human" is an awesome song with menacing demon attitude. A great filler track and complements the hits from *Love Gun*.

TOM GIGLIOTTI *(SHOUT IT OUT LOUDCAST)* – Take my comments from "Got Love for Sale" and apply them here. One of the greatest Demon deep cuts. The effects and that haunting chorus combined with the noisiest and craziest solo that Ace has ever done (with the exception of maybe "Dark Light"). Another song that appears nowhere but here and I like it that way, another song I consider "mine". *Love Gun* is my album and Gene is my guy, so it's no wonder I love this. And let's not forget that opening… "AAAARRRRRGGHHHHHH!"

Tom and Zeus on KISS Kruise XI, Halloween 2022

PLASTER CASTER

TOM HIGGINS *(KLASSIC '78)* – My childhood friend Shawn had the LG album before I did. This and "Hooligan" always make me think of him. This is Gene at his pinnacle. The music, lyrics and feel are all perfect. Great leads by Ace, great vocals all around and great drum work from Peter on the intro too.

ZEUS *(SHOUT IT OUT LOUDCAST)* – A Gene song about the Plaster Casters. A rare Gene pop culture song. Gene is using his "Beatles voice" on this one. Love the bass opening, then guitar, then drums. The pre-chorus is surpassed only by the incredible catchy chorus. I love how on the first chorus there's no call back, and then on the second turn, here it comes. Ace's little guitar fill after "collection" is just awesome. The part that always gets me is the outro call backs when the band changes to "Last her, last her." Ace is also wailing on the outro. This has so many great parts that it is one of the best KISS songs, period.

AHMET ZAPPA *(MUSICIAN)* – "Plaster Caster" works on so many levels for me. Cynthia Plaster Caster is famous for having made these molds of rock 'n' roll icons' dicks. Not that that's something I'm interested in, but I heard the stories as a kid from my mother and father because Cynthia was a family friend. And I was surprised to find out that KISS wrote a song about her. And a little anecdotal fact here; Cynthia was always nervous that her mom was going to find out that she made these proud statues of band members' members. At one point I was trying to work on a deal with Larry Flynt to go to Doc Johnson or one of these dildo manufacturers to help Cynthia put out a line of Rock Cocks. So this song just reminds me of those moments in time, trying to get that business off the ground. Apparently, Jimi Hendrix's member statue required two hands to get a hold of it.

SHANDON SAHM *(MEAT PUPPETS)* – The open E simple bass line is so great because it's thick and like hard rock Paul McCartney. The lyrics and the guitar playing are just great. The rhythm guitar really shines. Peter again just has this infectious swing with that deep Pearl snare drum sound. The vocal delivery is off the hook, real killer. The tom-tom fills right before he says, "Baby's getting anxious," is quintessential KISS.

CHRIS L. *(POD OF THUNDER)* – Over the course of doing my show and following other KISS podcasts, it's surprising to me that this one doesn't get way more love. The inclusion in the *MTV Unplugged* set gave it a little extra juice, but the original studio version on *Love Gun* is just amazing – mainly because of the slow, steady increase in intensity from start to finish – and the guitars are quintessential KISS.

THEN SHE KISSED ME

WES BEECH *(THE PLASMATICS)* – KISS have always worn their love of '60s music on their sleeves, and this tribute to Phil Spector and cover of the Crystals' girl group classic continues in the vein of "Any Way You Want It". Again, a straightforward cover with a heartfelt Paul vocal delivery and interesting and melodic guitar work make for something unexpected on an otherwise hard-rocking album. And when's the last time you heard castanets on a KISS song?

JOEY CASSATA *(ZO2, Z ROCK)* – As a kid I never knew this wasn't a KISS song. It just sounded like another great Paul Stanley song to me. Not sure why this gets so much hate. KISS could do no wrong for me, whatever they put out, I ate up like it was the best thing ever created.

BRAD RUSTOVEN *(SLAMFEST PODCAST)* – I've always liked this song. Of course, when I was 7 years old, I didn't know it was a cover of a Crystals song. I thought it was a KISS original since it had "Kissed" in the title. Paul's vocal and his harmonies with himself are fantastic. While listening as a kid, I would imagine Paul meeting her mom and dad and him getting down on one knee to ask her to be his bride… all while in makeup.

IZZY PRESLEY *(MUSICIAN, COMIC)* – You know, it is so easy to shit on this BUT I shan't. I take myself back to when I heard this record as a kid. No clue that it wasn't a KISS song. No clue that it would be shunned by the KISS masses. The kid in me remembers it like I heard it as a kid as well as the 51-year-old me does, not the snobonian KISS elitist that many of us have become. I like it. Yeah, I said it. Big whoop, wanna fight about it?

MURPH *(SHOUT IT OUT LOUDCAST)* – I understand the criticism this song receives from KISS fans but on its own, it is a great cover. Ace does a nice job of putting his own little style on the song throughout the track, and let's face it, Paul was tipping his hat to future solo projects. The song clearly does not mesh with the rest of the album or the band at that particular moment, but musically, I have always enjoyed their take on this classic.

CHAPTER 7

"ALIVE II, SIDE 4"

Released: October 14, 1977

KISS's *Alive II* album featured five new studio recordings. Released as part of the *Alive II* double LP in 1977, these tracks provided an exciting addition to the live recordings and showcased the band's evolving sound.

These tracks served as a bridge between KISS's earlier hard rock sound and their exploration of more diverse musical styles in the late 1970s. These songs demonstrated KISS's ability to create catchy, hard-hitting rock tunes while adapting to the evolving musical landscape of the time.

In 1977, KISS was riding high on the success of their live albums and their larger-than-life personas. *Alive II* was a culmination of their live shows, but it also offered something new: five studio tracks that showcased the band's versatility and adaptation to changing musical trends.

In retrospect, the new songs on *Alive II*" remain an interesting chapter in KISS's history that bridges the gap between *Love Gun* & the solo albums.

ALL AMERICAN MAN

BRUCE KULICK *(KISS)* – Bob had energy and excitement. Playing those blues riffs like Page, Clapton, Hendrix. Bob comes right out of the gate on *Alive II* with "All American Man". The solo, the harmony parts. He could mix it up and do stinging vibrato and regular vibrato, whammy bar, and dig into the strings.

CHARLIE BENANTE *(ANTHRAX)* – This is one of my favorite Paul Stanley songs. It's so heavy. His delivery on this song is so classic Paul Stanley. He was untouchable at this point. He came up with some great fucking songs and delivered them well.

RAISE YOUR GLASSES:
A Celebration of 50 Years of KISS Songs
by Celebrities, Musicians & Fans.

TOM HIGGINS *(KLASSIC '78)* – A childhood friend, Paul B, gave me a very scratched (and possibly stolen) vinyl of the sides 3 & 4 LP from *Alive II* in 1977. He kept the sides 1 & 2 LP, the gatefold and the booklet. At 7 years old, I didn't ask questions, I just played it over and over. This is 100% Paul Stanley attitude & swagger... musically & lyrically. If someone asks, "What song best represents Paul's persona in the '70s?", this song is it.

NICHOLAS BUCKLAND *(AUTHOR, Hottest Brand in the Land)* – With the knowledge this was co-written by Sean Delaney, the chorus lyrics "… you want to land a six-foot, hot look, all-American man!!" take on an almost shopping-list vibe, conjuring 'Tom of Finland' mental imagery of the highest order. Paul comes to the party and sings it with so much red-blooded macho you can practically see the chest hair coming at you through the speakers!

Tom and Zeus, Halloween 1994

JASON BAKKEN *(COBRAS & FIRE PODCAST)* – "A six-foot, hot look, All-American Man". Right up there with the opening line to "C'mon and Love Me" as far as killer Stanley lyrics. I talked to Bob Kulick about this as it was a song I wasn't getting on guitar. He showed me how to play that main riff. In hindsight it's obvious this isn't Ace on the record. But at the time, I was drinking the Kool Aid.

RUSSELL PETERS *(COMEDIAN)* – I don't know why, I just really like this song. It's one of those songs I wish I could have heard live. Whenever I get in the shower and the water hits me I go "uhhhhh." The song is in the pocket. That was the start of the decline.

ROCKIN' IN THE U.S.A.

BRUCE KULICK *(KISS)* – Bob is doing some tasty boogie-woogie rock 'n' roll riffs. Playing the role of a good time rock 'n' roll guitar player.

JOE McGINNESS *(KUARANTINE, KLASSIK '78)* – What I find amazing about this song is how autobiographical it is. Gene was at the height of his rock stardom, and the song describes clearly how different touring life was in other countries. Even though the lyrics certainly are a little basic at times, it's very rock 'n' roll and a fun listen. I've been hooked on this song since the first time I heard it.

COURTNEY CRONIN DOLD *(COMEDIAN)* – Something had to follow "All American Man", I feel sorry for whatever song that is.

But it's this one and I LOVE it! It's fun to dance to and the lyrics have some of that "Demon poetic gold" we love so much. "Germany was really neat, Japan had much to eat, Denmark was great, but I just can't wait..." He's a poet and he knows it. Spotify messed up the lyrics so it says, "Germany was really neat, there's just wasn't much to eat." Oops. Somebody just got fired.

JOE POLO *(PODCAST ROCK CITY)* – I often wondered if fans in other countries would be upset by this song proclaiming that there is no place to rock like the USA. Really kind of alienates fans from everywhere else, but it is an awesome song.

TOM HIGGINS *(KLASSIK '78)* – This song has so many hooks in it. The riff, the chorus, Bob Kulick's solo and his little lead licks during the last verse. Peter's snare work on this is excellent. I think Paul said once that when it comes to this song and "Larger Than Life", that it was Gene attempting to write songs influenced by the first Montrose record. I can hear that too, but I think it's a good thing. Takes me right back to 1977.

TOM GIGLIOTTI *(SHOUT IT OUT LOUDCAST)* – *Alive II* treated us to a few new originals and here is one that flies under the radar. The band sounds great, and they are in prime power pop form here. Catchy verses and a great chorus that is somewhat unique for the band, especially at this point in their career. KISS could pretty much do no wrong at this point.

LARGER THAN LIFE

BRUCE KULICK *(KISS)* – My brother's contributions are huge on this one. Bob comes in with the bends and the riffs. Some of those riffs, Bob was just nailing it. He's all over the neck like a madman, going high then low. I really feel that no one could've done that better than Bob.

Eddie Trunk with Gene Simmons

EDDIE TRUNK *(RADIO DJ & TV PERSONALITY)* – I love the guitar solo on it. I love the drums on it and there's massive speculation about who played on it, but I'm not going to doubt Peter when he says it's him. Even when I was 13, my eyebrows raised because I knew that the guitars were not in the style of Ace. The tone, the string bends, the whole approach. I didn't know what ghost players were, but I remember hearing it and thinking it was such a cool song. I'm partial to Paul songs but this is the perfect Gene song.

I also love the part of the chorus where you can hear Paul very clearly in the harmonies.

JEREMY ASBROCK *(ACE FREHLEY)* – Sides 3 and 4 of *Alive II* was my FIRST KISS record. After "Shout It Out Loud", "Larger Than Life" was my other favorite. Later on, I'd find out that Bob Kulick played one of my favorite Ace solos, which is actually very obvious to me now. When I got the opportunity to tell Bob how amazing and influential this solo was to me, he told me that he wouldn't play that solo the same now, which I thought was a weird way of saying "thank you". A lot of people don't think that is Peter, but if you really listen, you can tell it is, and Gene told me it was, and that's good enough for me. Another tune we tried to get him to do to no avail. I'll try harder next time.

GREG PRATO *(AUTHOR, Take It Off: KISS Truly Unmasked* and *The Eric Carr Story)* – I just can't get enough of that massive Bonham drum sound (which KISS would wisely return to for *Creatures of the Night*), can you? And Bob Kulick's soloing is outstanding (especially when you hear him digging his guitar pick into the strings, and wildly over-bending).

LISA LANE KULICK *(BRUCE KULICK'S WIFE)* – This song was my introduction to KISS. Of course I had heard the songs, "Beth" and "Rock And Roll All Nite" but that was the extent of my KISS knowledge. I was a sophomore in high school and my boyfriend at the time was a huge KISS fan. He had just gotten his driver's license and picked me up for our first ride in his new car. He was especially proud of his car radio and speakers. He turned the key and blasted "Larger Than Life." Oh my! Bob Kulick's bad-to-the-bone, hard-ass opening guitar riffs followed by Gene's slithery snake-like vocal tone on the words "believe" and "be" changed everything. It was on that day that I needed to know all about this band KISS, and soon gained an appreciation for their music that continues to this day.

JAMES CAMPION (*AUTHOR*, Shout It Out Loud – The Story of *KISS's Destroyer and the Making of an American Icon*) – Is this the best phallic-brag song of the rock era? Discuss. Until then, let's marvel at the sound of "Larger Than Life," which matches its audacious title. The guitars, played by the late-great axe-maven and brother of future member Bruce, Bob Kulick, are an impenetrable wall of crystal distortion, gloriously interrupted by the cavernous drum pounding of future David Letterman "World's Most Dangerous Band" stalwart, Anton Fig. There has been some debate on whether this is Peter Criss, but it sounds like nothing he ever played, so... no. But at least Gene is at his beastiest and the bridge into the searing guitar solos kicks my butt every time.

BRIAN TICHY *(THE DEAD DAISIES, GENE SIMMONS BAND)* – Oh yeah! Love it top to bottom! And yes, it's Bob Kulick on lead and he really rose up and played super-exciting, tasty licks! Oh, and to those who say it's not Peter: stop! It is... Eddie Kramer knows how to capture ambient drum sounds. Peter has a great touch and knows how to make that snare drum sing and crack! That is Peter's same snare tone as *Alive II* sides 1-3, and the *Love Gun* LP. It's HIS sound. I love it! Gene sounds great on vox! The riff is heavy! The chorus and post-chorus are so hooky! The song didn't even need a post-chorus but it's a great surprise!

ROCKET RIDE

MIKE PORTNOY *(DREAM THEATER, WINERY DOGS)* – Even though I'm a drummer, Ace was always my favorite member of KISS. Even when I was in elementary school, my nickname was Ace. I think "Rocket Ride" is an even cooler song than "Shock Me". It has real swagger. It's a cool, cool riff. It was Ace at his coolest. I think my 2 favorite Ace songs would be this and "Rip It Out" off of his 1978 solo album.

Mike Portnoy, age 12

JOEY CASSATA *(ZO2, Z ROCK)* – As a kid Ace was always my favorite member of KISS, until Eric Carr came along. I always liked

"Rocket Ride" even more than "Shock Me". That opening guitar riff is absolutely mesmerizing. I loved that they added the studio tracks to side 4 of *Alive II*. It was like having the best of both worlds – a killer live album and a new studio album wrapped into one. *Alive II* is my favorite record of all time. I must have stared at that centerfold for a hundred hours growing up.

BRIAN TICHY *(THE DEAD DAISIES, GENE SIMMONS BAND)* – Such a nice surprise to get on *Alive II*! This song is so Ace! It's the perfect follow up to "Shock Me"! The production is perfect! Peter's snare tone and crack rules!

SONNY POONI *(PODCAST ROCK CITY)* – In my late teen years, a friend and I put a rock band together. We had everything we needed except for a lead guitar player. I met this guy named Tony at work… found out that he played guitar and asked if he would come and audition for the band. I gave him a few KISS songs that we would like to try, and when he showed up at the audition, he was prepared and absolutely blew us away. We took a quick break, had a quick band meeting and decided that if he could play "Rocket Ride" on the fly… he would be our new lead guitarist. We asked Tony if he knew the song. Tony goes into his guitar case, pulls out this purple pedal, plugs in and starts playing the "Rocket Ride" riff. BOOM! We had a new lead guitarist. Tony and I have been inseparable since that day in 1987. I have "Rocket Ride" to thank for that.

RAISE YOUR GLASSES:
A Celebration of 50 Years of KISS Songs
by Celebrities, Musicians & Fans.

JAMES CAMPION *(AUTHOR, Shout It Out Loud – The Story of KISS's Destroyer and the Making of an American Icon)* – The best song off of side 4 of *Alive II*. Period. It's not heavy competition, mind you, but this may well be Ace's finest song, at least of the ones he sang. It is a fuel-injected, scorching hell-ride of a guitar intro into a runaway diesel truck, driven into overdrive by Frehley's otherworldly simpatico with drummer Anton Fig. These two pretty much gave us the Ace solo effort, and that is my fave of those. And his guitar gymnastics here are beyond words. I'll give it a shot, how about *fucking incendiary*. Okay, that's two words. Can you blame me? This solo is a Spaceman's greatest hits of wailing hammer-ons and speed-freak euphoria. When I was a teenager, I could make the world spin listening to it without the aid of chemicals.

ANY WAY YOU WANT IT

CHRIS L. *(POD OF THUNDER)* – I remember feeling a bit let down when I first purchased *Alive II* because all four sides weren't live. Over time I came to appreciate the new studio cuts, and this is the one I initially liked the most. The hooks drew me in, of course, but I really enjoyed hearing the bad boys of KISS pay homage to the British invasion with such passion and energy. And the vocals might be better than the original!

COURTNEY CRONIN DOLD *(COMEDIAN)* – Is this about sex or a sandwich? I think The Dave Clark Five would be happy with this "hard-ish" rock cover of their song. Paul's vocals on the "It's alright, it's alright" part and Ace's heavy guitar turn up the heat on this cool, clean-cut pop song and make it hot enough for KISS.

RAISE YOUR GLASSES:
A Celebration of 50 Years of KISS Songs
by Celebrities, Musicians & Fans.

Courtney Cronin Dold roasting Bruce Kulick

WES BEECH *(THE PLASMATICS)* – I was always a big fan of side 4 of *Alive II*, and this cover of one of my favorite British invasion band's songs has always stood out to me. The Dave Clark Five are right up there with the Beatles for me and were one of Gene's favorite bands as well, and this is his tip of the hat to one of the bands that influenced him. A straightforward cover with great gang vocals makes for a fun listen, with once again Peter's drumming powering the song along. Love the "Beatle chord" at the end. Wasn't until years later I learned Bob Kulick played guitar on the side 4 tracks, and he gets it just right.

JOEY CASSATA *(ZO2, Z ROCK)* – Growing up I never knew that this was a cover song. I just thought it was another fun KISS song! I remember one of the first bands I was ever in wanted to do a cover of "Any Way You Want It" and I was super excited. I went home and learned it that night and had it ready for the next rehearsal. When the band started to play it, it wasn't the KISS song. I said, what the hell is this? That's not the right song!! They actually wanted to do the

Journey song "Any Way You Want It". I had never even heard of it before. All of my musical knowledge was 100% KISS.

JEFF TROTT *(ART DIRECTOR)* – Originally written and performed by the Dave Clark Five on their 1964 album *Coast to Coast*, "Any Way You Want It" appeared on the studio side of *Alive II* as one of five studio tracks. This feel-good, straightforward rock song stays true to the original arrangement, with KISS omitting the saxophone. "Any Way You Want It" is an awesome song and a fun listen—I never skip it when it comes up on my playlist.

RAISE YOUR GLASSES:
A Celebration of 50 Years of KISS Songs
by Celebrities, Musicians & Fans.

CHAPTER 8

"THE SOLO ALBUMS"

Released: September 18, 1978

In 1978, each member of KISS released their own solo album simultaneously, marking a unique and ambitious move in rock history. The albums featured Gene Simmons, Paul Stanley, Ace Frehley, and Peter Criss each stepping into the spotlight with their individual artistic expressions.

The KISS solo albums were a groundbreaking endeavor that showcased the individual talents of each band member. Each delivered a diverse set of songs, revealing their personal influences and musical styles. While the albums received mixed critical reception, they remain a fascinating snapshot of KISS's creative diversity.

As the late 1970s unfolded, KISS was at the peak of their fame, and the decision to release solo albums simultaneously was both bold and unprecedented. Each member was given the creative freedom to explore their own musical inclinations, resulting in four distinct records that collectively captured the spectrum of rock and its various subgenres.

While the KISS solo albums received mixed critical reviews, they are significant for revealing the diverse musical influences within the band. The experiment demonstrated that beyond their collective force as KISS, each member brought a unique flavor to the table. Collectively, the solo albums are a testament to the band's willingness to take risks and explore their individual musical identities during a period of rock music marked by experimentation and eclecticism.

RAISE YOUR GLASSES:
A Celebration of 50 Years of KISS Songs
by Celebrities, Musicians & Fans.

"ACE FREHLEY"

Ace Frehley became the standout of the four. Filled with guitar-driven rock, including the hit single "New York Groove," Frehley's album solidified his status as a guitar virtuoso. The record reflects his bluesy influences and became a fan favorite, demonstrating Frehley's ability to shine both as a guitarist and a vocalist.

RIP IT OUT

STEVE BROWN *(TRIXTER)* – From the first 30 seconds of the songs, I was completely hooked. To this day, it's still one of those songs that, no matter what, I still get transformed back to 1978 and hearing the energy of that. I knew there was something different about that song and such an incredible lyric, and then hearing the drums and that middle drum section and realizing, "Wow, that's not Peter Criss!" It's the great Anton Fig. It's one of the top 5 Ace Frehley songs.

Steve Brown onstage with Ace Frehley

RAISE YOUR GLASSES:
A Celebration of 50 Years of KISS Songs
by Celebrities, Musicians & Fans.

BRIAN TICHY *(THE DEAD DAISIES, GENE SIMMONS BAND)* – The whole Ace solo LP rocks top to bottom! But to kick it all off with the anthemic "Rip It Out" just takes the cake! Not to mention, Anton Fig's drum solo breaks are badass!

CHRIS CAFFERY *(TRANS-SIBERIAN ORCHESTRA, SAVATAGE)* – Ace was by far my favorite KISS member. Ace's solo record was definitely my favorite of the 4 for many reasons beyond that. This song was definitely one of those reasons. Ace's singing voice was charming. It was light and jovial, just like Ace himself. This song is my favorite Ace vocal. It's just a crazy fun listen and made me super-excited as a huge Ace fan to hear what he could do on his own.

JOEY CASSATA *(ZO2, Z ROCK)* – There might not be a better opening track in the history of music for me. This completely sets the tone for the whole album. I also have two words for you... ANTON FIG! What a monster player he is. His drumming and Eddie Kramer's production is what sets this record apart from all of the other solo albums. I must have played the middle drum break 500 times as a kid. What a surreal moment it was to play this song live with Ace at the *KISS Cancer Goodbye* event in 2023.

TONY MUSALLAM *(RESTRAYNED)* – What a great way to start a record! This song kicks you in the face right from the opening riff. Ace's vocal delivery conveys his anger and frustration. The chorus is simple and catchy. The drum fill section is an awesome way to build up into the guitar solo.

MARTIN POPOFF *(AUTHOR)* – "Rip It Out" is one of the big contributors to Ace's album, being far and away the most highly regarded of the four solo albums. It's both KISS-like but fresh in that context, given the sort of tribal, clumpy, punky drumming, with the punk vibe heightened by Ace's bed-headed Dennis the Menace vocal. Also punky is the dumb fun of the chorus, with its dependable "Louie Louie" chords. At the polar opposite of punk is the drum break from Anton Fig, where he gets flashy like Steve Gadd on "Aja" (okay, let's not get carried away).

JAMES CAMPION (*AUTHOR, Shout It Out Loud – The Story of KISS's Destroyer and the Making of an American Icon*) *– Ace Frehley* has since been celebrated as the most popular and consistently solid of the four. This all starts with "Rip It Out" – a guitar assault buttressed with incredible dynamism by drummer, Anton Fig. The two of them really shine on this entire album, an almost intrinsic musical collab that proved that maybe Ace would have spread his wings far wider by himself, which likely led to his going bye-bye within three years of this record. And it all begins with "Rip It Out."

SONNY POON (*PODCAST ROCK CITY*) – One of the best opening tracks on a rock album, EVER! Having this song as your first "non-KISS involved song" showed the rock world that Ace was for real and had serious chops as a songwriter. Anton is the hero of the song thanks to the drumming "interlude" before the guitar solo.

SPEEDIN' BACK TO MY BABY

MARTIN POPOFF (*AUTHOR*) – Here's the second-silliest song on the beloved *Ace Frehley* album, second after "New York Groove" en route perhaps to "Wiped-Out." All told, it's an engaging combination between power pop and Foghat or ZZ Top, given the shuffle feel. Put Ace's holler-along voice up top, and then cramped drums underneath (Anton Fig does the whole album), and it's a bit punky too.

IZZY PRESLEY *(MUSICIAN, COMIC)* – Quintessential song from *Ace Frehley*. The riff. The rhymes. The female vocals. The backwards solo. A staple in the *ACK! A Tribute To Ace Frehley* set and was one hell of a song to cover. I have loved it from the 1st time I heard it.

Keith Roth with KISS

TONY MUSALLAM *(RESTRAYNED)* – Arguably one of coolest guitar riffs ever. And can we talk about that killer guitar solo with reverse intro? Guitar playing like this is what makes Ace a guitar hero.

RAISE YOUR GLASSES:
A Celebration of 50 Years of KISS Songs by Celebrities, Musicians & Fans.

ZEUS *(SHOUT IT OUT LOUDCAST)* – What a guitar intro. Ace is blazing on this song. His vocals, lyrics and guitar are all spectacular on this track. I was in middle school when I got back into KISS, and I remember a friend air guitaring this song to me and I was hooked. That abrupt stop and then solo is classic. This song is proof Ace has been underutilized by KISS.

SONNY POONI *(PODCAST ROCK CITY)* – Having four distinct characters in the band was great because most of us connected to one of the guys more than the other 3. For me that was (and still is) Ace. The spacy feel, the laid-back attitude, the party guy, he always seemed a little off... I totally connected with it. Although many regard *Ace Frehley* to be the best of the solo albums, no one ever mentions the 1-2 punch of the first two songs on the actual album. Another well-written song by Ace that even has a tinge of a gospel feel towards the end when the female backing vocal comes in. Love this song!

KEITH ROTH *(SIRIUS XM, THE DICTATORS)* – I got Ace's record the Saturday after all the solo records came out. Only had enough bread for his album. After him making his singing debut on *Love Gun*, that was the one I was most excited for. "Speeding Back to My Baby", that riff was so amazing to me at that time!!! Loved the campy background vox. The Donnas did a great version of this. When I still listen to this record, I never cherry-pick songs. Eddie Kramer captured the magic. Still sounds fresh to me after all these years. ICONIC!!!

BRAD RUSTOVEN *(SLAMFEST PODCAST)* – One of my favorite songs from the album. Great harmonized lead guitar melody during the intro. Love the vocal melody and his delivery during the verse – great "Oh yeahs" and "Uh-huhs" at the end of each line. Gotta love the drum fill from Anton leading into the second chorus and the plane sound effects during the outro.

SNOW BLIND

MARTIN POPOFF *(AUTHOR)* – Here's the "Rocket Ride" of the entire four-record experiment, namely the most exciting and cockle-warming heavy metal song. Black Sabbath had "Snowblind", but Ace's "Snow Blind" has Black Sabbath, most recognizable in the devil's tritone/*diabolus in musica* of the chorus riff. But, hey, I think Tony Iommi would have been happy to come up with what Ace does in the verses as well. Plus, Nashville Pussy covered the song on their 2005 *Get Some!* album—how cool is that?

PETER DANKELSON *(PETE'S DIARY)* – One of my favorite solo Ace tunes. His vocals sound great and I love how the guitar solo section goes into double time – it elevates the excitement that's already in the track, and the licks that Ace is playing during the solo are fantastic.

JASON HOOK *(FIVE FINGER DEATH PUNCH)* – What can you say... pure cool, edgy rock 'n' roll Ace Frehley. Great riff! I think Ace's record is only record of the 4 solo albums that really sounds like a KISS record. It's my favorite of all the solo albums.

MAC *(UGLY AMERICAN WEREWOLF IN LONDON PODCAST)* – This song plods a little which is strange given that it's obviously a song about cocaine. The lyrics sound a little drug-induced and there is the token reference to feeling lost in space. Things heat up on the solo, so just as you hope it's building into a fast-paced rocker, it devolves back into the plodding talk/singing, which is a signature of Ace. Great drumming by Anton Fig, but the end just slows down further until finally our sight returns when this one ends.

TOM GIGLIOTTI *(SHOUT IT OUT LOUDCAST)* – Heavy, dark and plodding along like a lost Sabbath song. Ace sounds great vocally which is something you may not hear every day. He gets us to sing along with that catchy chorus and of course, he doesn't disappoint with a blazing solo as we've come to expect during that sped-up section of the song. Many proponents of Ace's solo album point to this one.

OZONE

MARTIN POPOFF *(AUTHOR)* – There's a bunch of ambitious writing and arranging and playing on *Ace Frehley*, but "Ozone" contains the largest quantity of vaguely proggy parts and passages. It's interesting throughout and consistently loud and full-band, even beyond full-band, with Ace adding his signature acoustic guitar track to the sculpted sound. Also putting the listener in a familiar place is Ace talking about getting high. Call this one an instrumental with lyrics, which can only exist in Ace's ozone zone.

STEVE WRIGHT *(PODDER THAN HELL PODCAST)* – Layered clean and distorted guitars strum to get us going. This has more of an instrumental feel to it. It takes 1:15 to get to the lyrics. This fits

Ace to a tee, space-y feel and about getting loaded. Tempo change for the running type of solo. Anton Fig has some fantastic drum fills throughout the track. It does drag a little long for me. But definitely a song for Ace for the time.

GREG PRATO *(AUTHOR, Take It Off: KISS Truly Unmasked* **and** *The Eric Carr Story)* – Sure, there are quite a few more obvious Ace tunes that I could have selected ("Parasite," "Shock Me," "Rocket Ride," etc.), but what about this oft-overlooked rocker from *Ace Frehley* – which I still firmly believe was the best solo offering of the four. Great guitar riffs and bits throughout. Ever hear the Foo Fighters' cover?

MAC *(UGLY AMERICAN WEREWOLF IN LONDON PODCAST)* – Despite some decent riffs from Ace on this one, the lyrics and rhythm of his singing are terrible. Like so many songs from Ace, the guitar work saves the song. The band are jamming well but when that is interrupted by Ace's less-than-stellar lyrics about getting high, it not only makes the song less of a favorite but that earns Ace ridicule. Oooooooo-zoooooooone…

JOEY CASSATA *(ZO2, Z ROCK)* – I really love every song on this album! Each song has its own unique vibe, yet the album gels perfectly together. The drone-y feel of this song is so ACE! "I'm the kind of guy, who likes feeling high".

Joey Cassata and Steve Brown onstage with Ace Frehley

WHAT'S ON YOUR MIND?

MARTIN POPOFF *(AUTHOR)* – "What's on Your Mind?" could have been a cozy hit for KISS, given its easy-drinking verse chords, strong vocal melody and Byrds-y, descending chorus, which, oddly, is followed by a sort of post-chorus break. As well, Ace utilizes something he credits Eddie Kramer for teaching him, this idea of massaging in an acoustic guitar track to go along with the power chords. I would like to have seen an original like this in place of "Then She Kissed Me" on *Love Gun* or "Any Way You Want It" on the studio side of *Alive II*.

JOEY CASSATA *(ZO2, Z ROCK)* – I love when Ace writes pop songs. He has such a feel for melody and pop sensibilities. This song is a preview of what's to come on *Dynasty* and *Unmasked* from Ace.

He didn't go the "Rip It Out" path when he presented his next KISS songs, he went more of the pop route.

SHANDON SAHM *(MEAT PUPPETS)* – This is probably Ace's best pop tune ever. The lyrics are fantastic, like when he says, "You make me crazy, crazy." "Things look hazy, hazy." This song and the whole *Ace Frehley* album was lightning in a bottle. I know Ace tried to replicate this, but you can't rerecord that one-time brilliant thing. You just can't. This song and LP was a great snapshot of a record that's just brilliant from beginning to end.

MAC *(UGLY AMERICAN WEREWOLF IN LONDON PODCAST)* – With some ringing acoustic 12-string guitars, this song is a little warmer and different from most of the rest of the songs on *Ace Frehley*. There are still big chunky riffs, sophomoric lyrics and the usual hallmarks of an Ace song, but "What's On Your Mind?" stands out as a pop/rock ditty on this album.

MIKE BRUNN *(THE ROCK EXPERIENCE)* – This is a deep cut from Ace's classic '78 solo album, and has been a favorite of mine for decades. I love the acoustic guitar parts during the verses, and in my opinion it's one of Ace's greatest melodic songs. I wish he would do this in concert more often.

JEFF TROTT *(ART DIRECTOR)* – *Ace Frehley,* according to most, is the best of the four solo albums. "Speeding Back to my Baby", "New York Groove" and "Rip It Out" are amongst some of the greatest songs on the album, but the track I gravitate to is "What's On Your Mind?" "What's On Your Mind?" resonates as a standout from the album, showcasing his signature style with a groove that's both infectious and soulful. In my opinion its Ace's greatest vocal performance on any song that he's recorded, whether KISS or solo.

JASON HERNDON *(KISS MY WAX PODCAST)* – My favorite track off Ace's solo album by far. I love the use of the 12-string. As everyone knows, Ace was at the top of his game on his solo album. And this song proves it.

NEW YORK GROOVE

CRAIG GASS *(COMEDIAN)* – I did a lot of cocaine as a teenager, and very few things sound better when you're going out for a night on cocaine than this song. You could be driving into downtown Lincoln, Nebraska on coke while listening to this song, and it will somehow make Lincoln really, really incredible until the song ends and your buzz wears off.

MARTIN POPOFF *(AUTHOR)* – The biggest hit across all four solo albums, "New York Groove" was written by Russ Ballard and first covered with moderate success by late-fer-dinner UK glamsters Hello, circa 1975. Against the other all-business songs on *Ace Frehley*, this constitutes a guilty pleasure and we're all guilty! It's pure T. Rex, and we're laughing *with* Ace not at him.

PAUL JANIK *(GENE SIMMONS MONEYBAG SODA)* – The funky guitar riffs are second to none. One of Frehley's best. This song makes me want to groove. I have fond memories of getting down at the local roller rink while this title was spinning.

RAISE YOUR GLASSES:
A Celebration of 50 Years of KISS Songs
by Celebrities, Musicians & Fans.

TOMMY LONDON *(OZZY'S BONEYARD, SIRIUS XM)* – Being a native New Yorker, how could I not choose this song? I remember I put the needle down on this tune at least ten times when I first heard it. The song was originally recorded by the English glam band Hello, but Ace Frehley definitely made it his own and his version has stood the test of time. Best KISS solo album. Hands down.

Tommy London with Ace Frehley

JAMES CAMPION *(AUTHOR, Shout It Out Loud – The Story of KISS's Destroyer and the Making of an American Icon)* – Drum machine? Disco groove? Female background singers? Funky chicken-scratch guitars? A cover? What the hell is going on? Ace is going on, and he went and had himself a hit with "New York Groove," which today is the only KISS-related song to survive the changing zeitgeist beyond "Rock and Roll All Nite." I hear this damn thing all the time. It is an earworm hit made by an anti-hit guy — the cool, detached rocker blitzed on champagne and coke stumbling into a Top 20 smash. In other words, 1970s NYC. This is an ode to possibility of decadence by a world-class decadent. "Forget about tomorrow!" Ace shouts with knowing glee. Props goes to Eddie Kramer, who really did direct this album into places I doubt Ace could have imagined he might find himself, and to his credit, KISS's lead guitarist embraced and performed it all flawlessly.

KENNY BEGLEY *(KISS LIVE AUCTIONS)* – Although a remake, Ace makes this his own and even with the disco feel to it, it is still dominated by rock!

I'M IN NEED OF LOVE

JOEY CASSATA *(ZO2, Z ROCK)* – To me, Ace's solo record was by far the best of the four. The main reason being it had absolutely no filler at all. Every single track is strong. "I'm In Need Of Love" is no exception. The call and answer in the verses with Ace's lyric and that cool guitar effect is incredible. Great song!

MARTIN POPOFF *(AUTHOR)* – The hook in this one is that piercing, repeating, echoing guitar lick, but subconsciously we're invited in by the relaxed Anton Fig groove, augmented by big hanging chords. Not much of a chorus, but all told, the song serves a purpose in this sequence of tracks as something at a different speed and texture. Speaking of speed, there's a double-time lead break which finds Ace doing what he does best: simple old-school solos that are both musical and aggressive, like Ace is wringing hooky licks out of the neck.

Joey Cassata with Ace Frehley during the *10,000 Volts* recording sessions

ZACH THRONE *(COREY TAYLOR, BRUCE KULICK)* – Super-sexy, glammy, kind of Hendrix-y psychedelic heavy soul song. One of Ace's best solos EVER and one of my favorite guitar solos of all time. Pure 100% uncut Ace.

STEVE WRIGHT *(PODDER THAN HELL PODCAST)* – Cool "Space-y" fade in with some echoey guitars and Eddie Kramer's great production really shines through on this one. The panning in the speakers is crazy! Anton Fig's drumming is fantastic. Lots of crashing cymbals and great fills. Great tempo change for the ripping, solo and listen to the music underneath: just KILLER! Amazing deep track!

NICHOLAS BUCKLAND *(AUTHOR, Hottest Brand in the Land)* – This song is pure Ace, and if his vocal delivery were any more laid back they'd be horizontal. The song flicks between an otherworldly echoing space-age guitar part in the verses and then, almost as though the ketamine has been laced with an amphetamine and only just kicked in, it flies into hyperdrive in the middle section with an incredibly nutty guitar solo that could only come from the batty mind of Mr. Frehley!

WIPED-OUT

STEVE BROWN *(TRIXTER)* – Love this song. Anton (Fig) with the old school "Wipe Out"-style drumming intro. Gotta love that. I think what's really cool about this tune, what I really dig, is the tempo changes. Very unique, very Anton, very Ace. I love the chorus, the vocal. It's classic Ace with the delays. I like the short, anthemic, classic Ace guitar solo where he's doing one phrase over and over. That double-string thing that he's so famous for doing. I really like the harmony guitar solo that he does in the third chorus. Very cool and very unorthodox, but as we know, very Ace because Ace doesn't do anything orthodox.

JOE McGINNESS *(KUARANTINE, KLASSIK '78)* – I really dig the inverted drum beats on this track. Anton is a true genius. Without the phenomenal drums, the song is only half as good. Anton is the true star on this track.

RAISE YOUR GLASSES:
A Celebration of 50 Years of KISS Songs
by Celebrities, Musicians & Fans.

MARTIN POPOFF *(AUTHOR)* – Ace likes to write songs about being wasted, and fortunately for the selling of them they are believable. This starts like surf classic "Wipe Out" before collapsing into a three-legged race of a verse, with Ace getting goofy. It's hugely elevated with a shift in tone and rhythm to the pure metal chorus, first at halftime four-four and then an anxiety-inducing three-four.

MAC *(UGLY AMERICAN WEREWOLF IN LONDON PODCAST)* – The opening sounds like an ode to the old surfer tunes of the '60s. The song starts as a rocker talking again about partying and drinking. But then the chorus plods into an odd slowdown to get the point across that all that partying had taken its toll. Ace's singing on the verses is fast and he doesn't try to hold notes too long, which better suits his style. It's almost two songs in one – if that's supposed to show that you're upbeat and fun when partying but it's no fun to be wasted (wiped out) then it does a good job. But at the end of the day, it's a bit disjointed and not his best on the album.

ZEUS *(SHOUT IT OUT LOUDCAST)* – A silly but fun song. A real deep cut from Ace's solo album. However, the lyrics and verses are great and so is the guitar riff. It has a rare third verse from an Ace song. Ace also accents every last word from each verse. I love the booze references that would probably never be allowed on a KISS album.

Tom and Zeus with Ace Frehley

FRACTURED MIRROR

TOM HIGGINS *(KLASSIC '78)* – This is a great piece of music. Ace's power chords on this are so fat and cool sounding. The acoustic guitars and church bells are killer. Ace's talent was undeniable. This song takes me back to my childhood every time I hear it. Great memories.

TOM GIGLIOTTI *(SHOUT IT OUT LOUDCAST)* – I love instrumentals, and this is absolutely one of my favorites. The sound of the guitars overlayed and the way each instrument is introduced as the song progresses make this almost haunting for the listener. Ace really is musically gifted and this track on his '78 solo album is an achievement for him.

RAISE YOUR GLASSES:
A Celebration of 50 Years of KISS Songs by Celebrities, Musicians & Fans.

COURTNEY CRONIN DOLD *(COMEDIAN)* – I love an instrumental. The first time I heard this I wondered, "this is beautiful! When is Ace going to start singing and ruin it?" I'm kidding of course. But of all the solo albums you would expect it most from the lead guitarist. It's quite beautiful and was a real special treat seeing Ace and his band play the entire album at the *KISS Expo* in Parsippany 2018. Heads exploded with delight. It was awesome.

GARY "ACTION" JACKSON *(UGLY AMERICAN WEREWOLF IN LONDON PODCAST)* – Loved this track ever since the first time I heard it. It builds from the acoustic intro into a fairly complex track. This shows that Ace can play a mean rhythm part as well as lead. I also liked that he kept this theme going with "Fractured Too" from *Frehley's Comet*, and "Fractured III" from *Trouble Walkin'*.

JAMES CAMPION *(AUTHOR, Shout It Out Loud – The Story of KISS's Destroyer and the Making of an American Icon)* – What seals my opinion that *Ace Frehley* is the best of the four is this stellar instrumental that concludes it. Reminding KISS fans of the opening strains of "Rock Bottom," which the Spaceman penned back in '75, its atmospheric guitar fugue is worthy of what producer Eddie Kramer was able to massage with the incomparable Jimi Hendrix in his prime. The meshing of the elegantly executed prelude using a double-neck Gibson tuned to open E (keeping both pickups to capture an eerie echo effect) with crunchy Townshend-esque power chords, Frehley displays a deft alacrity for melody, including a countermelody he brings in at the 3:30 mark. This underscores his underrated melodic contributions to the KISS canon through his bombastic solos. Then, to further spread his experimental wings, Ace adds a tasty bass line beneath the kind of piercing synth lines that evoke the spacey milieu reflected in his character. I remember vividly being blown away with this as kid and glad I'd spent my meager funds on Ace's effort and most of all staring at the cover of my Bronx-bro's album while the Yankees took the 1978 World Series.

STEVE BROWN *(TRIXTER)* – The classic Ace instrumental. This started the tradition of him having an instrumental on all of his solo albums. I've always loved this from the first time I heard it. I kind of wish they had put vocals on it because I think it could've been a cool song. We continued this tradition of instrumentals on *10,000 Volts* with "Stratosphere", and that was very much influenced by "Fractured Mirror". A majestic arpeggio guitar melody that Ace is doing on the 12-string guitar. It's perfection, and you really can't finish off the brilliant 1978 solo album better than this. It's one of his signature styles.

RAISE YOUR GLASSES:
A Celebration of 50 Years of KISS Songs
by Celebrities, Musicians & Fans.

"GENE SIMMONS"

Gene Simmons is a diverse mix of hard rock, funk, and ballads. With tracks like "Radioactive" and "See You in Your Dreams," Simmons flexes his musical muscles, showcasing a range beyond his role as the Demon in KISS. The album also includes a cover of "When You Wish Upon a Star," adding an unexpected twist.

RADIOACTIVE

JOEY CASSATA *(ZO2, Z ROCK)* – This is the perfect song for Gene to lead off his solo album. The beginning is so haunting and satanic. It's something right out of the exorcist. It was rumored to have what they call "The Devil's Triad" in the opening. Which if heard 13 times in a row is said to make the listener go crazy. In complete contrast, when the song kicks in, it's pure pop. I love it! The verse is just as hooky, if not more so than the chorus. Gene at his absolute best.

Joey Cassata's pass, hanging with KISS's wireless packs on the Rock *The Nation* tour

TOM GIGLIOTTI *(SHOUT IT OUT LOUDCAST)* – One of my all-time favorite songs in the entire catalog. That creepy haunting intro still packs a punch over 45 years later. One of the hookiest, poppiest songs Gene has ever done. An infectious chorus and an overall groove that make this song enjoyable from the start (regardless of how scary it may be!)

PAUL JANIK *(GENE SIMMONS MONEYBAG SODA)* – The intro to this song scared the shit out of me as a kid! Solid song. One of Gene's best from his solo album.

TONY MUSALLAM *(RESTRAYNED)* – I remember the first time I heard this song, I thought there was a mistake and I got the wrong record. The intro was terrifying to me as a young boy. I thought it was some kind of satanic chant that was going to release demons into my house! But once the music finally started, I was singing along almost immediately.

KENNY BEGLEY *(KISS LIVE AUCTIONS)* – This song always reminds me of a horror movie with the intro, and to me that represented Gene's persona. Just a great song to me!

BURNING UP WITH FEVER

STEVE WRIGHT *(PODDER THAN HELL PODCAST)* – Gruff Gene count-in to an acoustic guitar, then he gives it a "Lovely". Drums bring it into a cool funky riff, played by Jeff "Skunk" Baxter from Steely Dan fame, that caught me right away as a 10-year-old. And I still bob my head to it to this day. And the great backing vocals supplied by the Disco Queen, Donna Summer. We do get sort of a "Demon" Gene vocal as well. Definitely a bright spot on a strange album. Skunk has some really good lead fills throughout the song and rather Ace-like short solo. Fun track.

RAISE YOUR GLASSES:
A Celebration of 50 Years of KISS Songs
by Celebrities, Musicians & Fans.

JEFF TROTT *(ART DIRECTOR)* – Love this song: "One, two, one, two, three, four… lovely / I'm a gifted giver, not a woman mistreater". Is there anything more Gene than that? I love the menacing intro that feels "Almost Human"-ish. From its pulsating rhythm to its electrifying vocals, you can feel the positivity drawing you into its infectious energy. Donna Summer's unforgettable backing vocals add another layer of brilliance to this track.

IZZY PRESLEY *(MUSICIAN, COMIC)* – As I have stated in previous and future ramblings in this high-quality publication in book form, I think of a lot of this stuff in the mind of my childhood self. I love this song. I love this record. As an opinionated douchebag adult? I love this song. I love this record.

ZEUS *(SHOUT IT OUT LOUDCAST)* – We all know that Gene's 1978 solo album is all over the place. But like Peter's, it may not be a KISS album but it's still a good album and fun. This song is one of those when you play it and go, "What the hell is this doing on a KISS album?" From the count-off, to the classical guitar and "lovely" remark, to the soulful backing singers, it is quite different to say the least. However, the song is catchy as all hell. Gene's delivery, his whispering "She said", his bass playing – all top-notch. Got to love the Jeff "Skunk" Baxter solo and of course Donna Summer's wailing. Sean Delaney kills it with the production on this track and the whole album. Try listening and not snapping your fingers and moving your neck back and forth while going, "I'm burnin' up with fever!"

RAISE YOUR GLASSES:
A Celebration of 50 Years of KISS Songs by Celebrities, Musicians & Fans.

Tom and Zeus with Gene Simmons, *An Evening with Gene Simmons*, May 7, 2023

TOM GIGLIOTTI *(SHOUT IT OUT LOUDCAST)* – I have always loved Gene's solo album and this groovy, sleazy song is one I really enjoy. It's 1978 and he is still peak Demon at this time. But he turns up the melody with that killer gang chorus. The bass line carries this song. Might not be something KISS would do as a band, but that's why the solo albums exist.

SEE YOU TONITE

ZACH THRONE *(COREY TAYLOR, BRUCE KULICK)* – Gene's Beatle-y songs always charmed me. He really can nail those when he wants to. His voice is perfectly suited and VERY Lennon-esque. Plus, he always sounds like he's truly enjoying singing this song when he sings it. This is the song I would play for musician friends that didn't like KISS and they would all say, "Gene Simmons wrote that?"

JOEY CASSATA *(ZO2, Z ROCK)* – Gene's album as a whole is a little underrated. Where it might not be as strong as Ace's or Paul's, it definitely still has some great moments. This is one of them. I think the main problem that people had with Gene's solo album was that they were expecting "God of Thunder" and instead got things like this Beatle-esque "See You Tonite". Over the years, I've come to appreciate Gene's album more and more.

JAMES CAMPION *(AUTHOR, Shout It Out Loud – The Story of KISS's Destroyer and the Making of an American Icon)* – What is with the "nite" thing? "Rock And Roll All Nite" and "See You Tonite." Where is the "gh", love? Okay, beyond the literary critique, this song is great. People call it Beatle-esque, but that's only because the Beatles introduced the idea of cheesy-cool; this weird amalgam of confection with depth, and Gene loved them for it. He was made into the Demon by their "looking like a gang" on *Ed Sullivan* and even acquiesced on putting strings on "Beth" because "if the Beatles did it… it's good enough for us." But mostly Gene, and his solo album bears this out, is an old softie for pop music from his childhood. It's what seduced a young Israeli into America's cheap, exploitative silliness as a hidden portal to unfettered freedom of imagination. And he was not wrong. If not for KISS and his well-designed persona, this was the music he was born to make. The *MTV Unplugged* version is sublime.

DARREN PALTROWITZ *(AUTHOR, How David Lee Roth Changed the World)* – If anyone tries to argue that Gene Simmons primarily wrote childish lyrics rooted in sexual double-entendres and/or third-rate hard rock, I immediately point them towards "See You Tonite," which only has Gene listed as a songwriter. Featuring guitar work by Jeff "Skunk" Baxter, it is arguably Gene's most overt homage to the Beatles and British invasion 1960s pop of anything he recorded in the 1970s. It is also rare within the KISS catalog – and I do consider the 1978 original members' solo albums to be part of the KISS catalog, given how they were marketed and released by Casablanca Records –to have an equally-definitive "unplugged" version, thanks to MTV. I have never had the pleasure of hearing this song performed live, unfortunately.

TONY MUSALLAM *(RESTRAYNED)* – Gene shows his influences on this song. A mellow, acoustic, almost Beatles-esque song that shows off a different, more gentle side of Gene's vocals, which is a nice change from the usual Demon growl.

TUNNEL OF LOVE

RICHIE RANNO *(STARZ, GENE SIMMONS SOLO ALBUM)* – I have to say, "Tunnel Of Love" is great. Not just because I play all the guitars, but I just really like it.

MARTIN POPOFF *(AUTHOR)* – Gene's album sold best of all of them, but it's the third most-loved by the base; as far as I'm concerned, it's due for a reassessment. "Tunnel of Love" is a nice example of an under-rated track, ambling along like an under-stated KISS song, restrained at the drum end (like Peter) courtesy of Allan Schwartzberg. But the best part is the chorus, where we get female backing vocals weaving in and out of some nice harmonies. On guitars, we get Joe Perry from Aerosmith and Richie Ranno from Starz.

NICHOLAS BUCKLAND *(AUTHOR, Hottest Brand in the Land)* – You've heard of a double entendre, well this was jam-packed with the singular variety making it a standout track on *Gene Simmons*. The heartbeat-like bass part comes directly from the crotch area, and you'd have to be the sourest individual on the planet to not smile at the lyrics, which gently plead "Tunnel of love, tunnel of love… let me visit your tunnel of love". Not sure if the 1987 Bruce Springsteen single of the same name speaks with the same urgency…

JASON BAKKEN *(COBRAS & FIRE PODCAST)* – By 1978 a very large portion of the KISS Army was male children. I would like to see a study of that group to see if we can determine just how stunted the sexual growth amongst that demographic was because of songs like "Tunnel of Love".

TOM GIGLIOTTI *(SHOUT IT OUT LOUDCAST)* – Gene's solo album has definitely grown on me over the years. I have really come to appreciate what he's doing, and this song has such a cool groove to it and a really catchy chorus. Gene's singing voice (not his Demon voice) is tremendously underrated and he gets to show it off on songs like this.

RAISE YOUR GLASSES:
A Celebration of 50 Years of KISS Songs
by Celebrities, Musicians & Fans.

TRUE CONFESSIONS

COURTNEY CRONIN DOLD *(COMEDIAN)* – I always thought this song could fit in *The Rocky Horror Picture Show*. It was also my alarm tone, for years. If Gene Simmons and Helen Reddy are telling you to get up, you listen. Plus, it has one of Gene's best, "Yeahs" of all time. End of second chorus.

MARK CICCHINI *(THREE SIDES OF THE COIN)* – Like "Cadillac Dreams", this is another autobiographical song and another of my favorites off Gene's (woefully underrated) solo album. *Gene Simmons* always reminded me of mid-70s Alice Cooper, meaning you had to look beyond the surface to see the humor in all of it. Gene politely (a "demon" asking politely? That's the humor!) asks his love/lust interest to be straight up and honest with him as he's being straight up and honest with her... "I'm not your social security, I'm not your star opportunity, you can have me absolutely, won't you give me TRUE CONFESSIONS? That's all I'm asking for". In other words, let's just enjoy the moment and let's not get ahead of ourselves. I'm sure Gene (especially in 1978) was having woman literally throw themselves at him (not only to be with a rock star but to maybe attach themselves to what dating a rock star is hyped up to be). Gene's advice to them? True confession! I'm only here for the fun! If you want a relationship, you're barking up the wrong tree. Song wise? Love the laid-back electric riff and the church choir break at the end make this song a rollicking, fun rocker! A highlight on an album with more highlights than it gets credit for.

ERNIE PALOOZA *(TOP 5 WITH JOEY CASSATA)* – First off, what a great bass line! Gene's melody in the verse is true pop. It actually makes me curious if he really wrote it. Where they start to lose me is the pre-chorus. Not a fan. Notice how they actually skip the pre-chorus in the second stanza. The riff in the chorus is my favorite thing about this song.

MARTIN POPOFF *(AUTHOR)* – This sounds like a heavy Eagles song, a nice sort of breezy California rock 'n' roll twist for KISS, solo or otherwise. And then come chorus time, I hear Blue Öyster Cult's "True Confessions" from 1976 and Mott the Hoople at the break. But anything with Gene singing is a joy to behold; here he's in a sort of middle gear, matching the meat-and-potatoes old-timey rock 'n' roll noise of this happy song.

LIVING IN SIN

MARTIN POPOFF *(AUTHOR)* – Like "Tunnel of Love," "Living in Sin" starts ill-advised, but then we're into an uptempo rocker with a sturdy frame, nice bass line, Gene variously doubling himself on vocals and dueting with others. As well, the song proper begins with its KISS-like chorus and then goes into the verses, which are a little more amusing, shall we say. There's also a long phone call sequence (featuring Cher!) and all sorts of attentive production touches, most zesty being the simple piano accompaniment from Eric Troyer and the complex vocal harmonies at the catchy chorus, with one of those voices being none other than Bob Seger.

IZZY PRESLEY *(MUSICIAN, COMIC)* – Kindergarten. Show and tell. I brought the Gene solo record in to show off and play a song. What does 5-year-old Izzy Presley pick? The song about banging groupies. While not knowing what it was or what it meant, I am pretty sure it shaped me good!

BILL STARKEY *(FOUNDER, KISS ARMY)* – In the early days before KISS started playing stadiums it was common knowledge that you could find your heroes at the local Holiday Inn. Gene was the ONLY member who checked in under his REAL name. I know because that's how I found him a few times. He didn't care. I myself never witnessed ANY debauchery, but Gene DID show me his scrapbook while we were at a Holiday Inn. I was way too naïve for such inventive perversity.

TONY MUSALLAM *(RESTRAYNED)* – "Living in Sin" is a fun, campy song with corny lyrics. The chorus is silly but super-catchy. Gene adds more and more vocal layers as the song progresses. The break down in the middle with the phone call takes it over the top.

BRAD RUSTOVEN *(SLAMFEST PODCAST)* – Between the cheesy intro and the phone call from Cher during the breakdown, this song is ridiculous… but it's so fun. As a 7-year-old, my mom asked me what I thought "Living in sin at the Holiday Inn" meant. My response… did they spill coffee on the carpet?

ALWAYS NEAR YOU/NOWHERE TO HIDE

MITCH WEISSMAN *(BEATLEMANIA, SONGWRITER)* – That is Gene doing the high part during the outro. There is talk that he may have slowed the machines down to get the voice on there then sped it up. But it doesn't sound like a Vinnie Vincent Invasion record (laughs).

RAISE YOUR GLASSES:
A Celebration of 50 Years of KISS Songs
by Celebrities, Musicians & Fans.

ZEUS *(SHOUT IT OUT LOUDCAST)* – Two songs in one. The song is always building and building. Gene back to his "Beatles voice." The Gene falsetto in the back part of the song is cool. Gene showing a different side of himself, and that's what the solo records were for…people!

JASON HERNDON *(KISS MY WAX PODCAST)* – The "Always Near You" part of this song is so haunting. And again, I just love Gene's smooth vocals when he uses them. His falsetto in the "Nowhere To Hide" part is impeccable. A brilliant song by Gene and one of my favorites from his solo album.

JOEY CASSATA *(ZO2, Z ROCK)* – The first half of this is a song I always skipped when I was younger. It was hard to appreciate it for what it is. It has such an *Elder* feel to it. The second half absolutely kills. There's not much to it, but Gene's vocal range really shines in this song.

TOM GIGLIOTTI *(SHOUT IT OUT LOUDCAST)* – The solo albums were a way for the members of KISS to express themselves and showcase their influences and individuality – and Gene surely goes that route here. It's no secret he loves the Beatles and he is channeling them strongly here. When the song transitions into the second half with the backing vocals and Gene hitting notes that no one had ever heard him hit before, you can feel his passion.

MAN OF 1000 FACES

ZEUS *(SHOUT IT OUT LOUDCAST)* – Gene's tribute to Lon Chaney and his love of the old black and white horror movies. This is another song that fits the phrase, "not a KISS song," but I still like it. It's a fun little pop song that works for me. The outro at the end with Gene saying, "I'm the man" is pretty cool.

WES BEECH *(THE PLASMATICS)* – Gene's love of horror movies is well known, and this tribute to the great actor and truly a "Man of 1000 Faces", Lon Chaney, has always been one of my favorite songs off *Gene Simmons*. And the fact that he named his publishing company Man of 1000 Faces just reinforces how much it means to him. His vocals on this track are straight from the heart. The guitar intro goes into an orchestral backing track that sounds like it could have come right off the Beatles *Sergent Pepper* album, a nod perhaps to another of Gene's biggest influences. It would be interesting to hear him do a rock version of this with his solo band.

PAUL JANIK *(GENE SIMMONS MONEYBAG SODA)* – Being a relentless horror movie nerd since a young age, I took to this song right away. I knew right away about the Lon Chaney reference in the title. Great melody and composition.

RAISE YOUR GLASSES:
A Celebration of 50 Years of KISS Songs by Celebrities, Musicians & Fans.

The guys from Gene Simmons Moneybag Soda with Gene Simmons

LISA MARTINI *(THREE SIDES OF THE COIN)* – Christmas 1978 was magical! For me it was the 4 solo albums that I was anxiously waiting to see if Santa Claus would bring me. I received the LP and the 8-track. The first one I played was Gene's. My cousin and I listened to it over and over all Christmas Day. I will always remember "Man of 1000 Faces" fading out on Program 1 (of the 8-track) and fading back in on Program 2. It's still strange listening to that song without that break.

STEVE WRIGHT *(PODDER THAN HELL PODCAST)* – Cool little riff at the beginning, and then we get an intense symphonic sort of stomp that does have a horror movie feel to it. Gene says he was sort of channeling Lon Chaney for this song. And stated that it was sort of autobiographical, with him being an immigrant and then putting on and taking off the makeup for the band. The chorus has a dreamy feel to it. Cool track on this diverse solo album.

MR. MAKE BELIEVE

MARTIN POPOFF *(AUTHOR)* – You couldn't say Gene missed his calling, because his calling turned out awesome, but man, on top of being a great singer in fourth and fifth gear, he's gorgeous of tone and persona in first and second gear. Plus, he's got a knack for the Beatles-esque, as evidenced on this sincere and smart ballad, which, with these gratuitous production touches, is perhaps more Wings-esque.

MITCH WEISSMAN *(BEATLEMANIA, SONGWRITER)* – By the time we got to this song, it's just me and Gene doing the vocals. Our voices seemed to mesh very well.

CLAUDIO SPERA *(KISS ARMY NATION PODCAST)* – If you would like to see how versatile Gene is in terms of music, you should listen to this song. It shows how much he loves the Beatles. The clean and crisp guitars coupled with a solid bass line gives the song a very "British" atmosphere. I really love the background vocals and how the song is constructed. The strings and orchestral part in the second part of the song are supreme. I would listen to this song over and over again.

TOM GIGLIOTTI *(SHOUT IT OUT LOUDCAST)* – It's no secret that Gene was massively influenced by the Beatles. This song could have been a lost Beatles demo. He sounds fantastic vocally and even hits those high notes quite well. The sweet-sounding acoustic guitar throughout the song combined with the harmonized vocals showcase a really important and impressive side to the Demon.

RAISE YOUR GLASSES:
A Celebration of 50 Years of KISS Songs
by Celebrities, Musicians & Fans.

Tom with Gene Simmons, *An Evening with Gene Simmons*, May 7, 2023

JOEY CASSATA *(ZO2, Z ROCK)* – What a great song!! The melody is so hooky that you can't help but sing it all day. Knowing how much Gene loves the Beatles, you can really appreciate this song, but as a kid it was just so far away from THE DEMON that I don't think it got the credit it deserved.

SEE YOU IN YOUR DREAMS

PASQUALE VARI *(KISS ARMY NATION PODCAST)* – A song that originally came from a near-perfect KISS album, *Rock and Roll*

Over, to being redone on a less than perfect solo album, leaves a lot to be desired for this new version. Did we really need those backup singers? If something is not broken, don't attempt to fix it. I don't understand why Gene felt it necessary to redo this song.

MARTIN POPOFF *(AUTHOR)* – We've already heard this one back on 1976's *Rock and Roll Over*, but we're in a happy place hearing it once again, given the song's bright and politely epic chorus refrain. At the verses, this one's illustrative of KISS's past in boogie, which you also hear on the verses of "Strutter." Guesting on guitar is Cheap Trick's Rick Nielsen, and on backing vocals, Detective's Michael Des Barres.

NICHOLAS BUCKLAND *(AUTHOR, Hottest Brand in the Land)* – Ever wanted to know what would happen if Gene's excesses were left completely unchecked? His remake of a KISS track from two years previous smacks of songwriting nepotism. And everything is thrown at this one, even a kitchen sink would show more restraint. Cheap Trick's Rick Nielsen and Michael Des Barres stop by to add even more cherries to the already over-cherried top of this ode to excess.

BRAD RUSTOVEN *(SLAMFEST PODCAST)* – I'm in the camp of preferring this version over the *RARO* version. More energy, an added pre-chorus, great backing vocals by the 'Kissettes' and a Rick Nielsen guitar solo. I especially love the build of the chorus after the solo and dig Michael Des Barres' vocal interjections throughout the song.

JEFF TROTT *(ART DIRECTOR)* – Electrifying guitar intro by Rick Nielsen and the scream is infectious. I love the short first verse that brings you quickly to the powerful chorus. Rick continues to shred and once you hear Katey "Peg Bundy" Segal's backing vocals you can never unhear them. Love the layered backing vocals and production on this track. It's a non-skippable track in my playlist.

WHEN YOU WISH UPON A STAR

JOEY CASSATA *(ZO2, Z ROCK)* – I never really cared for this song on this album when I was a kid, but I have come to respect Gene for putting it on the album. He loved this song and its meaning when he was a boy, and it took guts for the God Of Thunder to put this as the last song on his solo record.

PETER CORY *(KISS LIVE AUCTIONS)* – To me, this brings me back to when I was 4 years old listening to the 8-track in my living room. Gene was supposed to be this demon monster who spits blood, and he pulls off this amazing ballad from a Disney classic! Not a lot of great songs from the solo albums, but this is one of the good ones for sure.

JASON BAKKEN *(COBRAS & FIRE PODCAST)* – Some people shit on this. But I think it's the perfect ending to Gene's album. Gene likes to minimize his skill as a musician and songwriter, preferring to talk about trademarks and banging famous people. But motherfucker does he deliver a killer vocal on this.

JAMES CAMPION *(AUTHOR, Shout It Out Loud – The Story of KISS's Destroyer and the Making of an American Icon)* – All right, I'll be the one to defend this. And I do it not out of duty but authenticity. I love this. I love that Gene wanted to do it and end his solo album, a sonnet to his first loves as a kid, with it. Gene wished upon that star, as an entire generation of Boomer Disney-ites believed was their birthright. When Gene breaks up while singing it, you get Chaim Witz sitting in front of the tube making his own destiny one cartoon and comic book at a time. Gene Simmons is the hero's journey come to life. Never was there a more self-aware statement to conclude a solo album since John Lennon sang "My Mummy's Dead" to the tune of "Three Blind Mice." It is raw sense-memory. I applaud Gene's choice here, for no other reason than this was his chance to step out of the KISS bubble and give his confession. Testify!

ROBERT CONTE *(AUTHOR)* – The Demon singing Disney?! *Pinocchio* was theatrically re-released in 1978, the same year Gene Simmons covered this track on his KISS solo album—the first musical remake I ever heard. While the orchestra's performance in this version is genuinely beautiful and certainly rivals the original composed by Leigh Harline and Ned Washington, the vocals don't fit in some places. Despite its beautiful co-production by Sean Delaney and Gene, it's apparent he struggled to hit some of the highs. While some believe Gene's rendition of this song is the epitome of the album's self-indulgence, its message resonates with those who came from nothing and made something of themselves. Sorry, Gene, Jiminy Cricket wins this one!

RAISE YOUR GLASSES:
A Celebration of 50 Years of KISS Songs by Celebrities, Musicians & Fans.

"PAUL STANLEY"

Paul Stanley's solo effort leans towards the melodic side of rock, featuring anthemic tracks like "Tonight You Belong to Me" and "Hold Me, Touch Me." Stanley showcases his songwriting abilities and vocal range, offering a glimpse into the more romantic and melodic aspects of his musical sensibilities.

TONIGHT YOU BELONG TO ME

BRUCE KULICK *(KISS)* – His intro notes are so melodic. His high notes are crazy, he gets the riff out at the end. Bob was all over his bag of tricks. This is power pop at its best.

MARTIN POPOFF *(AUTHOR)* – There's over a minute of acoustic intro to this one, which is pretty daring for an album opener. But the message is that Paul's serious here. Soon we're into an emotional hard rocker, highly melodic and signature Starchild. And at 4:40, Stanley is in no hurry to move on to "Move On," letting us marinate in these melancholy melodies, setting the tone for a record that will nicely reinforce our opinion of Paul as the (only) believable love song guy of the band.

JOEY CASSATA *(ZO2, Z ROCK)* – The perfect Paul song. Another incredible way to start one of the solo albums. The acoustic intro, that slowly gives way to the heavy melodic rock song is perfectly put together by Paul. The solo albums were and still are one of the most daring and incredible feats by a band. Possibly never to be done again.

TONY MUSALLAM *(RESTRAYNED)* – My favorite song from my favorite solo album. The way this song goes from the tender acoustic intro to the crunchy riffs is very reminiscent of the KISS classic "Black Diamond". Paul flexes his vocal muscles, showing off his range as well as selling the emotion behind the lyrics. This is a very well-written and well-executed song.

SONNY POONI *(PODCAST ROCK CITY)* – *Paul Stanley* is not only my favorite of the solo albums but it's one of the best albums I own, period! The mix of the mellow and rocking parts of this song highlights the dynamics of Paul's vocals. I am a believer that if KISS ended in the early '80s, Paul would have done well as a solo artist.

KENNY BEGLEY *(KISS LIVE AUCTIONS)* – This song is just one of several soothing songs off this album, great to put on and just unwind with. Paul's solo is my favorite of the four.

MOVE ON

BRUCE KULICK *(KISS)* – Bob gets to play all over this song. How could someone listen to this record and not say "who's this guy playing guitar?" Paul just let Bob play. He's loud, he's up there in the mix. I was very impressed. It's a great song.

MARTIN POPOFF *(AUTHOR)* – Kinda cool that Paul used mostly lesser-knowns on his record—perhaps it makes for more of a band feel, certainly over and above Peter's and Gene's records. "Move On" sounds like a mid-league Starz song, a little hard rock, a little old rock 'n' roll. To be sure, there's piano and female backing vocals (Diana, Miriam, Maria), but otherwise it's a song that goes to work, with that pushing and shoving chorus sticking in the brain nicely and precisely.

STEVE WRIGHT *(PODDER THAN HELL PODCAST)* – Crunchy guitars for the main riff, Paul Stanley at his story-telling best. It was awesome to see Paul bust this one out for the *Live to Win* tour. Fast cadence for the verses. Great feel with the female background singers from Rouge. The main riff is really heavy for a Stanley-penned song. There's a soft bridge right before the amazing Bob Kulick solo, he really shines on this album. Great second track on the album. Bob also plays some killer leads on the outro! Rest in Peace Bob Kulick!

Tom and Zeus at the KISS pop-up store, New York, December 1, 2023

ZEUS *(SHOUT IT OUT LOUDCAST)* – When I hear this song I always think about the "what if" scenario about Bob Kulick. What if Bob was picked as the lead guitarist during auditions instead of Ace? Does KISS succeed? Does it do better or worse? I'll save the debate for the SIOL podcast or another book, but his guitar playing on this specific song shines bright, especially the solo and outro. The song itself is fun. Paul with his rapid delivery telling the story of his mother's advice with women. One of the great backing singers is Maria Vidal from Desmond Child and Rouge, and the "Gina" from the Bon Jovi song, "Livin' On A Prayer." There's a ton of foreshadowing to come on this collaboration.

TOM GIGLIOTTI *(SHOUT IT OUT LOUDCAST)* – Paul's solo album is pure power pop loaded with incredibly catchy choruses and hooks, as you would expect from the Starchild. This simple song with an undeniable groove was chosen as the one from his album that became part of their setlist during the *Dynasty* tour. Bob Kulick's guitar grooves and solo make this a song, which could've easily fit on a classic '70s KISS album.

AIN'T QUITE RIGHT

BRUCE KULICK *(KISS)* – This song I'm really impressed with. Starts mellow and Bob has some beautiful, tasty notes happening. Then he does a couple of jazzy notes. A killer '70s vibe kind of tune. It has the mellow parts then gets a little more aggressive.

CLAUDIO SPERA *(KISS ARMY NATION PODCAST)* – I think Paul's solo album has great vocals, material, players and production. The album is a good reflection of who Paul was and where he was at that point in his career. This song takes the listener to different melodic zones. The solo is sensational. Lots of feeling in every piece of the arrangements. In Paul's voice I can feel a mix of drama and darkness, but still positive. Hard to explain in words.

RAISE YOUR GLASSES:
A Celebration of 50 Years of KISS Songs
by Celebrities, Musicians & Fans.

CHRIS JERICHO *(WRESTLER, FOZZY)* – I love this song. I love the fact that in comes in almost like "Kiss You All Over" (by Exile). Keep in mind this is 1978. Paul sings great on it. When sequencing a record mattered, it's the perfect place for that song because it takes you down a little bit but it's still pretty cool. Once it kicks in with the instrumental section it's great, and the riff is great.

JEFF TROTT *(ART DIRECTOR)* – Co-written by Mikel Japp. I've always said *Paul Stanley* is the best, with *Ace Frehley* as a close second. The song starts with a soft acoustic intro and gentle vocals from Paul, followed by ripping guitar from the late Bob Kulick. I love how the song ramps up, slows down, and then picks back up—it's a rollercoaster ride and an overall fantastic track. Bob plays both acoustic and electric guitar on this song, with background vocals by the great Peppy Castro.

Chris Jericho with Paul Stanley

TOM GIGLIOTTI *(SHOUT IT OUT LOUDCAST)* – An interesting song on Paul's album that I think really is a fantastic deep cut. We get a very thoughtful Starchild here, with a groove that we don't see often from the band. The song builds up halfway through with incredible guitar work from Bob Kulick and then settles back into its quiet mood. It picks up the pace near the end and really creates a great classic sound.

WOULDN'T YOU LIKE TO KNOW ME

BRUCE KULICK *(KISS)* – Always a big fan of the drone-y, Cheap Trick-type of guitar, power pop stuff. So catchy, and Bob's solo is very memorable. I really like the way this one sounds, and the production on this one wouldn't work on other songs on the album.

MARTIN POPOFF *(AUTHOR)* – This one's fun because it shows Paul in bubblegum power pop mode, full-on guitars, spirited vocal, heroic but traditional chords… an adorable song all around, with more New York to it than any other geographical touchstone. Which is nice when you find it, because New York under-punches when it comes to musical influence. But yeah, I hear the Dolls, the '60s girl groups, and maybe a little bit of post-punk CBGB new wave.

CHRIS CZYNSZAK *(DECIBEL GEEK PODCAST)* – Paul Stanley with a nod to Eric Carmen's Raspberries. This tight, efficient power pop song is filled with jangly guitars and a snotty vocal delivery. While KISS did go too far at times with their pop aspirations, they do it well when they balance it with crunchy guitars as they do here.

RAISE YOUR GLASSES:
A Celebration of 50 Years of KISS Songs
by Celebrities, Musicians & Fans.

IZZY PRESLEY *(MUSICIAN, COMIC)* – From the album that sounds like demos for what would be '80s KISS, this song stands above the rest of the record. I know, it's sacrilege to scoff at Paul's solo record – but facts are facts. But the riff and Paul's vocals take this over the top.

Murph, Tom and Tom's son, Michael

JOEY CASSATA *(ZO2, Z ROCK)* – I didn't fully appreciate some of the songs on Paul's solo album until I saw him at L'Amour in Brooklyn on his solo tour in 1989. Something about the production on the album always fell short for me. His solo band was on fire that tour, led by Bob Kulick with Dennis St. James and of course Eric

Singer. Eric's playing on that tour made me a fan of all of these songs. Electrifying.

TAKE ME AWAY (TOGETHER AS ONE)

BRUCE KULICK *(KISS)* – Melodic 12-string guitar intro. I hear a little phaser on my brother's guitar. His solo is really melodic. This song was built for Carmine Appice to be the madman on the drums. There's a guitar part near the end that's an homage to Vanilla Fudge for Carmine.

CARMINE APPICE *(VANILLA FUDGE, ROD STEWART)* – When I play and record, I play whatever comes to mind. I went and actually bought the record. At my clinics everyone always asks me about that song. I had just come back from Asia with Rod Stewart and I went right into the studio; I was fried and Paul had been hanging out with me. So I played on the record.

STEVE WRIGHT *(PODDER THAN HELL PODCAST)* – I consider this an epic track. Acoustic start with soft Paul vocals. Some subtle leads from Bob Kulick. This would have been amazing live. When it kicks up, we get the cool pick scrape then the bombastic drums from Carmine Appice. Then it goes back down. Then builds back up again. Paul's vocals are stellar and so powerful in the chorus. Fantastic drum fill going into the very melodic solo from Bob Kulick. After the solo it stays in the more bombastic realm, then it goes into a sort of dreamy ending with the guitars and crazy drum fills from Carmine. Fades off into space. Amazing song and maybe the best song on any of the solo albums.

RAISE YOUR GLASSES:
A Celebration of 50 Years of KISS Songs
by Celebrities, Musicians & Fans.

Carmine Appice with Paul Stanley

RUSSELL PETERS *(COMEDIAN)* – I'm big on drum fills, I couldn't be a drummer because I'd put drum fills on everything. That's what "Take Me Away" has at the end. I'd love to hear what got cut off.

ZACH THRONE *(COREY TAYLOR, BRUCE KULICK)* – Great song by Paul. Spooky and rocking. Emotional, soulful vocal from Paul. Guitars sound so killer.

IT'S ALRIGHT

BRUCE KULICK *(KISS)* – There's not even a guitar solo on it but you can tell that Bob is chugging along on it. It's such a Rod Stewart or Faces type of song.

MARTIN POPOFF *(AUTHOR)* – Man, this one's got huge KISS hit written all over it. The wall of glammy guitars is downright giddy-making, and then with Paul singing high and energetic with that huge, attention-getting voice—that was KISS's secret weapon: three great singers across four great voices — "It's Alright" is much more than all right. What's more, I can see this one holding its own on *Revenge* or *Sonic Boom* or *Monster* as well, and it would've crushed the competition on *Psycho Circus*.

ZEUS *(SHOUT IT OUT LOUDCAST)* – What a fucking up-tempo rocking song. Paul is on fire and a badass on this song. This song is the quintessential Paul Stanley. An undeniable catchy hook, melody and chorus. Bob Kulick is a beast on this album. Imagine if this made it to *Love Gun* or *Dynasty*. Might be in the running for best KISS deep cut ever.

CHRIS L. *(POD OF THUNDER)* – I had never heard a note from Paul's solo album before doing my show. Back in the day, I only owned Ace's and Peter's. I've since ranked it above *Ace Frehley* as my favorite of the four, largely due to this song. An upbeat rocker about a one-night stand that may or may not lead to something more – as we often say on Pod of Thunder, "what's not to like?"

TONY MUSALLAM *(RESTRAYNED)* – "It's Alright" starts off with a cool guitar riff reminiscent of "Mr. Speed". This song always gets me singing along and bobbing my head. A super-catchy, well-written song.

Tom and Zeus, *End of the Road*, Mohegan Sun, March 23, 2019

BRAD RUSTOVEN *(SLAMFEST PODCAST)* – By far, the best song on the album. Amazing riff and one of Paul's best verse vocal performances ever. The backing vocals are perfect as well – not overwhelming and not too many layers of harmonies. Great live-sounding ending – it doesn't fade out! Only negative – no guitar solo.

JAMES CAMPION *(AUTHOR, Shout It Out Loud – The Story of KISS's Destroyer and the Making of an American Icon)* – "It's Alright" is straight out of *Dressed to Kill* land. Boasting one of the most infectious choruses of a songwriting career silly with infectious choruses, it is a banger. Stanley was always going on and on about loving British bands with their chant-addled anthems, and (clears throat) this is one hella example. This would have been a huge hit for KISS and should have been the album's single.

HOLD ME, TOUCH ME (THINK OF ME WHEN WE'RE APART)

BRUCE KULICK *(KISS)* – Bob isn't on it because it doesn't really require a guitar part, it wasn't appropriate. Paul was going for the big ballad. It doesn't really fit the rest of the album. I bought the single because the B-side is "Goodbye".

COURTNEY CRONIN DOLD *(COMEDIAN)* – Ah, the KISS song with the longest title. Of course, it's one of Paul's. Do you think when the solo albums came out, he said, "Hey guys, my song title is bigger than yours"? It's a little sappy for a Paul Stanley love song, but I love it. It's romantic, melodic, and a lot less creepy than his others. It would make an EXCELLENT theme song for a daytime soap opera.

MURPH *(SHOUT IT OUT LOUDCAST)* – I wonder if Paul had a do over if he would have put a tad more grit to the sound. The lyrics are solid and heartfelt, but I just listen to it and think of "Beth". I just felt if the sound was just picked up a tad (closer to "Hard Luck Woman"), would it have become more popular. I really want to like this song.

PASQUALE VARI *(KISS ARMY NATION PODCAST)* – Call me cheesy but I love Paul Stanley ballads. I loved this song as a 10-year-old and still love it as a 56-year-old man. This song comes from a solo album that was the closest thing to a KISS record. I'm not sure this song would actually fit on a KISS record, but I love it, nonetheless.

TOM HIGGINS *(KLASSIK '78)* – I may be the only person commenting on this one. Haha! This is a really well-crafted song. Sure, its sugary and sappy, but it was 1978. If this was recorded by Andy Gibb, Olivia Newton-John or Rod Stewart in 1978, it would have been a massive hit in the USA. A really cool and expressive guitar solo by Paul too.

LOVE IN CHAINS

BRUCE KULICK *(KISS)* – Starts with Bob's leads that are very thematic. There's a big solo from Bob in there and it's great. Another great song from Paul's record.

MARTIN POPOFF *(AUTHOR)* – "Love in Chains" is the heaviest song on *Paul Stanley*, but despite the sort of recurring note-dense "Creatures of the Night" lick, Paul doesn't forget to make a sturdy song of it. This is accomplished by the Stanley-esque chord changes at the verse, with the sum total resulting in another song that could have become a popular KISS anthem, even more so given a flashier title. Add in the tension of a sophisticated pop pre-chorus and a pregnant-pausing proto-hair metal chorus and this one's a winner all round.

RAISE YOUR GLASSES:
A Celebration of 50 Years of KISS Songs
by Celebrities, Musicians & Fans.

TONY MUSALLAM *(RESTRAYNED)* – From the first notes of its fiery intro, I was hooked. The vocal melodies throughout are super-catchy and memorable, especially the pre-chorus.

PETER DANKELSON *(PETE'S DIARY)* – This Paul Stanley tune is firing on all cylinders! The main guitar riff has this great muted attack and Paul's vocals sound huge, and I love the overall energetic swagger of this song!

TOM GIGLIOTTI *(SHOUT IT OUT LOUDCAST)* – One of the many songs on this album that could've easily fit on *Love Gun* or *Rock and Roll Over*. A spectacular rocker that is classic Starchild. It's got melody, passion, and kickass rock all rolled into one. Bob Kulick absolutely burns through an amazing solo here. Paul means what he says in this song, you can feel it in every word. An absolute go-to track on what has always been my favorite of the 1978 solo albums.

GOODBYE

BRUCE KULICK *(KISS)* – A killer ending song. It's a track that makes you want to hear more. The riff is so ahead of its time. Every riff that Bob placed in there is magic. There isn't a solo but there are tasty riffs.

ZEUS *(SHOUT IT OUT LOUDCAST)* – What a great closing track to the best KISS solo album from 1978. Yes, I said it. If you have the KISS Box Set you know this song came from the early demo called "Keep Me Waiting." It has a great bass line credited to Eric

Nelson. Although Paul played this on his solo tour, I would have loved to hear what it would be like to have this close a KISS concert.

MARTIN POPOFF *(AUTHOR)* – I hear top-shelf Starz in this one, classic '76 to '78 KISS and, because it's Paul, some of that heart-throb passion at the melody end that for some reason I associate most with the *Asylum* album from 1985, specifically "Tears Are Falling" and "Who Wants to Be Lonely." As well, "Goodbye" is performed like a KISS song, from the drums on up, so you can play those games of wishing (upon a star) that this would have replaced some dumb thing on *Rock and Roll Over* or *Love Gun*.

JASON HERNDON *(KISS MY WAX PODCAST)* – Paul Stanley perfection. The bass line is superb. Everything about this song is perfect. Especially Paul's vocals. A perfect ending to an album as well. A top favorite of mine from the solo albums.

RAISE YOUR GLASSES:
A Celebration of 50 Years of KISS Songs
by Celebrities, Musicians & Fans.

"PETER CRISS"

Peter Criss's solo album has a bluesy and soulful vibe, emphasizing his roots as a jazz and R&B drummer. Tracks like "You Matter to Me" and "Don't You Let Me Down" showcase Criss's soulful voice. The album presents a more laid-back and reflective side of KISS's Catman.

I'M GONNA LOVE YOU

JOEY CASSATA *(ZO2, Z ROCK)* – God, I love this album! I will admit that as a kid I kind of didn't understand it. But I also didn't get the Beatles, the Stones, Motown, or anything that wasn't classic KISS. Haha. "I'm Gonna Love You" is classic R&B. Great stuff.

ZEUS *(SHOUT IT OUT LOUDCAST)* – One of Shout It Out Loudcast's favorite opening lyrics, "Don't let me find you sleeping with another man." This can be said about almost the whole album – this song is not a KISS song, but it's a great song. The production on this whole album is excellent. The saloon-type piano playing on this song and the whole album sounds like it's being played by Rowlf from the *Muppets*, but it works. A song by Peter's original band Lips. A trio with co-songwriter Stan Penridge and Michael Benvenga, who is the only non-KISS member given a dedication on the back of the 1978 solo albums. Peter's whiskey voice and the horns and the piano make this a fun R&B number.

CHRIS L. *(POD OF THUNDER)* – When the four KISS solo albums came out, I only bought Ace's and Peter's, because they were my favorite members. *Peter Criss* gets a lot of flak for being too soft, but I enjoyed it from the beginning, and I feel like he and Gene are the ones who got the memo that a solo album is supposed to be different from what you do in your regular band. This song set the tone for the rest of Peter's album, and the veiled threat in the opening lyric is a masterstroke.

RAISE YOUR GLASSES:
A Celebration of 50 Years of KISS Songs by Celebrities, Musicians & Fans.

Zeus proudly wearing his Peter Criss costume, Halloween 1978

ROBERT CONTE *(AUTHOR)* – I fell in love with this song immediately after first hearing it. The track sets the tone for the entire blues-jazz-rock tone of the record. Dare I say *Peter Criss* is just as good, and in some ways better, as the *Ace Frehley* and *Paul Stanley* albums; it exemplifies Peter's sonic contributions from the original era. *Peter Criss* is underrated and, in my honest opinion, would have benefitted from higher sales and critical acclaim had it not been branded as a KISS album. Vini Poncia's production is top-notch, leading to his hiring on the next two KISS albums, *Dynasty* and *Unmasked*.

TOM GIGLIOTTI *(SHOUT IT OUT LOUDCAST)* – Over the years, I have become a huge fan of Peter's much-maligned solo album. I love jazz, swing and big band music, and most of his album incorporates that since those are his roots. This has such an incredible groove and classic rock vibe to it. The change during the chorus and the addition of the horns as the song progresses is just spectacular. Peter sings his ass off and you can't help but have fun here. And it has one of the all-time great opening lyrics of any KISS-related song… "Don't let me find you sleeping with another man".

YOU MATTER TO ME

JOEY CASSATA *(ZO2, Z ROCK)* Being that Casablanca was the "disco" label, they should have realized what they had with this song. This song could have easily been in *Saturday Night Fever*. I can see it now, Tony Manero (John Travolta) driving his giant Cadillac DeVille down 86th St. in Brooklyn, while this song is playing.

ALEX SALZMAN *(PRODUCER, ACE FREHLEY, PETER CRISS)* – Another favorite of Peter's and his fans. The opening synth riff is a classic and the great chorus hook is delivered with passion and conviction. A Japanese woman fan flew in to see Peter at The Cutting Room in New York and we added this song to the set at the last minute, as he knew she was coming and it was her favorite. He dedicated It to her, and she was balling.

CLAUDIO SPERA *(KISS ARMY NATION PODCAST)* – This song has a special meaning to me. When I was a kid, I used to live in a small house and everybody in the family could listen to the music blasting through the speakers. My mom, rest in peace, used to love this song so much. She used to say this was some kind of white R& B song with a bluesy singer. Peter's voice has the emotional resonance of singers like Rod Stewart or Joe Cocker.

IZZY PRESLEY *(MUSICIAN, COMIC)* – The *Peter Criss* solo album is the most underrated album with the KISS logo on it while not being a "KISS" record. This album SCREAMS the 1978 pop charts. Every song sounds like the Top 40 of September '78, and "You Matter To Me" screams it the loudest. GREAT POP/ROCK SONG!

Tom and Zeus, Madison Square Garden, December 1, 2023

TOM GIGLIOTTI *(SHOUT IT OUT LOUDCAST)* – I am an unapologetic fan of '70s soft rock and disco, and this amazing song has all of that. The keyboard harmonies that run through this along with one of Peter's catchiest choruses make this a song I have loved since the first time I heard it. And when Peter starts wailing near the end, it's just so good and enjoyable. Yes, I love Peter's solo album!

TOSSIN' AND TURNIN'

JOEY SASSO (*THE CIRCLE, NETFLIX*) – This shines as a particularly captivating tune for a variety of reasons. The intensity of emotion in Peter Criss's vocal performance, paired with moving lyrics, grabs the audience's interest immediately. Its memorable melody and brisk pace set a compelling rhythm that's difficult to ignore. Additionally, this song presents a different facet of Peter as an artist, underscoring his capabilities in songwriting and his knack for forging a personal connection through his music. The song's nostalgic feel engenders warmth and familiarity, marking it as a highlight of his solo work. In summary, "Tossin' and Turnin'" serves as a powerful demonstration of Peter's artistic prowess and stands out as a premier selection in his solo repertoire.

TOM GIGLIOTTI (*SHOUT IT OUT LOUDCAST*) – The much-maligned *Peter Criss* album has some really great songs if you can separate yourself from this being a true KISS album. This cover version of a classic song is so catchy and groovy, it's always been my go-to song on this album which I have grown to really respect and enjoy. His vocals combined with the funky vibe of the band playing behind him make this such a cool tune.

RAISE YOUR GLASSES:
A Celebration of 50 Years of KISS Songs by Celebrities, Musicians & Fans.

Brennan Mileto with KISS

DALE TORBORG *(THE DEMON WCW)* – My cousin Cathy gave me the *Peter Criss* album and I was thrilled. I liked that it was different, and I liked "Tossin' and Turnin'" because it was completely different, I didn't know the original song, for me it was Peter Criss, it was KISS.

JOE POLO *(PODCAST ROCK CITY)* – When I was a kid Peter Criss's solo album was the first one I got because my mom thought that the "Kitty Cat" was safe. I actually really enjoyed this record and enjoy this song.

BRENNAN MILETO *(SISTERS DOLL)* – What a song this is –such a catchy sing-along number. I loved watching it as a kid when they did this one on tour. Peter's voice shines through, especially when he belts it out at the end. The cowbell shuffle beat throughout the song is cool. I love how they sped it up live as opposed to the record.

JEFF TROTT *(ART DIRECTOR)* – "Tossin' and Turnin'" kicks off with a riff reminiscent of "All Right Now", setting it apart from Bobby Lewis's original version. This cover of the 1961 number one hit by Bobby Lewis was featured in KISS's live performances during the 1979 *Dynasty* tour, where each member played a song from their respective 1978 solo albums.

DON'T YOU LET ME DOWN

JOE McGINNESS *(KUARANTINE, KLASSIK '78)* – I've always thought Peter's solo album was criminally underrated. This song in particular is a great ballad, and to be honest, Peter's voice alone makes it worth listening to. It may not be a "KISS" song but who cares? If you take that out of the equation it's an excellent song that is well written and deserves recognition.

COURTNEY CRONIN DOLD *(COMEDIAN)* – And he didn't. Get your best girl, put down your Mai Tais and enjoy a nice little samba in the moonlight to this beauty. I love the backup singers, the soul in Peter's voice. This is my favorite slow dance song of all the solo albums.

KENNY BEGLEY *(KISS LIVE AUCTIONS)* – I have to confess, was not a fan of Peter's solo album as a teenager and into my 30s, but as I got older and listened, the more I got into it. This song is my favorite, I feel he sang it with passion for whatever reason!

ALEX SALZMAN *(PRODUCER, ACE FREHLEY, PETER CRISS)* – Peter shows his love for and influence by '50s- and '60s-era American music, and effortlessly delivers the vibe with both music and lyrics. We would sometimes go into "Stand By Me" and "Under The Boardwalk" at rehearsals, to his delight.

BRENNAN MILETO *(SISTERS DOLL)* – Peter's soulful voice in this song is so passionate, and you can tell where his influences come from in this song. When we played this with Peter on his final two shows ever, it was a highlight of the set, and singing the back-up harmonies along with Peter's one-of-a-kind voice blew me away every night.

THAT'S THE KIND OF SUGAR PAPA LIKES

JASON HOOK *(FIVE FINGER DEATH PUNCH)* – This was the first solo album I bought from the four KISS members. I have to give Peter props here, he did a great job with this record. The opening snare fill is 100% the Peter Criss sound. The song/album reminds me how fun and uplifting the sound was in 1978. Highlights include a killer guitar solo from Steve Lukather.

STEVE WRIGHT *(PODDER THAN HELL PODCAST)* – Good build into this song. One of the few non-ballads on *Peter Criss*. It has a good rock 'n' roll" feel to it. Good female background vocals and accents throughout the song. The drums sound really crisp and are produced really good. Peter's vocals are in the raspy range that I really like. The solo is supplied by Steve Lukather. Give this track another try, you may be surprised!

RAISE YOUR GLASSES:
A Celebration of 50 Years of KISS Songs
by Celebrities, Musicians & Fans.

JOEY CASSATA *(ZO2, Z ROCK)* – Probably my favorite song on the album. The quintessential Peter Criss shuffle leads this infectious track. Peter's raspy vocal mixed with the soulful female background singers makes this song untouchable.

Joey Cassata with his son and daughter

ZEUS *(SHOUT IT OUT LOUDCAST)* – Another old Lipps song brought back for Peter's solo album. Sugar? What kind of sugar is Peter singing about? Anyway, the song is a fun, catchy and upbeat number, but perhaps hurt by the silly song title. Steve Lukather kills it on the solo on the song. The backing singers are great as well. The chorus stays with you long after the song is over.

ERNIE PALOOZA *(TOP 5 WITH JOEY CASSATA)* – Peter's voice sounds so strong in this song! It makes me wonder, if KISS never happened, would he be in a different musical genre. His voice is perfectly suited for this poppish soul! The scream at 1:14 reminds me of Ian Gillan from Deep Purple on the song "Highway Star".

EASY THING

ZACH THRONE *(COREY TAYLOR, BRUCE KULICK)* – I decided awhile back to give the *Peter Criss* album a chance after dismissing it back when I bought it in '78. It's not a good album, but there are more good musical moments than I remembered. The song that shocked me (no pun intended) was "Easy Thing". This is actually a really good song – very John Lennon in its approach, arrangement and melody. Great vocal from Peter, particularly in the verses and choruses. If it had a better arrangement, a huge guitar solo in the middle and a lead vocal that builds and builds at the end, it could've been a Nazareth or Guns N' Roses ballad. If it was submitted to a KISS album and reworked by Bob Ezrin and I think it could've been another "Beth".

AUSTIN MILETO *(SISTERS DOLL)* – Such a beautiful song. Love the choice of chords and the vocal harmonies in the chorus. Can really hear the emotion in Peter's voice, which I also love.

RAISE YOUR GLASSES:
A Celebration of 50 Years of KISS Songs
by Celebrities, Musicians & Fans.

Sisters Doll with Peter Criss

JOEY TATTO (*THE CIRCLE, NETFLIX*) – "Easy Thing" stands out for various compelling reasons. The song's relaxed and soulful ambiance immediately captivates listeners, drawing them in. Peter's unique vocal style shines through in this sincere ballad, conveying vulnerability and authenticity that deeply resonates with this listener. The heartfelt lyrics are complemented by melodious guitar work and subtle instrumentation, enriching the emotional complexity of the song. "Easy Thing" exemplifies Peter's versatility as an artist, showcasing his capacity to deliver a moving and emotive performance that lingers with this guy long after.

In essence, "Easy Thing" emerges as a standout track on *Peter Criss* due to its poignant storytelling, genuine delivery, and overall musicality. It serves as a testament to Peter's artistry and continues to be cherished by fans for its authentic and heartfelt expression.

RAISE YOUR GLASSES:
A Celebration of 50 Years of KISS Songs
by Celebrities, Musicians & Fans.

Peter's solo album and his entire solo career have been widely misunderstood by numerous KISS fans over the years. A track such as "Easy Thing" can reveal Peter's genuine passion if approached with an open mind, appreciating it for its own merits rather than criticizing it for what it lacks.

TOM HIGGINS *(KLASSIK '78)* – I remember falling in love with a girl when I was in 3rd grade, and this was our song. She didn't know it was our song. I was too shy to tell her :) A very emotional vocal by Peter on this track. He could have had a successful solo career with this stuff, but even if Peter was in tip-top form, releasing his first few solo albums on Casablanca was always going to be a conflict of interest/dead end.

JOEY CASSATA *(ZO2, Z ROCK)* – The more I listen to Peter's album, the more I like it. In fact, it's the exact opposite for Paul's album. *Paul Stanley* has gotten weaker for me as time goes by and *Peter Criss* keeps getting stronger. "Easy Thing" is such a heartfelt vocal with an arrangement that is absolutely beautiful. Vini Poncia's production sets it apart from Gene's & Paul's albums for me.

ROCK ME. BABY

JOEY SASSO *(THE CIRCLE, NETFLIX)* – Considered a remarkable addition to Peter Criss's discography, "Rock Me, Baby" stands out for various reasons. The song emanates an infectious sense of fun and energy, attributed to its lively tempo and memorable hooks. Peter's distinctive gravelly vocals imbue the track with a raw, distinctive quality. The dynamic interplay of rhythmic beats and compelling guitar riffs in "Rock Me, Baby" establishes an energetic ambiance, ideal for audience participation and fostering enthusiasm. Its simple yet impactful lyrics strike a chord with rock enthusiasts, elevating its position as a standout piece on *Peter Criss*. In essence, "Rock Me, Baby" underscores Peter's adeptness in delivering a high-octane rock anthem with lasting appeal. By blending catchy tunes, potent vocals, and vibrant instrumentals, the song solidifies its stature as a standout from his solo work, appealing to both established fans and new audiences.

RYAN "BB" BANNON *(PODDER THAN HELL PODCAST)* – Jaunty piano, horn section, female background singers, Peter's raspy, New York City vocals. That's Peter's foundational sound. The music where Peter came from. Paul always ragged on Peter's solo album. Isn't that the sound Soul Station is producing today?

JOEY CASSATA *(ZO2, Z ROCK)* – Of course, Peter is best known for his ballads, but this is where Peter shines! Good old rock 'n' roll. His soulful voice is second to none. Once again, the music and production on this song are stellar. It's funny how all the KISS solo albums have tons of female background vocals. They really do add a richness to all of these songs.

ZEUS *(SHOUT IT OUT LOUDCAST)* – When Peter needed help getting songs for his 1978 solo album he turned to the great jack of all trades, Sean Delaney, who was busy producing Gene's 1978 solo album. This song, with its "Rowlf-like" piano groove and horns which could have been taken straight from an Earth Wind & Fire or Kool & The Gang song is a catchy upbeat soulful tune. Peter once again delivers vocally, and the backing singers do too on this deep cut. Vini Poncia's production on this works so well, unlike whatever he did on *Unmasked*.

TOM GIGLIOTTI *(SHOUT IT OUT LOUDCAST)* – Peter's solo album is much maligned because it's not a KISS record. As I said, I am huge fan of jazz and big band and I really enjoy this album, and especially this track. You can't help but tap your toes and bob your head while listening. He has such a knack for creating catchy and jazzy grooves, and this song is so fun to listen to; the album absolutely needs to be given a chance with fresh ears.

KISS THE GIRL GOODBYE

MARK CICCHINI *(THREE SIDES OF THE COIN)* – Arguably the best vocal on this album and to be fair, Peter's vocals were never the issue why this album has been so mercifully panned over the years... unfairly so in my estimation. This song is the most mature of the songs on *Peter Criss,* and in my opinion is one of the best-written songs on all the solo albums. A perfect melodic guitar arrangement complements Peter's perfectly pitched and soulful vocal delivery. A most beautiful ballad! Everything about this song shines. Unfortunately, the underwritten songs on this LP (not sure why Aucoin did not demand better writers be brought in to help tighten up the material) get more of the focus than the few truly bright spots like Peter's performance here.

COURTNEY CRONIN DOLD *(COMEDIAN)* – Another candlelight-dinner-stare-googly-eyed-at-each-other song. The soft acoustic guitar and Peter's sultry singing just feels like a big ole cat purr in your face.

JOEY SASSO *(THE CIRCLE, NETFLIX)* – Alright, listen up, folks, because "Kiss the Girl Goodbye" isn't just a song; it's a soulful journey that grips you from the get-go. Picture this: melodic guitar riffs and rhythmic drumming setting the stage for Peter's raw and emotionally charged vocals that hit you right in the heart. The lyrics? They aren't just words; they're a poignant message of love, nostalgia, and the heartache of goodbyes – relatable and touching to anyone who's felt that tug at their soul.

Now, let me tell you about Peter's distinctive sound and style in this track – it's like his musical fingerprint stamped all over it. "Kiss the Girl Goodbye" epitomizes why Peter's fans rally to defend his solo endeavors when critics challenge his musical prowess. Peter Criss, the heart of the band, bared his soul in this track, revealing a softer side beneath his Brooklyn-bred toughness. Through this song, he lays bare his vulnerabilities and desires for love and acceptance, shedding the bravado that often masked his true self. It's a poignant reminder that behind the rock-star persona lies a man yearning for connection and understanding, a testament to Peter's emotional depth and sincerity as an artist. This song still resonates today because it's timeless, folks. Its universal themes and crafted musical arrangement speak to the soul, making it a standout piece that showcases Peter's solo artistry like no other.

JOE POLO *(PODCAST ROCK CITY)* – I literally remember the first time I heard this song. I was a little kid and remember that all I thought was, "this song is sappy"! As an adult, I understand what he was saying in the song. I guess it was kind of personal.

IZZY PRESLEY *(MUSICIAN, COMIC)* – I am a big softy. I love a good love song. This is a good love song on an album that many of you humanoids would rather wipe your ass with than listen to. If you listen to it as a late-'70s pop/rock record, you may just change your mind... no, you will. Love this tune.

HOOKED ON ROCK 'N' ROLL

JOEY CASSATA *(ZO2, Z ROCK)* – I always loved this song due to it being very relatable to me as a drummer. The lyrics always hit home for me… "The boy could play before he learned to crawl", "Every mornin' at the break of dawn, you could see him draggin' home his drums", "I'm hooked on rock 'n' roll".

Joey Cassata with Peter Criss holding his autobiography

ZEUS *(SHOUT IT OUT LOUDCAST)* – What a fun rock, soul and R&B number. Once again, the production is top-notch and the band is just top-notch, as are Peter's vocals. I love the horns and piano on this one. I also like that this makes it to the alternate version of *KISS Meets The Phantom Of The Park – Attack Of The Phantoms*. Guest guitarist, Steve Lukather does a sweet little solo. If the horns and piano were replaced with Ace's guitar this would have been a great KISS song.

STEVE WRIGHT *(PODDER THAN HELL PODCAST)* – Some Motown feel for you with some jaunty piano and some great bass lines. Great raspy Peter vocals and some really good female background singers. I love the line "I was vaccinated with a victrola needle". Excellent solo from Steve Lukather. There's a big horn section and a steady drumbeat. Good "boogie-woogie" song! Peter says, "This is New York Yo".

BRYCE MILETO *(SISTERS DOLL)* – We played this song with Peter in Australia and New York City for his final show. We had the full orchestra backing our band Sisters Doll, along with Peter behind the kit, singing & belting lead vocals. Every time I hear this song, it takes me back to these life-pinching moments.

TOM GIGLIOTTI *(SHOUT IT OUT LOUDCAST)* – Peter really channels his love of classic old-school rock 'n' roll here. The pianos, the horns and the bouncy sing-along vibe sometimes remind me of the classic *Muppets*, with Rowlf banging away on the piano. Then throw in an amazing guitar solo and you have it all here. It's catchy, fun, hooky and another great track from his solo album.

I CAN'T STOP THE RAIN

BRYCE MILETO *(SISTERS DOLL)* – I've always loved this amazing song. Peter's vocal is just amazing and untouchable. We got the opportunity to play this song live for the first time with Peter in New York and Melbourne, and it was a real tear-jerker when the intro kicked in and Peter started singing. This song hits every emotion; I just love it.

MARTIN POPOFF *(AUTHOR)* – Last track on the most denigrated of the solo albums (and the only Peter Criss song on my list), "I Can't Stop the Rain" is in fact the second most-played song from the record on Spotify. I've picked it for writing about because it's a straight ballad with no R&B, rock 'n' rollsy nonsense added. There's real strings, and a chorus that improves it rather than makes it more maudlin. Cool George Harrison-like guitar solo too, courtesy of John Tropea. Oh, how it all could have been different. With a voice like that, had Peter made the heaviest solo album rather than the lightest, and then taken his drumming to the limit as well (i.e. beyond KISS, garnering increased respect), he could have left the band and been a big star. I can see him prowling the stage like a cat as a front man, howling out vocals (again, like a cat) like he did on "Black Diamond" and "Hooligan."

Britt Lightning and Tommy London with KISS

RAISE YOUR GLASSES:
A Celebration of 50 Years of KISS Songs
by Celebrities, Musicians & Fans.

ZEUS *(SHOUT IT OUT LOUDCAST)* – Quite possibly Peter's best ballad ever. A beautiful song that just soars. This is written by the underrated Sean Delaney. What an influence he had on the band. If he never had a falling out with the band who knows if KISS ever loses steam. Again. I have to give credit to producer Vini Poncia because the music is gorgeous. Peter's vocals, phrasing and delivery are just superb. The fills after Peter sings, "Lightning," give me chills. A gorgeous song done by Peter at his best. Another hidden gem of a deep cut.

ALEX SALZMAN *(PRODUCER, ACE FREHLEY, PETER CRISS)* – Peter's affinity for ballads is undeniable, as witnessed by the huge success of "Beth". I am not sure if this was written around the same time, but it obviously refers to the latter. The opening spoken, "This is New Yawk...yo" is indicative of his attachment to and love for the city he grew up in.

JAMES CAMPION *(AUTHOR, Shout It Out Loud – The Story of KISS's Destroyer and the Making of an American Icon)* – Of course, Peter would sing a ballad on his solo album. The massive success of "Beth" demanded the whole solo albums foray in the first place. Peter's spastic mood swings and coke-fueled demands had reached a saturation point by mid-'78, and to be frank you could make a cogent argument he might be KISS's best vocalist. He is by far its most soulful. And he uses that rasp to sell emotion that appears on the surface to be beyond him. But he brings it with this sappy treacle of a tune. And I write that with all due respect. If you're going to sell the sap, *sell* the fucking thing! I loved every ballad Alice Cooper dreamed up and I am already on record swooning on "Beth," but those songs have a load more musical and lyrical density than "I Can't Stop the Rain." Conflating rain with pain and yearning is as old as literature, never mind the odd ditty. Those '70s strings really bring that sentiment home. Sentiment being the operative word here. Or is it sentimental? Oh, and one minor complaint: how does this not end cold with a swelling string coda? Fade out? Come on, Catman!

JASON HERNDON *(KISS MY WAX PODCAST)* – Peter's solo album was my favorite of the four when I was a kid. But I love all four very much. Also, I play drums because of Peter Criss. I've been blessed to work with and spend a tremendous amount of time with Peter personally the last couple of years. "I Can't Stop The Rain" is an incredibly well-written song by Sean Delaney, and one of Peter's best vocals he's ever recorded in my opinion. Every time I listen to this song, I'm immediately transported back to being a young kid playing this record in my bedroom. I just love it.

RAISE YOUR GLASSES:
A Celebration of 50 Years of KISS Songs
by Celebrities, Musicians & Fans.

CHAPTER 9

"DYNASTY"

Released: May 23, 1979

Dynasty marked a pivotal moment for KISS. This album showcased the band's evolution, incorporating elements of disco and pop while retaining their signature hard rock roots. With standout tracks like "I Was Made for Lovin' You" and "Sure Know Something," *Dynasty* reflected KISS's ability to adapt to changing musical landscapes, appealing to a broader audience without losing their distinctive sound. *Dynasty* emerged at a time of musical transformation, and KISS embraced the changing tides with an album that blended their classic hard rock style with contemporary influences. *Dynasty* represented a new chapter for the band.

The album opens with the anthemic "I Was Made for Lovin' You," a disco-infused track that became one of KISS's biggest hits. With its catchy chorus and danceable rhythm, the song showcased the band's willingness to experiment with different genres while maintaining their trademark energy.

While disco influences were evident, tracks like "2,000 Man" and "Charisma" demonstrated that KISS hadn't abandoned their hard rock roots. These songs maintained the band's signature guitar-driven sound, providing a balance between the new and the familiar.

While *Dynasty* faced criticism for its departure from KISS's traditional sound, it also demonstrated the band's adaptability and resilience. In the face of changing musical landscapes, KISS successfully embraced new influences while maintaining their core identity.

In retrospect, *Dynasty* stands as a snapshot of a band navigating the complexities of a shifting music industry. The album's success affirmed KISS's ability to connect with audiences across genres and solidified their reputation as a band capable of reinvention. *Dynasty* remains a crucial chapter in KISS's discography, capturing a moment when rock legends dared to venture into uncharted musical territories.

I WAS MADE FOR LOVIN' YOU

ACE FREHLEY *(KISS)* – Paul has a lot of different tastes in music that I don't. There's nothing wrong with that. Unfortunately, when it came to KISS, he would go on tangents that I normally didn't agree with. Like for example when we did the disco song. I was 100 percent against that, but it's one of our biggest hits, what are you gonna do.

DESMOND CHILD *(SONGWRITER)* – I met Paul at SIR Studios in New York and Paul told me to meet him when they took their lunch break. There was a grand piano there and we sat together, side by side, and started writing this song. He loved the sound of Desmond Child and Rouge, which was Motown sound with rock sound, so we said let's do something with a Motown beat and put heavy rock guitars to it. We changed the course of popular music; no one had tried this before. This was different 'cause it had this grand operatic beginning. It was more akin to Motown, but with rock guitars. The song gets licensed every 5 minutes, it's a classic and an American standard. Then I saw them in the final concert in New York and I saw Paul fly across the stage when the song played. I thought to myself, "Gene can't even be on the same stage as Paul when that song plays!" Haha!

CARMINE APPICE *(VANILLA FUDGE, ROD STEWART)* – Paul wrote this after we (Rod Stewart) did "Do Ya Think I'm Sexy?" Paul was hanging out with us then and he always wanted a song like that. I thought it was a pretty cool song. How big did that song go.

RAISE YOUR GLASSES:
A Celebration of 50 Years of KISS Songs
by Celebrities, Musicians & Fans.

Desmond Child with Paul Stanley

BOBBY ROCK *(VINNIE VINCENT INVASION, LITA FORD)* – If you were a hard rock fan back in the late '70s, it was your obligation to hate disco. And if you were a musician, it was double the rage. We all thought it was a worthless, watered-down, and limp-wristed form of music, and we resented its encroachment on *our* airwaves and *our* record store shelves. So... when KISS came out with this track, many of us viewed it as an unfortunate selling of the soul to the devil. And to those who were already put off by their "lunch-box" marketing tactics, the sense was, there was no limit to how low this shamelessly commercial enterprise might stoop. Still, a good song is a good song, even if it has the misfortune of such a production. And Paul's vocals on this track were exceptional. We can't be too surprised that this remains one of their biggest—and certainly most streamed—tracks. Well... maybe we can! I honestly don't mind the song, though...

RAISE YOUR GLASSES:
A Celebration of 50 Years of KISS Songs
by Celebrities, Musicians & Fans.

JOE LYNN TURNER *(RAINBOW, YNGWIE MALMSTEEN)* – Desmond Child, Vini Poncia and Paul proved they could write a disco hit! Pure brilliance for the commercial market!

JOEL HOEKSTRA *(WHITESNAKE, TRANS-SIBERIAN ORCHESTRA)* – OK, OK, OK … What? You're leading with this, Joel? BUT, the simple fact remains that this is the first KISS song I heard. My mom and my sister were very much into disco at a time when I was trying to act like I didn't like music at all. I wanted to be a baseball player. I know that the chorus is one hell of a hook. I didn't understand production at the time, but looking back, even at that very young age I loved that signature KISS backing vocal sound and it grabbed me.

PETE EVICK *(BRET MICHAELS BAND)* – I loved this song from the minute I heard it. I was too young to be a purist and think kids had abandoned all that they were to venture into disco; I thought the guitar was cool, and I loved Paul's super-high vocal parts. The drum fills were epic to me, and I just thought the song had such a big hook.

MISTRESS CARRIE *(RADIO DJ)* – This song takes me back to Roll On America, the roller-skating rink that I spent so much of my childhood at. I had an orange satin jacket, and wheels on my white skates to match. I was just a kid, but all the teenagers used to skate to this, and I thought they were so cool. I had my first kiss at the roller rink, it's a place tied to so many of my memories from my youth, and this song takes me right back there!

JAMES CAMPION *(AUTHOR, Shout It Out Loud – The Story of KISS's Destroyer and the Making of an American Icon)* – Paul Stanley is the best overall songwriter in KISS, and this one wraps up my triumvirate of his spectacular efforts. Let's get this out of the way, "I Was Made for Lovin' You" is NOT a disco song. Okay, so technically it's silly with a "four-on-the-floor beat," but it doesn't fully give it up until the bridge, when Paul goes all Gloria Gaynor falsetto for all he's worth. Mostly though, it is a pop staple from a hard-edged pop band written by guys (with assistance from producer, Vini Poncia and soon-to-be pop/rock impresario, Desmond Child) who lived the zeitgeist.

Firstly, I adore the polish on this recording, the opening "oooh-oooh-oohs" and that stunningly catchy low-tone verse melody, which then reaches a beatific summit come high-register chorus time. The instrumental bridge, after Paul's falsetto breaks glass, is as close as this comes to dance-a-teria, but it is nonetheless supreme song arranging. The entire thing is pure ear candy *and* it fucking rocks, a helluva balancing act if you can pull it off. I don't think I'm going out on a limb here to state that "I Was Made for Lovin' You" might very well be one of the most underrated songs for any band ever. It is a masterwork in pop song structure and shit yeah, you can dance to it, but then again, I dance to KISS songs all the time.

DAVID PEA *(KISS REPLICAS)* – I was in the car when "I Was Made For Lovin' You" came on the radio and instantly I knew it was KISS's new single. Paul's voice is unmistakable and to this day it's one of my favorites. Some say it's a disco-ish sound, but I say it's pure rock 'n' roll. I love cranking it up and it instantly brings me back to a time when KISS was everything to me... and all these years later KISS is still a major part of my life and I still seek out "I Was Made For Lovin' You" on my playlist every time I get into the car. This one hits hard and I love hearing it live!!

AHMET ZAPPA *(MUSICIAN)* – There are so many fucking reasons why I love this track. One, I love disco. Two, I love combining disco and rock. Has anyone else tried to do a disco rock track? Was KISS the first? I do think they were taking advantage of that moment in time and influenced by other things on the radio, but the end result is just fucking rad. I also love that sound effect. I don't know if it's a lightning strike or what. It's like a laser claw sound. Like a fucking laser tiger that's slashing something. I just live for that.

2,000 MAN

STEVE BROWN *(TRIXTER)* – One of my favorites and it's near and dear to my heart because the *Dynasty* tour was the first time I saw KISS, in 1979 at Madison Square Garden. I got to see Ace play it live. I didn't realize for a while that it wasn't even an Ace song. It's a perfect cover song for Ace, a Mick and Keith Rolling Stones cover tune. We used this as an influence for "Cherry Medicine" on the *10,000 Volts* record. Still one of my favorites, and I had the honor of being able to play it with Ace a few times.

BRENNAN MILETO *(SISTERS DOLL)* – This song takes me right back to my childhood. It's my first KISS memory because as a 2-year-old I used to play this song on the drums and sing along to the *MTV Unplugged* DVD. We have some video footage somewhere, haha! To play this song alongside Ace Frehley almost 28 years later in Nashville was a real dream come true.

PETE EVICK *(BRET MICHAELS BAND)* – I always was a fan of anything Ace sang on, and I'm also a huge sci-fi guy so the premise of the song being about the future sold me. The chugging guitar riff is perfect, this was a perfect song for Ace, I love the "understand me" vocal. What a great song.

RAISE YOUR GLASSES:
A Celebration of 50 Years of KISS Songs
by Celebrities, Musicians & Fans.

BRITT LIGHTNING *(VIXEN)* – I always loved this version of the Rolling Stones classic. Honestly, it was never a song I cared for until Ace Frehley put his spin on it. I was fortunate enough to jam this song with the Spaceman himself last year at a Rock 'n' Roll Fantasy Camp. And that was truly a fantasy!

ROBERT CONTE *(AUTHOR)* – Co-written by The Rolling Stones' Mick Jagger and Keith Richards for their album, *Their Satanic Majesties Request*, KISS's cover of this track on *Dynasty* is a great example of one artist taking another's song and making it their own. A side-by-side comparison of the two versions helps one understand why the original Stones cut blends well with the entire album's presentation, while KISS's take sung by Ace Frehley has the rare distinction of becoming more known throughout the world. It's almost as if "2,000 Man" was specifically written for the Spaceman!

KEITH ROTH *(SIRIUS XM, THE DICTATORS)* – I was always a Rolling Stones fan, as far back as I can remember. Being very aware of the original, I was anticipating how KISS could possibly cover this. By the pre-chorus I was floored, how they made it their own, plus Ace singing it… it's a quintessential moment of that record (*Dynasty*) for me and must admit, better than the original.

Keith Roth with Gene Simmons

SURE KNOW SOMETHING

HOLLY KNIGHT *(SONGWRITER)* – It's not a typical KISS tune, it's more of a pop song, and it's musically more sophisticated than their usual stuff. I *love* that song.

MATT STARR *(ACE FREHLEY)* – This is one of a few songs Paul wrote about getting burned in a relationship around this time. I love the guitar chords and how the verse is melodic and '70s pop, then it explodes into the chorus. Great bass playing as well.

RAISE YOUR GLASSES:
A Celebration of 50 Years of KISS Songs
by Celebrities, Musicians & Fans.

PETE EVICK *(BRET MICHAELS BAND)* – I'm such a fan of these kind of KISS songs, generally Paul's mid-tempo pop/rock stuff is great to me. What a killer bass line, great melody and great vocal on Paul's part.

ALLISON HAGENDORF *(MUSIC JOURNALIST, TV HOST & PRODUCER)* – I just love that this song comes at you with this injection of funk and disco right in the very first measure, and I can't help but start dancing. It also sounds equally powerful stripped down; I loved the *MTV Unplugged* performance of it as well.

Allison Hagendorf with Gene Simmons

RAISE YOUR GLASSES:
A Celebration of 50 Years of KISS Songs by Celebrities, Musicians & Fans.

TOMMY SOMMERS *(THREE SIDES OF THE COIN)* – In my opinion, this song has the best bass line any KISS song. The moment I hear it, it always takes me back to my bedroom when I was in the 9th grade and "Super KISS" was in full swing. I think it's often a very overlooked song because it's medium tempo and they typically would never play it live other than in an acoustic setting.

JAY SCOTT *(THE HOOK ROCKS PODCAST)* – Who doesn't love this song? This is the highlight of *Dynasty*. It may not have been received by the fans at the time, but it holds up extremely well.

ACE VON JOHNSON *(FASTER PUSSYCAT, L.A. GUNS)* – One of the first memories I have of KISS was hearing this song, off *Dynasty*, and thinking "wow, these guys really have some pop sensibility." This was before the internet came along and told me about everyone's opinion of the record, which I still think is great, despite its "disco" leanings. Paul does his best Donna Summer and I'm here for it.

PJ FARLEY *(TRIXTER, FOZZY)* – This song always stuck with me because of the melodies. It was classic Paul, and that chorus hook was forever ingrained in me to the point of it showing up in Trixter's song, "One In A Million." Steve originally had the answer part on the downbeat but nudged it to the upbeat like "Sure Know Something".

DIRTY LIVIN'

SHANDON SAHM *(MEAT PUPPETS)* – They were saying say that Peter couldn't play at this time, yet this drum track is tight as hell, so much so that there's a dance version of this and it's just great. I just love the four-on-the-floor tight drumming. Peter's performance vocally was great. I love the guitar solo. I think that Peter just didn't want to play with them anymore, plus he was very coked out – that's what ruined KISS. Had Peter and Ace not had drug and alcohol problems, maybe they'd have never left. That's just my observation.

PETE EVICK *(BRET MICHAELS BAND)* – Classic Peter Criss, tough guy from the streets doing whatever it takes, always with a real touch of R&B with Peter's stuff, what a great groove, some real soul in this song. I always felt like Peter did the most with the least, not the best voice of the bunch but you always heard soul, almost pain in his voice.

STEVE WRIGHT *(PODDER THAN HELL PODCAST)* – I really got an NYC hit on this song right off the bat. This would be the only Peter Criss contribution to the *Dynasty* album and really his last in the band until the reunion era. Even with the female background singers the song has grit to it. The bass lines are incredible. And Ace pulls off a great solo. They should have played this one live on tour instead of "Tossin and Turnin". It remains one of my favorite deep tracks.

NICHOLAS BUCKLAND *(AUTHOR, Hottest Brand in the Land)* – Down and sleazy Studio 54-style track sung by Peter Criss at the most gun-toting, nose candy-snorting, dangerous part of his life. His sole track on *Dynasty* has a pulsating disco bass line and rhythm (and the original demo even more so). As KISS shifted more towards the younger kiddie market, Peter's lyrics portrayed a man at the crossroads of his position in the band and literally 'Out of Control'!! With lyrics like "Mainline out of China is due in tonight…" and "I can't wait any longer to set myself free" you can hear the cries for help coming from the very grooves of the vinyl. If this song doesn't have you searching for a mirror and a twenty-dollar bill, I don't know what will…

MITCH LAFON *(ROCK JOURNALIST)* – This was Peter Criss's swan song for KISS. An upbeat disco-influenced tune with gritty lyrics and even grittier vocal. Peter always had a knack for bringing some 'street cred' to KISS. It was "Hooligan" part 2 (the dance edit).

CHARISMA

JEREMY ASBROCK *(ACE FREHLEY)* – "Charisma" was one of my favorites to play in the Gene Simmons Band, and he must have loved it too, because we did it pretty much every show. The chorus has a very weird 3rd harmony on the "What is Mah". It's kinda tough to sing. But when you hit the "Charisma!", there's this huge lift that makes the chorus so strong. GREAT solo by Ace too. The first half is just some notes that he hangs on, then some slow bends, and it's just SO TASTY. It definitely works live, and it's a shame that KISS never did it. But then we wouldn't have been the first to bring it to the fans, so maybe it's good that they didn't.

RYAN SPENCER COOK *(ACE FREHLEY)* – Gene Simmons announced that he would tour as a solo artist. This would be a first.

RAISE YOUR GLASSES:
A Celebration of 50 Years of KISS Songs
by Celebrities, Musicians & Fans.

While he had released solo albums up to this point, he had never stepped outside of KISS to perform on his own. Flashback to the KISS Kruise 2016... Gene invited me to lunch... while I had been tipped off that he wanted to discuss future solo dates, I still wasn't sure what to expect. "So... I'm planning on doing a few solo dates, nothing too big, U.S.A. only" he explained. (NOTE: "nothing too big" turned into almost two years and "U.S.A. only" turned into worldwide). "Do you think you could put together a band for me?" he asked. My prerequisite for selecting my bandmates? Know, live and breathe KISS. You've gotta know it all, not just the hits, 'cause we are gonna go DEEP.

Our first US show took place at The Agora Ballroom in Cleveland, OH. The word was out... Gene Simmons has gone solo, now fronting The Gene Simmons Band. "Will he be in makeup? Will his band be in makeup?!? What about pyro?!" The most pressing question was, "Which songs will they play?" This is where it got really interesting, really fast. Gene was fearless. He knew the World was watching and he wanted to prove once and for all that he DID in fact listen to the fans. From Note One, Gene let everyone know that this night was one for the KISStory books.......

Opening the set with the demonic intro music to his 1978 solo album, we slammed directly into "Radioactive". Buckle up folks... this is a setlist to be remembered. While the classics were there – "Nothin' To Lose", "Calling Dr. Love" – the obscure tunes received the accolades, "Got Love For Sale", "Almost Human", "Are You Ready", "She's So European". It was KISS heaven. It was not lost on me that this was indeed a special moment... the band was having just as much fun, if not more, than the fans.

The moment that resonated most with me that evening was "Charisma". This was always my favorite track from 1979's *Dynasty*... the always-constant guitar chug laid a thick, heavy groove punctuated by Gene's grainy bass tone. We could always tell when Gene was feeling it each night, extending the intro riff, allowing the band to stretch. "Sounds GOOD!!" he'd say in his best Demon voice. We were a locomotive, accenting the song's battle cry chorus with perfect three-part harmonies. Once again, my out-of-body experience took hold... *"HOW DID I GET HERE?!!"*

Tom and Zeus with Ryan Spencer Cook

TODD KERNS *(BRUCE KULICK, SLASH)* – *Dynasty* in general gets a bad rap. It is a collection of great songs. Period. Yes, it has that Vini Poncia sheen to it and Peter isn't even on it – but when it came out it was the new KISS record and we bought it and LOVED it. There isn't really a clunker in the bunch in my opinion. "Charisma" is classic Gene. A few albums earlier this song would have had a different presentation to it, which might have made it more classically KISS. Another song where Gene is singing about... well, being Gene.

JOE McGINNESS *(KUARANTINE, KLASSIC '78)* – An underrated and catchy tune. I feel that it totally encapsulates the late '70s Gene Simmons ego and attitude. This should've have been released as a single. I have always wondered what their business manager Howard Marks' contribution was to this song? He is credited as a co-writer.

PAUL JANIK *(GENE SIMMONS MONEYBAG SODA)* – I had to have been no more than 3 years old. *Dynasty* had just come out and when this song came on it scared the fuck out of me!!! I would stare at the turntable and it felt like Gene was gonna crawl out of the vinyl and get me. For some reason, I couldn't stop listening.

PETE EVICK *(BRET MICHAELS BAND)* – I remember the first time I heard this song, I was going to really understand the sexual message. I just loved Gene's voice and the lyric, "Is it my fortune or my fame". It was something I felt was unique. While I wanted KISS to sound like KISS, I was always excited when there was a little something different, and this was it for me. I didn't think at the time Gene was trying to be sexy with the super-low voice saying "charisma" – I just thought it was unbelievably cool. Just a couple years ago Gene played a solo gig at a venue the night before I played there with Bret. When we got there the set list was still on the stage, and "Charisma" was in it – my heart sank thinking I had missed seeing this song live.

MAGIC TOUCH

STEVE BROWN *(TRIXTER)* – *Dynasty* was the third KISS record I ever got. Near and dear to my heart, it was also the first time I saw KISS, on the *Dynasty* tour. I love the record, love every song. I had already started playing guitar by this point. I learned "Magic Touch" and I would sing along and play along in front of my mirror thinking I was Paul Stanley. It was actually a very instrumental song in teaching me how to sing. That song just resonated with me. It was a little bit different, and I think it's one of the best songs Paul ever wrote. It has a little of the *Paul Stanley* solo album vibe to it.

JOEY CASSATA *(ZO2, Z ROCK)* – This could have been on Paul's solo album! It has that same vibe to it. *Dynasty* is an extremely underrated album in the KISS catalog. Even though "I Was Made For Lovin' You" was a smash hit, KISS took a lot of backlash for what the media deemed as them turning disco. What a bunch of bullshit, *Dynasty* absolutely rocks!! The difference was, with Vini Poncia at the helm producing, I think there was a much stronger emphasis on songwriting. "Magic Touch" is a masterpiece.

PETE EVICK *(BRET MICHAELS BAND)* – Similar to "Sure Know Something", mid-tempo pop; to me this is where Paul always excels. Great use of keys and great textures in the song. "She's got the magic touch / And you're walking around in a dream" – great lyric.

HAL SPARKS *(COMEDIAN)* – A song that feels like a never-ending chorus. The guitar arrangement is always folding in on itself and only lets up for half a measure once. And then it gets two breakdowns one, from the '70s and one from the '80s. People overuse "glam rock," but I think this tune exemplifies the term. It's like Broadway with balls.

JEFF TROTT *(ART DIRECTOR)* – Like *Unmasked*, *Dynasty* was an album I never went to a lot. *Dynasty* was just the album that had "I Was Made For Lovin' You", "Hard Times", and "Sure Know Something". When I saw Paul Stanley perform "Magic Touch" live on his *Live to Win* solo tour, I went back to revisit the *Dynasty* album. "Magic Touch" captivates with its powerful vocals and thunderous groove. It's a standout track from *Dynasty* and it was great to hear Paul pull this one out for his solo tour.

HARD TIMES

ACE FREHLEY *(KISS)* – It's about growing up in the Bronx. It's pretty much self-explanatory, the lyrics came very easy for me, 'cause I just drew from reality. I think I came up with a great guitar riff. Anton did some amazing drumming. Counterpoint stuff. Working with Anton, I don't have to explain to him what to do, he just does a fill, I got to laugh, he does a fill and I was just going to say to him, "do a fill here."

JEREMY ASBROCK *(ACE FREHLEY)* – I have this memory of seeing *The Empire Strikes Back* at the theater, then going to Sir Pizza afterwards, and putting "Hard Times" on the jukebox. While *Unmasked* was released the day before, "I Was Made For Lovin' You" was still the popular single, and occupied space in jukeboxes nationwide in the U.S. I was an Ace kid, so I always went to that B-side. I still feel 4 years old when I hear that song. Ace's bass playing is as good any rock bass player, and the bass line to this song is proof. Check out the bass in the verses if you don't believe me. The song has two different choruses, and the second one takes this melodic turn with a great harmony. It's odd that this song didn't make the *Dynasty* tour. It's one of my favorites to play live with him because my inner 4-year-old comes alive, and I look over and THE voice is directly to my right.

KEN KEENAN *(KISS FAQ)* – I was pleasantly surprised when I flipped over my "I Was Made For Lovin' You" 45rpm single, then spinning "Hard Times" for the first of many times. It's definitely an autobiographical New York street song from Ace. What a great song with a groove and riff that only Ace could come up with. Great vocal from Ace and super drums from Anton Fig.

PETE EVICK *(BRET MICHAELS BAND)* – I always called this Ace's Peter song. Life is tough on the New York streets, so I was fascinated by these kinds of songs. I came from a safe middle-class family in a safe town, so it was so exciting and dangerous to me: "Out in the street, we had to take it / Friends around, we couldn't fake it / What wasn't there, we had to make it / Hanging out down in the city". I couldn't relate in any way but I sure wanted to; what a great, great song. Great turnaround, I love how it goes from this rock groove to this real flowing pop thing. Great writing.

JOEY CASSATA *(ZO2, Z ROCK)* – Ace is so strong coming off the success of his solo album. You can hear the confidence in his voice on this track. Combo that with a killer drum track from Anton Fig, Ace captures more of the dynamic duo from his solo record.

X-RAY EYES

TOM GIGLIOTTI *(SHOUT IT OUT LOUDCAST)* – Gene only has two songs on *Dynasty* but he makes the most of them, especially with this awesome deep cut. The verses have a great classic rock style and then when the chorus kicks in, he really shows off what he can do vocally. A standout for me on one of my all-time favorite KISS albums.

AHMET ZAPPA *(MUSICIAN)* – This is another prime example of Gene being an incredible singer. He has such vocal control and sings the most interesting melodies. He is really, really talented.

KISS has to be one of the most underrated rock bands. They are so famous for their makeup and branding that people discount how awesome their music is. And Gene has got to be one of the greatest bass players, singer-songwriters, performers, of all time. And again, no disrespect to any of the other band members that played in KISS. Paul Stanley is the prototype for the greatest frontman of all time. In my opinion, David Lee Roth learned so much from Paul Stanley. The kicks, the jumps, the energy...

JOEY FATSO *(THE CIRCLE, NETFLIX)* – Let me tell you something about "X-Ray Eyes". This track, my friends, it's a gem that's been quietly shining in the shadows for far too long. You see, "X-Ray Eyes," it's not just good – it's a musical powerhouse that deserves to be celebrated. First off, the infectious rhythm and raw energy of this song, it's like a magnetic force that pulls you in from the get-go. Gene's provocative lyrics, they paint a vivid picture of desire and allure, drawing you deeper into the song's enigmatic world. And let's talk about the powerful vocal delivery – Gene's commanding voice cuts through the music with boldness and authority, leaving a lasting impression that's hard to forget. The dynamic instrumentation, the intricate guitar work, and that signature bass line, they all come together in perfect harmony to create a sound that's truly one-of-a-kind.

What makes "X-Ray Eyes" even more special is its unique sound and style. It's unmistakably KISS, yet it also showcases a side of the band that's often overshadowed by their bigger hits. This track exudes confidence and a certain edge that sets it apart from the rest. But here's the kicker – "X-Ray Eyes" is not just good; it's underrated. It's a hidden treasure waiting to be rediscovered and appreciated for its musical brilliance and timeless appeal. So, let's give credit where credit is due, and shine a spotlight on this underrated classic that's been quietly rocking our worlds all along.

ZEUS *(SHOUT IT OUT LOUDCAST)* – One of my favorite deep tracks. One of only two songs on *Dynasty*, but Gene makes this one count more so than "Charisma" for me. I love Gene's vocal delivery on this and the kiss-off lyrics too. The chorus is so catchy, along with the hook and guitar accent after every verse, and of course Ace's solo. The backing vocals by the band are fantastic.

DALE TORBORG *(THE DEMON WCW)* – *Dynasty* is one of my all-time favorite albums. Growing up I was a huge Gene fan, the Demon character and the boots, so I always went towards the Gene songs. I love that chorus on the song and Gene's voice, and because it wasn't played all the time it was a go-to song on *Dynasty* for me.

SAVE YOUR LOVE

ACE FREHLEY *(KISS)* – It was a little nutty. It was a little unorthodox, it wasn't straight-ahead rock 'n' roll, but you know, sometimes I think outside the box. I mean listen to "Torpedo Girl".

JOEY CASSATA *(ZO2, Z ROCK)* – I really love this song… up until when the chorus comes in. The background vocals always annoyed me. Very drone-y and not melodic at all. It doesn't completely ruin the song for me, but it comes close.

Joey Cassata playing on the KISS stage, 2004

ZEUS *(SHOUT IT OUT LOUDCAST)* – The third Ace song on *Dynasty*. This is the benchmark for Ace for me. Three solid songs on an album. His high point in KISS. Unfortunately, this would be the last to feature all four original members. Ace's vocals on this are very solid. He actually puts some passion into his vocals when he sings, "Save your love I don't want it!' A good straightforward song with decent lyrics, guitar solo and melody.

JASON BAKKEN *(COBRAS & FIRE PODCAST)* – "Shock Me" and "Cold Gin" get all the love. But this is Ace's best song on a KISS album. The outro is cool, and this really wraps up the album sequence. Even that little rap he does just before the solo is bad ass.

BRAD RUSTOVEN *(SLAMFEST PODCAST)* – Great intro. Love the use of vocal delay during the verses and pre-choruses. With the "Baby it's over" and "It's over now" lines, you can really feel the pain in Ace's voice. The guitar solo is long, melodic and memorable. And Paul's 'Save your loves' during the outro are fantastic.

RAISE YOUR GLASSES:
A Celebration of 50 Years of KISS Songs
by Celebrities, Musicians & Fans.

CHAPTER 10

"UNMASKED"

Released: May 20, 1980

Unmasked marked a distinctive phase in KISS's career. Departing from the heavier sound of their earlier albums, the band embraced a more pop-oriented approach. The album features catchy melodies, upbeat rhythms, and a polished production. With tracks like "Shandi" and "Talk to Me,"

RAISE YOUR GLASSES:
A Celebration of 50 Years of KISS Songs
by Celebrities, Musicians & Fans.

Unmasked is a reflection of KISS's willingness to explore different musical avenues and connect with a broader audience.

The album opens with the upbeat and infectious "Is That You?"— a track that sets the tone for the album's pop-oriented direction. With its catchy chorus and vibrant energy, it showcased a different side of KISS, embracing a sound more aligned with the pop/rock of the early 1980s.

One of the standout tracks, "Shandi," is a melodic ballad that demonstrated the band's ability to craft emotionally resonant songs. Sung by Paul Stanley, it became a hit in Australia, showcasing KISS's continued global appeal.

"Talk to Me" is another highlight, featuring a dynamic blend of pop/rock elements and KISS's signature style. The song's infectious hooks and harmonies made it a radio-friendly hit and highlighted the band's commitment to crafting accessible and memorable tunes.

While *Unmasked* faced criticism from some longtime fans for its departure from the band's traditional hard rock sound, it found success in reaching a new audience and expanding KISS's commercial appeal.

While *Unmasked* didn't achieve the same level of commercial success as some of KISS's earlier albums, it remains a fascinating chapter in their discography. It represents a period of experimentation and adaptation, showcasing the band's ability to evolve with the ever-changing landscape of rock music. *Unmasked* stands as a testament to KISS's versatility and their determination to explore new musical territories while remaining true to their core identity.

I҂ THAT YOU?

PETE EVICK *(BRET MICHAELS BAND)* – What an incredible song. I just listened to it the other day. I know this was part of the pop disco-era KISS but this song truly still rocks, production is great, vocals are great, "Cheap, seventeen and trashed out / You went too far, bein' a bitch you are". I didn't know what he meant, but man it was cool! Paul's voice is so dynamic in this song, going from full-on tough-guy rock singer to the Bee Gees-esque falsetto stuff. A very, very underrated KISS song, I'll probably go listen again right now!

BRENNAN MILETO *(SISTERS DOLL)* – This song just takes me back to my childhood. I remember watching an old VHS that my dad had of this song being played live in Sydney when KISS first came to Australia in 1980. This song literally sums up memories of my childhood. That chugging guitar intro/verse is just awesome.

JOE POLO *(PODCAST ROCK CITY)* – Second-favorite song off *Unmasked*. I love this song! Like a lot of KISS songs, I didn't understand the meaning when I was a kid. But as teenagers, we all knew this girl. I wish they played this more often.

RAISE YOUR GLASSES:
A Celebration of 50 Years of KISS Songs
by Celebrities, Musicians & Fans.

Brennan Mileto with Gene Simmons

CHRIS L. *(POD OF THUNDER)* – By the time *Unmasked* came out, I had moved on to Van Halen, AC/DC, the Big 4 of corporate rock (Styx, Journey, Foreigner, and REO Speedwagon) and others. So when I saw the cover, I actually thought it was a *MAD* magazine parody and not a real album. It wasn't until years later that I finally became aware of this song, but had I heard it back in the day, I probably wouldn't have been so quick to jump off the KISS train. Great groove and brimming with classic Paul Stanley attitude.

PASQUALE VARI *(KISS ARMY NATION PODCAST)* – I remember getting *Unmasked* and thinking, "What the heck is this?" I wasn't crazy about this record then, but I always loved this song as its opener. KISS has always had strong openers on their records and "Is That You?" was no exception.

SHANDI

PETE EVICK *(BRET MICHAELS BAND)* – Truth be told, I absolutely love *Unmasked*, and "Shandi" is a huge part of it. I understand that I was much younger than the KISS fans that started to give up by this time, but I still wanted to live and breathe KISS, I couldn't get enough. A lot of times, production can really change the feel of a song, and this is a perfect example – it's clearly produced to be pop in the early '80s, but just under the surface you can hear a pure rock song. Years later Paul performed this in his solo band with that more rock feel and it was great! And again, Paul's voice was better than ever moving into the '80s, and such a killer lyric: "I just can't pretend no more, I keep runnin' out of lies / Lovin' you is killing me inside / Every time I find the words to end it / Something in your eyes won't let it". Show me a songwriter alive that says they don't wish they wrote that and I'll show you a liar!

RUSSELL PETERS *(COMEDIAN)* – Sounds like a dog whining. The best thing about "Shandi" is the beverage, the beer and Sprite mixed beverage. That's the only "Shandi" I can rock with. It was annoying to me. It was an attempt to be deep.

COURTNEY CRONIN DOLD *(COMEDIAN)* – Not only is it an adorable name for a cat, "Shandi" is the song about a girl the female fans have been waiting for. Because it's real. The ladies LOVE this song because we want to be Shandi, even though she's about to get dumped. But it's still better than being Christine or Domino.

PASQUALE VARI *(KISS ARMY NATION PODCAST)* – I've always had a propensity for pop music as a young boy. Although I didn't appreciate *Unmasked* as a KISS record, I later began to appreciate it for its music and later accepted it as KISS. As pop songs go, "Shandi" was one of my favorite KISS pop songs, and yes, I still hold that song in high regard today.

PETER CORY *(KISS LIVE AUCTIONS)* – I guess if you are thinking of KISS and rock 'n' roll, this song doesn't really capture that, but everyone loves a good love song and that is what this is! Amazingly, this is one of the most popular KISS songs overseas. Something about Paul's voice in this song sounds very melodic. The live version of this song from Sydney, Australia is one of my favorites.

TALK TO ME

PETE EVICK *(BRET MICHAELS BAND)* – Ah, the one thing that I always looked forward to in a new KISS record: Ace's songs. I just loved them. This one has a great driving guitar riff almost like "2,000 Man", fun lyrics and Ace's almost lazy-sounding vocal. Love or hate Ace, the fact is no-one does what he does. Such a great pop hook at the end of the simple rock chorus, with the harmony and soaring "Talk to me" being held out.

JOEY CASSATA *(ZO2, Z ROCK)* – Easily my favorite song on *Unmasked*. When Ace writes a pop song, he is at his best. His rhyme scheme and rhythmic melodies are untouchable. This song also has one of my favorite Ace guitar solos, not to mention the Ace/Anton back and forth reminiscent of "Rip It Out". "Talk To Me" should have been a smash hit.

ZO2's Joey Cassata and Paulie Z in their KISS tribute band, KISSNATION

AUSTIN MILETO *(SISTERS DOLL)* – This song always takes me back to my childhood whenever I hear it. Can still picture my younger self walking into my dad's "KISS room" and hearing this song blaring through the speakers!!

BRANDON FIELDS *(MINEFIELD)* – This song features some really cool open tuning guitar playing by Ace. It's basically in the same vein as the tracks off Ace's solo record in the sense that Ace did all the vocals, guitars, and bass with Anton on drums. It always translated really well live, and in my opinion featured some of the best live harmonies KISS ever did. Another cool fact about this song is Ryan Cook told me it was the first song he ever played bass on live when he performed it with me and Kurt Frohlich at *KISSmas Masquerade* 2020. This is awesome considering Ryan ended up switching to bass in Ace's band.

JAY SCOTT *(THE HOOK ROCKS PODCAST)* – The most underrated Ace song in the catalog and the best song on *Unmasked.*

NAKED CITY

BRUCE KULICK *(KISS)* – I knew Bob had a co-write. I never realized what a cool song that was. He was really proud that this (and the "Mr. Speed" demo) appeared on the KISS Box Set.

AHMET ZAPPA *(MUSICIAN)* – This is more of an adult contemporary rock song from KISS. Even the lyrical content. The guys were at a different point in their lives. And it's an awesome Gene performance. The melodies are interesting, and I love the background harmonies. I listened to all of the makeup era albums and tried to pick two tracks from each. And on this album, not surprisingly, the two were Gene tracks.

MITCH LAFON *(ROCK JOURNALIST)* – The Gene Simmons-penned "Naked City" ushered in the 'KISS-lite' years, and I loved it. Street vampires and all… With *Unmasked*, KISS crossed over from leather-clad demons to Saturday morning cartoon heroes. The music changed as well, becoming more Leif Garrett than Black Sabbath. However, the odd gem could still be found, and "Naked City" was it. Pity it wasn't in the set list moving forward. Fun pop.

MURPH *(SHOUT IT OUT LOUDCAST)* – I like this song more every time I hear it. One of my favorite Gene tracks, and really demonstrates how good of a voice he had at this time in particular. This song should have received solid airplay but after

Dynasty it was probably difficult to determine whether it was Top 40, disco or traditional rock.

ERNIE PALOOZA *(TOP 5 WITH JOEY CASSATA)* – This song sounds like it should be on *The Elder*. It's very epic-sounding and not like the concise pop songs on the rest of *Unmasked*. Could this have been one of the last songs written for this album? It sounds more like the next release.

WHAT MAKES THE WORLD GO ROUND

PETE EVICK *(BRET MICHAELS BAND)* – Very pop production, very pop everything – certainly not my favorite KISS song but I also certainly love it. Still not sure what that sample or sound is happening with that snare drum, probably just an early '80s drum machine clap sound, but it fits. It's perfect – just a great pop song. It probably feels the least like KISS than anything, but you're a liar if you say it's not stuck in your head all day after you listen!

COURTNEY CRONIN DOLD *(COMEDIAN)* – I love when KISS gets "poppy", and this is the perfect example. I've always had a weird rock 'n' roll fantasy about singing this as a duet with Paul and Molly Ringwald '80s dancing through the whole thing. But are the last 20 seconds necessary? It's the longest fade out ever! Just end it by repeating the doo, doo, doooooo-doo, doo, doooooo. That's the best part.

MIKE BRUNN *(THE ROCK EXPERIENCE)* – *Unmasked* is an album that divides a lot of KISS fans because of its pop sound. Some love it, some hate it. I've always loved the album. When I interviewed Paul Stanley for his *Soul Station* album, I was surprised to hear him say that this KISS song was rooted in his R&B influences. I still don't hear it, but either way it's a fun pop-rock song to me.

JASON BAKKEN *(COBRAS & FIRE PODCAST)* – *Unmasked* is a bit of a dividing rod, but it might be the best collection of songs on one album up to this point. Another stellar vocal from Paul. The guitar solo is so perfect. Like everything on this record, if the production wasn't so pop, I think fans would feel different about this record. Hey man. A great song is a great song.

CHRIS JERICHO *(WRESTLER, FOZZY)* – Another huge chorus. I feel that the song was a victim of being on that record. I think if it would've been on *Dynasty*, but it's a little underrated because it's on *Unmasked*. But that's a really hooky, catchy chorus.

TOMORROW

PETE EVICK *(BRET MICHAELS BAND)* – Another amazing pop song. It may not be "Strutter" or "God of Thunder", but it's got hooks for days, simple love lyrics but a huge chorus, and like the rest of this record, Paul's voice is so dynamic between the chorus and verses – such versatility. Like most songs on this record, he slips in and out of "pop voice" to "rock voice" seamlessly. It gives this song and all of Paul's songs on this record such great dynamics.

RAISE YOUR GLASSES:
A Celebration of 50 Years of KISS Songs
by Celebrities, Musicians & Fans.

JOEY CASSATA *(ZO2, Z ROCK)* – This whole album is incredible. It's so misunderstood. KISS making different-sounding records over the years is what has made me the fanatical fan that I am. *Unmasked* is pure pop, which I happen to love just as much as, if not more than, rock. As great as the first six KISS albums are, I don't need another six. I love that KISS was releasing all different types of music during these years. Some days I want to hear "Take Me", some days I want to hear "Tomorrow". This song should have been a huge hit.

CHRIS CZYNSZAK *(DECIBEL GEEK PODCAST)* – This is the best Rick Springfield song that Rick never released! Having the name KISS attached to this song only served as a detriment. It's a 100% masterclass in pop/rock execution.

NICHOLAS BUCKLAND *(AUTHOR, Hottest Brand in the Land)* – If Paul Stanley wrote a commercial for Coca-Cola this would be the soundtrack. Pure Poncia-produced pop (try saying that three times) at its zenith, and the handclaps in the third verse surely were an inspiration for the theme from '90s sitcom *Friends*.

TOMMY LONDON *(OZZY'S BONEYARD, SIRIUS XM)* – In my opinion, *Unmasked* should have been called *Underrated* – because it is! Can't deny that some of the songs have a disco vibe, but nonetheless the hooks are amazing. "Tomorrow", with that huge Starchild chorus, was the third single released from the album and surprisingly never performed live. So many great tracks on this record: "Easy As It Seems", "Two Sides Of The Coin", and "Is That You?", just to name a few.

Tommy London with Paul Stanley

JEFF TROTT *(ART DIRECTOR)* – As a lifelong KISS fan *Unmasked* was never a go-to album for me. I knew it had some good songs but always thought of it as the insecure, confused power-pop album. However, once I heard Beth Blade and the Beautiful Disasters performed "Tomorrow" on the KISS Kruise, I revisited the album. "Tomorrow" has an infectious groove and catchy melody. It's a power-pop gem that deserves a place among KISS's top tracks.

TWO SIDES OF THE COIN

STEVE BROWN *(TRIXTER)* – Ace pop songwriting at its best. I love *Unmasked*. Props to Vini Poncia because he was a "song" guy. Incredible vocal by Ace, his melodic sense. Another unique thing is this is probably written using the same guitar as "Talk To Me". He uses the Keith Richards open-string tuning, and this song is very Rolling Stones. I love that there's no guitar solo in it. There's a beautiful guitar interlude where he does the arpeggios. It's classic Ace at its best.

PETE EVICK *(BRET MICHAELS BAND)* – Another Ace song. It's great, I don't know what else to say. Sometimes Ace's lyrics were so simple and to the point that you almost have to laugh – but that's the genius, you get his point. There's no hidden meaning or mystery to the message in this song. Pure Ace, what you hear is what you get.

JOEY CASSATA *(ZO2, Z ROCK)* – Nothing fancy here from Ace. Just a great, straightforward pop-rock song with hook after hook. The chorus is one of the most singable choruses on the record.

MAC *(UGLY AMERICAN WEREWOLF IN LONDON PODCAST)* – Even the most ardent members of the Ace Cult have to admit the lyrics on this one are pretty laughable. I guess when you're telling a story about having to choose which groupie you're going to bed for the night, you can take the lyrics too seriously. The bridge features some clean and melodic guitar work from Ace, which is very pop and fresh even to this day. But I always wondered if Gene wrote a song on the same concept, would he even choose or tell a story about cajoling them both to come back to the room with him.

MURPH *(SHOUT IT OUT LOUDCAST)* – Possibly my favorite song where Ace is the lead. I like everything about this song: the rhythm guitar throughout the tune, the tempo, the chorus, all of it. I can never tell if Ace is talking or singing, but either way, he just pulls it off well.

ΣHE'Σ ΣO EUROPEAN

ZEUΣ *(SHOUT IT OUT LOUDCAST)* – When we first started our podcast this was on my "worst KISS song" list. It has since grown on me a lot. It's a fun and catchy song, especially the pre-chorus. Gene, who is 30 at the time, is singing, "Her parents are still away." Yikes.

BRAD RUΣTOVEN *(SLAMFEST PODCAST)* – Great intro riff and percussion. The keys during the pre-chorus are a bit much, but don't ruin the song because Gene sounds so good. His lead vocal during the chorus is great, but the highlight of the song is the outro. Gene's interjections are amazing – ranging from "She's outta her mind" to a low-register "Yeah", to him holding a high note longer than he can hold without some studio trickery. Love it!

JOE MCGINNEΣΣ *(KUARANTINE, KLASSIK '78)* – Just like every other song on *Unmasked*, this song is insanely catchy. The opening guitar riff is so powerful. Once again Anton Fig delivers with his tasteful but technical grooves. This song is 10 out of 10 in my book! I wish they'd played it live on the *Unmasked* tour. It would be interesting to hear it without the keyboards.

AHMET ZAPPA *(MUSICIAN)* – The crowning jewel of *Unmasked* is "She's So European". This track is so good. They tried to do these new-wave synthesizer moments, which I totally appreciate. I feel like I'm repeating myself every time I talk about Gene's approach to vocals and the melodies he constructs. When he sings lead it's very odd and amazing. Not typical. I just can't get enough of "She's So European". I think it's kind of hilarious that he's singing about a fancy lady. A European lady that he wants to fuck, you know... it's pretty fun.

STEVEN MICHAEL *(GROWIN' UP ROCK PODCAST)* – For many years I hated this album, and it wasn't until I was old enough to accept this record as a great pop record, more so than an actual KISS record, that I really understood it. "She's So European" – again, a great hard rock riff that gives way to a pop melody from the Demon himself, and then that great bridge and pre-chorus with keyboards from a then-unknown songwriter Holly Knight just gives it a completely different feel. It's a pop gem and catchy as hell.

CHRIS L. *(POD OF THUNDER)* – Quite possibly my favorite Gene song of the entire '80s. It captures his increasing fascination with the exotic, jet-set lifestyle (and the women who populated it) that superstardom was allowing the band to enjoy. Musically, the keyboard line has me convinced that KISS was trying to be the Cars on *Unmasked*. And I loved the title of this song so much that I used it verbatim as the headline for a *Playboy* pictorial when I worked there.

EASY AS IT SEEMS

JOE MCGINNESS *(KUARANTINE, KLASSIC '78)* – This song has such a great melody. My favorite song from *Unmasked*. I can't help but sing when it comes on. The bass line is absolutely incredible. Anton Fig brings a lot of groove to this song, as well as to the rest of the album.

RAISE YOUR GLASSES:
A Celebration of 50 Years of KISS Songs
by Celebrities, Musicians & Fans.

The six-man Kuarantine

CHRI; JERICHO *(WRESTLER, FOZZY)* – I think this is just as good as "I Was Made for Lovin' You" and "Sure Know Something". It's still a disco-type tune. This new sound would've been a great follow-up. The bass line is great. It's super-funky and a great riff. They should have focused on that tune because disco was still going a little bit new-wave. It's got a great groove to it. It's got a keyboard solo in it, which is pretty cool (done by Holly Knight). I love that song. I would listen to it at any time.

;ONNY POONI *(PODCAST ROCK CITY)* – The bass line and groove of this song just makes it a pop-rock gem. When I introduce KISS to a non-rock fan, this is one of the songs that I use. As a whole, *Unmasked* is a very underrated record.

JOEY CA;;ATA *(ZO2, Z ROCK)* – This song is way more disco than "I Was Made For Lovin' You". But I guess by 1980 the whole disco movement was dying down, or this would have been a huge international hit. Such a great hook and feel.

JASON BAKKEN *(COBRAS & FIRE PODCAST)* – "When you're walking out on your dreams / You just walk away". Love it. Paul really delivered on *Unmasked*. While early Gene liked to write about nagging women, Paul would deliver a couple decades of great breakup songs. Some of his deeper cuts really hit. This one for sure does.

TORPEDO GIRL

PETE EVICK *(BRET MICHAELS BAND)* – Probably my favorite song on the record – such a great guitar riff and groove, very different from the other Ace songs on this record but still so Ace. I can't imagine what inspired the lyric or the story but it's unique; you've certainly never heard anything like it and probably never will again. To this day this lyric makes me smile: "I saw this thing that looked a lot like a submarine / With a pretty girl on the bridge, could this be a dream?" For some reason, as a kid I could visualize this – I had the music video in my head, before I think I even knew what music videos were!

RAISE YOUR GLASSES:
A Celebration of 50 Years of KISS Songs by Celebrities, Musicians & Fans.

Keith Roth interviewing KISS

CHRIS L. *(POD OF THUNDER)* – For me, Ace's contributions to *Unmasked* are my least favorite in terms of overall quality. It's almost as if he was trying to punk Gene and Paul after they tried to set him and Peter up to fail with the '78 solo albums (which didn't work, certainly in Ace's case). Of his three songs on this album, "Torpedo Girl" is my favorite because it's the funniest, due to a combination of Gene's bouncy bass line, the utterly ridiculous lyrics, and Ace's delivery of "I don't know" at the end of the second verse.

COURTNEY CRONIN DOLD *(COMEDIAN)* – I'm convinced that this is a song about pooping in a bathtub. "Man battle stations torpedo" is something a gross man would say before pushing one out in the jacuzzi. "I saw this thing that looked like a submarine?" What are you, twelve? It's just too silly for me to listen to without laughing, and dry heaving.

GARY "ACTION" JACKSON *(UGLY AMERICAN WEREWOLF IN LONDON PODCAST)* – When I first picked up this record and saw the title, I have to admit I thought this was going to be a silly throwaway track. Turns out this may be the best offering on the album. Ace on vocals, guitar and bass with Anton Fig on drums, this is all-day funky with a great beat. Yes it's silly with the opening sonar and submarine sound effects, but in the best way. I still say they stink.

JOE McGINNESS *(KUARANTINE, KLASSIK '78)* – Easily one of my favorite drum intros of all time. This is a perfect example of Ace firing on all cylinders. The bass line is one I play every time I pick up a bass guitar, in fact it was one of the first riffs I learned on bass guitar when I was a kid.

LISA MARTINI *(THREE SIDES OF THE COIN)* – *Unmasked* was the soundtrack to my summer of 1980. There are some solid tracks on *Unmasked* and you can see that they tried to get back to more rock 'n' roll roots, but the album had more of a pop vibe to it. I listened to that 8-track so much that it broke and my parents got me a new one. And let me also add that my friend and I made up dance routines to each song on the album, perfected our dance moves and then put on a show for our parents at the end of summer vacation!

YOU'RE ALL THAT I WANT

GENE SIMMONS *(KISS)* – We were on tour, and on the off days I would go and do demos. Usually, I would do all the instruments, but on that day Paul came in. I had this song, "You're all that I want, you're all that I need, you're all that I see you're everything to me". Once I had that, the chorus and melody came to me.

RAISE YOUR GLASSES:
A Celebration of 50 Years of KISS Songs
by Celebrities, Musicians & Fans.

ZEUS *(SHOUT IT OUT LOUDCAST)* – One of my favorite deep cuts in the KISS catalog. I think it's a dreamy, beautiful song. For some reason it takes me back to my childhood and has a lot of nostalgia for me. I cannot explain it. When I had the chance to meet Gene I had to ask him about this song. Prior to this song, I don't recall a Gene track on a KISS album proclaiming his endearing love for someone. At least not in this romantic way. The demo of this song on the Box Set is actually better with the acoustic guitar. I love Paul in the background on this track. Some songs just hit you for some unknown reason. This song does it for me. I absolutely love it.

JASON HERNDON *(KISS MY WAX PODCAST)* – My favorite KISS song in the entire catalog. I've loved this song since I first heard it back in 1980. An often-overlooked, criminally underrated pop/rock gem from Gene. I love his smooth voice on the track, and Paul's solo is incredible. I simply never tire of it.

BRAD RUSTOVEN *(SLAMFEST PODCAST)* – Great mid-tempo riff. Love Gene's vocal/lyrics during the verses, and the vocal harmonies during the pre-chorus are a great touch. The chorus is just okay, but the outro chorus is amazing with Paul's interjections. Only negative – they faded it out too soon!

JOEY CASSATA *(ZO2, Z ROCK)* – Anyone who knows me knows that I love *Unmasked*!! But for some reason this is the only song that I don't really care for. The verses are very forgettable, and the chorus seems lazy to me. The rest of this record is pure pop/rock gold!

CHAPTER II

"MUSIC FROM 'THE ELDER'"

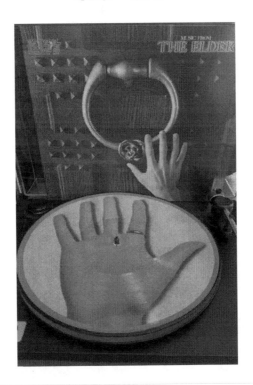

Released: November 10, 1981

Music From 'The Elder' stands as one of the most unconventional albums in KISS's catalog. Departing from their traditional hard rock sound, the band delved into progressive and art rock, crafting a concept album inspired by a fantasy storyline. While commercially unsuccessful at the time, *Music From 'The Elder'* has gained a cult following over the years, celebrated for its ambitious experimentation and willingness to defy expectations.

"A World Without Heroes" is a wonderful ballad that showcases the band's softer, more introspective side. Gene Simmons' vocals convey a vulnerability rarely seen in KISS's previous works, adding depth to the album's narrative.

"Mr. Blackwell" and "Escape from the Island" bring back a heavier rock sound, but the album's overall tone remains more subdued and experimental compared to KISS's earlier albums.

The ambitious concept of *The Elder* was inspired by a mythical story, but the complex narrative didn't resonate with fans at the time. The lack of commercial success led to the album being considered a commercial failure, prompting the band to shift gears in subsequent releases.

In retrospect, *Music From 'The Elder'* is a testament to KISS's artistic exploration and refusal to be confined by expectations. While it may not have achieved commercial success in its time, the album has found a place in rock history as a bold experiment that challenged the boundaries of what a KISS album could be. *Music From 'The Elder'* remains a fascinating and unique entry in the band's discography, celebrated for its artistic ambition and its role in KISS's evolution as a band unafraid of pushing musical boundaries.

FANFARE

ZEUS *(SHOUT IT OUT LOUDCAST)* – When listening to *Music From 'The Elder'* in the correct order as the band intended, this is the opening to the album. You're not sure if you are at a medieval fair or what. They even used medieval instruments. Gregorian chants too? Oh my. But for many people this is the beginning of the worst three songs in a row on a KISS album. I'm sorry but this still makes me laugh.

COURTNEY CRONIN DOLD *(COMEDIAN)* – Here ye, here ye! Welcome thee to the instrumental overture of the most debated album in the kingdom of KISSdom. Sir Complainsalot needs to shut it down – this is beautiful and gets me pumped up for what's to come!

NICHOLAS BUCKLAND *(AUTHOR, Hottest Brand in the Land)* – The sounds of a thousand KISS Army members staring open-mouthed in disbelief as their heroes go from hard rock heroes to mock medieval misfires. Certainly the strangest opening to any KISS album, and ironically an intro that would be more likely to induce the sounds of crickets rather than any kind of fanfare.

JAMES CAMPION *(AUTHOR, Shout It Out Loud – The Story of KISS's Destroyer and the Making of an American Icon)* – The flutes. The oboes. The medieval instrumentation. The vibe. The mood. The thunderous American Symphony Orchestra. The genius of Bob Ezrin. The arranging and conducting talents of the late, great, Michael Kamen. The dulcet tones of the St. Robert's Choir. It is, quite literally, a fanfare; planned as an aural prologue to the enthusiastic overreach of *Music From 'The Elder'*. But then a spooked Polygram fucked with the album's song sequence, so when I first heard the record in the winter of 1981, I was assaulted by a rocking number called "The Oath" instead. What was supposed to be the "story's" – if there is such a thing beyond the notebook musings of Gene Simmons ripping off *Star Wars* and *The Lord of the Rings* – eighth musical number was replaced by the album's best rock song (which it is) moved to the front to help soften the blow to what was assumed to be a shocked KISS-buying public (they were).

Nevertheless, when "Fanfare" was returned to its rightful place as the opening track, followed by the introductory protagonist piece, "Just a Boy" and his hero's Journey song, "Odyssey" in the 1997 CD reissue, it finally made sense. Much like Ezrin's opening car sequence on the brilliant *Destroyer* five years earlier, "Fanfare" was poised to gear up listeners that this was a different trip. KISS was taking a backseat to a running narrative à la The Who's *Tommy* or many of the Kinks' sojourns into "concept." Used in this way, it is great theater, something Ezrin knew well, and Simmons embraced it until (ahem) he didn't. Depending how you hear "Fanfare" – and I think it is up front in the current standard sequencing – is how good it lands.

TOM GIGLIOTTI *(SHOUT IT OUT LOUDCAST)* – *Music From 'The Elder'* was a concept album, and regardless of how ill-conceived you may think it was, they went all in – and this instrumental piece to start to the album paints the picture of something out of the old world, which is the message they were trying to convey. Not something you'd add to a KISS playlist, but as far as the imagery of the album, it does its job to get the listener prepared for what's ahead (or does it?)

Tom and Zeus at the *Elder* door, KISS Museum, May 7, 2023

JUST A BOY

ZEUS *(SHOUT IT OUT LOUDCAST)* – Maybe the most maligned KISS song of all time. To me, this is a good song, just not a KISS song. The melody is great, and it would make a great Broadway number. However, the timing of this album was all wrong. Had this project been really planned out, with a movie, storytelling in between songs and more, this would have probably been better received. Paul does a great job singing, but that falsetto is just not what the KISS Army wanted to hear.

KEITH ROTH *(SIRIUS XM, THE DICTATORS)* – I came way late to the party for *Music From 'The Elder'* – probably didn't hear this 'til like 1983. I think I got the record at Woolworth's for a dollar in Menlo Park Mall in Edison. Hearing of the story behind this record, how it was supposed to be the soundtrack to a film that got aborted. How Lou Reed writing with KISS and Bob Ezrin producing. I was always curious, especially people saying how bad it was. So, for $1.00, I'm in!! I got to be honest, I love everything about this album. Growing up on rock operas – *Quadrophenia*, *Tommy*, and my personal fave, *S.F. Sorrow* by Pretty Things, I felt like this tune especially was inspired from that Pretty Things record. Paul's falsetto, the acoustic guitar, LOVE IT!!!

NICHOLAS BUCKLAND *(AUTHOR, Hottest Brand in the Land)* – Could this possibly be the worst sequencing duo in the KISS catalog? Surely a contender. Between the cod-medieval quest theme of the verse lyrics wondering ("Who steers the ship through the stormy sea?") to the ill-advised falsetto of the chorus, this then segues into the schmaltzy orchestral "Odyssey".

TOM GIGLIOTTI *(SHOUT IT OUT LOUDCAST)* – Not held in high regard by most KISS fans, but the point of *Music From 'The Elder'* is to take the listener on a journey and welcome them to this world. Paul's falsetto often is a source of derision, but you have to hand it to him because at this time, this is what they wanted, and they went all in on these songs and themes.

RAISE YOUR GLASSES:
A Celebration of 50 Years of KISS Songs
by Celebrities, Musicians & Fans.

JOEY CASSATA *(ZO2, Z ROCK)* – Anyone who doesn't love *Music From 'The Elder'* is an IDIOT! Even this song is incredible. This album is why I love KISS so much. We can all agree that the first six records were just about perfect, but I didn't want 15 more *Love Guns* or *Destroyers*; what makes KISS so great is their diversity. The different ends of the spectrum between "Just a Boy" and something like "Take Me" is staggering. Much like the difference in "Dear Prudence" and "I Wanna Hold Your Hand" by the Beatles. Both are spectacular in their own way, and we are lucky to be able to have both.

ODYSSEY

JOE McGINNESS *(KUARANTINE, KLASSIC '78)* – I love *Music From 'The Elder'*, but this song is probably the worst KISS song ever recorded. I can barely get through the whole song when it comes on. Paul's operatic vocal kind of sounds like a bad Elvis Presley impression. I'm sure there is some musical genius hidden in this song somewhere, but it's not for me.

TOM GIGLIOTTI *(SHOUT IT OUT LOUDCAST)* – A very orchestral piece of music used to continue to tell the story of *Music From 'The Elder'*. The arrangement is very impressive here, and Paul's vocals during the verses are unusual and in a register we don't hear often. Another part of the storytelling that KISS is using to transport the listener to this world. Not very KISS-like of course, but then again, that was sort of the point at this time in 1981.

RAISE YOUR GLASSES:
A Celebration of 50 Years of KISS Songs
by Celebrities, Musicians & Fans.

Bully Ray, Velvet Sky and Dave LaGreca with Gene Simmons

ALEX SALZMAN *(PRODUCER, ACE FREHLEY, PETER CRISS)* – Never a commercial success, but I always connected the theatrical approach to what KISS was all about; it had to be instrumental in Paul getting the Broadway role. My favorite composition on the album, and a beautiful arrangement by Bob Ezrin. Sonically it does not sound like KISS and if one was not familiar with this album, they would never know.

ZEUS *(SHOUT IT OUT LOUDCAST)* – I could say, see my comments on "Just A Boy." This song is a punching bag for a lot of KISS fans, and me too at first. But as the song grew on me I realized there's a beautiful melody there. Paul's vocal delivery is just weird. Listen to how he sings the word "enchanted" at the beginning of the song. It's as if he's trying to find a bass in his voice that doesn't work. I really like the chorus, the music and the guitar solo, as well as the outro piano. Ezrin once again kills it on the production. But that bridge is just strange. "There's a child in a sundress looking at a rainy sky" should not be a KISS lyric. Regardless, this song would totally work in a Broadway version of *Music From 'The Elder'* – *The Musical!* C'mon Gene, do it!

NICHOLAS BUCKLAND *(AUTHOR, Hottest Brand in the Land)* – Dabbling with an outside songwriter, the lowlight brings forth the unintentional hilarity of Mr. Stanley singing the most unlikely KISS line: "There's a child in a sun dress looking at a rainy sky'. This must have had KISS fans both dumbfounded and rolling on the floor in laughter. Almost a career-killing deadly combo…

ONLY YOU

JOEY CASSATA *(ZO2, Z ROCK)* – I know this is a very polarizing album for some KISS fans, but to me it's just another epic KISS record. This was actually the first album I ever purchased with my own money. I was even unsure if it was a "real" KISS album because there were no pictures of them on the cover. I had bought some crappy bootleg albums near my grandmother's apartment in Greenwich Village and I thought this might be one of them. But I had an idea!! My brother had his Sony Walkman with him, so I decided to buy the cassette of *Music From 'The Elder'* to test it right away.

As soon as I heard it, I knew it was them. But when I read the liner notes my world was rocked. Paul Stanley, Ace Frehley, Gene Simmons and… Eric Carr! Who was this Eric Carr and what did he look like?? I was on a mission for the next year and a half to find what this mysterious, incredible new drummer looked like. It wasn't until I saw the *Creatures of the Night* album on the wall at Sam Goody that I got my answer… THE FOX!!!

RAISE YOUR GLASSES:
A Celebration of 50 Years of KISS Songs
by Celebrities, Musicians & Fans.

COURTNEY CRONIN DOLD *(COMEDIAN)* – I like to listen to all these songs with a fake musical like *Rent* meets *Rock of Ages*. This song is intense and has that splash of sexy that Gene puts on all his love songs. Even the non-creepy ones like this.

JOE POLO *(PODCAST ROCK CITY)* – *Music From 'The Elder'* is such a cool record for me. The band took a huge chance and alienated so many fans. I love this song. The bass line and the vocal go along together so well. It's really awesome that so many fans have caught onto this record. I have always liked it.

RUSSELL PETERS *(COMEDIAN)* – "Only You" and "Under the Rose" kind of bleed into each other. It's almost like the same song. They just belong together. You can't listen to one without the other.

ALEXANDER TALKINGTON *(KISS ARMY THINGS PODCAST)* – One of my favorite tracks from *Music From 'The Elder'*! Gene and Paul trading off lead vocals as the characters is brilliant. Reprising the melody from "Just A Boy" and using it as a story-telling device is brilliant. Maybe I need to relearn what the word 'brilliant' means? This is one track I can totally immerse myself in. I love the lyrics, the various vocal effects, and that part from 3:45 to 4:06 is infectious.

CLAUDIO SPERA *(KISS ARMY NATION PODCAST)* – One of my favorites from *Music From 'The Elder'*. The opening guitar sets the tone, and Gene's Beatles-esque singing is captivating. This song is like a movie in itself. The background sounds and voices prepare the listener for the second part of the song, where Paul kicks in with a strong rock 'n' roll riff and a powerful voice. While the riff is consistent, the song offers some interludes that make the song "breathe' beautifully.

UNDER THE ROSE

JOEY CASSATA *(ZO2, Z ROCK)* – This is such an eerie and dark song. I was always a big fantasy movie fan, and I also played *Dungeons & Dragons* with my friends when I was a kid (and still do), so I really connected with this album and song. Please make an animated series out of *The Elder*!!

LORETTA CARAVELLO *(ERIC CARR'S SISTER)* – Eric wrote that with Gene and I do know he was not happy with the chorus part. I'm not privy to what the original song was supposed to sound like, I don't know. I'm sure there's a demo tape that you may hear one day. He loved the way the song came out, but he was very unhappy with the chorus.

COURTNEY CRONIN DOLD *(COMEDIAN)* – Manheim Steamroller meets rock 'n' roll. Check out his albums *Fresh Aire I* and *II*, it will remind you of this song. Gene sounds AMAZING. These vocals are tingly and tantalizing. Ominous yet beautiful.

KEN KEENAN *(KISS FAQ)* – Dare I say that "Under the Rose" has the best riff since "Black Diamond"? It truly does. It's probably my favorite song off of *Music From 'The Elder'*. Love the opening with the guitar picking and bass, then Gene's smooth vocal that modulates, then comes the big riff and the gang chorus. Excellent effects for the guitar solo from left to right, like a follow the leader-type solo. Great song!

JOE POLO *(PODCAST ROCK CITY)* – Such an amazing song. The chorus blows me away. It's so powerful and almost regal. I am sure Bob Ezrin had something to do with this sound. But for a KISS song it is perfectly out of place and works so well.

DARK LIGHT

ACE FREHLEY *(KISS)* – I wrote it with Bob Ezrin in his basement in Toronto. We just jammed and I just came up with some crazy shit.

TOM GIGLIOTTI *(SHOUT IT OUT LOUDCAST)* – For all the crap that *Music From 'The Elder'* takes, if you take the time to listen, you will find some legitimately awesome songs here – and this is one of them. Ace sounds great, and his spoken-word "call and answer"-style vocals during the verses make this very unique. But the key to this song is arguably one of his greatest guitar solos. Filled with noise and amazing fretwork, it's too bad the album fell flat and they never toured for it, because this could've been a crowd pleaser.

COURTNEY CRONIN DOLD *(COMEDIAN)* – Is this the theme from *Jaws* or the coolest lead-in ever to another catchy Ace riff? It could be both. One of my favorite Ace songs for sure. The chorus is poppy and pretty and reminds me of "Hard Times", which is another fave.

JEFF TROTT *(ART DIRECTOR)* – Originally titled "Don't Run," "Dark Light" was written by Ace Frehley, Anton Fig, Gene Simmons, and Lou Reed. Featuring Ace on lead vocals, this track absolutely rips! The slow chugging intro into the great guitar riff makes "Dark Light" one of the most KISS-style songs on this unique album.

ZEUS *(SHOUT IT OUT LOUDCAST)* – The opening *Jaws*-like intro into the heavy Ace riff is cool. The lyrics are beyond parody, and Ace's vocals are ripe for impressions on Shout It Out Loudcast: "Or it's Sodom and Gomorrah." LOL! However, the song rips, as does Ace's insane guitar solo. I wish Ace would try this again live.

A WORLD WITHOUT HEROES

MITCH WEISSMAN *(BEATLEMANIA, SONGWRITER)* – The *Music From 'The Elder'* stuff is actually much better than anybody thought. Gene was writing that while I was hanging out at his apartment all the time. Lou Reed was leaving as I was coming in. When they released the song, after I said, "you know, after the guitar solo, you should've gone back to "well you don't know what you're after…" before you go into "a world without heroes". I thought that in the studio, and I knew I should've put in another bridge and I didn't do it.

JOEY CASSATA *(ZO2, Z ROCK)* – This song does not get the recognition it deserves. It's really only KISS's second ballad, "Beth" being the first. Gene's vocal and lyrics are phenomenal. Such a great message. The first thing people think of when they hear this song is when KISS showed the video for "A World Without Heroes" on

Solid Gold in 1981 and Gene cries at the end. I guess this turned a lot of people off, not me!

BRAD RUSTOVEN *(SLAMFEST PODCAST)* – The first time I heard this song was while watching KISS on *Solid Gold* – they showed the video during that episode. While I was confused by the arrangement and presentation of the song (is this KISS?), I liked the melody and thought Gene sounded great during the chorus. I also thought it was strange seeing Paul take the solo while Ace strummed an acoustic guitar.

The Demon Dale Torborg choking Joey Cassata

RAISE YOUR GLASSES:
A Celebration of 50 Years of KISS Songs by Celebrities, Musicians & Fans.

DALE TORBORG *(THE DEMON WCW)* – My grandmother gave me $10 and I went to Peaches record store and bought *Music From 'The Elder'*. I didn't understand what was going on, was it a movie? I just knew it was KISS. I saw the video for the "A World Without Heroes" and that was one my favorite songs from the album, and I took my Mego Gene doll and switched heads with my Christopher Reeve Superman doll and tried to make it match Gene and his *Elder* costume.

JAMES CAMPION *(AUTHOR, Shout It Out Loud – The Story of KISS's Destroyer and the Making of an American Icon)* – Man, this song had quite the journey from trite ditty to the lone single from *Music From 'The Elder.'* Taken from Paul Stanley's "Every Little Bit of Your Heart" and transformed by producer Bob Ezrin and NYC badass, and former Velvet Underground leader, Lou Reed from his throwaway line, "a world without heroes is like a world without sun," it was handed to Gene Simmons (aka the "God of Thunder") to croon. Poetic justice served, since the Demon credits comic book heroes with giving him a sense of self and moral direction as a kid. Crucially, "A World Without Heroes" ties up an opaque narration of a chosen one as a boy, the Council of the Elders, the Blue Meanies, and the Death Star somewhere in a futuristic Middle-Earth as best as any song can. It is certainly the preeminent composition on the album. Featuring perhaps Paul's best solo on record, it delivers melancholy with the finest KISS melodrama, but the quintessential version appears on *MTV Unplugged.*

JOE POLO *(PODCAST ROCK CITY)* – The first time I heard this song was on *Solid Gold.* Most of my friends talked about how different it was. Which it was, but all I ever heard was KISS.

THE OATH

ACE FREHLEY *(KISS)* – My favorite solo is "The Oath". when I go into the Echoplex, it's just timed perfectly, but I didn't time it that way. I can't tell you when I do stuff and it just happens.

EDDIE TRUNK *(RADIO DJ & TV PERSONALITY)* – So many people criticize *Music From 'The Elder'* but for me, it was a time and place for me as a KISS fan and I was holding on for dear life. It was not an easy thing to be in high school and be a KISS fan. Unless you lived it, you don't know how bad it was. I was all in on *Music From 'The Elder'*. Obviously it was a weird record, it was a different record. I remember hearing about a TV show called *Fridays* and I heard that KISS was going to play on it. The opened with "The Oath" and that riff, and for KISS, it's pretty heavy. Because they were so down in their career and just seeing them like that with the spotlight on national TV. And the fact that they actually played live. Most TV shows had bands lip sync. Kind of like *Lick It Up*, it signaled that they still had a heartbeat.

PAULIE Z *(ZO2, Z ROCK)* – Although *Music From 'The Elder'* is considered by many to be one of their worst albums, I love it and "The Oath" in particular. The song straddles the line between heavy metal and fantasy folklore. It's a rocker with delicate moments produced by the master, Bob Ezrin. It can be argued that *Music From 'The Elder'* was not a great record for KISS, but in general I think it's a great record.

RAISE YOUR GLASSES:
A Celebration of 50 Years of KISS Songs by Celebrities, Musicians & Fans.

Eddie Trunk at the *Elder* door, KISS Museum

DAVID LAGRECA *(BUSTED OPEN RADIO)* – Believe it or not, *Music From 'The Elder'* got me back into KISS. The disco/pop era of KISS completely turned me off, and I tuned out until I heard the opening (original) track of the album. The drums by Erik Carr grabbed me. Underrated song on a misunderstood album.

TODD KERNS *(BRUCE KULICK, SLASH)* – I first saw them perform this song live on *Fridays* and it blew my mind. I was too young to have much of an opinion on the haircuts or the absence of Peter Criss. I just thought it rocked. Soon after I bought the record and dug into all of it. The opening riff is a classic. Though it wasn't originally meant to be the opening track on the album, it was a wise choice for young rockers like me. It is a quintessential banger of a track, with Paul stretching out to attempt something new. Kudos. I'll always be a big supporter of *Music From 'The Elder'*.

RAISE YOUR GLASSES:
A Celebration of 50 Years of KISS Songs by Celebrities, Musicians & Fans.

Tom and Zeus with Todd Kerns

ALEX SALZMAN *(PRODUCER, ACE FREHLEY, PETER CRISS)* – This track combines the traditional KISS guitar riffs and vocal approach, but the changes and modulations are not conventional for them, so I have to assume that Ezrin wrote the falsetto chorus and the bridge and arranged the transitions.

MR. BLACKWELL

JOEY CASSATA *(ZO2, Z ROCK)* – This song is so goddamn good!! Thinking of this as being part of a movie makes it even better. It's creepy, groovy and evil. This song is easily one of the most underrated Gene songs in the entire KISS catalog.

ʃHΛNƊON ʃΛHΛ (*MEAT PUPPETS*) – Has a funky tight bass. A hard rock, funky bass line. You can really hear Gene's chops on this. The solo is stellar too.

JOƐY ʃΛʃʃO (*THE CIRCLE, NETFLIX*) – As a massive KISS fan with a deep passion for music, I can confidently say that "Mr. Blackwell" is one of the most underrated tunes from the Demon himself, as well as one of the most underrated from this polarizing record. This song, it's like a dark and mysterious journey through Gene's lyrical storytelling brain. The haunting atmosphere, the ominous vibe, it's all there, painting a vivid picture that transports you to a whole new world. Now, let's talk about the musicality of this track. The intricate guitar work, the pulsating bass line, the powerful drumming – they all come together in perfect harmony to create a sonic landscape that is both mesmerizing and unforgettable. Gene's raw vocals, they soar with intensity and passion, capturing the essence of the song's dark narrative with every note. What sets "Mr. Blackwell" apart is its unique blend of theatricality and rock 'n' roll grit. And that's what makes this track so special – it pushes boundaries, challenges expectations, and leaves a lasting impact on those who truly appreciate its depth and complexity.

ROBƐRT CONTƐ (*AUTHOR*) – I first heard this track during a middle-school trip in early Spring of 1984. *Music From 'The Elder'* was often considered the worst KISS album up to that point and, admittedly, it had to grow on me over time. "Mr. Blackwell" was my third-favorite song from the cassette because I believed that it was written to ridicule the once-famed clothing designer and fashion critic, Richard S. Blackwell, aka "Mr. Blackwell," who was known then for his annual "10 Worst Dressed Women List." I often thought that Blackwell had badmouthed KISS for their makeup and outfits and it got back to them, so the chorus, "You're not well, Mr. Blackwell, and we can tell. Why don't you go to hell!" perfectly summed it up for me.

TOM GIGLIOTTI *(SHOUT IT OUT LOUDCAST)* – A very haunting, creepy and unsettling song which is what we all expect from the Demon. The menacing intro that kicks it off followed by Gene's layered vocals and some spooky guitar effects make this a truly hidden gem for fans of the Demon. A very weird mid-section is something unexpected and unusual, but very cool to hear after some of the other songs we've heard on this album.

ESCAPE FROM THE ISLAND

MATT STARR *(ACE FREHLEY)* – The coolest instrumental ever. This is a great example of how unique Ace's writing style is. Primal, repetitive, and unique. Eric's drumming is fantastic on this song. The siren puts it over the top.

LORETTA CARAVELLO *(ERIC CARR'S SISTER)* – To me, it's one of the best songs on the album, and I'm partial because I love drumming songs.

JASON BAKKEN *(COBRAS & FIRE PODCAST)* – I'm guessing not a lot of people want to talk about this track. Co-written by Ace and new drummer Eric Carr. This quick instrumental rips, and fits perfectly into a record that gets too much shit. But the groove between Ace and Eric is killer, and it would have been fun to see a couple more albums with them both on it.

RUSSELL PETERS *(COMEDIAN)* – That is a good song, a pretty hard-rocking song. I used to play it on my fake drum kit.

TOM GIGLIOTTI *(SHOUT IT OUT LOUDCAST)* – I have always been a fan of instrumentals and this is no different. This is a very cool piece of music with an awesome Ace solo. Eric Carr is keeping the energy going, and the siren effects at the beginning of the song give the listeners the feeling that they are really trying to escape!

I

MITCH LAFON *(ROCK JOURNALIST)* – *Music From 'The Elder'* was not the album I wanted from my favorite band. It was lugubrious, labored, and quite frankly dull. Except for the song "I"... Yes, I believe in me! I believe in something more than you can understand! The KISS ethos on full display. The rallying cry for fans. It gave you strength. It gave you chills. It made you wonder why the album didn't have 10 other songs like "I"... anthems. *Music From 'The Elder'* needed more anthemic rock and less... well, less *Music From 'The Elder'*.

BRANDON FIELDS *(MINEFIELD)* – Paul and Gene sharing lead vocal duties makes this one an instant classic. It's probably the most KISS-sounding song on the album in regard to their older material. The only thing it's missing is a guitar solo, but I guess the finger snaps do just as well. This album definitely had them thinking outside of their normal box, and the climbing riff is a great example. It's an out of the ordinary chord structure for KISS but still pays homage to a more classic sound.

JOEY CASSATA *(ZO2, Z ROCK)* – I always felt this was one of the most underrated songs in the KISS catalog. It has everything in it to be a classic KISS anthem... the Gene and Paul trade-off vocals, the big sing-along chorus, and of course the message. It's a message that I have lived by my whole life... "I believe in me, and I believe in something more than you will ever know, yes I believe in me"!!

MAC *(UGLY AMERICAN WEREWOLF IN LONDON PODCAST)* – This song I can't stand. It sounds like some cheesy song from *Glee* or *High School Musical* with school chorus sing-alongs that was written by kids. I get you want to put out a positive message for kids to be confident in themselves. But to me it comes off as Paul desperately trying to write a hit and trying to convince himself he's good enough to do it. He is, but this isn't one of them.

DARREN PALTROWITZ *(AUTHOR, How David Lee Roth Changed The World)* – I give a lot of credit to KISS for what they were trying to do with *Music From 'The Elder'* since it may have been easier and more cost-effective to just keep doing what was already working for the band. Instead, they tried to go "mature" with a Bob Ezrin-produced concept album, which ultimately flops critically and commercially to the point that they cannot do a world tour in support of it. To me, "I" is the standout song on this album, even if it is one of many "we are KISS, we are strong, we are nothing without you" songs -- or team-building exercises set to music -- they would put out over the years. The only drawback of the song is its lengthy outro with non-musical sound effects, since that interrupts the flow of any mix or playlist.

ZEUS *(SHOUT IT OUT LOUDCAST)* – I love when Paul and Gene trade verses. This song rocks and has that "You can do it, Waterboy!" type of lyrics, which is empowering to many in the KISS Army. Amazingly, for some reason Bob Ezrin replaced Eric Carr on drums with Allan Schwartzberg. The song has that breakdown where Paul channels Elvis, which is a head scratcher. The song ends with the spoken words of the story and fanfare again. The rarely seen video is surreal, especially when the band is on the fans' shoulders looking like a chicken fight in the pool. But in the end, this song is a standout on an album that is not understood and very underrated.

RAISE YOUR GLASSES:
A Celebration of 50 Years of KISS Songs
by Celebrities, Musicians & Fans.

CHAPTER 12

"KILLERS"

Released: June 15, 1982

Killers is a compilation album that features four new studio tracks produced by Michael James Jackson.

A notable studio track is "Nowhere to Run," featuring a driving rhythm and catchy hooks. The song showcases KISS's knack for crafting infectious rock tunes while incorporating elements that hinted at the heavier sound that would dominate their later releases.

While *Killers* may not be a traditional studio album with all-new material, it serves as a significant chapter in KISS's discography. It captures a moment of transition for the band, offering a blend of their classic hits and a glimpse of their evolving musical direction. As KISS continued to navigate the changing landscape of rock music, *Killers* showcases their enduring impact on the world of hard rock and heavy metal.

I'M A LEGEND TONIGHT

BRUCE KULICK *(KISS)* – I loved it right away. What a great title. Bob has a fantastic, thematic solo. He's a little more controlled, he's not off the leash. Probably my favorite of the new songs on *Killers*.

ADAM MITCHELL *(SONGWRITER)* – Paul was never short of ideas or titles. He said he had this "I'm A Legend Tonight" and then we would just start working it out. When the song was written, we recorded the demo in the studio in my home.

AUSTIN MILETO *(SISTERS DOLL)* – This song gets me pumped, such a simple but effective song with a powerful chorus.

RAISE YOUR GLASSES:
A Celebration of 50 Years of KISS Songs by Celebrities, Musicians & Fans.

Adam Mitchell with Gene Simmons

JOE McGINNESS *(KUARANTINE, KLASSIC '78)* – I wish *Killers* wasn't a compilation but instead a whole album. Paul did an amazing job on all four of the newer tracks on this album. I feel like these songs don't get the attention that they deserve. This tune in particular has such a great riff and overall vibe.

RUSSELL PETERS *(COMEDIAN)* – I love *Killers* and I bought this record at a record store called Cheapies in Canada. What are these songs? But they're all good. I remember asking KISS fans in school, hey have you heard *Killers*? What? Iron Maiden?

DOWN ON YOUR KNEES

BRUCE KULICK *(KISS)* – Bob goes into his bag of tricks again. What was surprising to me was that it's a little Van Halen, a little AC/DC.

COURTNEY CRONIN DOLD *(COMEDIAN)* – For a song with a title that would normally turn me off, I actually love this one. Paul's vocals are fierce and forceful, and he works that raspy thang like he does (and should do more often). From creepy title to major pants-dropper. Love this song.

JASON BAKKEN *(COBRAS & FIRE PODCAST)* – The four new tracks on *Killers* give the KISS faithful rock boners, but they really are quite mediocre. While I like this song, it is a bit silly. That post-solo breakdown is fun. And maybe it's true that these songs served as a palate-cleanser from *Music From 'The Elder'* for the Starchild. It's easy to see why none of these made onto *Creatures of the Night*.

ZEUS *(SHOUT IT OUT LOUDCAST)* – Written by Paul, Mikel Japp and yes, *that* Bryan Adams, "Down On Your Knees" has an awesome beat, and great guitar by the late, great guitarist Bob Kulick. Love the call-back of "She's alight" by the band. This also has a great "Carlton" dance-type rhythm. In fact, friend of SIOL, Darryl Alber, the social media manager from Pantheon Podcasts, made a hilarious video clip of Carlton dancing to this song.

JOEY CASSATA *(ZO2, Z ROCK)* – All four songs on *Killers* are just great pop songs! "Down On Your Knees" is a really fun song, but I do think it's the weakest of the four songs on *Killers*. I wish Gene had a new song contribution on this record. There were a few demos from that era that he had that I thought were fantastic that never made a record – "It's Gonna Be Alright" and "Legends Never Die" in particular!

NOWHERE TO RUN

BRUCE KULICK *(KISS)* – Easily could've been on Paul's solo record. Some great Bob riffs. Clearly a standout on *Killers*.

Eddie Trunk with Peter Criss, 1981

EDDIE TRUNK *(RADIO DJ & TV PERSONALITY)* – I defiantly remained a fan, a supporter, a defender, and *Music From 'The Elder'* was a tough period. I was waiting in line to get into an Iron Maiden show and a kid comes up in line with a bag under his arm with a record. I asked him what it was and he said "It's a new KISS record, an import that just came out". My mind was blown because I thought I knew everything about KISS. He said, "It's called *Killers* and it's European only". I ran to the store and got a copy for myself. When I heard it, it sounded like a band that was getting their footing back.

"Nowhere To Run" is my favorite of the four. Paul's vocal on it is incredible.

TOM HIGGINS *(KLASSIC '78)* – Possibly the best Paul song of the '80s as far as I'm concerned. Vocally, he is on a whole new level. Very powerful and well written by Paul by himself. In my Top 10 Paul songs ever.

AUSTIN MILETO *(SISTERS DOLL)* – Such a heroic-sounding song, I feel you can really hear the emotion in Paul's voice for this one, which I love. Also, an amazing guitar solo by the incredible Bob Kulick, R.I.P.

Austin Mileto with KISS

PARTNERS IN CRIME

BRUCE KULICK *(KISS)* – I nicknamed that the Whammy Wildness song because of Bob's use of the whammy. It's not a bad song, but I see it as a showboat song for the Floyd Rose whammy.

JOEY CASSATA *(ZO2, Z ROCK)* – "Partners in Crime" is my favorite track from *Killers*! The drum intro hooked me immediately. Everyone always talks about "Nowhere to Run" as the standout song from this album, but I think it's this! It's Paul Stanley at his pop best! The version KISS released on the *Creatures* Box Set is absolutely fantastic!! I remember seeing the cover for *Killers* for the first time and losing my mind. I thought I knew all there was to know about KISS in the early '80s, so when my friend pulled out his *Killers* cassette with Eric Carr on the cover, I was so confused. There was no internet, and I had no idea what an "import" album was. I must have played the four new tracks a hundred times that first day.

JOEY SASSO *(THE CIRCLE, NETFLIX)* – During the *Killers* era, KISS was in the midst of a transitional period, exploring new sounds and pushing boundaries in their music. This song stands out as a testament to the band's versatility and evolution to deliver by any means necessary during one of the bands most struggling eras. This track, it's more than just a solid Paul Stanley song – it's a hidden treasure in the KISS catalog that demands our attention, and I can confidently say that "Partners in Crime" is one of the most underrated gems from the Starchild himself. "Partners in Crime" shines as a standout track on *Killers* for its infectious energy, catchy hooks, and Paul's charismatic vocal delivery. The song encapsulates that classic KISS sound while infusing it with a fresh, vibrant energy that sets it apart from their more well-known hits.

RAISE YOUR GLASSES:
A Celebration of 50 Years of KISS Songs
by Celebrities, Musicians & Fans.

What makes "Partners in Crime" so special is its anthemic nature and timeless appeal. Paul's passionate lyrics about camaraderie and loyalty resonate deeply, making it a song that speaks to the hearts of fans on a personal level. The driving guitar riffs, the powerhouse drumming, the melodic harmonies – they all come together to create a musical tapestry that's both captivating and unforgettable. As we look back on KISS's legacy, "Partners in Crime" stands out as a testament to the band's ability to reinvent themselves while staying true to their roots. It's a hidden gem that deserves to be rediscovered and celebrated for its contribution to the band's rich musical tapestry.

ZEUS *(SHOUT IT OUT LOUDCAST)* – *Killers* is the beginning of KISS repairing the damage of the last three albums, which were seen as the disco, pop and concept albums respectively. It is also the beginning of the great relationship KISS had with a great unsung hero in KISStory, Michael James Jackson, who produced *Killers*, *Creatures of the Night* and *Lick It Up*. The four songs are all Paul Stanley-led rockers. This song has grown on me over the years. Love the bass line and the guitar on the chorus, as well as Bob Kulick's fantastic guitar solo and the outro.

TOM GIGLIOTTI *(SHOUT IT OUT LOUDCAST)* – I think every KISS fan was thrilled and surprised to see that *Killers* had four brand-new songs! I think all of them are bangers, although some are better than others of course. Paul's vocals on all of them are spectacular, and this song here is one of them. It's got a slower groove than we've come to expect from this era of KISS, but at this point, we didn't care because it was brand-new music.

CHAPTER 13

"CREATURES OF THE NIGHT"

Released: October 13, 1982.

Creatures of the Night marked a significant return to KISS's hard rock and heavy metal roots. The album, characterized by its powerful guitar-driven sound, showcases the band's resilience and determination. With standout tracks like "I Love It Loud" and the title track, *Creatures of the Night* is hailed as a rejuvenation for KISS, reaffirming their status and delivering an album that has stood the test of time.

The title track opens the album with a thunderous roar. The driving guitar riffs, pulsating rhythm, and aggressive vocals immediately announce that KISS is back with a vengeance. The song captures the essence of heavy metal, establishing the tone for the entire album.

"I Love It Loud" became one of the standout tracks, featuring a chant-worthy chorus and Gene Simmons' commanding vocals. The song's anthemic quality and hard-hitting instrumentation make it a quintessential representation of KISS's return to their roots.

The album is also notable for "War Machine," a powerful and menacing track that further solidifies the band's commitment to a heavier sound. Gene Simmons' vocals, combined with Eric Carr's thunderous drums, create an intense and memorable listening experience.

Creatures of the Night saw the drumming of Eric Carr take KISS's sound to the next level in terms of a renewed energy and power. The lineup change, combined with a focus on heavier guitar-driven sound, contributed to the album's success in reestablishing KISS's presence in the hard rock and heavy metal scene.

The album cover, featuring the iconic KISS logo against a dark, stormy backdrop, depicting the band with glowing eyes and visually reflects the album's aggressive and menacing tone. The imagery emphasizes the band's return to a darker and more ferocious musical landscape.

While *Creatures of the Night* did not achieve the commercial success of some of KISS's earlier albums, it is revered by fans and critics alike as a crucial moment in the band's history. The album demonstrated KISS's adaptability and their ability to evolve with the changing musical landscape. Creatures of the Night remains a powerful and enduring testament to KISS's resilience and dedication to their hard rock roots.

CREATURES OF THE NIGHT

ADAM MITCHELL *(SONGWRITER)* – Paul had the title and the first line or two and we did the demo; I came up with that guitar lick and I did that on the record. It's not an easy lick to play because the first part is a shuffle, and the rest goes sixteenth notes. We used a drum machine. We came up with it fairly quickly.

JEFF PLATE *(TRANS-SIBERIAN ORCHESTRA, SAVATAGE)* – I had lost track of KISS for a number of years, but hearing this tune for the first time reminded of what I liked about them in the first place; they were a badass hard rock band. Eric Carr's drumming and his new energy brought some needed power and aggression to the band.

AHMET ZAPPA *(MUSICIAN)* – This is another thing I love about KISS: they have a few records where the title of the record is also a great song. "Love Gun", nailed it. "Hotter Than Hell", nailed it. And they do it again with "Creatures of the Night". This is around the time when they lost band members, and we were not sure who the next character would be. Would we get the Fuzzy Raccoon? But no, we got the Fox, Eric Carr. And they knock it out of the fucking park with *Creatures of the Night* (I'll skip *Music From 'The Elder'*). Anytime you can blend the supernatural and singing about gorgeous ladies, trying to hook up with them, and maybe, just maybe becoming a werewolf or fighting warlocks and dragons and shit... it's the best, right? "Creatures of the Night" is just that. It's très magnifique.

DON JAMIESON *(COMEDIAN)* – After the failed experiment that was *Music From 'The Elder'*, this album and its title track hit me like an asteroid from outer space. Unfortunately, this would be the first KISS album that the Spaceman himself, Ace Frehley, would not appear. Not only that, when I found out later that the guitarist from Mr. Mister did the solo on the song, my head started smoking like Ace's Les Paul. Still, the guitars on this track are aggressive and provide the perfect template for Eric Carr's huge drum sound. All the Paul songs on this album are strong but "Creatures of the Night" stands out and makes the perfect album opener.

TOMMY SOMMERS *(THREE SIDES OF THE COIN)* – After the disappointment that was *Music From 'The Elder'*, as a KISS fan all of us were a little concerned about what this new record was going to sound like. I'll never forget dropping the needle for the first time on this record in the fall of 1982. I remember falling in love with it from the first chord. This is my go-to song when I am low on energy and I need to get ready for a big appointment. Plus, it's a great song to crank in the summer driving around with the top down.

CHRIS CAFFERY *(TRANS-SIBERIAN ORCHESTRA, SAVATAGE)* – Just like any great band when the critics and naysayers attack, KISS always responded with a vengeance. The entire *Creatures* record was this level of intensity. The title track to me was just the most aggressive and straightforward. As a huge fan of Paul Stanley's singing voice, this song reaches that high-level rasp that is trademark Paul. I love the production of the lead, giving it that space-age sound and Steve Farris really fit in very well with the chemistry of this amazing song and record.

SAINT AND SINNER

KENT SLUCHER *(LUKE BRYAN, KUARANTINE)* – Eric Carr's drum part on this tune is sick and the drums are huge on the *Creatures* record. Always have dug this song big time, great guitar solo as well.

TOM HIGGINS *(KLASSIC '78)* – Eric Carr is AMAZING on this whole album. His drumming on the *Creatures* album is his *Back In Black* moment. He made his mark on the music world. On this song, Eric swings, drives and grooves throughout, and it's spectacular. This is one of my fav songs from the record. Gene's vocal personality on this is very cool. The drumming and the restraint on Vinnie's melodic guitar solo are both outstanding. They let Vinnie loose at the end with a great outro solo too. Great musical chemistry with KISS and Vinnie back then, but flawed personalities ruined what could've been.

RUSSELL PETERS *(COMEDIAN)* – A nice deep cut. I always liked the way the song built. I really dig the progression of that song. Eric's drumming was amazing. I liked the way it flowed.

RAISE YOUR GLASSES:
A Celebration of 50 Years of KISS Songs
by Celebrities, Musicians & Fans.

CHRIS CZYNSZAK *(DECIBEL GEEK PODCAST)* – A bit of a curveball in the KISS catalog; a shuffle beat and Beck-like guitar solo? Eric Carr's drum part on this song truly drives it along and Vinnie Vincent channels Jeff Beck with a slide solo that stands out. This song is the dark horse of the *Creatures* album, to me. I love it.

DAVID JULIAN *(SONGWRITER)* – My fascination with *Creatures of the Night* may be because I kind of remember when it came out and loved "I Love it Loud". It was also a crazy time for the band and a lot of people were involved in that record, including Bryan Adams! For me a standout track is "Saint and Sinner". The song is great and the guitar playing is cool.

LORETTA CARAVELLO *(ERIC CARR'S SISTER)* – This was Eric's favorite song on the album to play. It was the mood, it was very laid-back, but the drums made it happen. "

KEEP ME COMIN'

ADAM MITCHELL *(SONGWRITER)* – Paul came up with the idea. I just went with it, yeah let's do it. It's a rock 'n' roll band.

WES BEECH *(THE PLASMATICS)* – KISS does Zeppelin from my favorite KISS album – and the album that lets the world know they are a heavy metal band. I'll bet Kingdom Come wishes they would have written this song, as it's right in their vein. The big Michael James Jackson drum sound and Eric Carr's muscular drumming provides a solid foundation for the rest of the instruments and Paul's Plant-like delivery. Big fans of Zeppelin, this song may be their most blatant Zep-influenced tune. The guitar solo is reigned in and right on the money, exuding Jimmy Page vibes, and the song just grooves along. Surprising it was never promoted, as it might have brought more fans their way.

Wes Beech's pass, *Creatures of the Night* tour

JASON BAKKEN *(COBRAS & FIRE PODCAST)* – Blehh. A song that Paul insists upon us. The verse is annoying, and the chorus just sucks. Bad song on a killer record.

CLAUDIO SPERA *(KISS ARMY NATION PODCAST)* – I absolutely love "Keep Me Comin'". It's got a Zeppelin groove. It is the proof of KISS's attempt to get back at being loud, hard, and metal. The pounding, heavy drums and crispy guitars in perfect sync with the bass line make this song a real killer. I love the gang vocals on the chorus and how the song transitions towards it. Vinnie's solo adds an interesting layer to the heavy and consistent riff behind it.

JOEY CASSATA *(ZO2, Z ROCK)* – *Creatures* is considered a very heavy KISS album, but that's mostly because of the production. The infectious energy of "Keep Me Comin'" and the catchy chorus showcase the band's ability to blend hard rock with melodic hooks. That's really what makes this album stand out as an absolute gem in the catalog.

ROCK AND ROLL HELL

DON JAMIESON *(COMEDIAN)* – This is KISS's version of Foreigner's *Jukebox Hero* – the story of a young boy who has big rock 'n' roll dreams, not unlike Gene himself. I'm glad I didn't know that Bryan Adams and Jim Vallance were brought in to write this song with Gene, or I probably would've asked Gene to breath fire into my face. In the end though it's a great showcase for Gene's underrated vocal range, and is still one of my favorite tunes on the *Creatures of the Night* album. Even Ace Frehley did his version of "Rock And Roll Hell" on his *Origins, Volume 1* album.

JOEY SASSO *(THE CIRCLE, NETFLIX)* – This track, my friends, is not just your average Gene Simmons song – it's a hidden masterpiece that deserves our utmost respect. As a passionate KISStard with a deep love for rock music, let me tell you why "Rock And Roll Hell" is an absolute banger of a song off of a great record. Now, during the *Creatures of the Night* era, KISS was in a pivotal moment in their career. The band was undergoing a revitalization, redefining their sound with a heavier, more hard-hitting approach.

RAISE YOUR GLASSES:
A Celebration of 50 Years of KISS Songs
by Celebrities, Musicians & Fans.

This album, known for its raw energy and uncompromising attitude, marks a standout period in KISS's legacy as they embraced a new sonic direction.

"Rock And Roll Hell" emerges as a standout track on *Creatures of The Night* for its powerful lyrics, intense musicality, and Gene's commanding vocal presence. The song encapsulates the essence of classic KISS while infusing it with a new-found intensity that resonates with fans on a visceral level. What sets "Rock And Roll Hell" apart is its unapologetic grit and unbridled passion. Gene's raw, emotive delivery, coupled with the thunderous guitar riffs and driving rhythm section, creates a sonic onslaught that captures the very soul of rock 'n' roll rebellion. As we reflect on KISS's enduring legacy, "Rock And Roll Hell" stands out as a testament to the band's resilience and creative evolution. It's a song that embodies the spirit of rock music at its core, reminding us of KISS's unwavering dedication to their craft and their fans.

GREG PRATO *(AUTHOR, Take It Off: KISS Truly Unmasked and The Eric Carr Story)* – The sound of the Demon finally regaining his focus (give a listen to a tune such as "She's So European" to catch my drift concerning how far out to sea Mr. Simmons had drifted during KISS's wishy-washy '79-'81 period). Did you know that the chorus was an exact replication of the Bachman-Turner Overdrive song of the same name?

CLAUDIO SPERA *(KISS ARMY NATION PODCAST)* – I was so happy to feel that Gene was back in his Demon persona during the *Creatures of the Night* era. Being a drummer, I love when the pairing of drums and bass define a song. And I believe this song is such that. A well-rounded, solid bass line with huge-sounding drums. Just amazing. And Gene's singing is worth mentioning, it provides the song with an extra edge.

TOM GIGLIOTTI *(SHOUT IT OUT LOUDCAST)* – A very heavy, moody song which is quite shocking considering that '80s favorite, Bryan Adams, is the co-writer! Gene delivers here with the vocals and tone of this one. *Creatures* was obviously a return to form and this song has an incredibly dense sound during the verses and then explodes into one of the more powerful choruses on the album. And of course, anytime Genes sing a song with this type of storytelling, it makes it even more menacing.

DANGER

BRUCE KULICK *(KISS)* – Michael James Jackson talks about Bob's involvement in the liner notes of *Creatures of the Night*. Bob thought he would play on a lot of the record. He did not and it wasn't something to brag about. But it does sound like Bob starts the solo at the 3:20 mark. I think Bob played on "Danger". But it sounds like the beginning of the solo is Bob and then either Vinnie Vincent or maybe Rick Derringer finish it. But I know it's not Bob because of the certain chromatic style of playing.

ADAM MITCHELL *(SONGWRITER)* – "Danger" was always one of my favorite KISS songs. Paul and I had done the demo at my home studio and because it was pretty small and I didn't have a drum kit, I'd used one of Roger Linn's drum machines to do the drum track. In fact, I think it was the second one that Roger ever made. (Little known fact... Roger is also a great guitar player and used to play guitar in my band.) So, we used his drum machine, and it was perfect for that track because it's super up-tempo and the drum part really works like a machine gun driving it along. Super-fast, super-intense.

JOEY CASSATA *(ZO2, Z ROCK)* – *Creatures* has no filler at all. Every song is strong. "Danger" is no exception. I actually think the verses are catchier than the chorus. I know the first thing that everyone talks about when you say *Creatures of the Night* is Eric's drum sound, but I actually don't think it's praised enough. Not only the sonics of his drums, but his playing is so incredible on this record. The shuffle in songs like "Danger" and "Saint & Sinner" are some the most intricate and difficult patterns in the whole KISS catalog.

Joey Cassata as Eric Carr

ZEUS *(SHOUT IT OUT LOUDCAST)* – Drums, drums, drums, vocals, vocals, vocals, guitar, guitar, guitar. This song rips. Eric is a beast. Paul's voice is on fire. Vinnie is a killer on this song. Lyrically, the verses and the pre-chorus are off the charts. Paul is as passionate as I ever heard him. Musically, I'm not sure KISS is ever as good as this, despite the bass being played by Jimmy Haslip and not Gene. Bob Kulick had originally worked on this song with Paul, and who knows if a part of his playing made it to the album. This is a favorite deep cut of mine.

LORETTA CARAVELLO *(ERIC CARR'S SISTER)* – This a fast song that goes crazy. Another song where I just love the drumming. This is a drummer's record.

I LOVE IT LOUD

BOBBY ROCK *(VINNIE VINCENT INVASION, LITA FORD)* – I don't think you can talk about Eric Carr's drumming legacy without underscoring the enduring impact of this track. This record was nothing short of revolutionary when it first came out in the early '80s, in large part because of its cavernous drum tones. It turned out to be somewhat of a precursor to *Metal Health*, *Pyromania*, and *Shout at the Devil*: three records that would go on to shape that mammoth '80s drum sound for the rest of the decade. But *Creatures of the Night* was first! In the larger view, I always thought *Creatures* had everything necessary to resuscitate KISS from the fire-scorched rubble they found themselves in at the time, with this track as the flagship anthem. But it just seemed that the makeup thing had become too much of a liability by that point. Still, though, Eric would cement himself into drum hero-dom with this record.

RAISE YOUR GLASSES:
A Celebration of 50 Years of KISS Songs by Celebrities, Musicians & Fans.

Bobby Rock with Eric Carr

ROXY PETRUCCI *(VIXEN)* – Vixen toured with KISS and I couldn't wait to hear this song played live. I used to play the song with Madam X in the clubs and I always loved copying the huge heavy Eric Carr drum sound. The crowd would go nuts, it was a knee-dropper for sure. Perfect catchy anthem with Eric's signature drum work.

AHMET ZAPPA *(MUSICIAN)* – It's a true rock banger. When this came out, I would listen to it all the time. I first heard it here in L.A. on KNAC. And it was kind of a surprise. At this point you either kind of liked or didn't like KISS. This was not KISS at their zenith. I think it was maybe not so cool to like KISS as much as I liked KISS. This track clawed them back into the consciousness because it Is undeniably kick-ass, and I think you can stack this track up next to anthems like Judas Priest's "Living After Midnight". So sing-songy. So get up on your feet. Stand on your chair in the stadium, clap your hands over your head, light your lighters and sing along.

RAISE YOUR GLASSES:
A Celebration of 50 Years of KISS Songs
by Celebrities, Musicians & Fans.

FRANKIE KAZARIAN *(WRESTLER)* – The drum intro on this song, my god. The drum tone is magnificent. The drumming and Eric Carr is the star here, but this whole song is perhaps low-key my favorite KISS song. And you gotta love how the song fades out a bit at the end only to return, much like the band themselves have done a time or two!

DAVID LAGRECA *(BUSTED OPEN RADIO)* – The ultimate anthem. As a kid I had no idea that KISS was in a major slump and this album didn't sell. I thought it was the greatest, heaviest album ever. It wasn't until I read an interview in *Circus* magazine with the band that I realized what a bad state the band was in. Amazing album and my favorite song on it.

PAUL JANIK *(GENE SIMMONS MONEYBAG SODA)* – Eric's drums are huge and powerful on this track. The video is a masterpiece of '80s cheesiness. I love it really loud!!

CRAIG GASS *(COMEDIAN)* – Now I wanna change my declaration of Favorite KISS Song to this one, because the more I think about it, the more I realize that this song still sounds amazing live. Also, the line, "Rock on, I wanna be President" is something I was absolutely capable of saying on any given night when I was doing coke as a teenager. Just silly, attitude-filled lyrics, and in my opinion, the greatest example of what KISS is about.

LORETTA CARAVELLO *(ERIC CARR'S SISTER)* – It's phenomenal. Those drums. Eric told me the album had drums that could never be duplicated.

I STILL LOVE YOU

RUSSELL PETERS *(COMEDIAN)* – I love the album version but when I saw them do it live, I was geeked 'cause it was so cool, and 'cause they had the explosions again at the end. They made it build the right way and to me it was the beginning of the power ballads for everybody.

JEFF PLATE *(TRANS-SIBERIAN ORCHESTRA, SAVATAGE)* – The album version is great, but the live version from the *MTV Unplugged* show is brilliant. That whole performance is fantastic, and this song has always stood out.

PAULIE Z *(ZO2, Z ROCK)* – This is one of my favorite KISS songs because it is dark and emotional in a way that we rarely see from the band. I love Paul's voice in general, but on this song he delivers an especially moving performance that is hauntingly beautiful. I really love the acoustic version they did on *MTV Unplugged*, particularly Bruce's solo. I love the song so much that I sang it in dedication to my late brother David Z at one of his memorial concerts, with Bruce Kulick on guitar.

JASON BAKKEN *(COBRAS & FIRE PODCAST)* – Another masterful breakup song from Paul. Starts off a bit sluggish. An emotional vocal that doesn't grab you at first, but it soon does. I prefer hearing this live over the studio version. When Paul was in his prime, few were better.

RAISE YOUR GLASSES:
A Celebration of 50 Years of KISS Songs by Celebrities, Musicians & Fans.

ALLISON HAGENDORF *(MUSIC JOURNALIST, TV HOST & PRODUCER)* – A standout song for me. This is a vulnerable, heart-wrenching, bluesy, soulful power ballad, and Paul's vocals perfectly convey that heartbreak we have all felt at one point. Also, that epic guitar solo needs to be turned up to 11.

Allison Hagendorf with Paul Stanley

LISA LANE KULICK *(BRUCE KULICK'S WIFE)* – How can any female not fall in love with this emotional rock ballad? Paul Stanley's vocals, full of pain and anguish, cut deep into your soul. I've listened to this haunting melody hundreds of times and it still brings me to tears. "I Still Love You" is at the top of my favorite KISS song list.

JAY SCOTT *(THE HOOK ROCKS PODCAST)* – Is this the original power ballad? Paul's vocals are incredible. An amazing song and a forgotten gem.

SONNY POONI *(PODCAST ROCK CITY)* – One of the best rock ballads ever! The version on *Animalize Live Uncensored* is great. The version on *MTV Unplugged* is absolutely OUTSTANDING! Paul pours his heart out on this song. KISS missed an opportunity to re-release this song in the late '80s because this song would've done really well on the Billboard charts when all the other hair metal ballads were out there.

LORETTA CARAVELLO *(ERIC CARR'S SISTER)* – Eric played bass on that. My brother would sometimes have to teach them their parts. He had such a good ear. My brother sometimes would say 'well maybe like this…' and then he would pick up the guitar and it was perfect. I think there's nothing bad about that album."

KILLER

RUSSELL PETERS *(COMEDIAN)* – Music triggers your memory. I heard this song and I thought "hey, what was I when this song came out, oh my God I was jerking off. That was '82. It reminded me of when I started to… oh, I was 11". Wow I was a pervert.

JOEY CASSATA *(ZO2, Z ROCK)* – Let's pose the famous question… did Vinnie Vincent save KISS? Well, if the songwriting on *Creatures* & *Lick It Up* turned KISS around, then I would say he at least had a big part to play. Songs like "Killer" really brought KISS back into being a heavy rock band that moms didn't approve of. Paul's rhythm guitar playing on this song is fantastic. It's a sign of things to come through the next few albums. Paul's heavy rhythm is a staple throughout *Creatures*, *Lick It Up* & *Animalize*.

The Handsome Devils: Gabriel Connor, Charlie Parra,
Joey Cassata and Todd Kerns

TOM GIGLIOTTI *(SHOUT IT OUT LOUDCAST)* – Gene is in full classic Demon on this album. The riff and rhythm of this song make this deep cut an awesome song to play LOUD! That droning guitar during the chorus and of course Eric's bombastic drums, combined with the story he tells, is just classic Demon here. A standout that gets buried among the classics on this album.

ERNIE PALOOZA *(TOP 5 WITH JOEY CASSATA)* – The opening riff is classic New Wave of British Heavy Metal! The riff almost sounds like the song "Makin' Love" backwards.

ZEUS *(SHOUT IT OUT LOUDCAST)* – Love the slow build into the awesome Vinnie Vincent guitar riff. Since this is *Creatures of the Night*, Eric Carr's drums can't be denied. Gene's growl and vocal delivery is great, and so is Vinnie's solo. Love the sound effect after "crack the whip," as well. This is supposedly the first song Gene and Vinnie wrote together. It's probably the biggest shame in all of KISStory that Vinnie couldn't write and perform more songs with KISS.

WAR MACHINE

RUSSELL PETERS *(COMEDIAN)* – Bryan Adams and I are buddies. I was in his dressing room, and I asked, "Hey, did you write "War Machine" for KISS?" and he goes, "Yeah how did you know that?". I said, "Cause I'm a KISS geek". A couple minutes later he showed up in my dressing room with an acoustic guitar playing it, and then I started singing it and that's how that video came about.

FRANKIE KAZARIAN *(WRESTLER)* – With a killer riff to open the track, then that catchy groove that is the chorus. I also really dig the solo in this song. The wrestler Taz, who is a friend of mine, used some type of cover version of this song for entrance music back in the late '90s, for the ECW promotion, and it fit him perfectly.

RAISE YOUR GLASSES:
A Celebration of 50 Years of KISS Songs
by Celebrities, Musicians & Fans.

Joey Cassata and Frankie Kazarian

BRYCE MILETO *(SISTERS DOLL)* – This tune I grew more to love over recent years. Especially when they play it live to this day. HEAVY AF!!! I love it!!!

MARTIN POPOFF *(AUTHOR)* – Here's a big an' bashing doomy rocker from *Creatures of the Night*, which should have been bigger, given the good standing of metal on both sides of the pond in 1982. Gene bellows it boldly, skating across huge buffalo-burger chords and a massive backbeat from Eric Carr. God of Thunder, Demon, The Devil, War Machine… it's all of a character set consistent with Gene's makeup and costumes, which, if you think about it, ain't exactly Dr. Love.

CHAPTER 14

"LICK IT UP"

Released: September 18, 1983

Lick It Up stands as a pivotal album in KISS's career. The record marked the band's first venture without their trademark makeup, symbolizing a significant change in their image. Musically, *Lick It Up* is a return to straightforward hard rock, featuring anthems like the title track and "All Hell's Breakin'

Loose." The album's success not only revitalized KISS's commercial standing but also solidified their place in the 1980s glam metal scene.

The title track became an anthem for the band's revitalization. The song's infectious energy, catchy riffs, and Paul Stanley's spirited vocals immediately resonated with fans. It was a declaration that KISS was back, both visually and musically, ready to reclaim their place in the rock and metal scene.

"All Hell's Breakin' Loose" continued the hard-hitting theme, featuring a blend of rock and funk elements. Gene Simmons' bass line and the dynamic interplay of guitars added a groove to the track, showcasing the band's versatility.

While *Lick It Up* signaled a return to a more traditional hard rock sound, the album also demonstrated KISS's willingness to experiment. Tracks like "Not for the Innocent" and "A Million to One" added depth to the record, exploring different facets of the band's musical range.

The success of *Lick It Up* not only reaffirmed KISS's status as rock icons but also positioned them as influential figures in the exploding glam metal movement of the 1980s. The album's commercial success and critical acclaim marked a triumphant comeback for a band that had weathered various storms.

The album cover, featuring the band members without makeup against a plain white background, became an iconic image of KISS's new era. The visual shift, combined with the energetic and polished sound of the album, resonated with both longtime fans and a new generation of rock enthusiasts.

In retrospect, *Lick It Up* remains a crucial chapter in KISStory. The album not only revitalized the band's career but also showcased their ability to adapt to changing musical landscapes. *Lick It Up* stands as a testament to KISS's enduring impact on the hard rock and glam metal genres, proving that their influence could thrive in evolving musical scenes.

EXCITER

JOE McGINNESS *(KUARANTINE, KLASSIC '78)* – A great track to open an album. The song is an absolute rocker, but I'm not crazy about the guitar solos. I wish they had more emotion, vibrato and weren't covered in delay. I think it would be interesting to hear this song with Bob or Bruce Kulick writing and recording the leads on it. In my opinion Rick Derringer Is a great player but doesn't fit on this particular track.

HAL SPARKS *(COMEDIAN)* – Because of the title track there are several songs on *Lick It Up* that don't get enough love. With its galloping rhythm and its Starchild storyline, it feels like a song that was too heavy for Paul's solo record.

STEVEN MICHAEL *(GROWIN' UP ROCK PODCAST)* – For me, this era of KISS was huge, not only because they took their makeup off, but because I did not connect with them when I was younger, but now I was a teenager and really getting into harder and heavier music, so the timing was right. "Exciter" was the lead off track on this record and it kicks you in the face. It's also the introduction to Vinnie Vincent even though he does not play the solo. I love the chorus and the whispers of "Exciter". Love everything about this tune.

PETER CORY *(KISS LIVE AUCTIONS)* – I'll be honest with this one, I was never a fan of this song on the album, but hearing the song live is a lot different! I was too young to go to the *Lick It Up* tour to see it live from KISS, but I had the privilege of seeing Bruce Kulick and his band perform this on the KISS Kruise and they killed it! Some songs are just better live!

CLAUDIO SPERA *(KISS ARMY NATION PODCAST)* – Makeup is gone and KISS surprises the world with a new album and a new lineup. The opening track usually sets the tone for the rest of the record. I believe "Exciter" accomplished this task with high grades. The aggressive opening chords coupled with a strong bass-drums kick welcome Paul's vocals. This is 'in your face', fierce hard rock. Perfect opener to a great album. I love the sound on Rick Derringer's solo.

NOT FOR THE INNOCENT

JOEY CASSATA *(ZO2, Z ROCK)* – This is probably my favorite Gene track from the '80s. It's so mean and nasty!! Every section of this song is great. The lyrics are so strong and powerful. "You better lock up your daughters, we're coming to your town / We're here for the slaughter, kick you when you're down.../ We're not for the innocent!" This is the Gene I love. It was always fun for me to think that when they recorded *Lick It Up* they were still a makeup band. I could totally see Gene in Demon makeup singing this!! *Lick It Up* is the perfect sister album to *Creatures of the Night*!

RAISE YOUR GLASSES:
A Celebration of 50 Years of KISS Songs
by Celebrities, Musicians & Fans.

JOHN JANIK *(GENE SIMMONS MONEYBAG SODA)* – It was the summer of '84 and my best friend from my neighborhood would crank his boom box while we played basketball. The *Lick it Up* cassette was on repeat. We always got a kick out of the rawness of this track. Most people side with the innocent, that was not the case with Gene on this ditty and we ate it up!!!

The guys from Gene Simmons Moneybag Soda with Gene Simmons

GREG PRATO *(AUTHOR, Take It Off: KISS Truly Unmasked and The Eric Carr Story)* – Although I've written two books that focus largely on KISS's non-makeup era, I have to admit, it's the '70s era that remains my favorite. But that said, I can still pick and choose some worthy tracks from most non-makeup records, and my favorite by far is this largely forgotten ditty from *Lick it Up*. And to be honest, the reason why I fancy it so much is because it was probably the most Demon-like sounding Gene tune of the non-makeup era (until "Unholy"). Go on and give it another listen, close your peepers, and it's very easy to picture Señor Simmons in his *Creatures* garb and makeup growling this delightful number.

ROBERT CONTE *(AUTHOR)* – *Lick it Up* was the second KISS LP I ever owned. While the opening track "Exciter" failed to excite me at all, this second cut (co-written by Gene Simmons and new guitarist Vinnie Vincent) encouraged me to listen to the rest of the record with high anticipation. After "Lick It Up" the LP only got better and inspired me to seek out KISS's entire catalog, one album at a time. A local record shop that carried bootleg cassettes had a mix tape of various KISS demos with a rough version of this track with Paul Stanley singing some of its verses. Hearing this alternate take on an already awesome song began my passion for collecting other KISS demos and live concerts wherever I could find them!

MARK CICCHINI *(THREE SIDES OF THE COIN)* – Oddly enough, I always thought this song was a left over from the *Creatures* era. Turns out my instincts were correct... it was! Next to the title track, this is my favorite song on the LP. With that said, had the original arrangement remained (Paul and Gene sharing the lead vocal duty as it is on the original *Creatures*-era demo) I'm guessing it would have been my favorite instead. A great song on an album of great songs... but I still like the demo better! "Gonna tan your hide! Rip the flesh off your bones!"... indeed!

LICK IT UP

CHRIS JERICHO *(WRESTLER, FOZZY)* – It's like "Enter Sandman" or "Pour Some Sugar On Me", you've heard this song so many times. But when it comes on, you say 'oh this is a cool tune, it's "Lick It Up". Whenever it comes on, you love it. It's a huge song and one that they've made a career off of.

BOBBY ROCK *(VINNIE VINCENT INVASION, LITA FORD)* –
There is a genius in both the simplicity and impact of this song. It is an absolute masterclass in the study of "less is more," on every level. No guitar solo, no contrasting bridge section, and no distractions from the groove. I always saw this tune and the removal of the makeup as one unified statement: a 180-degree return to only that which is essential. It appeared to work! It's interesting to note that, when this song hit MTV, I was hardcore in the midst of a jazz phase (fresh out of the Berklee College of Music in Boston) and wasn't paying much attention to the rock world. So, when I first happened to catch the vid—bemused by the fact that KISS had actually taken their makeup off—I was confused. *"Where is Ace?"* I wondered. Little did I know at the time that my future boss had replaced him!

Bobby Rock with Vinnie Vincent

EDDIE TRUNK *(RADIO DJ & TV PERSONALITY)* – This song is so important for KISS and that period was so important for them. KISS was dead, nobody cared, they weren't selling tickets. When

KISS took the makeup off, the narrative at that time was, "Who cares?" But I loved that MTV gave them the opportunity to showcase them taking the makeup off live on TV. The video and the song made me think that maybe this band has a shot at coming back. I remember working at a record store and accidentally seeing a copy of the record a month before its release, and couldn't believe it when I saw the cover.

BRYCE MILETO *(SISTERS DOLL)* – Love this song… especially The Who "Won't Get Fooled Again" segment they did throughout the live shows.

JORDAN CANNATA *(SLAUGHTER)* – This song is just the perfect example of when everything goes right. Not only did they write a great song with a great hook and riff, but they had the perfect production and mix. The drum sound and guitar tones are perfect. The performances from everyone were exactly what they needed to be. The song sounds very open and spacious, yet big and epic at the same time. If someone asked what you could do to make the song better, the answer would be nothing. Each person played exactly what the song needed, and the production stands the test of time for me.

JOEL HOEKSTRA *(WHITESNAKE, TRANS-SIBERIAN ORCHESTRA)* – The bottom line is I fell in love with hard rock/heavy metal around 1981. AC/DC – "Back in Black" and Angus Young in particular – made me want to play guitar. Hence the direct segue to 1983 and the KISS "non-makeup" era. It's kind of hilarious that the '80s are associated with bands wearing makeup, but KISS had to take theirs off to thrive amidst the cultural change. Anyway, "Lick It Up" has everything. Like AC/DC, it's got that straight-ahead, mid-tempo eighth-note groove, and the riff leaves space. I love that the riff is the response to the vocal in the verse. Once again, that amazing KISS backing vocal sound in the chorus. Also, three chords, man. Less IS more.

Eddie Trunk with Vinnie Vincent

YOUNG AND WASTED

CHRIS JERICHO *(WRESTLER, FOZZY)* – Eric Carr singing it on *Animalize Live Uncensored* is incredible. It's another song that we grew up with on that DVD.

HAL SPARKS *(COMEDIAN)* – I mean, come on! Not only does this song rip on the album, Eric Carr's version live made it a gut punch. The riff harkens back to Budgie and late '70s proto-thrash, and the vocals on the record… what are there? 35 Genes? And Paul's wailing chorus adds a spooky cruelty to the story.

IZZY PRESLEY *(MUSICIAN, COMIC)* – Eric Carr's shining moment on *Animalize Live Uncensored*, probably because Gene could not sing it live, so we got Eric Carr gold! Great groove, very '80s KISS riff and driving drums. Izzy approves.

JOEY SASSO *(THE CIRCLE, NETFLIX)* – Let's talk "Young and Wasted", a true hidden gem that shines bright but was overlooked. During the *Lick It Up* era, a pivotal moment, KISS boldly unmasked, reinventing themselves with a new edge. This album marked a turning point in their legacy, and "Young and Wasted" embodies that raw, rebellious spirit with its infectious energy and powerful riffs. Despite flying under the radar, this track's punchy lyrics and vibrant sound make it a standout, deserving more recognition in the annals of KISStory.

CLAUDIO SPERA *(KISS ARMY NATION PODCAST)* – Fierce pounding rock 'n' roll. As simple as that. Gene's singing is superb.

The bass drives the song through different zones until the chorus kicks in. I absolutely love how you can notice Paul's voice in the chorus. Eric Carr's up-tempo drumming is another highlight on this track. And Vinnie's solo is the cherry on the pie. One of my favorites from *Lick It Up*. Worth mentioning the live version with Eric on vocals.

ROBERT CONTE *(AUTHOR)* – OMG — this is THE track on *Lick it Up* for me! I fondly recall listening to this album in my bedroom while fantasizing about the *Creatures*-era of KISS performing it in makeup! Although Mercury Records released "Lick It Up" and "All Hell's Breakin' Loose" as singles and videos, I wholeheartedly believed this track deserved the same treatment. Hard. Heavy. Fast... "Young and Wasted" is among the absolute best of Gene's non-makeup KISS songs! Producer Michael James Jackson deserves extra kudos for the album's sound; it is perhaps the closest to a true "heavy metal" record. No one could doubt KISS was back with a vengeance!

GIMME MORE

ZEUS *(SHOUT IT OUT LOUDCAST)* – "Fast KISS" in all its glory. Man, KISS proved they could hang with the metal acts of their day. Vinnie Vincent, along with Eric Carr, gave them an element in the arsenal they never had before. They could pull off this metal song and yet still have that KISS melodic sound. With lyrics like "lick my candy cane" and "make my juices flow", the KISS identity was still intact.

RAISE YOUR GLASSES:
A Celebration of 50 Years of KISS Songs by Celebrities, Musicians & Fans.

JOEY SASSO *(THE CIRCLE, NETFLIX)* – This song has been flying under the radar for too long. During the *Lick It Up* era, KISS rose from the ashes, ditching the makeup for a fresh start. This album marked a defining moment in their journey, bringing forth a rejuvenated sound that resonated deeply with diehard fans, many of which were happy to see the band sticking with the hard-hitting sound that made us all fall in love with them in the first place. "Gimme More" shines on this record, with its infectious groove and Paul Stanley's homage to his love of Led Zeppelin evident in the song's powerful, Zeppelin-esque vibe. Despite not receiving the credit it deserves, this track's blend of raw energy and melodic hooks cements its place as a standout in the iconic legacy of KISS, capturing the essence of rock 'n' roll rebellion that has defined the band's spirit to this day.

RYAN "BB" BANNON *(PODDER THAN HELL PODCAST)* –This fast-paced rocker was the B-side to the single "All Hell's Breakin' Loose" in Japan and was also in the rotation of live songs for the *Lick It Up* tour. It showcases what a crazy shredder Vinnie was. He also gets a writing credit on this song with Paul as well. But the real question is who came up with the lines, "Love is sweet, so insane / Come on lick my candy cane."

TOM GIGLIOTTI *(SHOUT IT OUT LOUDCAST)* – It's 1983, the makeup is off, and KISS is trying new things. The faster, up-tempo songs are what was happening in the rock music scene at the time, so of course KISS throws their hat in the ring with this one. *Lick it Up* is an amazing album and the incredible frenetic pace of this song that Eric Carr brings, along with Vinnie Vincent's guitar wizardry, make this a song that most KISS fans weren't used to hearing – but it certainly kicks ass from start to finish with no time to catch your breath. But at the end of the day, it's all about Paul telling everyone to "lick his candy cane"!

JOEY CASSATA *(ZO2, Z ROCK)* – It seemed like a conscious effort to have one of these "high-energy" KISS songs on every album through the '80s, starting with "Gimme More". I like the musicality of this song more than the vocal melody and delivery. The band with Vinnie was definitely firing on all cylinders.

Tom, Chris Jericho, Joey Cassata and Zeus

ALL HELL'S BREAKIN' LOOSE

CRAIG GASS *(COMEDIAN)* – Just a great rock anthem, and bonus for the Paul Stanley talk-up in the beginning of this song. As a teenager, though, I would advise against anyone using that speech when there is real potential for getting your ass kicked. Turns out you also have to know how to fight if some kids want to beat the shit out of you, and announcing, "I am cool, I am the breeze" will only make those punks hit you even harder while you lay on the ground crying.

JOEY CASSATA *(ZO2, Z ROCK)* – Very surprising that this was the second single and video from *Lick It Up*. I personally love the song, but it's very different for KISS. Especially with the Paul Stanley rap-type verses. I had the pleasure of recording this with my band ZO2 for Eric Carr's memorial album *Unfinished Business*. I also recorded a version of "Carr Jam" with Eric's drum solo. It was actually harder to recreate the killer groove on "All Hell's..." than to do the drum solo. I know that's crazy to say, but Eric had a swagger and feel that is very, very hard to duplicate. All the great drummers do. I always said, if you can recreate a drum track with a drum machine, then the drummer's feel wasn't that unique or great. Eric's right-hand hi-hat work had a feel that you cannot recreate.

LORETTA CARAVELLO *(ERIC CARR'S SISTER)* – He was really proud of that song because he had a writing contribution. It's a heavy song. There were a lot of songs that weren't put on the album, but this is one they could use because it's really good.

RAISE YOUR GLASSES:
A Celebration of 50 Years of KISS Songs
by Celebrities, Musicians & Fans.

ZEUS *(SHOUT IT OUT LOUDCAST)* – Another rare song where all four members are credited as songwriters. KISS rapping? You know what? It works. Was KISS at the forefront of the rock/rap movement? I don't know – but I do know that the riff on this song is one of the best in the KISS catalog. Man, this song kicks ass. The chorus is one of KISS's best. It's so catchy. I love when Paul says, "Oh take it," then Vinnie rips his solo. Man, what a kick Vinnie provided on this album. By the way, did you know that Paul is cool? He is the breeze.

ZACH THRONE *(COREY TAYLOR, BRUCE KULICK)* – One of the best songs in the KISS katalog, and one of the BEST riffs they ever came up with. In G tuning. Eric Carr apparently was instrumental in putting this together.

KEITH ROTH *(SIRIUS XM, THE DICTATORS)* – That Motown-inspired chorus! The video was campy, but I loved it. Post-apocalyptic NYC, KISS running the streets, a takeoff of "Escape from New York". Badass!!

A MILLION TO ONE

STEVE BROWN *(TRIXTER)* – You can definitely hear the big '80s influence. A great song. Paul Stanley and Vinnie Vincent knocked this one out of the park. The chord progressions, definitely more chords than we're used to hearing in a KISS song. They use them very creatively. I love the lyrics and the whole storyline. Very powerful songwriting.

CHRIS CZYNSZAK *(DECIBEL GEEK PODCAST)* – I still think it's a crime that this song wasn't released as a single. It's a perfect song for 1983 and contains everything you'd want, including a great riff, strong vocals, and a melody that sticks with you.

CHRIS JERICHO *(WRESTLER, FOZZY)* – They (the record company) dropped the ball. This should've been a single. That would've been a huge hit in my opinion. It's such a great tune.

SONNY POONI *(PODCAST ROCK CITY)* – Vocally, Paul was untouchable from 1979-1992. The range and power of his voice was amazing. Add the songwriting chops… and you get some great songs. KISS made a major mistake here. This song should've been the second single from *Lick it Up*.

LISA LANE KULICK *(BRUCE KULICK'S WIFE)* – In my opinion one of the most underrated KISS songs. *Lick It Up* was the first KISS LP I bought as soon as it was released. Michael James Jackson's influence gave the guitars and drums a more aggressive '80s metal sound, which was a pleasant surprise. Paul Stanley's belief that he's the best man for the girl, sincerely comes through the lyrics and his gut-wrenching lead vocal note, extending from the bridge to the last chorus, always puts me over the edge. If you haven't had this song on your radar, give it a good listen. You won't be disappointed.

MITCH LAFON *(ROCK JOURNALIST)* – This is the be all end all '80s KISS song. Slow build, explosive chorus, Paul Stanley turned to 11. How this wasn't released as a single or played live forever is a modern-day mystery. The Vincent/Stanley writing partnership should have been the Lennon/McCartney of the '80s, but personalities and ego got in the way. Play this song NOW and make sure it's turned up to 11!

ZEUS *(SHOUT IT OUT LOUDCAST)* – When critics ridicule KISS, this is one of the songs you can throw in their face. This is an incredible song. Not sure what's better, Paul's vocals, the lyrics or Vinnie's solo. Paul is pouring his heart out and showing a side of himself that he does not usually share. This song makes it a travesty that this KISS lineup of Paul, Gene, Eric and Vinnie had just this album and a portion of *Creatures of the Night*. This is one of the best KISS lineups; the songwriting on this whole album, because of what Vinnie brought, could be the best in the KISS discography.

FITS LIKE A GLOVE

CHRIS JERICHO *(WRESTLER, FOZZY)* – Gene does have some good songs from the '80s and this is one of them. I used to bag on him for that era.

BRANDON FIELDS *(MINEFIELD)* – This entire album is quintessential KISS for me, and this is my favorite track of the bunch. Gene's vocals are some of his best and definitely one of the highest registers he used. It features great guitar work by Vinnie as well, with the guitar solo being one of my favorites of his. The final ascending riff in the solo is amazing. The lyrics are classic Gene: "My snake's alive and it's ready to bite".

CHARLIE PARRA *(KUARANTINE)* – What the hell is Vinnie doing?" was my first thought. I absolutely understood that quote

RAISE YOUR GLASSES:
A Celebration of 50 Years of KISS Songs
by Celebrities, Musicians & Fans.

Gene once said: "Vinnie is like Yngwie on crack". Well, he probably is – and in a good way on this record. Fun riff and song to rock out to. One of my favorite songs with Gene doing the main vocal section. I've become a bigger fan of this song (and the whole *Lick it Up* album) recently after being able to play this with The Handsome Devils (Gabriel Connor, Todd Kerns, Joey Cassata and me). Even though this is my favorite track off *Lick it Up*", my favorite lyric in the album is in "Dance All Over Your Face": "Well listen B*TCH, I got news!".

JOE McGINNESS *(KUARANTINE, KLASSIC '78)* – I have always loved this song. Especially the *Animalize Live Uncensored* version. Gene has an uncanny ability to write guitar riffs that will get stuck in your head for days. This is one of them! It's a shame they stopped playing it live.

DARREN PALTROWITZ *(AUTHOR, How David Lee Roth Changed The World)* – To me, the definitive version of this song is the live version from the *Animalize Live Uncensored* video filmed in 1984 and released in 1985. That performance in Detroit is faster than the studio version -- reportedly the preference of Paul Stanley for everything to be played faster in concert -- and more aggressive, vaguely sounding like Motorhead's "Bomber." An aggressive song simply based on feel and groove, aside from the guitar and bass tone. It is also one of the rare KISS songs of note written solely by Gene without a co-writer.

STEVE WRIGHT *(PODDER THAN HELL PODCAST)* – Killer riff starts then you get the "Uh" and the band kicks it in. Fast rocking and what has been known to be called one of Gene's "f**k me s**k me" songs. The aggression of this song has always attracted me, from the riff to the gritty Gene vocals, and the amazing pre-chorus and gang-type vocals for the chorus. Then the famous stop and start: "Cause when I go through her / It's just like a / HOT KNIFE! Through butteahhhhhhhh..." "Oh yeah" to the blazing Vinnie Vincent solo. This was always a highlight live for me whenever it would be played live. KISS at their rocking best!

Chris Jericho with Gene Simmons

ĐON JAMIEĐON *(COMEDIAN)* – Despite some of the most childish lyrics Gene Simmons has ever written ("Well goodness sake's my snake's alive and it's ready to bite") I'm still somehow drawn to and somewhat obsessed with this song. It's such a weird track for KISS, and maybe that's what appeals to me. You never know where the song is going and there's a surprise around every corner. It's not a conventional song structure at all. Particularly love the extended Gene screams, and I was thrilled when they included it in their live set on that tour. "Cause when I go through her, it's just like a hot knife through butter"? Come on Gene!

DANCE ALL OVER YOUR FACE

TOM GIGLIOTTI *(SHOUT IT OUT LOUDCAST)* – Everything on *Lick It Up* is thick and heavy, and this is a stomper of a song with a great Demon tone. The chorus shows his range and that howl we all love from Gene. The lyrics are not very subtle, but is KISS ever subtle? No – and that's why we love them.

JAY SCOTT *(THE HOOK ROCKS PODCAST)* – I remember when I first heard this at the age of 9, I imagined how it must hurt when someone dances on your face. And then years later when I saw my first porn movie the light bulb went on.

BRAD RUSTOVEN *(SLAMFEST PODCAST)* – Aside from the subject matter, I'm a fan of this song. Great mid-tempo riff and I'm a sucker for vocal delay and it's used well in the chorus. Welcome to the non-makeup era of the '80s! Gene writes a "debonair" line and for one of the first times ever, calls the woman in the song a bitch… twice.

KENNY BEGLEY *(KISS LIVE AUCTIONS)* – Such a great song referring to a cheating significant other, awesome Gene song!

ZEUS *(SHOUT IT OUT LOUDCAST)* – Nice riff and chorus. Vinnie has a nice little outro, but this forgotten deep cut is about as crude as it gets. This song is for those that think "Burn Bitch Burn" is too romantic. "Dance All Over Your Face?" Gee, what could Gene be referring to when he says 'dance'?

AND ON THE 8ᵀᴴ DAY

TOM HIGGINS *(KLASSIC '78)* – One of my favorites from *Lick It Up*. This is Gene and Vinnie collaborating and coming up with something new that is still very much KISS. The mix is a bit muddy compared to other songs on this album, but the song holds up. It should've been a staple in the set list.

WES BEECH *(THE PLASMATICS)* – Always one of my favorite songs from *Lick It Up*, this song has a very melodic structure, and the intro sounds like something from the Alice Cooper band circa *Billion Dollar Babies*. Once again, the great Michael James Jackson drum sound is in play and Eric Carr proves yet again that he's the heaviest drummer KISS has ever had. Is it just me or is the verse motif a bit reminiscent of Eric Burton's "Spill the Wine"? Love when Gene breaks into the chorus and his voice cracks as he reaches the high note. Gives it character. A short and sweet guitar solo from Vinnie that just barely keeps from going out of control fits perfectly. Gene plays some great bass lines throughout; his playing is often overlooked. Again, another song that should have attracted more attention.

RAISE YOUR GLASSES:
A Celebration of 50 Years of KISS Songs by Celebrities, Musicians & Fans.

Wes Beech with Vinnie Vincent

JOEY JASSO (*THE CIRCLE, NETFLIX*) – Lemme school ya on "And On The 8th Day", a tune that's been hiding in the shadows for way too long. Picture this: KISS in the post-makeup era, redefining rock 'n' roll with a gutsy raw sound on *Lick It Up*. This album? A game-changer in their legacy, and "And On The 8th Day" is a mighty gem that often gets overlooked. Now, let's talk Michael James Jackson, the man behind this record, bringing serious fire to KISS's sound for the third and final time. This track? It stands out like a blazing comet, blending fierce guitars, killer vocals, and an anthemic vibe that screams quintessential KISS. If there is a negative I can say regarding the track, it's that I wish the band would have consciously looked back to try to give us more tunes that carry the cool and loose atmosphere and vibe of this track.

METAL MIKE (*80's GLAM METALCAST*) – Any KISS song that says "rock 'n' roll" in it is great in my book! Then they mix in some killer Vinnie riffs (from the original "Boyz Gonna Rock"). Gene's voice is in its nastiest top form, and Eric cracks your ribs with his EPIC drumming. A classic way to end *Lick It Up*.

RAISE YOUR GLASSES:
A Celebration of 50 Years of KISS Songs
by Celebrities, Musicians & Fans.

ZEUS *(SHOUT IT OUT LOUDCAST)* – This underappreciated deep cut is one of those non-makeup songs that would work with Gene in makeup. Gene with his Demon voice really channels his former character. The guitar riff and Eric start this song on the right path. Gene loves that "legends never die" line. I like the chorus and the whole concept of God creating rock 'n' roll on the 8th day. That's clever, Gene.

RAISE YOUR GLASSES:
A Celebration of 50 Years of KISS Songs
by Celebrities, Musicians & Fans.

CHAPTER IS

"ANIMALIZE"

Released: September 13, 1984

Animalize is a hard-hitting and energetic album that solidified KISS's presence in the glam metal scene of the 1980s. Featuring the hit single "Heaven's on Fire" and other anthems like "Thrills in the Night," the album showcases a reinvigorated band with a sound that aligns seamlessly with the glam metal aesthetics of the time. *Animalize* is a celebration of high-energy rock, marking KISS's continued relevance in the ever-evolving world of hard rock and metal.

Animalize arrived at a time when glam metal was dominating the rock scene, and KISS, always adept at adapting to trends, fully embraced the genre's excesses. Released in 1984, the album exudes a vibrant energy and a polished production that aligns perfectly with the glam metal aesthetic of the era.

The standout track, "Heaven's on Fire," became one of KISS's most successful singles from the 1980s. Paul Stanley's powerhouse vocals and the infectious chorus made it an anthem that resonated with fans and cemented KISS's status.

The album's lineup featured Gene Simmons, Paul Stanley, Eric Carr, and Mark St. John. This incarnation of the band brought a renewed energy and contributed to the album's success.

Animalize may not be considered a groundbreaking departure for KISS, but it served a vital purpose in solidifying their place in the glam metal movement. The album's commercial success, coupled with its energetic and anthemic tracks, reaffirmed KISS's ability to stay relevant in the ever-changing landscape of rock music.

In retrospect, *Animalize* stands as a testament to KISS's resilience and adaptability. The album showcases the band's commitment to evolving with the times while staying true to their core identity as rock icons. *Animalize* remains a vibrant and essential entry in KISS's discography, capturing a moment when the band embraced the glam metal era with gusto and continued to prove their enduring impact on the genre.

I'VE HAD ENOUGH (INTO THE FIRE)

DESMOND CHILD *(SONGWRITER)* – That was done at Paul's apartment in New York, I think. I think Paul comes in with that riff, then we would be improvising and then the hook would just pop out. Usually, Paul was driving that. He had an idea for a song. He was very complete. I was just there to lend a helping hand and fill in with lyrics.

HAL SPARKS *(COMEDIAN)* – This song has gotten me through some of the worst moments in my life. Everyone needs their pick-me-up song, and this one gets me back in the fight. This song is priceless.

STEVEN MICHAEL *(GROWIN' UP ROCK PODCAST)* – Arguably one of my top 5 favorite '80s-era KISS songs. If you didn't lose your shit when you dropped the needle down on this album for the first time and got your hair blown back by this riff, you may not have been breathing. This riff, right out of the gate from then-new guitarist Mark St. John, was all I needed to be sold on this guy. Again, decent melody and chorus, but the riff and Eric Carr's drums along with Paul's vocals sold it for me.

JOHN JANIK *(GENE SIMMONS MONEYBAG SODA)* – One of the most mind-melting openers to any KISS record! The band was back!! Paul's lyric, "kick it and break it" still makes me wanna destroy something with my foot!!!!

RAISE YOUR GLASSES:
A Celebration of 50 Years of KISS Songs
by Celebrities, Musicians & Fans.

Desmond Child with KISS

TONNY POONI *(PODCAST ROCK CITY)* – My KISS fandom started later than most. I was 14 when I first heard KISS. It was 1984 and MTV was showing these guys with girls all over them, some dude jumping through a hoop of fire, lots of grunts, etc. and I remember thinking to myself… that's what I want to do for the rest of my life. That December I pooled all my birthday and Christmas money and purchased my first set of albums. *Animalize* was part of that purchase. I got home, threw it on the turntable and when I heard the onslaught of guitar and vocals on the opening track… I instantly fell in love with "fast KISS" forever.

JOEY CASSATA *(ZO2, Z ROCK)* – Another incredible song to start off a KISS album. The last three have been fantastic… "Creatures of the Night", "Exciter", and now this! I always felt *Animalize* never got the credit it deserved. The Paul songs are some of the strongest of his career! This song has one of my favorite bridges ever! The melody with Eric's drum fills is absolutely mesmerizing!

HEAVEN'S ON FIRE

CHRIS JERICHO *(WRESTLER, FOZZY)* – I feel it's the best written song of the '80s, and one of the best choruses in rock 'n' roll history.

DESMOND CHILD *(SONGWRITER)* – I learned from Bob Crewe to write titles that have tension of opposites. Those kinds of titles write themselves. You mean hell's on fire? No – HEAVEN's on fire. That gave it a sexual double entendre. There's a lot of Stones in that song. I used that intro when I wrote Joan Jett's "I Hate Myself For Loving You".

JOE LYNN TURNER *(RAINBOW, YNGWIE MALMSTEEN)* –You can't beat collaborating with Desmond Child. I worked with him in the studio on several occasions and wrote a few songs for other artists... including a Bon Jovi tune that was never released for reasons unknown...

FRANKIE KAZARIAN *(WRESTLER)* – Paul opening this song the way he does is just so rock 'n' roll to me. Great hook, great verses, and such a cool and singable chorus. Just a great rock song. KISS at their best.

JOEL HOEKSTRA *(WHITESNAKE, TRANS-SIBERIAN ORCHESTRA)* – So, the non-makeup era section continues for me. What am I supposed to say here? Paul's opening bluesy vocal riff? Once again, the space in the verses lets the rock breathe! Then, BAM!!!!... you're hit with that magic KISS vocal sound in unison with the riff itself. The then-14-year-old me said… "THIS KICKS TOTAL ASS!"

DAVID JULIAN *(SONGWRITER)* – I first discovered KISS during *Creatures*, but most of my time listening was during the non-makeup era, beginning with *Lick it Up*. When *Animalize* came out I was totally hooked. I started playing guitar and formed a short-lived band with my brother on drums, and I made him play that song over and over again until he basically quit playing drums. Great times.

BURN BITCH BURN

CHRIS JERICHO *(WRESTLER, FOZZY)* – We used to laugh at that, and how bad the "I wanna put my log in your fireplace" was, but it's a pretty cool tune!"

CHRIS "THE WALLET" HAICK *(GENE SIMMONS MONEYBAG SODA)* – I was always a sucker for Gene's so-called filler songs (I never thought they were filler). When I was in my teen years, all I thought about was sex. I wanted to put my log in any girl's fireplace. I would honestly use this song to pump me up before hanging with girls hoping I'd get some tail. I had no game, so things never went my way, lol.

RAISE YOUR GLASSES:
A Celebration of 50 Years of KISS Songs
by Celebrities, Musicians & Fans.

Kuarantine on the Chris Jericho Cruise

JAY SCOTT *(THE HOOK ROCKS PODCAST)* – This song caused a battle between my parents and me. I played this one day with the volume turned all the way up and my freaked-out old-school catholic mother had a fit. After this I started a covert operation of hiding my music in my bedroom while also asking for a good set of headphones for my birthday.

SHANDON SAHM *(MEAT PUPPETS)* – OMG. Just awful. I about spit out whatever I was drinking at the time when I heard, "I wanna put my log in your fireplace." That lyric alone would make John Lennon jealous. Just kidding. Terrible and cringeworthy.

TODD KERNS *(BRUCE KULICK, SLASH)* – Now I will be flexing for Gene. It's too easy at this point in the band's journey to point out all of Paul's strengths. They were all on full display. I loved Gene's contributions during this phase. He gets flak for under-participating, but when Gene shows up, he shows up. This song has all the Spinal Tap-isms it gets ribbed for, but it is a no-apologies barn-burner from top to bottom. Yes, it's goofy. Yes, it's completely unacceptable by today's standards. But it is what most rock 'n' roll should be: Fun. Not enough is said about Gene's voice in the '80s. He shreds his vocal cords for us and it's glorious.

COURTNEY CRONIN DOLD *(COMEDIAN)* – I LOVE THE GUITAR at the top! OMG it is hot, "You know what I'm talking about". Paul at his best with his dancing, entrancing, sound barrier-lancing vocals. And oh oh my, that chorus! Those deep manly harmonies make this a fun one to sing in the car. But with the windows closed. You're gonna crack on those Paul parts, you know it.

Todd Kerns onstage with Bruce Kulick

GET ALL YOU CAN TAKE

MITCH WEISSMAN *(BEATLEMANIA, SONGWRITER)* – The song had about 10 verses to it that I kept writing. I wrote verse after verse until we whittled it down. It was Paul's idea eventually (to throw the F-bomb in there). We couldn't come up with "what (blank) difference does it make?" We came up with every word you could possibly think of and one night, we were on the phone for about two hours trying to think of what word it should be. Paul just said, "what fuckin' difference does it make" and he said, "this is what we're singing." Paul and I wrote that song with me on drums and him on guitar and then we would switch.

JASON BAKKEN *(COBRAS & FIRE PODCAST)* – Another boring-ass, side-one closer from Paul. Notable as I think it's the first use of the F word on a KISS song? Not enough to make it worth listening to. Fast forward and flip the cassette.

JEAN BEAUVOIR *(SONGWRITER)* – I like the groove because it's a little bit funky. Paul throws his vocals in and it offsets it.

CLAUDIO SPERA *(KISS ARMY NATION PODCAST)* – Paul's jangly riff is bombastic. It is a Led Zeppelin kind of tune. It has that groove. I love the ballsiness of the line, "What fuckin' difference does it make?" You can easily notice Mark St. John's style on lead guitar. His solo is something KISS fans were not used to. But I have to say, it fits with the song style and makes it flow. Really good song for a very interesting album during shaky times for the band.

Jean Beauvoir and Keith Leroux with Paul Stanley

LONELY IS THE HUNTER

TOM GIGLIOTTI *(SHOUT IT OUT LOUDCAST)* – This album is mostly deep cuts that don't appear anywhere else, and this song is no different. It has a really cool riff and a great vocal melody from Gene. Another catchy chorus makes this a go-to track for me on *Animalize*.

JOEY SASSO *(THE CIRCLE, NETFLIX)* – Now, picture this: KISS in the '80s, navigating uncharted waters as they evolve with the ever-shifting music scene. *Animalize* marked a new chapter for the band, steering away from their '70s roots into uncharted territory where they were now making it known that they were no longer the trendsetters they had been in the previous decade, but now fully committed to copying every current trend of the moment in an effort to survive more than thrive. "Lonely is the Hunter" captures this transition, showcasing a different side of KISS as they adapt to the changing musical landscape while still staying true to their rock 'n' roll roots. So yeah, maybe not a chart-topper, but a respectable addition to the band's journey through musical evolution. The track may not soar to greatness but still holds its ground solidly in the KISS catalog, while being super-interesting to show new KISS fans when schooling them on their KISStory.

JEFF TROTT *(ART DIRECTOR)* – This is why fans and critics often joke that Gene was asleep at the wheel during the '80s. These lyrics are just absurd. "Eggs in one basket but she threw me a bone"? It's hard not to cringe, especially compared to gems like "Log in the fireplace" from "Burn Bitch Burn." Despite the questionable songwriting, Bruce Kulick shines brilliantly here. I believe this marks Bruce's debut on a KISS album, and his signature sound is unmistakable. The tempo shift in the middle, leading into the solo, adds great energy. "Lonely is the Hunter" took some time to grow on me; it's not a track I immediately gravitate towards, but it has its own charm.

ZEUS *(SHOUT IT OUT LOUDCAST)* – This Gene deep cut is the first Bruce Kulick appearance on a KISS album. Bruce does what Bruce does – he makes every song better. However, I still don't get it. You have a new guitarist join the band, Mark St. John, and yet he doesn't play on the whole album, just like Vinnie didn't perform the solo on "Exciter" on *Lick it Up*. Regardless, I always liked this laid-back, sleazy song, especially Bruce's fills and solo.

RAISE YOUR GLASSES:
A Celebration of 50 Years of KISS Songs
by Celebrities, Musicians & Fans.

JOEY CASSATA *(ZO2, Z ROCK)* – This is actually a pretty good song with a catchy lyric. I remember one of my first real drum lessons I had, my instructor asked what I was currently listening to and I put on the *Animalize* album and showed him I could play "Heaven's on Fire" and "Thrills in the Night". He then said put on another song and try to play to it. I put on this and even though Eric is playing a straight groove, he's turning the beat around because of a measure of three. It was extremely confusing for me!!

UNDER THE GUN

CHRIS JERICHO *(WRESTLER, FOZZY)* – It is a fast KISS song; usually they don't work but people equate it with that *Animalize Live Uncensored* video. Paul just starts playing that riff after his amazing Eddie Van Halen-esque guitar solo. It's got great lyrics to it as well.

DESMOND CHILD *(SONGWRITER)* – Laughing at "Let's hit the highway doing 69". I mean honestly, it's very sophomoric, but that was the fun of it. Naughty little things that they can giggle at.

JEAN BEAUVOIR *(SONGWRITER)* – It's a fast one, and I love the groove and the double-kick on that. Eric Carr really kicked ass on that record. It was really good to play with it because as a bass player, that's the key. If you don't have that drummer that's really in the pocket, you're just never going to get that grooving. I really enjoyed working with him (Eric Carr).

MARK CICCHINI *(THREE SIDES OF THE COIN)* – KISS goes metal!!! Paul embraces his inner W.A.S.P. and goes full-bore

Blackie! Paul briefly rivals Gene for the stupidest lyrics ever on a KISS LP... "Let's hit the highway doing 69?" That makes "Burn Bitch Burn" seem like Shakespeare! Regardless, a kick-ass, full-bore '80s KISS rocker that could NEVER have been performed by the original band. The drumming and guitar solo are light years away from anything within Peter's or Ace's wheelhouse. Regardless, a fun song as KISS continued to chase trends.

THRILLS IN THE NIGHT

JOEY CASSATA *(ZO2, Z ROCK)* – This was actually the first full song I ever learned on the drums. I was 10 years old, and I had just gotten *Animalize* and Stryper's *Soldiers Under Command*. I learned "Thrills in the Night" & "Soldiers Under Command" over the same weekend. Weirdly, "Thrills in the Night" was more difficult for me to play. It had a pattern that I didn't quite understand yet. I am still anxiously waiting for someone to leak the unreleased video for this song!!

PASQUALE VARI *(KISS ARMY NATION PODCAST)* – In the early '80s, I checked out of KISS. I began to rediscover them in '89 and as I was listening to their '80s catalog for the very first time, "Thrills in the Night" quickly became one of my favorites. To this day, it's in my top 5 alongside "Detroit Rock City" and "I Stole Your Love", if you can believe that.

COURTNEY CRONIN DOLD *(COMEDIAN)* – Favorite song on *Animalize*. It's as mysterious as the girl in it, and the perfect song to put your makeup on to. The part where Paul sings, "... as she's walking around like a mystery" gives me chills in the night, every single time.

JEAN BEAUVOIR *(SONGWRITER)* – I like the subject, the mystery that I think the song creates in its vibe altogether. I like the groove. I really like the stuff that Paul and I did together because they always had a different groove. There was always a feeling with the bass line vs the guitar line. And I think the chorus is very catchy too. It was the first song I ever wrote.

Jean Beauvoir with Gene Simmons

KENNY BEGLEY *(KISS LIVE AUCTIONS)* – One of my favorite Paul songs ever. His voice was at this point is approaching the best it will ever be (from *Lick It Up* to *Revenge* is my favorite Paul voice).

WHILE THE CITY SLEEPS

MITCH WEISSMAN *(BEATLEMANIA, SONGWRITER)* – I had this riff and we would write and record demos together. It was pretty much my riff, and if you know the song "Wishing Well" by Free, you can hear it (hums riff). I like that song.

BRAD RUSTOVEN *(SLAMFEST PODCAST)* – I'm not sure why this song gets so much crap – I always thought it was Gene's best song on the album. Cool extended intro riff into a verse riff with lots of space. I love the dual vocals between Gene and Paul during the chorus and how they overlap with each other at times.

JASON BAKKEN *(COBRAS & FIRE PODCAST)* – I dig this song and I would've liked to have heard a second Mark St. John KISS album. Gene writing a song not about misogyny or sex or… both. Is a unicorn. Especially in the '80s. The main guitar progression that opens up the song is cool. Underrated singer that Gene.

TOM GIGLIOTTI *(SHOUT IT OUT LOUDCAST)* – *Animalize* is an album loaded with deep cuts. And most of them are the Gene songs. This is one of them and I will admit, I love it. The guitar groove during the verses is very cool, and the chorus is typical '80s sing-along style. I've always waved the flag for '80s Gene songs, and although I won't try to convince anyone that this is a classic, I've always liked it very much.

JOEY CASSATA *(ZO2, Z ROCK)* – OK, I will be honest, these next two songs are a few of the only songs that I really never listen to in the whole KISS catalog. This song feels like a throw away.

MURDER IN HIGH HEELS

TODD KERNS *(BRUCE KULICK, SLASH)* – A not-so-guilty pleasure. The Aerosmith riff. Of course, there is the inclusion of my friend Bruce Kulick on guitar on this song and "Lonely is the Hunter". Gene's spoken-word chorus is a killer. The broken-up, odd time signature at the end is very uncharacteristic but effective. Coulda been a *Done With Mirrors* Aerosmith track.

MITCH WEISSMAN *(BEATLEMANIA, SONGWRITER)* – I had the main riff. It was one of those songs from the closet. The way Gene and I worked together, he would orchestrate the songs and I would play the guitars and bass. We would sing the lyrics together and write it all down. I'm actually playing the guitars on that. It was me coming up with those guitar parts. When it came time to record the song, Gene was gone and doing the movie *Runaway* so I'm doing the bass parts and I'm doing it wrong. Jean Beauvoir had to play that part.

RAISE YOUR GLASSES:
A Celebration of 50 Years of KISS Songs
by Celebrities, Musicians & Fans.

Todd Kerns with Bruce Kulick

COURTNEY CRONIN DOLD *(COMEDIAN)* – High heels are murder on your toes but on this song I think Gene is talking about murdering some ass. That funky bass keeps me grooving and those silly Gene sexual innuendos keep me smiling.

TOM GIGLIOTTI *(SHOUT IT OUT LOUDCAST)* – As mentioned in my comments for "While the City Sleeps", this falls into that same category of Gene deep cuts that go unnoticed. This has such a sleazy, dirty groove to it, and you can tell Gene needed music to go along with the song title. Bruce Kulick makes an appearance on guitars, which is always a welcome addition to any KISS track. Now: the chorus on this one? Gene tries to make the song seem even dirtier when he growls the song title… IT'S MURDER.

JOEY CASSATA *(ZO2, Z ROCK)* – The music in this song is actually pretty cool. It's got a driving riff with a really nice groove. What's missing is melody!! The verse has no flow and no hook until the very brief pre-chorus. Then we get one of, if not the, worst chorus in KISStory!

CHAPTER 16

"ASYLUM"

Released: September 16, 1985

Asylum is a dynamic and energetic album that further solidified KISS's place in the '80s metal scene. With a lineup featuring Gene Simmons, Paul Stanley, Eric Carr, and Bruce Kulick, the album delivers a mix of anthemic rockers and melodic ballads.

RAISE YOUR GLASSES:
A Celebration of 50 Years of KISS Songs
by Celebrities, Musicians & Fans.

The track "Tears Are Falling" became a notable hit for KISS. Paul Stanley's emotive vocals and the infectious chorus made it a radio-friendly anthem, showcasing the band's ability to craft melodic rock tunes with mass appeal. The song's music video received heavy rotation on MTV, contributing to its success.

"Uh! All Night" is a high-energy rocker that exemplifies rock music of the time. With its catchy hooks, driving rhythm, and anthemic chorus, the track reflects KISS's commitment to delivering the kind of hard-hitting rock that resonated with audiences during this period.

While *Asylum* embraces the glam metal look and sound, it also features moments of diversity. "Who Wants to be Lonely" demonstrates KISS's ability to infuse emotional depth into their music. Gene Simmons's "Secretly Cruel" brings a dose of swagger and attitude, showcasing the band's ability to balance hard-hitting tracks with a touch of glam.

The album's cover art, featuring the band members against a vibrant and chaotic background, reflects the visual aesthetic of the glam metal era. The colorful and bold imagery aligns with the album's overall theme of energetic and larger-than-life rock.

In retrospect, *Asylum* remains a significant chapter in KISS's discography. *Asylum* stands as a testament to KISS's resilience and adaptability, showcasing their ability to thrive in the dynamic world of glam metal during the mid-1980s.

KING OF THE MOUNTAIN

BRUCE KULICK *(KISS)* – It's a scary song on lead guitar. I was petrified when we were going to open a set with it. On the *Asylum* record, at that time, everyone had adopted the Eddie Van Halen thing. Those techniques, I was absorbing them but I didn't always excel at them.

DESMOND CHILD *(SONGWRITER)* – Wrote this at Paul's apartment in New York. It's got the KISS brand, bigger than life. What could be bigger than king of the mountain.

CHRIS JERICHO *(WRESTLER, FOZZY)* – The rumor is that Eric was just messing around and warming up at the beginning of the song and they liked it so much, they kept it. The middle section is something from an early '70s Rush song, almost prog rock, and I've always liked that. You can't go wrong with any Paul vocal from that era. He was at the peak of his power.

BRYCE MILETO *(SISTERS DOLL)* – That intro… c'mon. What a tune! R.I.P to the late great Eric Carr.

TODD KERNS *(BRUCE KULICK, SLASH)* – KISS was always dependable on a great opener, and this song might be top 5. Just a slayer of an opening track. The thunder of the late, great Eric Carr right out of the gate, Paul singing with more conviction than ever, and officially introducing Mr. Kulick on lead guitar. Big vocals. Big guitars. HUGE chorus. A+ '80s RAWK! *Asylum* is definitely one of the best non-makeup KISS albums.

Zach Throne, Brent Fitz, Todd Kerns and Bruce Kulick

KENT SLUCHER *(LUKE BRYAN, KUARANTINE)* – Any song that starts with a drum solo gets my vote :). Overall, a musical masterpiece and Bruce plays an incredible solo as usual. The prechorus sets up the choruses perfectly. The perfect non-makeup KISS tune in my opinion. Again… Paul's vocals were untouchable.

ANY WAY YOU SLICE IT

BRUCE KULICK *(KISS)* – We tried playing this live once during the first show, and never again. The band wasn't really feeling it.

JOEY CASSATA *(ZO2, Z ROCK)* – If I've said it once, I'll say it a thousand times, Gene's songs from the '80s are very underrated!! I know it's been commonly said that Gene was checked out during the

'80s, but I call bullshit!! Yes, Gene didn't have a strong showing on *Animalize*, but his songs on *Lick it Up*, *Asylum*, *Crazy Nights* and *Hot in the Shade* are fantastic.

Bruce Kulick, Joey Cassata and Ace Frehley at KISS Cancer Goodbye

MARTIN POPOFF *(AUTHOR)* – I couldn't bring myself to include anything from *Crazy Nights* or *Hot in the Shade*, but I've always dug *Asylum*, even if it's the Paul songs that elevate it. But here we are at track two with Gene singing high up his range on a party rocker that takes us back to a *Lick it Up* vibe. Of note, "Secretly Cruel" from this album made my honorable mentions, but neither is quite at "King of the Mountain," "Who Wants to be Lonely" or "Tears Are Falling" levels, all of which are Paul tracks.

STEVE WRIGHT *(PODDER THAN HELL PODCAST)* – Choppy chug at the start to the very catchy riff once the band gets going. Kind of high vocals for Gene. I love the sound of the guitars here, some really cool riffing. Great background vocals. The transition from the chorus back to the verse is very well done. Eric Carr has some amazing drum fills throughout the song. Bruce Kulick really shows off his chops with this kick-ass solo that totally fits the song but doesn't overdo it. Very tasteful. We even get a bluesy ending, which is kind of weird but cool at the same time. Fantastic deep track.

IZZY PRESLEY *(MUSICIAN, COMIC)* – "Gene's stuff in the '80s sucked". "Gene wasn't there". "Gene looked like Phyllis Diller". OK that last one may be true. In all honesty, Gene's '80s stuff is VERY underrated. This song is proof of that. Great vocal, driving guitars, Bruce shines. *Asylum* rules. Get your heads out your backside cavities and appreciate Gene in all of his '80s glory!

TOM GIGLIOTTI *(SHOUT IT OUT LOUDCAST)* – Gene's entire '80s catalog of songs is pretty much all deep cuts since the '80s was Paul's decade. That being said, anyone sleeping on Gene's songs are missing out, and this is absolutely one of them. Great groove, awesome bridge and a great call and response chorus. A killer Bruce solo and a very cool breakdown make this one of the standouts on *Asylum*. Sadly, it gets buried due to the all the classic Paul songs from the album. So let me be your king bee, I want your hornet's nest!

WHO WANTS TO BE LONELY

DESMOND CHILD *(SONGWRITER)* – This is my favorite KISS song. Love Jean Beauvoir. He broke the mold and broke barriers. What made this song is the bass line, because he's a bass player and he had that funky bass part. This has what Paul and I love – that

Motown driving bass line that later shows up on stuff I worked on with Bon Jovi. Who wants to be lonely? Nobody, that's the answer to that. Now we have the phone, and we are never lonely.

CHRIS JERICHO *(WRESTLER, FOZZY)* – It's one of my favorite KISS songs and it was never actually a single.

JEAN BEAUVOIR *(SONGWRITER)* – First of all, a lot of people can relate to a song like that. You don't have to go any further than that. I've had such a hard time trying to find bass players to play that song properly. But Gene is a very good bass player. I'm a fan of his and his playing. Some of the songs that he's singing and playing at the same time is not easy. I felt an honor that I got a chance to be a part of history and playing bass on KISS albums.

Doc McGhee and Jean Beauvoir with Paul Stanley

RAISE YOUR GLASSES:
A Celebration of 50 Years of KISS Songs
by Celebrities, Musicians & Fans.

AUSTIN MILETO *(SISTERS DOLL)* – A solid and killer drum beat! The guitar solo by Bruce on this song is nothing but top notch.

LISA LANE KULICK *(BRUCE KULICK'S WIFE)* – This kick-ass song, with its galloping guitar riffs, hooked me as soon as I first heard it. Even though the band never performed it live, the video of Paul walking through a steamed-filled tunnel, wearing his "Tears Are Falling" robe and hot-pink fringed gloves, will always visually stand out as the perfect '80s KISS image and the soundtrack of my young adult life.

JOEY TASSO *(THE CIRCLE, NETFLIX)* – The KISS catalog has many songs that could have been massive hits if performed by any other band. "Who Wants to be Lonely" is a prime example of this. Although "Tears Are Falling" was the big hit from *Asylum*, "Who Wants to be Lonely" is just a great song overall, KISS or not. As time has passed, more people have come to embrace this song as a lost hit and recognize it for what it truly is. It is a shame that Paul wasn't more vocal about his thoughts and feelings on this song and didn't find more opportunities to play it. If *Asylum* had a more popular band name on the cover, it would have been one of the highest-selling albums of the period. With "Who Wants to be Lonely", "Tears Are Falling", and "Trial By Fire", *Asylum* should have been one of the best-selling albums in the band's catalog, with "Who Wants to be Lonely" surpassing the biggest hit of the decade, *Lick it Up*. If '80s KISS was truly Paul's band and he was calling all the shots, then "Who Wants to be Lonely" represents the pinnacle of what he was able to achieve during that time.

HAL SPARKS *(COMEDIAN)* – One of my favorite KISS riffs. This song always gets turned up when it comes on. I was psyched to see it was co-written with Paul by Jean Beauvoir. I really dug "Feel The Heat" on the *Cobra* soundtrack, which led me to his *Drums Along the Mohawk* record.

DAVID JULIAN *(SONGWRITER)* – I really liked *Asylum* and this song was a standout for me. I would later go on to mix a version with Jean Beauvoir singing the song for a charity project. A huge honor given he co-wrote the song, and his vocals on the charity track sounded killer!

TRIAL BY FIRE

JOEY SASSO *(THE CIRCLE, NETFLIX)* – It's interesting how many people tend to focus on Gene's absence during the '80s, but very few acknowledge the other side of Gene during that decade. The part of him that would suddenly appear out of nowhere and deliver some of the most exceptional tracks of the era. One such example is "Trial By Fire." The song is a testament to Gene's immense talent and musical prowess. It's hard not to love it. Gene's highs during the '80s far outweigh the lows, and "Trial By Fire" is a perfect example of that. But, there's one more song off *Asylum* that surpasses it.

MARK CICCHINI *(THREE SIDES OF THE COIN)* – I love this song despite it containing some of the elements of '80s hair metal that I despise (a soulless drum intro that a four-year-old could play, stupid, unnecessary gang vocals where they are not needed, and a paint-by-number arrangement). With that said? One of the better

Gene songs of the era, but that doesn't say much. I wish I could magically present this song to the band circa 1975 and give them a shot at it. Why? Because I think the song is really good but the era when it was recorded? Uh, not so much.

METAL MIKE *(80's GLAM METALCAST)* – Feels like '70s KISS seeped into this one a bit. One of my favorite '80s Gene tracks from the first KISS album I ever bought! It's got a hard driving beat and chug that complements Gene's rebellious lyrics. Watch out for that huge monstrous chorus!

COURTNEY CRONIN DOLD *(COMEDIAN)* – ONE OF MY ALL-TIME FAVORITE KISS SONGS. This song is everything. Starts hot and never quits, and that guitar! Fun chorus that you can sing along to, and the best part is the band asks us in unison... "Just who do you think you are!?" Someone who loves this song.

JOEY CASSATA *(ZO2, Z ROCK)* – What a fun song! Gene is full of hook and melody on this song. Something that was definitely missing in a few of his *Animalize* songs.

I'M ALIVE

DESMOND CHILD *(SONGWRITER)* – Paul's title, that's like KISS brand, upbeat, powerful, in charge, victorious. That's the signature of KISS, because we as human beings need to hear that.

RAISE YOUR GLASSES:
A Celebration of 50 Years of KISS Songs
by Celebrities, Musicians & Fans.

PAULIE Z *(ZO2, Z ROCK)* – To me this song has a Van Halen feel to it, from the drum intro to the guitar riff and the vocal approach Paul takes. Even that falsetto high note at the end of the bridge had that Diamond Dave quality to it. All that being said, it still sounds like a KISS song, which is a testament to their ability to put their stamp on everything they do.

ZEUS *(SHOUT IT OUT LOUDCAST)* – "Fast KISS" is back and this time Bruce takes the lead. This song has everything: Desmond Child, great chorus, Bruce's sizzling guitar and solo and fun, silly and cheesy '80s lyrics, like "Man if it kills me, I know that I'll go, dead, stiff and smiling." Man, Paul was in his element in the 1980s.

Paulie Z winning a $20 bet from Gene Simmons

IZZY PRESLEY *(MUSICIAN, COMIC)* – Rumor and innuendo would tell us that Gene wanted Edward and Alex Van Halen in the band. This is the song that sounds like that would have sounded. Bruce SHINES on this song and Eric Carr was in beast mode. Fast and driving like a great hard rock song should be. Another great Paul vocal.

JOEY CASSATA *(ZO2, Z ROCK)* – I LOVE the drum intro by Eric! Taken straight from his solo during those years. This is the *Asylum* "Fast KISS song". Like I mentioned earlier, I think KISS felt they needed one of these on every album. It's an OK song, I just wish that I could hear Eric's drums better. The drum production on Asylum is terrible. Eric is doing so much double-bass work that is just getting buried.

LOVE'S A DEADLY WEAPON

BRUCE KULICK *(KISS)* – A very guitar-driven track!

CHRIS JERICHO *(WRESTLER, FOZZY)* – You really listen to it, it's really intricate. There's lots of different parts. Almost "proggy" at times. But it's also very fast.

JOEY CASSATA *(ZO2, Z ROCK)* – *Asylum* is a much heavier KISS record than people give it credit for. Partly because of the singles and mostly because of the stage outfits. People tend to listen with their eyes sometimes. This is a great song that has so many incredible parts. When I had to learn this to play with Chris Jericho's Kuarantine, it kicked my ass!! There's a turnaround in the middle that is very prog-like. I actually think it might have been a mistake when they recorded it and then they just went with it.

WES BEECH *(THE PLASMATICS)* – Of course I have to include the song I originally wrote for Wendy O. Williams called "Party" from her second solo album, *Kommander of Kaos*. I wrote it in the vein of Motörhead, so was surprised when Gene appropriated it for the *Asylum* album. He was slated to produce Wendy's follow-up to the *W.O.W.* album, but scheduling conflicts got in the way so he had to bow out. He came down to a rehearsal and heard the song and said "I like that. I think I'll use it." He changed the main riff a little and put the words from another KISS demo, "Deadly Weapons", to it and it became kind of a speed metal song. Eric's drums are like thunder and Bruce just shreds on it. Long overlooked by KISS fans, it has taken on new popularity, helped perhaps by Chris Jericho's band Kuarantine's recent cover. Gene is in full Demon mode on it, and the band rips through it like someone's chasing them! When I saw Bruce backstage on the *Asylum* tour he told me it was a "great song, but too fast for Paul to play live." Gene's solo band has played it on a few occasions.

Joey Cassata and Chris Jericho on the Chris Jericho Cruise

TOM GIGLIOTTI *(SHOUT IT OUT LOUDCAST)* – Another Gene song from *Asylum* that gets no love from most fans. Maybe because it's "Fast KISS" and doesn't have the melody that we come to expect from their '80s music. But the song rips! Bruce delivers an insanely heavy but melodic riff and Gene's vocals soar. When our buddies from Kuarantine covered this, they gave it new life and introduced it to fans who may not have already appreciated it.

TEARS ARE FALLING

PJ FARLEY *(TRIXTER, FOZZY)* – Even the video couldn't hurt this song. Just a standout track with another GREAT guitar solo by Bruce. One of my favorites from that era.

JEAN BEAUVOIR *(SONGWRITER)* – That's a really good song, a REALLY good song. I remember when Paul played that for me in his apartment and I was like, "Hey, that's a hit!".

JOE LYNN TURNER *(RAINBOW, YNGWIE MALMSTEEN)* –Paul did an excellent job of writing and performance on this one!

JOHN JANIK *(GENE SIMMONS MONEYBAG SODA)* – On spring break of '86 with my family at a resort in Florida, all the kids were playing at the pool. Not me. I was inside repeatedly calling *Dial MTV* voting for this song. Still love the song and video to this day!!!!

CHARLIE PARRA *(KUARANTINE)* – Fun thing is the whole song has got three chords, no bridge and it's still a perfect hard rock track. That guitar solo by master Bruce Kulick is still to this day not matched by anyone who dares to play it. Not even the longest-time guitar player in KISStory has ever nailed it. Bruce is untouchable in this one. The lyrics, chorus and Paul's vocals in his absolute prime make it my favorite (or at least in my top 3) non-makeup-era song.

PJ Farley doing his best Paul Stanley

ACE VON JOHNSON *(FASTER PUSSYCAT, L.A. GUNS)* – Peak '80s KISS at its finest. Kulick doesn't get the credit he deserves, but his skill still shines even 40 years later. I love the chorus, and will break out singing it anytime someone mentions "shedding a tear". I think they mastered the art of making a heartbreak still sound like a good time, as only KISS can.

BETH-AMI HEAVENSTONE *(GRAHAM BONNET BAND)* – I love this song. I love that video with that pretty girl and she's crying, I feel that. KISS is more than just music, it's theatre, it's a Broadway show, and I just love KISS.

SECRETLY CRUEL

TOM GIGLIOTTI *(SHOUT IT OUT LOUDCAST)* – People always go to Paul during the non-makeup era, and for good reason. But Gene has some amazing songs during this era that get buried because they weren't singles or videos. This is such an awesome upbeat rocker with a really cool gang-style chorus. *Asylum* has such a great sound thanks to Bruce's amazing guitar work, but this song is another from Gene that deserves more attention!

CHRIS JERICHO *(WRESTLER, FOZZY)* – Another one I could see Kuarantine doing at some point. Once again, Gene's porn lyrics. I'm in, it's KISS, it's Gene. Great chorus, super-catchy. I always had this prejudice against Gene songs because I was such a Paul guy. But *Asylum* is a great record from top to bottom. There isn't a bad song on it, and Gene's stuff is really cool. This is probably the best of his four songs on the album.

STEVEN MICHAEL *(GROWIN' UP ROCK PODCAST)* – To me this riff seems like it could have fit right in on *Rock and Roll Over*. It has an old-school KISS feel. The chorus is a little lazy, but still not bad. I like that some of the verses are in harmony. I like the break coming out of the solo.

RAISE YOUR GLASSES:
A Celebration of 50 Years of KISS Songs
by Celebrities, Musicians & Fans.

JASON BAKKEN *(COBRAS & FIRE PODCAST)* – A little "Mr. Speed" flavor to kick this song off. Paul likes to crap on Gene's work in the '80s, but his songs hold up better than a lot of Paul's. Here Gene tells the tale of a groupie skipping the foreplay. The lyrics have the subtlety of porn dialogue. Actually, it may be porn dialogue.

JOEY SASSO *(THE CIRCLE, NETFLIX)* – "Secretly Cruel" is undoubtedly the best Gene tune off *Asylum* and deserves to be recognized as one of the top KISS songs of the decade. The song brilliantly infuses Gene's iconic '70s style with contemporary elements, resulting in an instant classic. Whenever I listen to it, I can't help but imagine what the '70s version would sound like, and I can feel the raw energy that it would have had. "Secretly Cruel" showcases Gene's versatility and proves that he can excel in other styles apart from his Demon persona. Personally, I never get tired of listening to this track. As a proud member of the '80s Gene cult, I firmly believe that if Gene had remained focused on his music, he could have given Paul a real competition for the top spot.

RADAR FOR LOVE

DESMOND CHILD *(SONGWRITER)* – I may have had the title. There's something sci-fi about it. Like '60s sci-fi. I really love this song.

SONNY POONI *(PODCAST ROCK CITY)* – First, let me point out… *Asylum* is my favorite KISS album. Now that you've recovered from that… read on. Even though the record has some great classic "Fast KISS" hits, I've always loved "Radar for Love". I remember folks telling me in '85 that the song was a Led Zeppelin rip-off, but I didn't even know who Led Zeppelin was at that time... so I didn't care. Yes... I now know who Led Zeppelin is, and guess what... I still don't care. This song rocks!

TOM GIGLIOTTI *(SHOUT IT OUT LOUDCAST)* – The rare Paul deep cut from *Asylum*, and if you're a fan of Led Zeppelin, you have to be a fan of this one. Paying homage to the classic start/stop riffing of "Black Dog", the song has become a favorite of mine over the years, and Paul's voice suits it very well. The bridge into the chorus reminds us of the incredible melodies that Paul delivers all the time.

JOEY CASSATA *(ZO2, Z ROCK)* – Fantastic song! Great riff by Bruce, followed by a fun Zeppelin-type vocal by Paul in the chorus. Throw in a Bon Jovi pre-chorus and an anthemic chorus and you have all the ingredients for a killer tune.

UH! ALL NIGHT

DESMOND CHILD *(SONGWRITER)* – It was like caveman talk: this is well-branded for KISS. That was Paul all the way. Just writing these songs taught me everything about stadium anthems. This is a song you know when Paul sings, "Uh!" you're gonna throw your fist in the air. It's an automatic response. Like kicking someone in the balls, you know how they are going to respond. "Uh!" means "fuck", but we didn't dirty the song making it unplayable, unlike 30 years later.

RAISE YOUR GLASSES:
A Celebration of 50 Years of KISS Songs by Celebrities, Musicians & Fans.

Evan Stanley, Nick Simmons and Desmond Child

COURTNEY CRONIN DOLD *(COMEDIAN)* – The pre-chorus is so good it makes me want to "Uh" for at least 10 minutes. I know what 'Uh" meant in 1985, but now in 2023 the only time KISS can go "Uh! All night" is alone, on the toilet.

JOEY SASSO *(THE CIRCLE, NETFLIX)* – It's time to face the truth: deep down, we all love it when Paul Stanley turns up the corniness to unprecedented levels. And there's no shame in admitting it. This song is the perfect example of how Paul can make even the cheesiest material work without playing it up for laughs. When he commits to a song, he goes all in, and he hardly ever misses. "Uh! All Night" is one of those forgotten songs that deserves more recognition. Yes, the title is dumb, and yes, Paul talks about people doing time for the hundredth time. But that's what makes it a quintessential '80s KISS tune. Don't overthink it. Just let go and enjoy the ride. *Asylum* is a fantastic '80s KISS album, and "Uh! All Night" is one of its highlights. So let's stop judging it.

CHRIS JERICHO *(WRESTLER, FOZZY)* – It's a great Paul song but it's not a very talked-about Paul song. It very much goes into his Zeppelin influence. It's kind of like "Black Dog". It's got this kind of real snakey riff, and then it stops and it's just vocal. I like that tune. It's not my favorite Paul song, but I appreciate where he's coming from because I know what he was thinking when he wrote it. Like I said, this is a real Jimmy Page-type of a riff. And if you're into that, it's very cool.

JEAN BEAUVOIR *(SONGWRITER)* – Paul and I spent a lot of time in the clubs, and females were quite on our mind. So you start thinking about things and you come up with a song like "Uh! All Night". It is over-the-top, it's fantasy. Rock 'n' roll to me is supposed to be fantasy, and I think that that's one of the reasons why they're as successful as they are – because it creates another world for people to be able to go to for a minute and get out of the realities.

NICHOLAS BUCKLAND *(AUTHOR, Hottest Brand in the Land)* – Paul's ode to a "work/life balance" is big, dumb and an absolutely perfect piece of '80s hard rock. His buddy Jean Beauvoir filled in for an absent Mr. Simmons and you can hear the stark difference stylistically; the bass line practically bounces along in the verses as though the instrument itself is racing upstairs to jump in on all the night-time fun…

RAISE YOUR GLASSES:
A Celebration of 50 Years of KISS Songs by Celebrities, Musicians & Fans.

PJ Farley and Chris Jericho with Gene Simmons, *An Evening with Gene Simmons*, May 7, 2023

JASON BAKKEN *(COBRAS & FIRE PODCAST)* – There is very little on *Asylum* worth listening to. Including this turd. Catchy chorus and a freaking guitar clinic put on by new member Bruce Kulick. The solo is worth your time. Dammit. As bad as this song is, it's a good hurt.

JEFF TROTT *(ART DIRECTOR)* – When I think of the KISS *Exposed* home video, other than the pool scene a few things come to mind. Gene spitting blood, "cut her out" and "Uh! All Night." *Asylum* is a fantastic album that has gained a lot of respect in recent years due to Bruce's band playing several of the tracks on the KISS Kruise. "Uh! All Night" captures the '80s sleaze and energetic rock 'n' roll persona. It's a testament to Paul's commanding presence as a front man and Bruce Kulick's growing influence within the band.

RAISE YOUR GLASSES:
A Celebration of 50 Years of KISS Songs
by Celebrities, Musicians & Fans.

CHAPTER 17

"CRAZY NIGHTS"

Released: September 18, 1987

Crazy Nights is an album that encapsulates KISS's foray into the excesses of the late-1980s glam metal scene. Filled with anthemic choruses, catchy melodies, and polished production, the album includes hits like "Crazy Crazy Nights" and "Reason to Live." While the album showcases a more commercial and accessible side of KISS, it also sparked divisive opinions due to its departure from the band's traditional hard rock roots.

The title track, "Crazy Crazy Nights," serves as the album's energetic anthem. With its upbeat tempo, infectious hooks, and optimistic lyrics, the song perfectly captures the spirit of the era's glam metal scene. The accompanying music video, featuring the band's dynamic performance, added to the song's popularity and commercial success.

"Reason to Live" is a power ballad that showcased KISS's versatility. Paul Stanley's emotive vocals and the song's anthemic quality contributed to its success, marking a balance between the band's hard-hitting image and a more melodic, radio-friendly approach.

While *Crazy Nights* received commercial success and contributed to KISS's visibility, it faced criticism for deviating from the band's classic hard rock sound by (over-)relying on a keyboard-driven sound. Some fans and critics viewed the album as a departure from the raw and edgier elements that characterized KISS's earlier works, expressing concerns about the band's evolution in the glam metal landscape.

Crazy Nights remains a polarizing entry in KISS's discography. While some appreciate the album's catchy and accessible tracks, others view it as a departure from the band's roots. Regardless, it stands as a testament to KISS's adaptability and their willingness to explore different musical territories during a period of significant change in the rock music landscape. *Crazy Nights* captures a moment in KISS's history when they navigated the evolving sounds of glam metal, leaving an indelible mark on the band's trajectory.

CRAZY CRAZY NIGHTS

BRENNAN MILETO *(SISTERS DOLL)* – This song holds my favorite lyric from any KISS song. "If life is a radio turn up to 10" – that lyric sums KISS up perfectly. The way they preach positivity and living life to the fullest is an amazing thing and something I love relating to. This song is everything a good song should be.

ADAM MITCHELL *(SONGWRITER)* – The thing I love about "Crazy Crazy Nights" - well, apart from the fact that it was a big hit and still gets played around the world – is that it really is a complete song. A songwriter's song. And I would say this even if I hadn't co-written it with Paul. It's a song that really stands on its own apart from being a KISS song. We had written it as a big arena-rock anthem, and it kills that way. But if you look at how many other versions of it there are – wow, it's amazing. Not just covers of it as an up-tempo rocker, but slow versions that are really, really good and make the song sound as if it had been written to be slow and moody. That's the sign of a great song – when it can be recorded with so many different ways and attitudes and still work. And the other sign of a great song is longevity; "Crazy Crazy Nights" still gets played all the time. I was in Rome recently and there was even a poster of "Crazy Crazy Nights" right outside the Hard Rock Cafe. I took a pic and texted it to Paul. When we sat down to write and he described to me this idea he had for a big arena rocker, we probably had no idea what a classic it would turn out to be.

RAISE YOUR GLASSES:
A Celebration of 50 Years of KISS Songs by Celebrities, Musicians & Fans.

Adam Mitchell with Paul Stanley

DARREN PALTROWITZ *(AUTHOR, How David Lee Roth Changed The World)* – This track is a divisive one within the KISS fanbase as its lyrics are over-the-top positive, the production is incredibly polished, and it has a spoken-word middle section, almost like a song written for an after-school TV special. The frequent key changes also push it further into wimpy territory. But at the end of the day, a sing-along chorus you remember long after you heard it is a great chorus, and this song has a chorus that is hard to forget. The underlying message of its lyrics – to ignore your critics, keep pushing forward and go where the love is – also is universal and applicable. The epitome of a guilty pleasure. And once sang at me impromptu by AFI's Davey Havok during an interview we taped via Zoom.

FRANKIE KAZARIAN *(WRESTLER)* – Another rock anthem from the kings of that topic. Unapologetic lyrics, "They try to tell us, we don't belong / That's alright, we're millions strong / This is my music, it makes me proud / These are my people, and this is my crowd". With lyrics and songs like this, it's no wonder this band has had a literal army following them for so long.

MURPH *(SHOUT IT OUT LOUDCAST)* – Before I heard this track, the last KISS song that grabbed my attention was "I Was Made for Lovin' You." I had forgotten about the band, but this was my reintroduction to KISS. While I did not pay any attention to the rest of the album, this will always be the song that I will say started me off as a KISS fan.

I'LL FIGHT HELL TO HOLD YOU

CHRIS JERICHO *(WRESTLER, FOZZY)* – Another great Bruce solo. Awesome lyrics. Awesome tune.

ADAM MITCHELL *(SONGWRITER)* – Wow. Not having listened to it for a while, this track is really special. It starts like it's coming from another planet! And Bruce's guitar intro is just phenomenal. One of my favorite things he ever played. I think it might've been at that point I realized that if I went home and practiced really hard for 200 years, I still wouldn't play that good! And Paul's vocal, it's phenomenal. Once again, singing higher and better than seems humanly possible.

JOE McGINNESS *(KUARANTINE, KLASSIC '78)* – In my opinion this could've easily been a huge hit for KISS. I love the chord progression and guitar solos. Every time I pick up my guitar I end up playing parts of this song as a warm up. Another underrated track from *Crazy Nights*.

TOMMY SOMMERS *(THREE SIDES OF THE COIN)* – I felt at this point, KISS was chasing other bands and trends. I was not a huge fan of the production of this particular record, but the guitar solo in this song and the incredible vocal performance by Paul make this another song that I have in heavy rotation. I can easily say it's my favorite of all the non-makeup songs.

JEFF TROTT *(ART DIRECTOR)* – "I'll Fight Hell to Hold You" emerges as one of Paul's most powerful performances from the '80s, with its epic build-up and soaring vocals. I'm not comparing this to *Destroyer* by any means, but at the end of "Detroit Rock City" you hear the buzz, and it goes right in the "King of the Night Time World". I get that same feeling when "Crazy Crazy Nights" is fading out and boom, "I'll Fight Hell to Hold You" starts with a bang and Bruce's ripping guitar punches you right in the face.

MARK CICCHINI *(THREE SIDES OF THE COIN)* – Paul's vocals on this track are nothing short of gymnastic! I really dig Eric's drum part and Bruce's tasty licks throughout. The chorus is strong and the verses passionate... quintessential '80s era Paul Stanley! One of the better tracks off this underachieving LP.

BANG BANG YOU

DESMOND CHILD *(SONGWRITER)* – My favorite song growing up was Cher's "Bang Bang". I brought this in with Paul. Then later I wrote "She Bangs".

RAISE YOUR GLASSES:
A Celebration of 50 Years of KISS Songs
by Celebrities, Musicians & Fans.

CHRIS JERICHO *(WRESTLER, FOZZY)* – I really like the chorus. I like the callback with the "I'll shoot you down with my love gun baby". I love the breakdown where it's got that guitar riff. I just really love that little part. It reminds me of like a Matthias Jabs part that he would do in the Scorpions, this little kind of background riff that really becomes the main riff. Is it a stupid song title? Of course it is. It's 1987 and it's KISS.

JEFF TROTT *(ART DIRECTOR)* – "Bang Bang You" – a modern-day "Love Gun" for the time? Well, not exactly, and let's not get crazy. But is there anything more '80s than "Bang Bang You"? Every time I hear that song it takes me back to the Paul stage rant / intro on the *Crazy Nights* tour. It's too bad this song is the butt of many KISS jokes and doesn't give the credit to Bruce Kulick that he deserves. It's a testament to Bruce Kulick's contributions to KISS's sound during the *Crazy Nights* era.

TOM GIGLIOTTI *(SHOUT IT OUT LOUDCAST)* – Sometimes KISS has a song that makes you laugh and smile but also reminds you why you love this band. Are the title and most of the lyrics the kind of cheese we've all come to know and love? Of course, and that's why I love this song. The callback to "Love Gun" is a nice touch, and Paul is definitely making sure you know what's on his mind here. The Bruce solo with Paul's little vocal breakdown is undeniable. Don't take everything so seriously and enjoy this piece of pop cheese!

ERNIE PALOOZA *(TOP 5 WITH JOEY CASSATA)* – The background vocals in the chorus are very BOOMBASTICAL! I like the production trick they are using to make it sound so big. The riff in the verse is very '70s KISS and almost goes to AC/DC land, and the drums really get to breathe.

NO NO NO

BRUCE KULICK *(KISS)* – Eric Carr and I were totally into the Van Halen vibe and we knew there was going to be this double-bass drum thing. We realized we were going to kind of do this homage to Van Halen. A music review thought the intro was done by a keyboard.

CHRIS JERICHO *(WRESTLER, FOZZY)* – I never really got it until we played it (with Kuarantine). It's a really hard song, it's difficult. Gene sings off-time. There's some weird time signatures to it. He jumps in at weird places. That's when I started realizing the musicianship of '80s KISS. How are they starting with this crazy guitar solo? It's a tour de force, a riff-tastic tune that I respect way more now.

LORETTA CARAVELLO *(ERIC CARR'S SISTER)* – I like the beginning of the song with Bruce and Eric going back and forth. I wish there was more of that. That was awesome. It was such timing and blends perfectly.

ZEUS *(SHOUT IT OUT LOUDCAST)* – What an opening. Bruce is given a chance to shine and of course he nails it. He kills this whole song, including the solo. I also love Gene's vocals as well. His delivery and phrasing are perfect. Always liked this song, but I love how Chris Jericho and his band Kuarantine picked this as their first song to record; it charted well and brought some good attention to this Gene deep cut.

Loretta Caravello with Eric Carr

SONNY POONI *(PODCAST ROCK CITY)* – The first 47 seconds of this song are Bruce Kulick's forever business card for rock/metal guitar. There were a ton of shredders in the '80s but Bruce had both the shredding ability and the feel. He did a great job of showing off when it was appropriate and played to make the song better when appropriate. There were some guitarists that KISS had that didn't quite understand that. Also, every time someone says that Gene's '80s songs sucked, I say "No, No, No", they don't. Get it? LOL.

HELL OR HIGH WATER

BRUCE KULICK *(KISS)* – I gave Gene that title and had most of the music. At first, he sang it differently. I knew it was something that would work for us, and thankfully Ron Nevison liked it and it wound up on the album.

ZEUS *(SHOUT IT OUT LOUDCAST)* – An underrated '80s Gene track. This is Gene's sexy voice. Lowering his voice but without the growl. It works because of his delivery. Written by Gene and Bruce. The pre-chorus with the harmonies is excellent. The chorus is great as well. Bruce's solo is sweet. He has a great tone on this track. The call-back at the end is great between Gene and the band. Bruce is ripping it on the outro.

CHRIS CZYNSZAK *(DECIBEL GEEK PODCAST)* – With *Crazy Nights* being my gateway album, I've only grown fonder of it over the years. Gene's vocal delivery is much different on this album, and I think it serves it well. While lyrically it's pretty pedestrian, the guitar work from Bruce Kulick really shines, especially the guitar solo. I think it's one of his best.

ROBERT CONTE *(AUTHOR)* – *Crazy Nights* was released just after I started my senior year of high school. I bought it at Record World after class, and then, with my buddy Joe, conducted a song-by-song analysis. He read the lyrics to me from the inner sleeve as my picture disc did not include it. We both agreed that, lyrically, this was the worst Gene song; it felt disingenuous coming from someone who long declared sleeping with thousands of women. Now he missed one particular female and felt lonely and despondent without her...? Really?! Later I speculated this was likely a love song penned for his partner of 40-plus years, Shannon Tweed.

JASON HERNDON *(KISS MY WAX PODCAST)* – More pop/rock perfection with Gene's smooth voice. This was my favorite from

Crazy Nights the moment I first heard it. There are really some incredible and overlooked songs from this album.

MY WAY

BRUCE KULICK *(KISS)* – I remember when we cut it, and I thought it was a bit operatic, like a show tune.

CHRIS JERICHO *(WRESTLER, FOZZY)* – It's such a high song, possibly Paul's highest vocals. It's got the great Paul Stanley lyrics to just believe in yourself and just do what you can to survive. That song is insanely high. Great solo. Love that one.

DESMOND CHILD *(SONGWRITER)* – Along the same lines as "I'm Alive", powerful and upbeat. I wrote this with Paul, and Bruce Turgeon may have come in before or after I wrote with Paul. Sometimes you jump into a song at any point. Like we say, it takes the Village People.

JOEY CASSATA *(ZO2, Z ROCK)* – I absolutely love everything about this song! The message, the music and of course the insanely high Paul Stanley vocals. KISS to me was always about believing in yourself and not listening to what other people thought. "I'm gonna talk like I talk and walk like I walk… MY WAY".

RAISE YOUR GLASSES:
A Celebration of 50 Years of KISS Songs
by Celebrities, Musicians & Fans.

Joey Cassata, Joe McGinness, Todd Kerns and Bruce Kulick

CLAUDIO SPERA *(KISS ARMY NATION PODCAST)* – KISS's sound during the '85-'87 years drifted apart from the hard rock guitar-driven sound that fans were used to during *Lick It Up* and *Animalize*. As such, the overload of keyboards made KISS sound like a different band. But hey… it was the '80s and it was the sound of the glam rock scene. I truly like this song, and Paul's high pitch is remarkable. I so love the melody on the part "Cause after it's all said and done, I won't be wondering why…" Absolutely magic.

WHEN YOUR WALLS COME DOWN

ADAM MITCHELL *(SONGWRITER)* – Wow, what a fun track. It's got such an arena vibe. Just a real, live, let's rock out and have fun kind of song. I love the lead vocal being answered with the backing vocals. And as always, great playing and singing! When people think of KISS, they often think of just the show and makeup. But this is a great band!

RAISE YOUR GLASSES:
A Celebration of 50 Years of KISS Songs by Celebrities, Musicians & Fans.

COURTNEY CRONIN DOLD *(COMEDIAN)* – Some of KISS's most infamous "what the fuck were they thinking" lyrics. But you can't deny the song is fun. And fun to sing. Well, up to the part where he says, "You'll swallow everything when you're with me." Eww. I really do love this song; I'm not a "liar liar with my pants on fire", but my pants do heat up when I hear it.

JOEY SASSO *(THE CIRCLE, NETFLIX)* – Alright, let's dig into "When Your Walls Come Down", a track that may not hit the pinnacle of greatness but damn, it holds its own solid spot in the album. A great deal of '80s KISS haters cite the reasoning for their distaste for the band's output of this era due to them abandoning who they were in an effort to try to copy trends. Are they right? Absolutely! Do I give a shit? Absolutely not!

"When Your Walls Come Down" stands as a testament to Paul's cool but obviously cheesy vibe during this era. His swagger and vocal prowess shine through, delivering those anthemic hooks that keep us rockin'. And let's not forget that killer lyric from the track: "The games we play are never fair / I'm caught in your reckless stare." Boom! Paul's lyrical magic, right there, adding that extra punch to the song. You're gonna tell me you don't feel that? I call bullshit, 'cause if you're sitting here and reading this book right now then you know you can love it or hate it but you can't escape your love for all things KISS, no matter how dumb they may be.

JOEY CASSATA *(ZO2, Z ROCK)* – *Crazy Nights* is one of my favorite KISS albums, probably in the top 5, but for some reason, this song never did anything for me. I'm actually not sure why. It has all the elements of a pretty good song.

TOM GIGLIOTTI *(SHOUT IT OUT LOUDCAST)* – *Crazy Nights* is filled with so many melodic hooks and amazing riffs from Bruce. It's also filled with some of the most tongue-in-cheek and hilarious Paul lyrics of the era. That being said, when a song is catchy, that's all that matters to us KISS fans. And the call-and-answer bridge into the upbeat sing-along chorus is pure '80s. Another deep cut off one of my personal favorite albums of the decade.

REASON TO LIVE

BRUCE KULICK *(KISS)* – It was meant to be like a big ballad. I really think Paul's emotion is fantastic in it.

DESMOND CHILD *(SONGWRITER)* – This may be my favorite KISS song. It had a lot of yearning. This was kind of personal. This existential idea, everybody's got a reason to live and it can't be your love. Meaning that goes with the idea I'm strong, I'm not a victim. The song tugs at your heart. The irony is, it IS your love. It means I'm suffering because of you and I'm telling myself, fuck you, but you're dying for the other person. That's why the song is intriguing.

LISA LANE KULICK *(BRUCE KULICK'S WIFE)* – What I love most about this song are the lyrics. We've all come out of a bad relationship and need to find ourselves once again. This song is full of inspiration, with its persuasive "Everybody's got a reason to live" chorus. You can't help but feel strong inside and ready to move on, after hearing the uplifting lyrics and melody of "Reason to Live."

RAISE YOUR GLASSES:
A Celebration of 50 Years of KISS Songs
by Celebrities, Musicians & Fans.

KENNY BEGLEY *(KISS LIVE AUCTIONS)* – Amazing vocal, inspiring lyrics, great music video and a great power ballad. Fan since '76 (5 years old), but 1987 was my first tour I got to finally see and will always have a special place in my heart!

JOEY SASSO *(THE CIRCLE, NETFLIX)* – The first time I heard "Reason to Live", I was taken aback by the non-KISS-like material, and struggled to accept that it was Paul Stanley himself who had willingly committed to it. But as time passed, something happened: the song grew on me. To be honest, I was initially embarrassed to admit that I was falling in love with it. But as a young man pursuing my dreams and career in Los Angeles, I was no stranger to being down and out. There were countless nights when I would drive through the Hollywood hills, battling bouts of depression, and overlooking the bright lights of Los Angeles below while blasting "Reason to Live" at full volume. I know that KISS can be over-the-top, but I stand by my opinion that "Reason to Live" delves into something deeper than what KISS typically produces. We'll never know for sure, but the mixture of hidden pain and inspiration in Paul's performance makes this song a one-of-a-kind original that we've never seen before or since. In fact, I firmly believe that this song, with its cheesy but powerful message, has the ability to save lives. And I'm living proof of that.

BRENNAN MILETO *(SISTERS DOLL)* – I've always loved this song and the whole *Crazy Nights* album. This song got me through a rough time in my life as a late teenager and it was on repeat all the time. The chorus is amazing, and it's just a great love song that hits all the feels.

RAISE YOUR GLASSES:
A Celebration of 50 Years of KISS Songs
by Celebrities, Musicians & Fans.

TOMMY LONDON *(OZZY'S BONEYARD, SIRIUS XM)* – This song should have been a much bigger hit than it was. In my opinion, this song is the jewel in the *Crazy Nights* album crown. The lyrics, the melody, Paul's vocals. Come on! This album also connects with me because it was the first tour I ever saw KISS on. I remember my brother bought the Paul Stanley t-shirt at the show that said, "Life is like sex, the more you put in the more you get out". Mom was livid. She wouldn't let him leave the house with it on.

HAL SPARKS *(COMEDIAN, ACTOR)* – There are some songs that when they first come out you like them. You appreciate them. But only later do you love them. "Reason to Live" has never stopped growing on me. It has my favorite Bruce Kulick solo.

CHRIS "THE WALLET" HAICK *(GENE SIMMONS MONEYBAG SODA)* – This was the music video/song that introduced me to KISS. I'd jump off the school bus and run inside to catch the *Top 20 Video Countdown* on the Canadian Station because we didn't have cable. I'd always try to see if I can catch a glimpse of *Playboy* Playmate Eloise Broady's tits when she jumped in front of the mirror. God, those were simpler times.

RAISE YOUR GLASSES:
A Celebration of 50 Years of KISS Songs
by Celebrities, Musicians & Fans.

Tom and Zeus with Bruce and Lisa Lane Kulick, *An Evening with Gene Simmons*, May 7, 2023

GOOD GIRL GONE BAD

TOM GIGLIOTTI *(SHOUT IT OUT LOUDCAST)* – The singles from *Crazy Nights* get all the accolades but don't sleep on the deep cuts, especially the Gene songs. His vocal approach on this album, including this song, is so dynamic and unexpected after years of "The Demon". A very melodic and hooky chorus make this such a great song that you wonder why it wasn't a single. And of course, Bruce is absolutely on fire on this album – and this track is no different.

RAISE YOUR GLASSES:
A Celebration of 50 Years of KISS Songs
by Celebrities, Musicians & Fans.

COURTNEY CRONIN DOLD *(COMEDIAN)* – That "Tears are Falling"-like heavy ominous guitar at the top grabs my attention and then actually saves this song throughout, those little riffs between the lines in the verses. Both Bruce's solos are pure fire. He is this whole song for me.

CHRIS JERICHO *(WRESTLER, FOZZY)* – The Gene songs were always a hard sell for me on this album. But on this one, I remember thinking that this isn't bad, and it's actually pretty good. It's a really catchy tune. It's a great chorus, and once again – Bruce Kulick. What a great fucking solo. Like I've said it before, and I'll argue with anybody that wants to argue with me, Bruce Kulick is the best guitar player in KISStory, in my opinion. And this is another perfect example of that.

ROBERT CONTE *(AUTHOR)* – Now this is real Gene — a song acknowledging that teen girls could be just as horny and unashamed of sex as their male counterparts. Lyrics like "Show me the way!" and "One kiss will drive you mad!" were the perfect language for my then-teenage self. Who wouldn't want to experience being seduced by a hot, lusty girl inside a car? A great highlight of the Stanley/Simmons/Carr/Kulick-era KISS that easily could have been a single. But, during that time, this was "Paul's KISS", and Gene hadn't had an A-side since 1982's "I Love It Loud", which I believed was unfair.

CHRIS "THE WALLET" HAICK *(GENE SIMMONS MONEYBAG SODA)* – I think this song is underrated and a hidden gem on the *Crazy Nights* record. Gene's vocals and lyrics fit the track perfectly, and Bruce's overall guitar work and solo are pretty fucking solid. Being sandwiched between "Reason to Live" and "Turn on the Night" seems to be the perfect placement on the record, and is part of the reason why side 2 is so much stronger than the first side of the record.

Courtney Cronin Dold with Bruce Kulick

TURN ON THE NIGHT

BRUCE KULICK *(KISS)* – We never did it live, but when I do it with my boys (The Bruce Kulick Band), people go nuts. There were a lot of songs like this that I always wondered why we never got around to playing it live.

CHRIS JERICHO *(WRESTLER, FOZZY)* – Should've been a lot bigger than it was, which it wasn't big at all. It's got a really fun video to it. Another song that when Todd Kerns and Bruce Kulick do on the KISS Kruise, it just kills.

JOE MCGINNESS *(KUARANTINE, KLASSIC '78)* – It may not have the raw power chords and heavy riffs from the early makeup years, but what it lacks in heaviness it makes up for in melody and feel. The song is well written and highlight Paul's vocal ability at its peak. This anthem should have been a huge hit. I really feel that Bruce Kulick's solo is one of his greatest from his era. I wish they would've played this on the *Crazy Nights* tour.

DARREN PALTROWITZ *(AUTHOR, How David Lee Roth Changed The World)* – You are likely to love or hate "Turn on the Night" for the same reasons which you love or hate "Crazy Crazy Nights." These two songs both have cheesy music videos and generally did not make their way onto KISS setlists after the 1980s despite being charting hits. For the record, KISS did do "Crazy Crazy Nights" as part of an encore I caught on the *End of the Road* tour, but that was the only time I heard them play it live. Besides having a great chorus, I appreciate how "Turn on the Night" shows off Paul Stanley's higher vocal register, which was in peak form for a lot of the 1980s and 1990s. Also significant about this one is that it was co-written by Diane Warren, preceding future hits like Chicago's "Look Away," Cher's "If I Could Turn Back Time" and Michael Bolton's "How Can We Be Lovers," further showing that KISS helped jump-start careers for lots of future A-list songwriters (e.g. Desmond Child, Bryan Adams, Jim Vallance).

ZEU*(SHOUT IT OUT LOUDCAST)* – Shout It Out Loudcast has been singing the praises of this song from day one. How was this not a huge hit? This is the quintessential summer KISS song. Written by Paul with THE Diane Warren, this should have been enormous. Not sure if there's a catchier chorus in the KISS catalog. Sure there are keyboards, but it works. Paul's vocals and delivery are unmatched. Bruce's solo is so good as well. This should be on all their compilations and should have been in the setlist – and definitely on the *End of the Road* tour. Plus, the video was filmed in Worcester, Massachusetts. This song makes me happy.

THIEF IN THE NIGHT

BRUCE KULICK *(KISS)* – Wendy O. Williams did this song. We cut it, Nevison approves it and it goes on *Crazy Nights*. And then when Paul found out it had been done before, he was not happy about it.

Joe McGinness, Joey Cassata, Todd Kerns and Bruce Kulick

RAISE YOUR GLASSES:
A Celebration of 50 Years of KISS Songs
by Celebrities, Musicians & Fans.

WES BEECH *(THE PLASMATICS)* – I originally played this Mitch Weissman-penned song on Wendy O. Williams' *W.O.W.* album and it was always one of my favorite songs to play live. Gene brought it to the *Crazy Nights* album as it was a finished song and he was busy with outside projects at the time. The story goes that Paul was furious when, after the fact, he learned that it had already been released on Wendy's album as he wasn't a big fan of hers. I don't think the KISS version is as heavy as Wendy's, and a number of fans agree. Gene's vocal delivery is good, but the backing track would have been better with *Creatures*-era production, and is a bit thin here. A perfunctory reading of the song. Bruce's solo is a bit disjointed and could have been stronger. All in all, a good groove and change of pace for the keyboard-driven album.

Chris Jericho wearing funny Paul shirt

METAL MIKE *(80's GLAM METALCAST)* – I'm not a huge *Crazy Nights* guy, but I've always loved this song. This originally was given to Wendy O. Williams, but the KISS version is far superior in my opinion. Gene's smooth vocal is more fitting for its '80s pop-metal vibe. From the start with that heavy chorus riff, you know you are in for a treat.

MITCH WEISSMAN *(BEATLEMANIA, SONGWRITER)* – It first appeared on Wendy O. Williams' *W.O.W.* album. Paul either forgot or never listened to that album because he actually sings on that album, so how did he never hear it?

ZEUS *(SHOUT IT OUT LOUDCAST)* – This is further proof that Gene songs in the 1980s are underrated. Love the riff and Gene's vocal delivery, switching from the smooth Gene voice to the growl on the chorus. The pre-chorus and chorus are great, and Bruce nails the solo. Written with SIOL friend Mitch Weissman, I love the story that Paul did not that Wendy O. Williams already recorded this on her 1984 *W.O.W.* album, which Gene produced, and was pissed about it.

RAISE YOUR GLASSES:
A Celebration of 50 Years of KISS Songs
by Celebrities, Musicians & Fans.

CHAPTER 18

"SMASHES, THRASHES & HITS"

Released: November 15, 1988

Smashes, Thrashes & Hits is a compilation album that served as a retrospective of KISS's most popular hits up to that point. Featuring classic tracks, re-recordings, and two new songs, the album aimed to reintroduce the band to both longtime fans and a new generation. While it provided a snapshot of KISS's commercial successes, it also stirred debates among fans about the re-recorded material.

One of the notable features of the album is the inclusion of a re-recorded version of "Beth" featuring Eric Carr on vocals, showcasing the band's commitment to honoring its current lineup.

The album also introduced two new tracks, "Let's Put the X in Sex, and "(You Make Me) Rock Hard", which aimed to capture the glam metal fans of the late '80s with their catchy hooks and risqué lyrics.

While *Smashes, Thrashes & Hits* may not be a traditional studio album, it served a valuable purpose in KISS's discography. It acted as a gateway for new fans to discover the band's classic material, and offered a nostalgic journey for longtime enthusiasts.

In retrospect, *Smashes, Thrashes & Hits* remains a snapshot of KISS's commercial successes. The album is a testament to the enduring appeal of KISS's timeless hits and their impact on the rock and glam metal genres.

LET'∫ PUT THE X IN ∫EX

DE∫MOND CHILD *(SONGWRITER)* – We wrote this at Paul's apartment. "Let's put the X in sex / Love's like a muscle and you make me want to flex" was Paul's line, I'm sure of it.

RAISE YOUR GLASSES:
A Celebration of 50 Years of KISS Songs
by Celebrities, Musicians & Fans.

CHRIS JERICHO *(WRESTLER, FOZZY)* – Probably the epitome of '80s KISS and more importantly, the epitome of Paul Stanley when he was taking over the band. It's super-catchy. To me, it's the best '80s sex song.

BRUCE KULICK *(KISS)* – The type of girls chosen for the video were probably not the right choice.

ZEUS *(SHOUT IT OUT LOUDCAST)* – This song is song one of Paul's trifecta of sexual innuendo masterpieces. There is a big difference in a song like this that works, versus "Bang Bang You" and "Read My Body." I absolutely love this song. The guitar riff is great. The lyrics are sleazy and clever, and there is a payoff at the end. Of course, this song is pre-cellphone and Internet. The chorus is great, as is Bruce Kulick's solo. A fun and catchy song; not everything has to be "Stairway to Heaven". The video has a lot to break down: Paul with no guitar, the legal issues due to the location, the females selected for the video, and Paul's pants hiked up higher than a senior at The Villages in Florida.

BETH-AMI HEAVENSTONE *(GRAHAM BONNET BAND)* – This one cracked me up. I thought this was so silly that it's brilliant. I love Paul. He's a real talented person.

(YOU MAKE ME) ROCK HARD

CHRIS JERICHO *(WRESTLER, FOZZY)* – Desmond Child said there's only one song that they wrote that's bad, and it's this. Paul said "Yup, that's the one."

RAISE YOUR GLASSES:
A Celebration of 50 Years of KISS Songs by Celebrities, Musicians & Fans.

Tom, Zeus and Chris Jericho

DESMOND CHILD *(SONGWRITER)* – Diane Warren became a great pal. I got her in some writing sessions with me, and one was with Paul. We were at a little café on Columbus Avenue in front of the Museum of Natural History and we were saying what she would bring to the session with Paul. What's a good title that would intrigue him, and someone came up with "You Make Me Rock Hard". We were laughing 'cause that title was so stupid and outrageous so it can either be an ice breaker or he's just gonna throw us out. Half-jokingly we presented the title and he loved it. It doesn't sound like real English. It was like a joke, but Paul made something out of nothing. It's more than a double entendre, it's downright dirty. It's such a fun song. I think it should be a commercial for Cialis.

JASON BAKKEN *(COBRAS & FIRE PODCAST)* – A parenthesis, or parenthetical phrase, is an explanatory or qualifying word, phrase, clause, or sentence inserted into a passage. Let me qualify this song and explain it. It's about Paul's dick. *Smashes, Thrashes & Hits* is a trainwreck.

IZZY PRESLEY *(MUSICIAN, COMIC)* – Desmond Child and Diane Warren wrote this to see if they could write the worst song ever written. They did. Paul loved it. It's brutal. I can't believe I had to listen to it again for this. The price you pay for Internet notoriety…

JEFF TROTT *(ART DIRECTOR)* – Despite its humorous origins, "(You Make Me) Rock Hard" shines with its infectious melody and undeniable charm. It's a testament to KISS's ability to rock out with unapologetic enthusiasm. When KISS released *Smashes…* I was disappointed that it was another greatest hits, but was pumped that it included a couple new tracks, just like *Killers* did years ago. "(You Make Me) Rock Hard" was new KISS and I didn't care about the cheesy content, hell I'm not even sure I really knew what it meant when I was 8 years old. It was a new KISS song from a new KISS album, and I still rock it often to this day.

ALEXANDER TALKINGTON *(KISS ARMY THINGS PODCAST)* – This is a Top 20 favorite KISS song of mine! (Pause for boos). Right from that iconic '80s snare in the beginning, this song makes me wanna "Turn it up!" Even though it's probably just a drum machine, the cowbell in the chorus is too good. The second verse is my favorite; "I'm under a physical spell / I'm a prisoner and your love is my cell / Once I get started, I can't stop / I can't cool down 'cause this love is so hot."

CHAPTER 19

"HOT IN THE SHADE"

Released: October 17, 1989

Hot in the Shade marks a significant chapter in KISS's discography as the band aimed to reclaim their hard rock roots. This album, featuring an extensive track list and a mix of rock anthems and ballads, showcased KISS's determination to stay relevant in the changing musical landscape of the late '80s. While it received mixed critical reception, *Hot in the*

RAISE YOUR GLASSES:
A Celebration of 50 Years of KISS Songs
by Celebrities, Musicians & Fans.

Shade holds a unique place in the band's evolution, capturing a moment when KISS sought to balance commercial appeal with a return to their classic hard rock sound.

The album features a total of 15 songs. This abundance of material showcases KISS's eagerness to deliver a diverse listening experience, offering a mix of uplifting rock anthems and heartfelt ballads. The band's dedication to providing fans with a substantial musical offering is evident throughout the album.

The standout track, "Forever," became one of KISS's most successful ballads. Co-written by Michael Bolton, the song's melodic and emotional qualities contributed to its commercial success. "Rise to It" and "Hide Your Heart" are among the hard-hitting rock tracks that exemplify the band's commitment to reclaiming their signature sound.

Hot in the Shade is also highlighted by the now long-tenured lineup featuring drummer Eric Carr and guitarist Bruce Kulick. The chemistry among band members is palpable, and their collaborative efforts result in a cohesive yet diverse collection of songs.

While *Hot in the Shade* received mixed critical reviews, it stands as a testament to KISS's resilience and adaptability, making it a noteworthy entry in the band's evolving discography.

RAISE YOUR GLASSES:
A Celebration of 50 Years of KISS Songs
by Celebrities, Musicians & Fans.

RISE TO IT

CHRIS JERICHO *(WRESTLER, FOZZY)* – When I first heard it, I thought it sounded like "Bad Seamstress Blues" by Cinderella. But it's a great tune, great opening song. As soon as it kicks in, I was all for it. It's got a lot of energy to it. Paul does this really cool vocal part at the end of the song during the fade out that I used to just crank out. I would always turn it up to listen to that part. The video was amazing.

PETER CORY *(KISS LIVE AUCTIONS)* – I think if I am going to talk about this song, I have to talk about the video. This is the first video and song that really gave me hope (and I think many other KISS fans) of the band coming back with makeup. The song was very catchy and more like a sing-along song, but the video was what made this song. The beginning, when they are backstage in 1975 putting makeup on and talking, to the end where they are in full makeup and outfits for the first time in 6 years. A true moment in KISStory and of hope!

CHRIS L. *(POD OF THUNDER)* – Most of the non-makeup era in the '80s didn't do it for me, either because I didn't dig the music or the band's aesthetic was a little too out there (or both). *Hot in the Shade* seemed different. The visual image was less androgenous (not that there's anything wrong with that) and the album's opening salvo sounded much tougher and straight-ahead. Plus, how can you go wrong with lyrics about Paul achieving an erection?

NICHOLAS BUCKLAND *(AUTHOR, Hottest Brand in the Land)* – A song massively overshadowed by its video featuring Gene and

Paul back in makeup. Song-wise this has a very sing-along chorus despite it being a euphemistic ode to one's erection!

STEVEN MICHAEL *(GROWIN' UP ROCK PODCAST)* – I love this riff. Nobody appreciates a rocking track to kick off an album more than me. For me the album track opener sets the mood and pace for the rest of the record. Even though many people said KISS was following trends with several of the songs on this album, I only listen to riffs and melodies, and for me "Rise to It" has both. It's a positive and upbeat tune with a driving bluesy riff and memorable chorus that kicks ass. I love it.

BETRAYED

CHRIS "THE WALLET" HAICK *(GENE SIMMONS MONEYBAG SODA)* – As a kid, I was never good at understanding what the lyrics were in a lot of songs. Before the Internet days of easily looking them up you'd have to rely on the band including the lyrics on the record sleeve or cassette insert, which didn't happen that often, so I'd ad-lib constantly. Back in middle school I'd play this song and used to think Gene said, "What doesn't kill you makes you scunger". What the fuck is scunger? My buddy at the time, John Janik, whom I'm still close with and one of my Gene Simmons Moneybag Soda partners, today broke the news to me that it was "stronger" and not "scunger". He left me in complete astonishment. To this day, we still say scunger when we crank the song and just laugh.

CHRIS JERICHO *(WRESTLER, FOZZY)* – I think it's really good. It's got a really catchy chorus.

RAISE YOUR GLASSES:
A Celebration of 50 Years of KISS Songs
by Celebrities, Musicians & Fans.

JEFF TROTT *(ART DIRECTOR)* – *Hot in the Shade* has a lot of great material but is often looked at as the "demos and drum machine" album. "Betrayed" from *Hot in the Shade* proves that Gene's vocal prowess extends far beyond his makeup-era performances. It's a testament to his underrated talent, delivering a powerful performance with a cool groove that embodies the essence of '80s Gene tracks.

MIKE BRUNN *(THE ROCK EXPERIENCE)* – The *Hot in the Shade* album suffers from poor production, and no song on the album suffers more (IMO) than "Betrayed". This song rocks, and if the production was better, I think many fans would point to this song as one of Gene's best from the decade. A great hard-rocking song, in the same vein as "Deuce" that came 15 years prior.

Tom and Zeus cracking up with Chris Jericho and Bruce Kulick

TOM GIGLIOTTI *(SHOUT IT OUT LOUDCAST)* – Gene has quite a few contributions on *Hot in the Shade* and this foot-stomper is one of his more kickass tunes. Lyrically, he's singing from the heart as he usually does. It has a huge gang-vocal chorus and Eric Carr's pummeling drums keep the song pulsating from start to finish. You get to catch your breath for a second before Bruce comes in with another spectacular solo, as we've come to expect.

HIDE YOUR HEART

BRUCE KULICK *(KISS)* – I don't care how many other versions there are of it, I think Paul delivering it is always the win.

HOLLY KNIGHT *(SONGWRITER)* – Paul came over one day and we jammed in my studio and recorded the session. I started to play some chords and sing a melody which basically ended up being the chorus and the chorus refrain to "Hide Your Heart." A few weeks later, Paul sent me a tape. He had gotten together with Desmond (Child) and they'd written a song around the chorus and hook that I'd initially come up with. I love the *Hot in the Shade* version and as time goes on, I love it more. I think it's great, but I like the Ace version even more. It's more raw, and I like his scruffy voice on it.

DESMOND CHILD *(SONGWRITER)* – Paul came to write with me in when I was in Santa Monica. He had started a song with Holly, called "Bite Down Hard". That's sorta her, she always had a bit of edge. I didn't think that title sounded commercial and feminine. But "Hide Your Heart" had alliteration, which is another principle of Bob Crewe. Paul asked if I wanted to join the song. So Paul called up Holly and said, "Desmond is going to write on this song". So Paul and I started pursuing this sorta *West Side Story* storyline. I had a similar song in Desmond Child & Rouge along those lines that was called "Rosa". So we all agreed to give it to Bonnie Tyler. The song also got cut by KISS, Ace Frehley, Robin Beck, and Molly Hatchet.

RAISE YOUR GLASSES:
A Celebration of 50 Years of KISS Songs
by Celebrities, Musicians & Fans.

JOE LYNN TURNER *(RAINBOW, YNGWIE MALMSTEEN)* – This song was a joint collaboration between Holly Knight, Desmond Child and Paul... it was first released by Bonnie Tyler and I sang background vocals on her version... then KISS finally covered it, as well as a few other artists...

BRAD RUSTOVEN *(SLAMFEST PODCAST)* – The classic of the album. One of the best KISS songs of the non-makeup era. Great riff and lead guitar melody. Amazing chorus – 'Ah, ah, ah, ah, hey, hey, hey, doo, doo, doo, doo, doo, doo, doo, doo' is so damn catchy. Outro chorus – classic Paul interjections. A perfect song!

JASON BAKKEN *(COBRAS & FIRE PODCAST)* – This song. What a weird history. Recorded and released by Bonnie Tyler and Molly Hatchet (Molly Hatchet?!?!) before KISS released in on *Hot in the Shade*, almost simultaneously with Ace Frehley on his record *Trouble Walkin'*. KISS's version is hands-down the best. Still weird.

PRISONER OF LOVE

JOE McGINNESS *(KUARANTINE, KLASSIK '78)* – One of my favorite Gene songs on *Hot in the Shade*. A very powerful chord progression with some insanely tasteful and bluesy Bruce Kulick riffs. The chorus is fun to sing along with. The song overall is very well written.

JOEY SASSO *(THE CIRCLE, NETFLIX)* – This track may not hit the top tier of greatness but it sits solidly in the album's lineup. Gene Simmons delivers his classic vibes as "Prisoner of Love" shapes up as a typical Gene tune that feels like it might've started as a demo. Throughout *Hot in the Shade*, Gene's presence is undeniable in a few ways. We all knew how checked out he was during the '80s. While this record gets its fair share of hate (some warranted, some unwarranted) it's heartwarming to see Gene at least attempting to bring some ideas and concepts to the table again. This track kinda cruises in the middle lane, not quite reaching the heights of KISS classics. However, there's a charm in its simplicity that resonates with me, a reminder of how Gene's signature style can win me over even when he's delivering a track that he never fully developed to its full potential. Classic Gene depth, good and bad, lives on this album and this song, capturing that raw, introspective essence Gene is known for. Gene evolves with the band on this track, finding a nice balance where he can confidently bring his persona of the time to the table in an effort to fully find himself again. So while "Prisoner of Love" may not steal the show, it's a testament to Gene's enduring presence coming back full swing, as well as preparing us for the full commitment that Gene would give us one album later on *Revenge*.

ALEXANDER TALKINGTON *(KISS ARMY THINGS PODCAST)* – This is one of those KISS songs you wanna be cruising to when it comes on! Perfect for open roads, sunny weather and windows down! As a matter of fact, that sums up the entire *Hot in the Shade* record for me. This is one of my favorite Gene cuts from the album, but it's Eric and Bruce that steal the show. Bruce's solo is gnarly, and Eric breaks out into that classic ride/snare beat he played during live solos (and also halfway through "Saint and Sinner" on *Creatures*).

RAISE YOUR GLASSES:
A Celebration of 50 Years of KISS Songs by Celebrities, Musicians & Fans.

Tom, Zeus and Tom's son, Michael,
End of the Road, TD Garden, March 26, 2019

JEFF TROTT *(ART DIRECTOR)* – Co-written by Bruce Kulick, "Prisoner of Love" kicks off with a killer riff followed by powerful gang vocals. Featuring Gene on lead vocals, this track carries a familiar vibe from his songs on *Hot in the Shade*, yet it stands out as another banger. I love this album and this song, especially Bruce's cool solo intertwined with drums that sound like a freight train approaching.

JOEY CASSATA *(ZO2, Z ROCK)* – A very strong song off of a very strong record. People always say that there are too many songs on

Hot in the Shade, but I would rather have more! As KISS fans, we all like something different. A song like "Prisoner of Love" might have been cut if it had only been a 10-song album. I always loved playing this song, especially Eric's triplet feel on the ride cymbal bell during the bridge. SO FUN!!

READ MY BODY

CHRIS JERICHO *(WRESTLER, FOZZY)* – I love this song. It's not one of the best Paul Stanley songs. It's definitely in that category of "(You Make Me) Rock Hard". But I love the opening drum part with some kind of weird canastas or something. As soon as you hear it, it's like, oh, that sounds like "Pour Some Sugar On Me" by Def Leppard. That's totally the riff for that. But this is once again Paul Stanley at the peak of his powers as a singer and as a songwriter. It's pure KISS cheese served on a platter.

PASQUALE VARI *(KISS ARMY NATION PODCAST)* – I know, I know, the majority of KISS fans hate this song. I'm in the minority. *Hot in the Shade* was the album that helped me rediscover KISS after I checked out in the early '80s. I found a lot of songs on this album fun and catchy. That is what I love most about KISS songs. Paul's attempt at rap, cringy lyrics and a catchy hook – c'mon, what's not to love? And I'm not being sarcastic.

RAISE YOUR GLASSES:
A Celebration of 50 Years of KISS Songs
by Celebrities, Musicians & Fans.

Tom and Zeus, Creatures Fest, May 27, 2022

CHRIS L. *(POD OF THUNDER)* – This may come as a shock to some die-hard KISS fans, but the band and its members can sometimes take themselves too seriously. They're always better when they're as outrageous and over-the-top as possible, especially when they add some silliness to the mix. "Read My Body" follows in the "Let's Put the X in Sex" tradition of featuring completely ridiculous (and decidedly horny) lyrical subject matter that's simply fun. Paul has disowned these songs over the years and would like to pretend they don't even exist. I like to pretend "Read My Body" ended up in a post-reunion set list sometime.

ALEXANDER TALKINGTON *(KISS ARMY THINGS PODCAST)* – I wish I didn't like this song so much. I wish I hated it like everyone else. But I don't. I love it. It makes me laugh and it makes me smile. The riff and simple drums are enough to hook me, but it's Paul's ridiculous lyrics that make me wanna, "wooooo shout it out!" I love that the song gets more unhinged as it progresses... to the point where Gene and Paul are trading back and forth "yeahs" and Paul is exclaiming, "Extra, extra! Read all about it!" Rock 'n' roll is supposed to be fun!

TOM GIGLIOTTI *(SHOUT IT OUT LOUDCAST)* – Let's be serious for a minute. On second thoughts, let's not. How can we be when this is song we're talking about? Definitely influenced by the rhythm and vibe of Def Leppard's "Pour Some Sugar On Me", it's just silly enough for KISS fans that it brings a big smile to your face. Paul isn't taking this too seriously and neither should we. Now, turn the page and get to the good stuff! Pure Paul poetry!

LOVE'S A SLAP IN THE FACE

ZEUS *(SHOUT IT OUT LOUDCAST)* – Another underrated Gene song from the 1980s. Written by Gene and the returning Vini Poncia, the producer of Peter's 1978 solo album, *Dynasty* and *Unmasked*. A catchy little tune. I like Gene's vocal delivery, the chorus and the backing vocals.

COURTNEY CRONIN DOLD *(COMEDIAN)* – Even though it sounds like Gene wrote these lyrics on the toilet, I still love it. I love the "na-na-na" part. It's like he's waving his finger at this heartbreaker hottie whose about to slap him, and telling her "No, No, No."

RYAN "BB" BANNON *(PODDER THAN HELL PODCAST)* – Most of KISS Nation can agree that *Hot in the Shade* is too long of an album. This is why. When Gene sings "na" 104 times, the song is just a filler. Personally, I think it could have been somewhat of a better song if Paul sang it and extended the opening music to more than seven seconds.

JOEY SASSO (*THE CIRCLE, NETFLIX*) – Once again we find Gene delivering a solid track that doesn't quite skyrocket to greatness but is undeniably cool, with its signature Gene demo-style that you are either here for or you are not. SPOILER ALERT: This guy is fucking here for it! What can make a great Gene demo-style, you ask? Let's see... undeniable presence with a classic flair that is true to only Gene. Very few could get away with what Gene can do, even Paul Stanley himself. Throughout all of the obvious Gene demos this album carries, I would argue his presence has not been more felt then right here on this tune.

ALEXANDER TALKINGTON *(KISS ARMY THINGS PODCAST)* – Gene filler, maybe. But Gene filler can still be fun, and who doesn't like saying "na, na, na, na" over and over? Bruce's guitar work is well done, as usual, and proves to be the most interesting aspect of the song.

FOREVER

BRUCE KULICK *(KISS)* – I love that I was able to be the same guy who can do the very aggressive solo on *Revenge* and also the very Jimmy Page-like acoustic solo here. A very memorable song that people get married to.

RAISE YOUR GLASSES:
A Celebration of 50 Years of KISS Songs
by Celebrities, Musicians & Fans.

CHRIS JERICHO *(WRESTLER, FOZZY)* – It's their biggest hit of this timeframe. Once again, one of the most well-written songs. Bruce said that Paul wanted something like Led Zeppelin with the acoustic solo. It's just a brilliant solo.

JOE LYNN TURNER *(RAINBOW, YNGWIE MALMSTEEN)* – Great song / lyrics by Paul Stanley and Michael Bolton. KISS has so many great songs that it's difficult to choose just a few, but coming from a songwriter's point of view I tend to favor the collaborations.

PJ FARLEY *(TRIXTER, FOZZY)* – Easily one of Paul's (and Michael Bolton's) best songs and vocal performances; the song just has an organic flow to it and one of my favorite acoustic guitar solos of all time. During a time when KISS was still kinda trying to stay relevant they sometimes tried too hard, but "Forever" sounds and feels very natural to me and not forced.

JASON HOOK *(FIVE FINGER DEATH PUNCH)* – What can you say, just a really well-crafted power ballad. Paul claimed in later years that Michael Bolton's contribution was limited.

BRENNAN MILETO *(SISTERS DOLL)* – This is my favorite rock ballad of all time. Paul's voice is on fire and the emotion he shows throughout is beautiful. The chorus is absolute magic, and I can never get enough of this song. An absolute classic.

LORETTA CARAVELLO *(ERIC CARR'S SISTER)* – The jacket he wore in the video was the jacket Eric wore when he auditioned for KISS, it was on his resumé photos and I still have it. When he got to

LA to do the "Forever" video, they had shipped a big box of KISS white logo sticks and someone walked off with them, so he had to use generic ones.

ЅILUEЯ ЅPOON

ZEUЅ *(SHOUT IT OUT LOUDCAST)* – A very different type of KISS song. The lyrics on this album, and this song particularly, are very different from the songs on previous KISS albums. This song is telling a story, which was happening a lot at this stage of "hair metal." Bands were moving away from the glam look and "Talk Dirty To Me"-type lyrics. The song is empowering and written by Paul and, again, Vini Poncia. The soul singers, The Sisters Of No Mercy, coming in at the end, add to the uniqueness of this song. One of the best on *Hot in the Shade*.

JOEY ЅAЅЅO *(THE CIRCLE, NETFLIX)* – When you talk about KISS deep cuts there is no other track to bring up then this slept-on Paul Stanley classic. That's right – if you know, you know. I am talking about the absolute masterpiece that is "Silver Spoon". That's right, you read that right. I said this song is a masterpiece in every way, a Paul Stanley song elevated to that next level of Paul perfection. This track is a testament to Paul Stanley's artistry, showcasing why he stands as one of rock music's greatest frontmen. With its infectious energy and anthemic quality, "Silver Spoon" emerges as a standout, offering a glimpse into Paul's brilliance during this era and on this album.

JAЅON BAKKEN *(COBRAS & FIRE PODCAST)* – Paul was quite good at tapping into that chip on his shoulder when looking for lyrical influence. *Hot in the Shade* may be a bit bloated, but that seems more of a sign of the times, when bands were trying to squeeze as many minutes onto a CD as possible, than a lack of quality. This song rips and reminds us that Paul wasn't done at this point by any means.

ALEXANDER TALKINGTON *(KISS ARMY THINGS PODCAST)* – This has become one of my favorite tracks off *Hot in the Shade* over the years. It's fun to rock out to and to sing at the top of your lungs! Paul's vocals are soaring, and so are the female vocalists who appear at the end!

RYAN "BB" BANNON *(PODDER THAN HELL PODCAST)* – I always enjoyed this song. I love how Bruce Kulick sprinkles sounds of his brother Bob in this song. It reminds me of Paul's solo album. I guess that's why I enjoy it. The female background singers towards the end of the song are an added bonus as well. It gives it that Paul solo '70s feel.

CADILLAC DREAMS

BRUCE KULICK *(KISS)* – I walked up to Gene and told him, I was comfortable enough at the time, and I said, "Gene, I really don't like that song."

MARK CICCHINI *(THREE SIDES OF THE COIN)* – I've always been drawn to this song as it resonates with me personally & professionally. Greed? No, I think people miss the point of this song. As it is said, "A rising tide lifts all ships." In layman's terms? Most people who have means first had "Cadillac Dreams." The song tells the story of someone who started with a dream, paid their dues and achieved their goals. "When you want all the best things money can buy / You gotta reach down inside of you, to reach up to the sky." About as autobiographical a KISS song can be from Gene's perspective. The American dream come true. Love the lyric, the music and performance. A shining diamond off an unremarkable album.

JEFF TROTT *(ART DIRECTOR)* – Who from KISS is always preaching you can do anything you put your mind to? In "Cadillac Dreams", Gene's ambition and personality shine through, embodying the spirit of Gene's enduring message of empowerment.

ZEUS *(SHOUT IT OUT LOUDCAST)* – Is this Gene's autobiographical story? I love the lyrics. Gene is always confident and bold to tell it like it is. He wants money, money that's all he needs. Gene certainly had Cadillac dreams and he's achieved that and beyond. His love of this country and its greatness is so endearing. That being said, am I hearing horns in a KISS song? Regardless, the lyrics, the chorus and the melody work.

JOEY CASSATA *(ZO2, Z ROCK)* – I love this song!! To me, as much as "God of Thunder" symbolized Gene in the '70s as the Demon, "Cadillac Dreams" symbolizes who non-makeup Gene really is.

KING OF HEARTS

CHRIS JERICHO *(WRESTLER, FOZZY)* – I think it's my favorite song on *Hot in the Shade*. The melody, the chorus, Paul's vocals. It's just great.

SONNY POONI *(PODCAST ROCK CITY)* – A song where the intro guitar melody immediately grabs you. I love the vocal melody and the way the backing vocals and Paul's vocal in the chorus play off of each other. I would label this as a sister song to "Hide Your Heart". It feels like the song was written to be a radio hit. If Bon Jovi had done this song on *New Jersey*, it would be a rock radio staple.

STEVE WRIGHT *(PODDER THAN HELL PODCAST)* – I'm not sure how this song is not touted as one of KISS's best songs of the non-makeup era. This song kind of sneaks up on you, being the tenth track on the *Hot in the Shade* album. There is a subtle build in this song that makes it even better for me. Great drumming from Eric Carr. Understated background vocals. The guitars are crisp. In parts of some of the verses there are layered vocals that add to it. Paul's vocals are amazing, and he is at the peak of his singing abilities. Bruce's solo is very tasteful and fits perfectly. This may very well be the KING of deep tracks.

MIKE BRUNN *(THE ROCK EXPERIENCE)* – This song is probably my favorite deep cut from non-makeup years. Often overlooked by many fans, this song has a great hook. I was so glad Bruce Kulick and his band performed this on KISS Kruise XI. For any fans who have slept on this song, give it another listen. You won't be disappointed.

PETER CORY *(KISS LIVE AUCTIONS)* – The beginning of this song with Bruce Kulick on guitar is just pure magic! I fell in love with this song as soon as I heard in 1989 because of the guitar, but then when you listen to Paul sing so deeply, like he is pleading, it is a song that didn't get as much love as it should have. Again, working with Bruce I was able to talk/persuade/beg him and his band to play it on the KISS Kruise and it instantly became a huge hit among the KISS fans in attendance, and is now a staple for the Bruce Kulick Band.

THE STREET GIVETH AND THE STREET TAKETH AWAY

BRAD RUSTOVEN *(SLAMFEST PODCAST)* – I was a delivery driver for Pizza Hut in high school when *Hot in the Shade* came out. When "Forever" was released as a single, it was added to the old-school juke box in the dining room, and this song was the B-side. I would always play it while on break, to the chagrin of the dining patrons. The gang vocals and the harmonies during the chorus are awesome. Strums of the acoustic lead into the outro – the chorus goes up a key and Gene adds some fantastic interjections.

JOEY SASSO *(THE CIRCLE, NETFLIX)* – Now, when it comes to awful song titles, this one definitely takes the cake, standing out as perhaps the pinnacle of KISS's eccentricity. Despite the title's, let's say, lack of subtlety, the song itself embodies everything that makes KISS so delightfully over-the-top and cheesy. It's a perfect example of the band fully embracing their kitschy, larger-than-life persona to the fullest extent. "The Street Giveth and the Street Taketh Away" revels in its own cheesiness, unapologetically delivering a dose of KISS magic in all its glory.

Now, amidst the campiness and flamboyance, there's a line in this song that truly captures its essence: "Life's a game, and it's play for keeps, no telling what waits." Classic KISS, right? Embracing the melodrama and theatrics that have defined their style from the beginning. So, despite its... questionable... title, let's give credit where it's due – "The Street Giveth and the Street Taketh Away" stands as a prime example of KISS fully leaning into their trademark cheesiness. It's a song that reminds us why we love this band – for their unapologetic flair, their larger-than-life personas, and their ability to craft anthems that transport us to a world of pure rock 'n' roll extravagance. Does the song accomplish all of those things? No, it does not. But it's swinging and giving everything it has trying to deliver on all of those qualities that can make up most of the band's most legendary tunes, and for that effort given I have to fully endorse this moronic song. You only love it when your band hits it out of the park? Fuck that. We got our boys' backs when they miss as much as we do when they kill it. So crank up the volume, embrace the cheese, and let KISS take you on a wild, over-the-top ride that's uniquely their own.

ZEUS *(SHOUT IT OUT LOUDCAST)* – Quite possibly the longest title in the KISS catalog, this song was co-written by the one and only future KISS member, Tommy Thayer. Tommy also played the electro-acoustic guitar on this deep cut. There's a fun breakdown at the 2:42 mark of the song where the acoustic guitar is isolated and then it goes back to the fun chorus. Good stuff.

JOEY CASSATA *(ZO2, Z ROCK)* – Super-solid offering from Gene here. The back half of *Hot in the Shade* doesn't get the recognition it deserves. Gene really loves coming up with a title for a song and then kind of working backwards. I remember when ZO2 was on tour with KISS, he would go around all day and say, "That would be a good song title" and then pull out his black book and write it down.

TOM GIGLIOTTI *(SHOUT IT OUT LOUDCAST)* – *Hot in the Shade* is loaded with deep cuts, which is to be expected when there's 15 tracks. This is the true definition of a deep cut, and of course it's a Gene track. It has a great slide-style guitar as they embraced this quite a bit on this album. Another big gang vocal in the chorus makes this a crowd pleaser, if only the crowd was exposed to it. Don't sleep on *Hot in the Shade*!

YOU LOVE ME TO HATE YOU

DESMOND CHILD *(SONGWRITER)* – This is like standard English for KISS. Very high school sophomoric. It has a sado-masochistic thing to it. "You're like a cat on a hot tin roof / I love it when you scratch and bite", that's Paul.

TOM GIGLIOTTI *(SHOUT IT OUT LOUDCAST)* – *Hot in the Shade* is a spectacular album filled with incredible deep cuts, specifically Paul songs. This is part of the trifecta from the album (along with "Silver Spoon" and "King of Hearts"). One of the greatest bridge sections into an awesome sing-along chorus combined with some of Paul's strongest vocals make this my favorite track on the album. A tasty little solo from Bruce adds to the awesomeness. Should've been a hit!

IZZY PRESLEY *(MUSICIAN, COMIC)* – Ahhh, *Hot in the Shade*... the album that needs a proper remaster and should have been about 3 or 4 songs shorter. I've always loved this tune. No bullshit. Paul sounds like he has a clamp on his balls during the chorus. Don't judge me...

SONNY POONI *(PODCAST ROCK CITY)* – What an awesome deep cut. The groove of the song is undeniable, and Paul is absolutely wailing on the song, especially when the vocal melody builds from the pre-chorus to the chorus. Also, playing with the words "love" and "hate" is done so well... "And the more that I hate you, I love you..."

JEFF TROTT *(ART DIRECTOR)* – This resonates as one of Paul's powerhouse performances from *Hot in the Shade*. "I Hate Myself for Loving You", "You Give Love a Bad Name", "You Love Me to Hate You"! While this track wasn't a hit for KISS, it is another great Stanley-Child collaboration, and a prime example of Desmond's "opposite" method of writing.

SOMEWHERE BETWEEN HEAVEN AND HELL

COURTNEY CRONIN DOLD *(COMEDIAN)* – If "Love Gun" is about Paul's penis, and "Nothin' to Lose" is about anal sex, then this song is definitely about Gene's taint. Somewhere... between? You get it.

RAISE YOUR GLASSES:
A Celebration of 50 Years of KISS Songs
by Celebrities, Musicians & Fans.

JOEY SASSO (*THE CIRCLE, NETFLIX*) – The fact that I have never heard somebody in the masses of KISS fans bring up "Somewhere Between Heaven and Hell" is a criminal act in the world of KISS fandom as far as I am concerned. This track is a hidden treasure that shines brilliantly as another prime example that showcases what Gene can bring to the table. "Life is like a jigsaw puzzle, and love's a game we play." These words carry the weight of experience and reflection, showcasing Gene's depth as a songwriter and adding a layer of emotional depth to an already captivating melody. That is a lyric that I have spent years getting pleasure out of and none of that pleasure is guilty! I will proudly state what many are too blind or afraid to say. Does this record get praised from many? Nope, it certainly does not. But for us KISStards out there, it's tracks like this – that show standout moments of the band attempting something with pure commitment – that absolutely deserve our recognition.

PASQUALE VARI (*KISS ARMY NATION PODCAST*) – I hated the majority of Gene Simmons songs in the '80s. It was only on *Hot in the Shade* that I began to appreciate his songs. I just love "Somewhere Between Heaven and Hell". It prods forward like a typical Gene song with a catchiness not typical of his usual '80s contributions. Barring his *Revenge* material, this is one of my favorite '80s Gene songs.

METAL MIKE (*80's GLAM METALCAST*) – A great Gene song that gets lost in this album with too many songs. Starts with a slightly eerie riff that harkens back to "X-Ray Eyes", but then quickly turns to typical '80s metal fare. Catchy bridge and chorus with an excellent vocal by Mr. Simmons.

ZEUS *(SHOUT IT OUT LOUDCAST)* – *Hot in the Shade* saw KISS bring back an old favorite, Vini Poncia, the producer of Peter's solo album, *Dynasty* and *Unmasked*, as a songwriter. He has a co-write with Gene on this deep cut. I really enjoy Gene's vocals on this song, the pre-chorus on this song is great.

LITTLE CAESAR

BRUCE KULICK *(KISS)* – I found another version that is slower and then I realized that everything about it was Aerosmith. It was more obvious during the slower version. Eric is on bass and I'm on guitar. I don't even think Paul or Gene are on that track.

EDDIE TRUNK *(RADIO DJ & TV PERSONALITY)* – It's here because I was very good friends with Eric Carr. I loved him and I still miss him to this day. He so desperately wanted to sing on a KISS record, and he was a lead singer in his previous band. Eric wasn't happy with the process of making *Hot in the Shade,* but he was excited to have a song on the record. And it was a song that he wrote and played bass on.

LORETTA CARAVELLO *(ERIC CARR'S SISTER)* – Bruce would come over and they would play, and they were just jamming. There's a couple of versions of "Little Caesar". There's "No One's Messin' With You" on *Unfinished Business*, released in 2011 and re-released for Record Store Day 2024. The lyrics are totally different than what ended up on *Hot in the Shade.* Then KISS actually got into trouble for this, because they took a Beatles song and used lyrics when they did "Ain't That Peculiar", which ended up on the KISS Box Set. Those lyrics were dummy lyrics so that he could sing something.

There's a version that's very sluggish but the music is totally cool. Bruce's solo is drop-dead perfect, it's awesome. A couple of those demos will be released eventually.

Eddie Trunk with Eric Carr

TODD KERNS *(BRUCE KULICK, SLASH)* – Some may see it as a novelty track 'giving the drummer some', but all of us fans were more than aware of Mr. Carr's vocal prowess from when he took the lead on "Black Diamond" and "Young and Wasted" live. It was high time to give him a song on an album, and "Little Caesar" is a highlight on the *Hot in the Shade* album. The crime and shame of it is that it was Eric's only showcase, but thank God we have it.

ADAM MITCHELL *(SONGWRITER)* – Was Eric's idea, and he and he Bruce Kulick and I were working on Rock Heads. We wrote it at Bruce's condo. It's a totally different type of feel, and it's definitely an Eric feel. It was Eric's moment to shine. I love the drum part and the drum sound.

BOOMERANG

JOE McGINNESS *(KUARANTINE, KLASSIK '78)* – I've always loved the KISS tracks that highlight the musicianship from Eric and Bruce. Both were clearly in their prime musically. This is one of my favorite Bruce Kulick solos of all time.

JOEY SASSO *(THE CIRCLE, NETFLIX)* – There are many KISS tracks that have divided fans for many years but there is only one song that sits atop that list: "Boomerang". This is a track that has stirred quite the debate among die-hard KISS fans and even the members themselves. The song stands out as one of the most divisive in the catalog, with opinions ranging from staunch defense to outright disdain. Despite the conflicting views, "Boomerang' has managed to carve a unique place in the hearts of fans and within the band's own history, adding to its enigmatic allure. The song carries such an infectious rhythm and energy that makes me fully get behind it. When the band embraced what they were trying to do without feeling bad about it, one could not turn away from them – and that is evidently clear on this often-hated song. How can you not get behind it? It is unapologetic KISS at its finest. It encapsulates the band's steadfast mission to entertain and captivate us every moment they have our attention. Beyond the polarizing reception, it sits as an underrated gem in the KISS repertoire. I appreciate the song having its own unique charm that shows the band continuing to attempt to push boundaries and defy expectations. "Boomerang" is a reminder that even in controversy, there lies beauty and artistry worth celebrating whenever we discuss the enduring legacy of KISS and their ever-evolving sound.

NICHOLAS BUCKLAND *(AUTHOR, Hottest Brand in the Land)* – All sizzle, no sausage in this tune that starts off by showcasing the breakneck drumming of Eric Carr and the nimble fingers of Bruce Kulick. After such an exciting intro this one seems to be lacking one vital element present in most KISS songs, a discernible melody. And we've never really figured out what "Get the noose, I know I'm gonna hang, 'cause you're like a boomerang."

RYAN "BB" BANNON *(PODDER THAN HELL PODCAST)* – I always thought this song would have been perfect as an instrumental song. It is easily the heaviest, musically, on the album. Bruce and Eric take this song into another KISS level of heaviness. And the lyrics!?!?!? After 35 years I still don't know what it means.

JOEY CASSATA *(ZO2, Z ROCK)* – There are not many KISS songs that I don't like, this is probably one of them. "Boomerang" is *Hot in the Shade*'s "Fast KISS" song. But this one just feels like they added it just because they thought they needed the quintessential high-energy double-bass song that they have on every non-makeup record.

RAISE YOUR GLASSES:
A Celebration of 50 Years of KISS Songs
by Celebrities, Musicians & Fans.

CHAPTER 20

"REVENGE"

Released: May 19, 1992

Revenge stands as a powerful and impactful chapter in KISS's discography. In a deliberate return to a harder-edged sound, the album marked a departure from the band's previous efforts and showcased a rejuvenated KISS. With a renewed focus on heavy guitar riffs, *Revenge* is often hailed as a late-era gem in the band's catalog, reaffirming their status as hard rock pioneers.

The album kicks off with the thunderous "Unholy," a track that sets the tone for the entire record. With its gritty guitar riffs and Gene Simmons' snarling vocals, "Unholy" announces a departure from the glam metal sound that characterized KISS in the late '80s. Instead, *Revenge* embraces a heavier, darker sonic landscape.

"God Gave Rock 'n' Roll to You II" became a standout anthem from the album, featuring an uplifting message underscored by powerful instrumentals. The song was also featured in the film *Bill & Ted's Bogus Journey*.

Other tracks like "Domino" and "I Just Wanna" continue the assault of heavy riffs and catchy hooks, illustrating the band's commitment to delivering hard-hitting rock. The inclusion of "Every Time I Look at You" adds a touch of balladry, displaying KISS's versatility in balancing heavy metal aggression with heartfelt emotion.

Revenge also marked the first appearance of drummer Eric Singer, following the devastating and untimely passing of Eric Carr in November 1991. Despite having huge shoes to fill, Eric Singer was a great fit for KISS, and the lineup, consisting of Gene Simmons, Paul Stanley, Bruce Kulick, and Eric Singer proved to be a dynamic force.

In retrospect, *Revenge* is often celebrated as a triumph in KISS's later years. The album's return to a harder-edged sound resonated with both longtime fans and a new generation, solidifying *Revenge* as a memorable and influential entry in the KISS discography.

UNHOLY

CHRIS JERICHO *(WRESTLER, FOZZY)* – All of us love KISS for the same reason we love any rock 'n' roll band. Your favorite song is always going to be a rock song because they're a rock band. 'Unholy" is still one of my favorite KISS songs and possibly my favorite Gene song ever. I'll never forget this. We had MuchMusic in Canada, not MTV; it was called the *Power Hour* and they would advertise the new KISS. And when the video was done, I said, "holy shit, it's the return of Gene Simmons". It's the perfect return of the Demon and it's a great Bruce Kulick solo. It's my favorite KISS lineup ever.

ROXY PETRUCCI *(VIXEN)* – The riff and vibe are dark, sexy and evil. I dig that. I'm all about groove and this one lays it down and dirty.

JEFF PLATE *(TRANS-SIBERIAN ORCHESTRA, SAVATAGE)* – Again, I had lost track of KISS for some time, but this song let everyone know they could be as heavy and as metal as they wanted to be when they wanted to be. Great riffs and vocals, great production, and new drummer Eric Singer was a perfect addition.

PJ FARLEY *(TRIXTER, FOZZY)* – I feel this song was sooo important in keeping KISS's head above water when it came out. Tough time for non-grunge bands, and this song spoke to the hardcore KISS Army and we rallied. I enjoyed hearing this EVERY NIGHT on the *Revenge* tour :).

RAISE YOUR GLASSES:
A Celebration of 50 Years of KISS Songs by Celebrities, Musicians & Fans.

Tom and Zeus with Eddie Trunk, Rio Hotel, May 6, 2023

CRAIG GASS *(COMEDIAN)* – My favorite KISS song for a few reasons... Besides the power behind it, it's the fact that this song was released long after they sold a ton of records, a ton of tickets, a ton of merch and had no reason to be hungry, but this song sounds REALLY hungry and hostile. Also, the image in the video of Gene's eyes rolling into the back of his head is what I believe I'll be seeing right before he chokes me to death (I'm being a realist with all the jokes I've done about Gene on stage).

ACE VON JOHNSON *(FASTER PUSSYCAT, L.A. GUNS)* – The best Danzig riff ever to not be written by that band. I love this song, and Gene's sermon of what I always assumed was an ode to the Demon character he portrays onstage is top-notch. Definitely their most evil riff, and I love it. As a kid in the '90s, this was the heavier stuff I was craving from the band. Definitely one of my favorite songs in their catalog.

MARTIN POPOFF *(AUTHOR)* – Man, *Revenge* might be my favorite KISS album, although it's considered a little nutty to pick anything other than *Destroyer* (and sure, I oscillate between the two). Here's the opening track, crushingly recorded by Bob Ezrin, back again after being forgiven for *Music From 'The Elder'*. Everybody's trying harder here because the competition coming from the grunge world and the death of hair metal demands it. KISS responds, thoughtful of riff, pounding of performance, with Gene essentially playing the guy from "Sympathy for the Devil" to delectable perfection.

TAKE IT OFF

BRUCE KULICK *(KISS)* – There's a connection to "Won't Get Fooled Again" in this song with some of the rhythms.

ZEUS *(SHOUT IT OUT LOUDCAST)* – This song is song two of Paul's trifecta of sexual innuendo masterpieces. The sexual and sleazy lyrics are genius. The ultimate stripper song. Paul's vocals are great, the guitar riff is awesome. Kevin Valentine's (Eric Singer was on tour still with Alice Cooper) kicks are great, and there's Gene with his awesome bass slides. I love the Ezrin breakdown, it made you feel like you were in the mind of the sex fiend of the story. When played live there were strippers/dancers on stage with the band. Oh, how the rated-R KISS has tamed over the years. There are so many classic lines from this song like, "So I hop into my car, hit the local titty bar, uh-huh," or how about, "Wave your panties in the air, lick your lips and shake your hair, uh-huh. As Tom would say, "Poetry."

RAISE YOUR GLASSES:
A Celebration of 50 Years of KISS Songs
by Celebrities, Musicians & Fans.

SHANDON SAHM *(MEAT PUPPETS)* – I stopped listening after *Creatures of the Night*, but when I heard this song, I was like, "Yup, KISS is officially stupid now. Just a horrible song with horrible lyrics. It wasn't even tongue-in-cheek funny. It was just silly. I cringed when I heard, "Well my mind is getting dirty around 11:30, uh-huh." Just gross. Yuck.

MAC *(UGLY AMERICAN WEREWOLF IN LONDON PODCAST)* – To see this song live on the *Revenge* tour is the only way to best understand the song. Paul announces, "You've got a lot of pretty girls out here, some girls who like to strut their stuff!" And we think wow, he's going to play "Strutter"! Then he announces "Take It Off", a song that was no doubt made to get played in strip clubs. But as the disappointment of no "Strutter" starts to wash over you with the average riff and sophomoric lyrics, suddenly women (we'll call them dancers) emerge to shake, rattle and roll on stage. It went from worst to first live in my book.

JASON BAKKEN *(COBRAS & FIRE PODCAST)* – True story. Around the time of *Revenge*'s release, I called my boss and quit. Loaded up the car with some buddies to hit the strip clubs. One of the guys with us was not a KISS fan and when this song came on he bitched about how stupid it was. Later on at one of the clubs, a dancer danced to this song. On the drive home he proclaimed he suddenly "got it" and asked to hear it again. Stupid stripper anthem. Love it.

TOUGH LOVE

BRUCE KULICK *(KISS)* – With the Ezrin-produced record, it was tough to get co-writes. They even brought back Vinnie Vincent. And they did that because they're smart. I'm throwing riffs at these guys, and nothing was clicking, and then fortunately, Ezrin heard this and said, 'Let's do that'. Ezrin jumped in and Paul came up with a great chorus. I had to change the key it was in because if it wasn't in the right key then Paul wouldn't be able to sing it, and it wouldn't be on the record. I was really happy to have it on there, and glad to be represented on the *Revenge* record with a co-write.

CHRIS L. *(POD OF THUNDER)* – Given the overall sound and band aesthetic on *Revenge*, it makes sense that one of the songs had the word "tough" in the title. Paul's ode to the edgier side of lovemaking was the perfect candidate, replete with an infectious groove and great syncopated playing by the whole band.

CLAUDIO SPERA *(KISS ARMY NATION PODCAST)* – One of the high points of one my top 5 favorite albums. *Revenge* has no fillers, and you can really feel KISS was hungry and angry. Bob Ezrin's contribution is undeniable. Bob clearly knows how to get the best out of the band. Paul's singing pairs perfectly with a melodic heaviness and depth that hadn't been heard in a long time. The up-tempo bridge preceding Bruce's solo is memorable. This is '90s KISS at its peak.

JOEY SASSO *(THE CIRCLE, NETFLIX)* – *Revenge* packs fan favorite after fan favorite, which was a breath of fresh air for all diehards worldwide. While we give deserving praise to Gene for his full commitment again, it's easy to overlook Paul, because whether we are aware or not, we always know he will deliver for us. Even still, we have to give credit where it's due, and that's why we need to shine a spotlight on a rarely discussed song, "Tough Love". This song packs a punch with its gritty, no-nonsense attitude and powerhouse performance, making it a standout among the stellar lineup of songs on the record. Within "Tough Love", one lyric truly captures its raw energy and unyielding spirit: "You wanna taste it, you gotta face it." These words embody the essence of the song, reflecting its bold and uncompromising nature, while also showcasing Paul's ability to deliver hard-hitting cock rock in every era.

JOEY CASSATA *(ZO2, Z ROCK)* – A very under-appreciated song. I had a bootleg of *Revenge* months before it was released, and when I saw KISS on the club tour at L'Amour in Brooklyn I was really hoping they would play this song. It was one of my favorites from the first time I heard the record. Should have been a single.

SPIT

BRUCE KULICK *(KISS)* – I hint at "The Star-Spangled Banner" in this one. I love Hendrix and I was always bringing in things that I was influenced by.

TOM GIGLIOTTI *(SHOUT IT OUT LOUDCAST)* – *Revenge* is my go-to non-makeup album, and "Spit" has a great mix of tongue-in-cheek Gene along with the hook and melody you expect from KISS. The spoken-word style during the verses combined with Paul jumping in during the chorus makes this such a fun song. Throw in some scat vocals from Gene and an awesome musical breakdown and solo from Bruce and what's not to love!?

Tom and Zeus with Vinnie Vincent

MARK CICCHINI *(THREE SIDES OF THE COIN)* – A fun, "dirty Gene" riff rocker (great work by Bruce!) Love the backing vocals, and having Gene and Paul swap vocal lines is always a treat to hear! I once asked Bruce about the "Star-Spangled Banner" part at the beginning of the solo section and he said, "The original lyrics mentioned something about the 4th of July or something like that." Speaking of lyrics? "The bigger the cushion, the better the pushin'" and "What you are is what you eat" – I'm sure somewhere, St. Hubbins, Tufnel & Smalls approve!

MIKE BRUNN *(THE ROCK EXPERIENCE)* – Oddly, this was the first song I ever heard from the *Revenge* album (besides "God Gave Rock 'N' Roll To You"). Weeks before the album was released, I knew someone who had an advance copy cassette. For whatever reason this was the first song played for me and I loved it. Paul and Gene trading vocals again like they did in the past! Are the lyrics a bit cheesy? Sure. But who cares! This is pure KISS and such a fun song!

ROBERT CONTE *(AUTHOR)* – I laughed out loud when I first heard this duet between Gene and Paul. Its musical groove is amazing but the lyrics are clichéd, especially "The bigger the cushion, the better the pushin" which had already become synonymous with "Big Bottom" in the film *This is Spinal Tap*. I wonder if it may have first been called "Shit" or "Whole Lotta Woman" and someone got cold feet before it was recorded. Its message? Okay, some of us prefer pleasantly plump, curvy women over skinny ones. Not a bad thing. The "Star Spangled Banner" bit exemplifying the freedom of admitting it is amusing, too.

GOD GAVE ROCK 'N' ROLL TO YOU II

BRUCE KULICK *(KISS)* – Such a fantastic song that I think represents the band in a strong way, especially the arrangement from Ezrin. The vocals trading off between Gene and Paul and the breakdown which features Eric Carr on vocals. It's been the anthem for my era.

TODD KERNS *(BRUCE KULICK, SLASH)* – Call it too obvious a choice, but there's a reason it has prevailed as a classic. I've been fortunate enough to sing this song many times and I feel it's as powerful as any classic. The line "If you wanna be a singer or play guitar / Man you gotta sweat or you won't get far / Cuz it's never too late to work 9 to 5" always stays with me. Music isn't a luxury. It's

RAISE YOUR GLASSES:
A Celebration of 50 Years of KISS Songs
by Celebrities, Musicians & Fans.

a privilege. You have to work at it – and boy have KISS worked for it. It's a powerful, effective sentiment all gussied up by the great Bob Ezrin. The third time's the charm. I say that only as the second (*Music From 'The Elder'*) was a bit of a misstep. Not for me though. I love all three of his efforts with the band.

Zach Throne, Todd Kerns and Bruce Kulick onstage at Creatures Fest

BLAS ELIAS *(SLAUGHTER)* – Amazing rock 'n' roll anthem, again catching the vibe of being in the music business and the love between the fans and the music.

CHARLIE PARRA *(KUARANTINE)* – Not just one of my favorite KISS tracks, but also one of my favorite rock anthems ever. That clean guitar bridge featuring Eric Carr's backing vocals is breathtaking. A positive message filled with guitars, love and hope. Those key changes and guitar arrangement are top-notch. I really don't even care the song was on *Bill & Ted's Bogus Journey*, it's just a masterpiece.

JORDAN CANNATA *(SLAUGHTER)* – The first time I heard this song, I was watching the movie *Bill & Ted's Bogus Journey*. I heard the guitar riff, which then becomes the chorus hook. I immediately said, "Who is this?" I had no clue that it was KISS. After that, I listened to the song in its entirety and loved it. The melody is perfect. The harmonized guitar solo is beautiful. The arrangement is awesome. I love the breakdown near the end with the clean guitar and the vocal harmonies. Then it just gets huge again. Once you hear it, it's stuck in your head. It's the kind of melody that you never forget and find yourself humming without even realizing it.

LORETTA CARAVELLO *(ERIC CARR'S SISTER)* – I remember Eric going back and forth to record that. I think he went back three times to LA. I was told that Eric laid down the tracks for *Revenge*. The tracks were laid down. They were used but duplicated for the album.

ALLISON HAGENDORF *(MUSIC JOURNALIST, TV HOST & PRODUCER)* – One of my favorite anthems. Period.

GRAHAM BONNET *(RAINBOW, MICHAEL SCHENKER)* - I knew the original version of the song because of Russ Ballard. It is a very typical Russ-type of chorus. I like KISS's version.

DOMINO

CHRIS JERICHO *(WRESTLER, FOZZY)* – I love it. It's such a simple riff. It's another strange Gene song where he just pulls his pants down and bangs chicks at random.

JORDAN CANNATA *(SLAUGHTER)* – When Joey asked me to do this, I was excited, but then also realized…there is a ton of KISS music that I'm honestly (and regrettably) not familiar with. So, I decided to just put the whole KISS catalog on shuffle to find something that was new for me. That's how I discovered this song. I had never heard it before. But once I heard it, I played it on loop. It's just a badass rock tune. Straightforward. The opening sounds like it would fit on an AC/DC album. The low verse vocals, into the heavily accented riff for the pre-hook, back into the main riff for the chorus. Pure rock 'n' roll.

MARTIN POPOFF *(AUTHOR)* – It's back to the can-do *Revenge* album for a low an' lascivious vocal from Gene, who then kicks it into high gear, showing us that he's got lots of gas in the tank still up into KISS's 16th album in 18 years. Yeah, it's a bit odd putting this popular albeit later track this high, but I just think the band was the best mature version of their golden-era selves on this album, Gene and his voice included.

DAVID JULIAN *(SONGWRITER)* – I wasn't as into the more commercial ballads of the late '80s (all rock all the time—ha!) so when *Revenge* came out, I thought like many fans that it was a true return to form. Great record, and "Domino" sounded great. The production was very dry and in-your-face, and the song was awesome.

CHRIS "THE WALLET" HAICK *(GENE SIMMONS MONEYBAG SODA)* – I'd listen to this over and over because it is my wife's favorite KISS song and every time I'd play it, she'd want to have sex. I don't think there is a better reason to play a KISS song!

JASON BAKKEN *(COBRAS & FIRE PODCAST)* – Should have been the second single. Not exactly a hot take, but this song should still be a staple in their set. Great riff and fun Gene anthem.

HEART OF CHROME

CHRIS JERICHO *(WRESTLER, FOZZY)* – Another one written by Vinnie (Vincent) and Paul. Killer tune. If the album had had a little more legs, they probably could've released it as a single.

KENT SLUCHER *(LUKE BRYAN, KUARANTINE)* – Not only one of my favorite songs, but off one of my favorite albums. Sonically and structurally incredible, the band was on fire. Paul's voice was second-to-none and the choruses are super-strong.

SONNY POONI *(PODCAST ROCK CITY)* – A song that definitely gets overlooked because of some of the hits on the *Revenge* record. This song has a ton of groove. The uniqueness of Paul's passionate singing in the chorus playing off the backing vocals became somewhat of a staple in Paul's songwriting style in the late

'80s and early '90s. Bruce also does some really cool guitar fills throughout the verses. Great deep cut!

AUSTIN MILETO *(SISTERS DOLL)* – I love the heavy approach KISS took on this album. Paul's voice blows me away on this track every time I listen to it, and Bruce's guitar work and tone are incredible.

ZEUS *(SHOUT IT OUT LOUDCAST)* – Angry, bitter and pissed off Paul is great! What a great kiss-off song. Written with Bob Ezrin and Vinnie Vincent, this song couldn't be anything but great. This song has everything – unmistakable catchy Paul chorus, Ezrin breakdown, a tip of the hat to "Love Gun" at the 3:10 mark, and badass lyrics, "You taped our sexy conversations and sold 'em to the BBC." And with the addition of Ezrin, Vinnie and even the late, great Eric Carr, *Revenge* may be the best combination of talent ever assembled for a KISS record.

THOU SHALT NOT

BRUCE KULICK *(KISS)* – In the solo, I hint at a classical piece of music ("Hall of the Mountain King").

CHRIS L. *(POD OF THUNDER)* – "Unholy" is the Gene song on *Revenge* that rightfully gets most of the accolades. "Thou Shalt Not" should be a close second on any discerning listener's list. I'm sure the true identity of the man in black has been stated somewhere, but it adds to my enjoyment that I have no idea who he's calling a son of a bitch or telling to kiss his ass.

COURTNEY CRONIN DOLD *(COMEDIAN)* – OMG, if you don't like this one you can "kindly kiss MY ass!" The guitar, the anthemic chorus, all of it. This is non-makeup era KISS at its best. You got that right.

MARTIN POPOFF *(AUTHOR)* – "I lived most of my life in New York City!" hollers Gene, as this kick-ass *Revenge* track heats up, slamming of beat, world-beating like the KISS of 1976 (commercially, if not on record). This is Gene at his conquering best, not taking no for an answer, striding through a vocal and lyric that is a metaphor for how professional *Revenge* is, top to tails. The chords are a little "Smoke on the Water", but the excitement level is all Mötley Crüe circa *Shout at the Devil*.

TOM GIGLIOTTI *(SHOUT IT OUT LOUDCAST)* – The Demon returned on *Revenge* and there was no one happier than me. Obviously "Unholy" is the epitome of his return, and rightfully so. But this song has long been one of my all-time favorite Gene songs. An absolute powerhouse, with a killer chorus and a riff for the ages. Then comes in the face-melter of a solo by Bruce, and my love of Gene and *Revenge* goes off the charts! A spectacular track!

EVERY TIME I LOOK AT YOU

BRUCE KULICK *(KISS)* – There's some sadness in there, and it's really not a love song like "Forever". I played bass on that track.

RAISE YOUR GLASSES:
A Celebration of 50 Years of KISS Songs
by Celebrities, Musicians & Fans.

CHRIS JERICHO *(WRESTLER, FOZZY)* – They had a big hit with "Forever" and they went to the well again. I appreciate a good KISS ballad, but this one just missed the mark for me. It stops *Revenge* from being a perfect album.

BRYCE MILETO *(SISTERS DOLL)* – I've had many sleepless nights in my feels crying over a girl listening to this song. A real tear-jerker, an incredible song I've related to on every level.

JAY SCOTT *(THE HOOK ROCKS PODCAST)* – This is what a ballad should sound like. Great lyrics, great performance by the band. This is what the song "Forever" wanted to be.

SONNY POONI *(PODCAST ROCK CITY)* – One of the best ballads from the '90s that no one ever talks about. Paul wrote a masterpiece here and I would encourage everyone to put this song on their romantic time playlist. What really irks me about amazing songs like this is that "Every Rose Has Its Thorn" and "Something to Believe In" were both top 5 hits on the *Billboard Hot 100*, but nobody even remembers "Every Time I Look at You". So frustrating...

JEFF TROTT *(ART DIRECTOR)* – "Every Time I Look at You" stands as one of KISS's most powerful ballads, with Paul delivering a soul-stirring performance. It's a testament to the band's versatility, and in my opinion the *MTV Unplugged* version is even more powerful than the original studio recording.

LISA LANE KULICK *(BRUCE KULICK'S WIFE)* – What a beautiful gem in the midst of the rough and tumble *Revenge* LP. The sincerity and passion executed by Paul's heartfelt lyrics is just another example of the softer, more vulnerable side of KISS, which is what I love most about the band.

PARALYZED

BRUCE KULICK *(KISS)* – Gene wanted to have a rapper in that section and I said, 'Are you out of your mind?' That was a real rapper, and I don't remember his name. We tried it, I wasn't really for it. It was a big thing with rock and rap – just look at Run-DMC and Aerosmith.

ZEUS *(SHOUT IT OUT LOUDCAST)* – This song is further proof that *Revenge* is the best Gene album in years. This solid deep cut written by Gene and Bob Ezrin has one of the best choruses on *Revenge*. It also features an Ezrin breakdown with Gene talking and some mumbling right before Bruce's great solo. However, one of the proudest moments of Shout It Out Loudcast was our 100th episode, which featured Bruce Kulick and Chris Jericho, who we had on for *KISS Draft VIII – the Bruce Kulick Draft*. Bruce played the unheard middle rap that was on "Paralyzed" and was eventually deleted. What a thrill, and what an episode.

JOEY CASSATA *(ZO2, ZROCK)* – As soon as the bass slide hit, I knew I would like this song! I had a bootleg copy of *Revenge* months before it was released and this was one of the first songs that stuck out to me. The bootleg didn't have any song titles on it, so I always thought the name of this song was "It's Alright".

RAISE YOUR GLASSES:
A Celebration of 50 Years of KISS Songs
by Celebrities, Musicians & Fans.

Rikki Rockett, Eric Singer and Joey Cassata – the
drummers on the *Rock The Nation* tour

JASON HOOK *(FIVE FINGER DEATH PUNCH)* – Great song
from Gene Simmons. I love the heavy guitars. Gene does a great job
on lead vocals, and the spoken voice / swung middle breakdown is
super-creative and fun.

JEFF TROTT *(ART DIRECTOR)* – For me, "Paralyzed" was just
another song on *Revenge* for a long time. However, it has emerged
as a standout track, driven by Bruce's powerful guitar work and
Gene's gritty vocals. It's a solid cut that deserves more recognition
for its raw intensity and emotional depth. Zach Throne has
performed this with Bruce's band on the last few KISS Kruises and
it's unbelievable how he channels Gene in his delivery when
performing this song. "Paralyzed" is a solid cut that rarely gets
brought up when the *Revenge* album is being discussed or reviewed.

I JUST WANNA

ZEUS *(SHOUT IT OUT LOUDCAST)* – This is the last song of Paul's trifecta of sexual innuendo masterpieces. This features three of five lead guitars of KISS. Old friend Vinnie Vincent returns to co-write some songs on *Revenge* (like this one), and Tommy Thayer is a background singer on this too. Another sexual and sleazy lyric-filled romp, but again done so cleverly, like "Let's Put The X In Sex" and "Take It Off." Paul has a "body built for sin and an appetite for passion!" Bruce has an awesome slide guitar solo and Eric is killing it on the drums. The performance video for the song is a lot of fun.

CHRIS L. *(POD OF THUNDER)* – "I got a body built for sin and an appetite for passion" is the second-best opening line in the entire KISS catalog (first, of course, is "She's a dancer, a romancer, I'm a Capricorn and she's a Cancer"). Then there's the part where you think they're saying "fuck," but they really aren't. In between are all sorts of other brilliant lyrical nuggets. Great video too.

HAL SPARKS *(COMEDIAN)* – This was KISS's return to good-time rock 'n' roll. "Unholy" set the tone for the album and let the haters know this was a real record, but it didn't scare off the fun and excitement of KISS as a band. The tongue-in-cheek lyrics and the Americana riff gave this song all the wink and nod it needed.

COURTNEY CRONIN DOLD *(COMEDIAN)* – I just wanna listen to this song over and over and over! Thank goodness for The Bruce Kulick Band for bringing this back to us live and in full-frontal fierceness. If you're not singing along then you probably just had some dental work done. This one will even get an introverted narcoleptic with a club foot on his feet. Foot.

MURPH *(SHOUT IT OUT LOUDCAST)* – This may be the last song in the catalog where I really enjoy listening to Paul. He sounds great, the tune is catchy, and he is hitting all of the notes. He's still having fun. I still recall the video, and it's a version of Paul, without makeup, that I like to remember. Solid track from front to back.

CARR JAM 1981

JOEY JASSO *(THE CIRCLE, NETFLIX)* – This instrumental showcases the iconic Eric Carr feeling his way through a groove that transports us back to memories of musical bliss that warmed all fans' hearts for more than a decade. This instrumental showcases his incredible talent and significance within the band and for KISS fans worldwide. As the formidable drummer who brought a new energy and sound to KISS during a pivotal era, Eric Carr's legacy continues to resonate, making "Carr Jam 1981" a poignant tribute to his lasting impact on the band's evolution. With its thunderous drums and infectious groove, "Carr Jam 1981" captures Eric Carr's unparalleled skill and passion for his craft. Despite being an instrumental track, its emotive power and dynamic composition stand as a testament to Carr's musical prowess and creative spirit, solidifying its place as a standout piece in the history of KISS.

IZZY PRESLEY *(MUSICIAN, COMIC)* – "Eric's only recorded drum solo on a demo from 1981 that we fixed and Bruce put a solo over it"… or however the hell they said it in *KISS X-treme Close-Up*, with NO mention of the fact that it was "Breakout" on the

Frehley's Comet record. Anything they can do to bury Ace. Great playing by Bruce and Eric, of course.

JOEY CASSATA *(ZO2, Z ROCK)* – What can I say about the person who has been my biggest inspiration in my drumming career? The most incredible thing about this track is that it most likely wasn't even a real take. This is more than likely just Eric messing around in the studio. I was honored to be asked by Eric's sister Loretta to recreate "Carr Jam 1981" for Eric's memorial album *Unfinished Business*. Eric's feel and overall creativeness during his solos are unmatched! His solo is constructed like a song. Each solo has different sections with meaning and purpose. I was absolutely devastated when I heard of Eric's passing. I am so very happy that KISS paid tribute to him on revenge by including "Carr Jam 1981".

Joey Cassata (as Eric Carr) with Paul Stanley and Gene Simmons
at the KISS Box Set release party

RAISE YOUR GLASSES:
A Celebration of 50 Years of KISS Songs
by Celebrities, Musicians & Fans.

PETER CORY *(KISS LIVE AUCTIONS)* – Not one of the best KISS songs in my opinion, but again, seeing Bruce and his band play this live at Creatures Fest in Nashville in 2022 was really, really good. Everyone loved Eric Carr, and having Ace be part of the song is a true gem in KISStory.

JEFF TROTT *(ART DIRECTOR)* – What can I say? It was a tough time for KISS. Coming off the road from the *Hot in the Shade* tour and preparing to enter the studio for *Revenge*, Eric Carr fell ill. Including this track on the *Revenge* album as a tribute to Eric was a heartfelt gesture. Everyone loved Eric, and this track is a small example of the powerful, bombastic drumming Eric brought to KISS. R.I.P. Eric.

RAISE YOUR GLASSES:
A Celebration of 50 Years of KISS Songs
by Celebrities, Musicians & Fans.

RAISE YOUR GLASSES:
A Celebration of 50 Years of KISS Songs
by Celebrities, Musicians & Fans.

CHAPTER 21

"CARNIVAL OF SOULS"

Released: October 28, 1997

Carnival of Souls: The Final Sessions offers a glimpse into an experimental phase of KISS's career. The album, originally recorded in the mid-'90s but shelved until 1997, showcases the band's exploration of darker, grunge-influenced sounds.

Marked by heavy guitar riffs and introspective lyrics, *Carnival of Souls* is an intriguing departure from KISS's traditional hard rock roots, sparking both curiosity and debate among fans.

The opening track, "Hate," sets a darker and more aggressive tone, featuring heavy guitar riffs and a departure from the glam metal aesthetic that characterized KISS in the past. Throughout the album, Gene Simmons and Paul Stanley deliver vocals with a raw and gritty quality, complementing the overall mood of the music.

Songs like "Master & Slave" and "I Walk Alone" further emphasize the band's foray into a grunge-inspired sonic territory. The album's stripped-down production style also contributed to its distinctive atmosphere.

The delayed release of *Carnival of Souls* in 1997 added an element of mystery to the album, as it had been recorded several years earlier and shelved. This timing contributed to the album's reception as a retrospective glimpse into KISS's exploration of alternative sounds during a period of significant musical evolution.

In retrospect, *Carnival of Souls* remains a polarizing but intriguing chapter in KISS's discography. While it may not have achieved the commercial success of some of their earlier works, it stands as a testament to the band's willingness to push boundaries and experiment with their sound, making it a noteworthy and distinctive entry in KISS's extensive catalog.

HATE

BRUCE KULICK *(KISS)* – For the intro, I have a real high-gain amp and had a crazy pedal. I knew that if I wasn't plugged in, that's what it would sound like. You hear me getting close to plugging in and that's what it sounds like. It's like someone trying to communicate from another planet. You can kind of hear Paul saying something during that intro, but it's actually backwards. He's actually saying, "little Billy Corgan!"

CHRIS JERICHO *(WRESTLER, FOZZY)* – I like how they opened *Carnival of Souls* with another heavy Gene song. The heaviest, meanest KISS song. The song is fucking crazy. The drums are fucking nuts. "Hate" is the perfect title for it. Because when I listen to it, I get mad. Like anybody that I fucking hate, I want to just punch them in the face when I hear this song. And Bruce is on fire this whole record.

Chris Jericho with Eric Singer

RAISE YOUR GLASSES:
A Celebration of 50 Years of KISS Songs
by Celebrities, Musicians & Fans.

WES BEECH (*THE PLASMATICS*) – Like many hardcore KISS fans I procured a bootleg copy of *Carnival of Souls* and this opening track made it plain that this wasn't just another KISS album. The sound was dark and heavy, grunge-like and almost industrial, a total departure from anything the band had done before. Clearly, they were hitching their wagon to the modern sound of Alice In Chains, Soundgarden, Pearl Jam, and even a touch of Nine Inch Nails. Sadly the album was put on the back burner and not released until after the fact, which, coupled with them not touring it or playing any of the songs live, hurt sales. Bruce supplies a great solo with the appropriate-for-the-era wah wah, and the drums and bass churn along nicely. Gene's vocal delivery is also suitably dark and demonic and sets the tone for the rest of the album. Not an album that I revisit often but it is a nice departure from the poppier *Dynasty* and *Unmasked*.

MARK CICCHINI (*THREE SIDES OF THE COIN*) – Like "Unholy", Gene delves into the topic of religion, which not only Gene, but the rest of the band rarely ever did. "Don't you think it's odd / Man was created in the image of God?" Easily one of my top 20 favorite KISS songs of any era. Bruce and Eric shine! Aggressive riffing and soloing throughout, and easily one of the greatest drum parts in the entire KISS catalog. I also think *Carnival of Souls*, not *Music From 'The Elder'*, is the most overlooked gem in the entire KISS catalog.

MARTIN POPOFF (*AUTHOR*) – I've always been a fan of *Carnival of Souls*, and it's well-known that Gene was more on board with the dark, doomy grunge direction of the thing than Paul was. I think that seeps through the walls like killer mold on the album's crushing opening track "Hate," where Gene sells it well with an apocalyptic vocal, utilizing his barking-dog growl to delicious result over a vicious riff and rhythm combination that helps construct the most technical and heavy song on the album.

BRANDON FIELDS *(MINEFIELD)* – This is one of Gene's best tracks, in my opinion, off of any album. It just reeks of heaviness; the riff, Gene's vocals, Eric's aggressive drumming, and the dropped tuning. I'm a major fan of this genre of music and thought Gene was perfect for it. Bruce also showcases some awesome tremolo bar abilities in this. Not everyone is a fan of tremolo bars, but you can't deny how effortlessly and elegantly Bruce has utilized his throughout his career. It was a great choice as well to have a Gene song start this album. It was just an unfortunate victim of the reunion era. I don't know if it would have sold much better than it has if it had a proper release, but it definitely deserved one. "Hate" is a great example of Bruce getting to show more character on a KISS studio album as well. He was the perfect guitarist to be in KISS to make an album like this.

RAIN

CHRIS JERICHO *(WRESTLER, FOZZY)* – I love this song. People say it's such a grunge-type song. But you know what, they did it better than Mötley Crüe did it. And I love the chorus. I think the 1-2-3 punch of "Hate", "Rain" and "Master & Slave" is one of their strongest 1-2-3 punches, and stronger than *Revenge* because *Revenge* had "Tough Love" which I don't think is up to snuff.

TONY MUSALLAM *(RESTRAYNED)* – "Rain" starts with an incredibly heavy and sludgy riff. The song plods along incorporating some interesting time-signature changes. The subject matter is uncharacteristically dark and depressing. Still, I think this is a stand-out track from an album that is typically panned by most KISS fans.

JASON HERNDON *(KISS MY WAX PODCAST)* – I love the *Carnival of Souls* album, and "Rain" is easily one of Paul's best vocal performances on any KISS album. Such a killer, heavy, standout track. My favorite on the album.

CLAUDIO SPERA *(KISS ARMY NATION PODCAST)* – This song, as most of the *Carnival of Souls* album, uses a lot of detuned strings, where the low strings are tuned down. When all guitars are together in the mix, the sound is a bit bizarre, but it's a cool track. Bruce's riff is dark and heavy-footed. Paul has such a powerful voice, and it clearly shows his ability to sing dynamically. I like this song very much.

JEFF TROTT *(ART DIRECTOR)* – "Rain" kicks off with a sludgy, grungy bass intro and a down-tuned riff. Despite Paul's discomfort and struggle with the modern style of this album, "Rain" stands out as one of his strongest tracks on the album. Co-written by Bruce Kulick and Curtis Cuomo, the song features a standout moment in the middle with Paul singing, "Open your eyes you can't deny, it's just a fantasy, YEAH." This breakdown captures a pure KISS/Paul sound on an otherwise unique album.

MASTER & SLAVE

BRUCE KULICK *(KISS)* – We set out to do a heavier album than *Revenge*. I remember it was a little hard for Paul to totally get into it at first. The song is really based on his guitar riff. I came up with some other parts, like the bridge, but the rest of it was all Paul.

CHRIS JERICHO *(WRESTLER, FOZZY)* – The most KISS-like song to me on this album. Great tune. It sounds like it could've been on *Hot in the Shade* or *Revenge*. It's got some swing to it and I love the breakdown. What a great riff. And when I was pre-Fozzy, when I was starting to think about putting together a band and doing covers, that was one of the songs that I was working on because I was going to try and sing and play bass and I could play that riff. I was like, fuck, I really want to do "Master & Slave" live.

Tom and Zeus with Keith Leroux, KISS Kruise XI

RAISE YOUR GLASSES:
A Celebration of 50 Years of KISS Songs
by Celebrities, Musicians & Fans.

CHRIS L. *(POD OF THUNDER)* – *Carnival of Souls* is an album I didn't care for when it came out. It didn't sound "finished" to me, and it seemed to be too desperate of an attempt to get with the times (does anyone really want a depressed, downtrodden KISS?). I've since come to appreciate it, and this song – a natural progression from *Revenge*, specifically "Unholy" – showcases the great chemistry of four fantastic musicians throwing down and rocking out with flash, balls, and ability.

TONY MUSALLAM *(RESTRAYNED)* – This song has a killer, heavy riff. I like the way the verse is just bass and drums and continues to build into the chorus. It's very different for KISS. But I like it.

ROBERT CONTE *(AUTHOR)* – Best track on *Carnival of Souls*! Cassettes floated around Mercury/PolyGram referencing it as "Tell Me" — and then the album was shelved when the original band reunited. Later, some of us took a road trip from New York City to Detroit, Michigan to see the first full *Alive/Worldwide* concert, and a colleague surprised us with a copy! We must have listened to it a dozen times and this song described exactly how I felt about life at that moment: "Time, the race you'll never win…" Had this received radio play I believe *Carnival of Souls* would have had a chance, but the label and band didn't support it, hence its doom.

RAISE YOUR GLASSES:
A Celebration of 50 Years of KISS Songs by Celebrities, Musicians & Fans.

Robert Conte with Gene Simmons

CHILDHOOD'S END

ZEUS *(SHOUT IT OUT LOUDCAST)* – From the much-maligned *Carnival of Souls* album, where KISS went supposedly "grunge" with the help of Alice In Chains producer, Toby Wright. I get that people say KISS chased trends and that KISS supposedly had their disco, heavy metal, hair metal, and grunge albums, but guess what, they still were KISS albums and they still were done well. If this is a grunge album, then it's a damn good grunge album. This song proves it. The KISS formula is always still prevalent in all their songs. This song is dark, like most of the album, and so are the lyrics. Gene is singing about the suicide of an old friend. The melody is fantastic, as are Gene's vocals. The backing vocals overlapping on the outro is cool.

RAISE YOUR GLASSES:
A Celebration of 50 Years of KISS Songs
by Celebrities, Musicians & Fans.

PASQUALE VARI *(KISS ARMY NATION PODCAST)* – Like most KISS fans, *Carnival of Souls* was not one of my favorite albums, but man, Gene's contributions were awesome. *Revenge* and *Carnival* defined '90s Gene. From the first time I heard the bootleg version of this song, I was in love with it. I can't tell you how many times I listened to it when it first came out.

JASON BAKKEN *(COBRAS & FIRE PODCAST)* – This was the first song I heard bootlegged from this record via some shitty Geocities website. As bad as the audio quality was, I got excited by this song. Some of Gene's best lyrics in a long time, and nice use of the children's choir.

JOE McGINNESS *(KUARANTINE, KLASSIK '78)* – I remember the first time I listened to *Carnival of Souls* in its entirety this song in particular stuck out to me. I think the group vocals, the haunting lyrics and the melody made it memorable. I truly like the song a lot. I would love to hear it remixed someday with a little more reverb and more powerful drums.

TOM GIGLIOTTI *(SHOUT IT OUT LOUDCAST)* – *Carnival of Souls* is considered their grunge album and I won't argue otherwise, especially because I'm a massive fan of grunge and this album in general. This is one of those songs where Gene's various vocal styles really shine. This song seems to get dumped on way more than it should, and I blame that on the general dislike of the album and the style. I absolutely love the outro with the kids singing, and how can you not love when Gene does a callback to "God of Thunder" when he screams, "You got something about you! You got something I need!"

I WILL BE THERE

BRAD RUSTOVEN *(SLAMFEST PODCAST)* – Obviously, written for Paul's son – I loved it the first time I heard it. Lots going on in this song – it always felt like it was heavily influenced by Zeppelin. The arrangement is a slow build, from the opening 12-string acoustic to the orchestration and powerful vocal from Paul during the outro. I rewrote the lyrics to this song as a lullaby for my son.

COURTNEY CRONIN DOLD *(COMEDIAN)* – Ominous acoustic guitar will hook me into a song every single time. It's the fluffy pillow in the middle of all the hard rock. Were they listening to Alice In Chains and Styx that morning? Maybe... Plus, I like to pretend that Paul is singing this to me.

WES BEECH *(THE PLASMATICS)* – I certainly won't be there! This dirge-like song sung by Paul is easily my least favorite song on my least favorite KISS album. This is just self-indulgence as only Paul can deliver, and it just doesn't fit in with the heavier grunge direction of the album. To me it's just a bad song with cringeworthy lyrics that doesn't belong on this record. And for all of you keeping score at home it's one of three songs that start with "I" in the title.

JASON BAKKEN *(COBRAS & FIRE PODCAST)* – A heartful and emotional vocal from Paul. One his best. The post-solo chorus should make the hair on the back of your neck stand up.

JOEY CASSATA *(ZO2, ZROCK)* – I absolutely love *Carnival of Souls*! When KISS goes out of the box it's always fantastic. "I Will

Be There" is not like anything they have ever released. Great melody and message. Paul and Bruce kill this song. Pure emotion.

JUNGLE

CHRIS JERICHO *(WRESTLER, FOZZY)* – I think it's a great song, and the fact that it was actually on the radio in the '90s blew my mind. It's got a really cool slinky, slimy kind of riff. And it's got a cool chorus.

COURTNEY CRONIN DOLD *(COMEDIAN)* – What did Gene do to his bass to make it sound like a swamp creature? Because I LOVE IT! I find myself singing "Shine" by Collective Soul in the middle. I smell a mash-up.

TONY MUSALLAM *(RESTRAYNED)* – The intro jungle-rhythm drums might be a little on the nose. But paired with the heavy bass groove, it works perfectly. I like the vocal delivery in the pre-chorus, which sets up the chorus perfectly.

CHRIS L. *(POD OF THUNDER)* – Of the many KISS songs that are driven by one of Gene's badass bass lines, this could be my favorite. "Jungle" is the perfect bridge between the harder-edged cock-rock swagger of *Revenge* and the full-on grunge introspection of *Carnival of Souls*. The band even gets borderline jammy toward the end. I remember hearing this on rock radio when it came out and thinking, "wow, KISS might be on to something here."

TOM GIGLIOTTI *(SHOUT IT OUT LOUDCAST)* – An absolutely killer bass line gives this song a very cool, sleazy vibe. Paul makes us wait until the chorus to hear the vocals we all know and love from him. And when it comes, it's like a bomb going off with his screams and the band crashing in all at once. The verses give us time to catch our breath. The guitars are really doing some cool things in the background of the verses, and the overall sound of this track makes it no surprise it was one of the more popular ones on the album.

IN MY HEAD

CHRIS JERICHO *(WRESTLER, FOZZY)* – It's cool. It's another angry, dirty Gene song.

STEVE WRIGHT *(PODDER THAN HELL PODCAST)* – Dark, ominous start that goes into a heavy stomp. Growly Gene lead vocals, but Paul's vocals are laid in throughout the song. The grinding guitars that come in during the verses give it an even heavier feel. Bruce pulls off a sort of trippy convoluted solo with some cool effects. The "Look behind the mask" adds to the creepiness of the track. This is one heavy KISS song!

TONY MUSALLAM *(RESTRAYNED)* – "In My Head" is Gene being the Demon at a time when he wasn't really embodying that persona. Musically, the song plods along from start to finish, layered with some menacing lyrics and vocal melodies.

DARREN PALTROWITZ *(AUTHOR, How David Lee Roth Changed The World)* – History correctly shows that *Carnival of Souls* was KISS trying to "go grunge" via producer Toby Wright, and "In My Head" sounds like Gene Simmons channeling Alice In Chains, who Wright had produced. Yet interestingly, this one was co-written with guitarist Scott Van Zen and Black 'N Blue singer Jaime St. James. As a big fan of AIC, it sounds good to me. But I think all of that speaks volumes about how Gene and KISS kept up long-term relationships with a lot of people. When I interviewed Scott Van Zen two years or so ago, he referenced talking with Gene that week. When Gene stepped offstage after the final KISS show, on pay-per-view, he quickly referenced Jaime, who he had produced in the 1980s. The aforementioned Toby Wright was an assistant engineer on 1987's *Crazy Nights* album. So chew on that anytime people want to present the narrative of Gene and Paul being difficult to work with or be friendly with.

ZEUS *(SHOUT IT OUT LOUDCAST)* – Love the pounding heavy drums, then the chugging guitar. This is a heavy KISS song and very Alice In Chains-like, but Gene makes it work, especially on the chorus. The recurring "in my head" throughout the song gives it a dark foreboding theme.

IT NEVER GOES AWAY

COURTNEY CRONIN DOLD *(COMEDIAN)* – This HAS to be a song about herpes. No? My apologies.

RAISE YOUR GLASSES:
A Celebration of 50 Years of KISS Songs
by Celebrities, Musicians & Fans.

JOEY SASSO (*THE CIRCLE, NETFLIX*) – An unsung hero from an album where the band delved into the grunge genre. Despite the band's departure from their traditional sound, this track shines as a standout, with its haunting melody and introspective lyrics that capture the essence of KISS navigating unfamiliar musical territory. The core emotion of the song reflects a sense of enduring struggle and resilience. This poignance cuts deep if you let it in, underscoring the raw vulnerability and depth of "It Never Goes Away", making it a potent representation of KISS's experimental phase that was *Carnival of Souls* as a whole.

JASON BAKKEN (*COBRAS & FIRE PODCAST*) – *Carnival of Souls* has become a record KISS and some of the faithful shit on. Not me. I love what they did with this record. Maybe it's buried in subtext, but I couldn't find a lyric about Paul complaining about his butler, as he likes to joke. A well-constructed, dark tune.

JEFF TROTT (*ART DIRECTOR*) – Another track from *Carnival of Souls* co-written by Paul Stanley, Bruce Kulick, and Curtis Cuomo that showcases why Bruce Kulick is the MVP of this album. Playing both guitar and bass on this track, Kulick shines. The song starts with a slow build through the first couple of verses, but when the chorus hits, it takes off and continues to climb until the end.

ERNIE PALOOZA (*TOP 5 WITH JOEY CASSATA*) – This song lands between Black Sabbath's "Disturbing the Priest" and Alice In Chains' "Dirt". It really doesn't have a hook, which makes the song a no-go for me.

SEDUCTION OF THE INNOCENT

CHRIS CZYNSZAK *(DECIBEL GEEK PODCAST)* – A very strange song in the KISS catalog, but made more interesting by its origin story. The melody line came to Gene as a child in Israel and he carried it with him until recording *Carnival of Souls*. It's not the greatest riff ever, but the song is taken to a new level due to Bruce Kulick's blistering solo.

TOM GIGLIOTTI *(SHOUT IT OUT LOUDCAST)* – Gene was inspired by world music and various instruments and ways to create sounds here. This is definitely something different from him and the band in general. But I always love different, even if it's something I may not go to all the time as a KISS fan. The chorus picks up the pace and takes a few turns musically that give listeners more of what they expect from KISS. An incredibly awesome guitar solo with unique effects make it memorable, if nothing else, before the classic ripping sounds from Bruce make a welcome appearance.

PASQUALE VARI *(KISS ARMY NATION PODCAST)* – It's really a shame *Carnival of Souls* was tossed aside for the *Reunion* tour. I feel some of Gene's strongest '80s and '90s material came from this album. "Seduction of the Innocent" destroys anything Gene did after *Lick It Up*. I would love to hear this song, along with a few more from *Carnival*, on his solo tour.

COURTNEY CRONIN DOLD *(COMEDIAN)* – The guitar is the seductive hypnotic dance, and Eric's drums are low and slow like he's coming for you! Then BOOM! They got you.

ZEUS *(SHOUT IT OUT LOUDCAST)* – *Carnival of Souls* worked for Gene. Paul? Not so much. But this is another solid song, with Gene using his laid-back vocals with interesting lyrics. Bruce gets a very Jerry Cantrell tone out of his solo, probably with the help of co-producer Toby Wright.

I CONFESS

TOM GIGLIOTTI *(SHOUT IT OUT LOUDCAST)* – *Carnival of Souls* is a very divisive record, and I get it to some extent. But when KISS decided to record this album and become "dark", they crushed it – and this deep cut is a perfect example. Gene's vocals during the verses are somber and almost spoken word, and then when the chorus comes crashing in, it's an undeniable rocker with that KISS hook. I love this album and I will wave that flag constantly!

Tom and Zeus with Bruce Kulick

RAISE YOUR GLASSES:
A Celebration of 50 Years of KISS Songs
by Celebrities, Musicians & Fans.

STEVE WRIGHT *(PODDER THAN HELL PODCAST)* – Sinister feel from the start that feels like it was from Gene's '78 solo album. Great kick up for the chorus with the soaring guitars underneath. Then goes right back to the softer vocals. There's a build into the solo that doesn't go as I hoped it would, and a Led Zeppelin feel towards the end. I love the heavy stomping part at the end with some killer leads from Bruce. Fantastic deep track on an album full of deep tracks.

ZEUS *(SHOUT IT OUT LOUDCAST)* – The best song on *Carnival of Souls*. This dark, eerie song is written by Gene and Christian rock singer Ken Tamplin. Gene is so underrated as a singer. He uses so many different styles, and on "I Confess" he finds the right groove. Love the verses and the chorus. What a haunting song.

Zeus with Gene Simmons, *An Evening with Gene Simmons*, May 7, 2023

JEFF TROTT *(ART DIRECTOR)* – *Carnival of Souls* marks a bold evolution for KISS, defying trends and showcasing a new dimension of their sound. "I Confess" stands as a highlight, with its gritty tone and Gene's versatile vocal range. Bruce Kulick's sludgy but rhythmic guitar and Eric's hard-hitting drums fits the grit of the track perfectly.

JOEY CASSATA *(ZO2, ZROCK)* – An incredibly dark, eerie song from the Demon! The fact that KISS can make an album like *Carnival of Souls* and write songs like "I Confess" is a true testament to not only their level of musicianship, but also their diversity in songwriting. Their diversity in all of their albums is why KISS is my favorite band of all time.

IN THE MIRROR

KENT SLUCHER *(LUKE BRYAN, KUARANTINE)* – I personally love this tune, it has a fantastic drum break and the best Paul scream ever! I've always dug the main guitar are riff and love the four-on-the-floor choruses.

CHRIS JERICHO *(WRESTLER, FOZZY)* – It's a really cool tune. It's like a real Soundgarden song. I hear that riff and it's like, oh that sounds like Kim Thayil (Soundgarden guitarist). They really locked into their Soundgarden side with this song.

ALEXANDER TALKINGTON *(KISS ARMY THINGS PODCAST)* – This song is easily my favorite off *Carnival of Souls*. It feels like old-school KISS but with that '90s KISS drive to it. Eric Singer provides the best drum breaks in the entire catalog. From 2:49 to 2:58, Eric unleashes a flurry of tasty fills and fast double-bass that is by far the track's highlight.

CHRIS L. *(POD OF THUNDER)* – Just like the entire grunge movement, *Carnival of Souls* is often saddled with the blanket statement that the whole thing is gloomy, self-loathing, and an overall bummer. Not so with this song. It's an upbeat, powerful rocker that to my ears wouldn't have been out of place on *Lick It Up* or *Hot in the Shade*.

TOM GIGLIOTTI *(SHOUT IT OUT LOUDCAST)* – A straight-ahead rocker with no pretense, and it gives Paul a chance to shine vocally in a way that fans waited for on this album. Eric Singer is pounding away here and even gives us a mini drum solo. Listen closely for some slide guitar effects as the song progresses. As usual, Bruce burns it down with another incredible solo. A fantastic deep cut and one that I always go to when listening to *Carnival of Souls*.

I WALK ALONE

BRUCE KULICK *(KISS)* – This meant so much to me. It was going to be a Gene song, but I just kept working on the demo. I got clever with doing some of the backwards stuff and taking a bridge from a different version. It was (producer) Toby Wright who said, "Bruce has to sing it". He didn't know about the reunion tour yet. He felt that having someone else sing a song is important. I didn't realize how prophetic Gene's lyrics were.

RAISE YOUR GLASSES:
A Celebration of 50 Years of KISS Songs
by Celebrities, Musicians & Fans.

ZEUS *(SHOUT IT OUT LOUDCAST)* – Bruce Kulick finally gets to sing on his last KISS album. What shame he wasn't given more of a chance on earlier albums. I like the melody, Bruce's lyrics and Bruce's guitar work, especially his solos throughout the song. I like when Paul doubles on the vocals towards the end as well. The song is haunting and a fitting end to this album.

Murph, Tom and Zeus, Stonehill College, 1994

NICHOLAS BUCKLAND *(AUTHOR, Hottest Brand in the Land)* – On first listen I thought this was Kulick the Younger's ode to personal grooming ("I Wore Cologne"). Bruce goes full "Flying in a Blue Dream"-era Satriani by taking the reins of the microphone regardless of any actual vocal ability and gives his all in this quiet/loud/quiet/loud rocker, a formula in vogue at the time (or at least in vogue five years earlier). Eric's crisp drums and Paul's backing vocal give this song's chorus an energy boost only let down by the clichéd backwards tape sounds in the solo.

LISA LANE KULICK *(BRUCE KULICK'S WIFE)* – Bruce introduced me to "I Walk Alone" when we first started dating. Since then, it's become very special and near and dear to my heart. It was destined to be Bruce's song. Not only is the sentiment of the lyric perfect for that time in his life, but the melody and guitar work is the heart and soul of my husband. His creative approach is unique with his use of backward guitars and drums, as well as the double- and triple-tracking of the guitars and vocals, which gives the song a multi-dimensional, interactive sound. It's not just a song. It's an experience.

CHRIS "THE WALLET" HAICK *(GENE SIMMONS MONEYBAG SODA)* – *Carnival of Souls* was released as I started my career fresh out of college. I was at a time in my life where my close friends and I went separate ways and I really felt I had nobody. I identified with "I Walk Alone" because I knew I could only count on myself to accomplish my dreams. *Carnival of Souls* gets a bad rap, and Bruce Kulick fucking nails this song. I really enjoy this record.

WES BEECH *(THE PLASMATICS)* – For my money one of the better tracks on an otherwise dark and sludgy experiment, *Carnival of Souls*, KISS's foray into grunge. Bruce's vocals are a standout on this track tacked onto the end of the album almost as an afterthought. Sad that Bruce was never given more vocal opportunities as he had a distinctive voice that helps sell the song. The melody Is almost Beatle-y, and the band is tight and crisp throughout. A definite winner on an album that for me was played once and done.

CHAPTER 22

"PSYCHO CIRCUS"

Released: September 22, 1998

Psycho Circus marked a significant moment in KISS's history as the original lineup reunited for a studio album after nearly two decades. While the album is recognized for its ambitious concept and the return of the iconic characters, it received mixed reviews due to controversies surrounding the extent of the original members' involvement. Despite the criticisms, *Psycho Circus* embodies KISS's theatrical and anthemic style, offering a mix of classic hard rock and a glimpse into the band's enduring showmanship.

The title track serves as a bombastic introduction to the album, complete with a carnival-esque atmosphere and a declaration of KISS's enduring spectacle. The song encapsulates the band's theatrical approach to their music and performances, setting the stage for an album that aims to recapture the magic of their early years.

While the reunion was a cause for celebration among fans, controversies emerged regarding the extent of the original members' involvement in the recording process. Some tracks featured contributions from session musicians, sparking debates about the authenticity of the reunion. Despite the controversies, the album produced memorable tracks such as "I Pledge Allegiance to the State of Rock & Roll" and "We Are One."

Despite the mixed critical reception and controversies, *Psycho Circus* holds a special place in KISS's discography as a symbolic reunion of the original lineup. The album captures the essence of KISS's showmanship, combining theatricality with their signature hard rock sound. *Psycho Circus* stands as a testament to KISS's ability to create a grand spectacle, showcasing the enduring power of their iconic characters.

PSYCHO CIRCUS

BLAS ELIAS *(SLAUGHTER)* – This is the ultimate song to get your blood pumping and get psyched up for a show! When I played with the Blue Man Group band, we played this song almost every night while getting ready for the show. We had neon face paint and neon skeleton costumes, our room had black lights and weird props and things painted all over the walls. There was definitely KISS energy in the band!

TOMMY SOMMERS *(THREE SIDES OF THE COIN)* – When I dropped the needle for the very first time on this song I felt like a kid again. It could be the best opening track on any KISS album. I absolutely love this song and never tire of listening to it. It became a staple in their live shows and I'm glad that they kept it in the set.

CHRIS JERICHO *(WRESTLER, FOZZY)* – They made this a KISS classic by playing it live. It's another one that reminds me of a Bob Ezrin-type of song because it's got the breakdown to it. It's got a great harmony part, kind of a little bit of a "Detroit Rock City"-type vibe to it. It's very epic and very much a great opener.

JAY SCOTT *(THE HOOK ROCKS PODCAST)* – The return of the original KISS. I love this tune for so many reasons but mainly it felt like the return of all four legends together again, and it was special.

TONY MUSALLAM *(RESTRAYNED)* – When I hear this song, I am immediately transported back to 1998. We made the road trip from the Bay Area to Los Angeles for the opening night of the *Psycho*

Circus tour. This song was a perfect choice to open the show. It's a well-written song and a great return to the classic KISS lineup.

PJ FARLEY *(TRIXTER, FOZZY)* – This song was the first "back in makeup" original lineup song for KISS, and it did not disappoint. It's catchy as hell, with all the KISS elements firing, not corny or forced. I always revert to how important a song is to a band's career, and much like "Unholy", "Psycho Circus" HAD to be great. And it was.

WITHIN

ZEUS *(SHOUT IT OUT LOUDCAST)* – The reunion that wasn't. This song is real heavy. The drums when the chorus kicks in are fucking great. No it's not Peter, but Kevin Valentine. It sounds like a leftover from *Carnival of Souls*. The chorus when Gene sings over his own repeated verses is cool.

CHRIS JERICHO *(WRESTLER, FOZZY)* – I think it's a really cool riff. I know they played it live for a bit on the *Psycho Circus* tour. It's a very *Revenge*-sounding tune. It was kind of a cool Gene stomping song.

MARK CICCHINI *(THREE SIDES OF THE COIN)* – From Bruce's backward intro effect (yes, it's Bruce) throughout the grungy, groovy and trippy (well, trippy for KISS) groove, "Within" shines. I love Gene's lyric throughout, and the guitar tone too. My only complaint? I actually prefer the live version arrangement from the bonus disc. Why? I wish they would have let Ace play that same solo that he plays live on the studio album. The studio version, while great, sorely lacks Ace's feel from the way they played it live on the *Psycho Circus* tour.

JEFF TROTT *(ART DIRECTOR)* – "Within" is, in my opinion, the best Gene lead vocal on the album. Although Bruce Kulick had exited the band due to Gene and Paul reuniting with Peter Criss and Ace Frehley, he still played a significant role on *Psycho Circus*. "Within" features a unique vinyl click sound, reminiscent of a record playing backwards, and it's rumored to be a leftover track from *Carnival of Souls*, which makes sense. The song starts slow, leading into ripping guitars and Gene's powerful vocals. The soft breakdown in the middle, right before Bruce's solo, is fantastic. "Within" is one of the strongest tracks on *Psycho Circus*.

ALEXANDER TALKINGTON *(KISS ARMY THINGS PODCAST)* – Sonic. Heavy. Atmospheric. Other-worldy... Gene either had an unnamed co-writer or this is his lyrical magnum opus! "World Without Heroes" meets "Childhood's End" and then some. Musically, this song hypnotizes the listener— almost into a psychedelic trance. Heavy metal Beatles.

I PLEDGE ALLEGIANCE TO THE STATE OF ROCK & ROLL

HOLLY KNIGHT *(SONGWRITER)* – I find that song somewhat embarrassing, and I'm the guilty one that came up with that title. No other band could get away with it. I pride myself on the quality of my work and what I consider a well-written song. But that's not one of them. I don't think that any of the KISS songs I co-wrote are reflective of the quality of songs I've written. I'm trying to say that in a way that's delicate.

JOEY FATONE (*THE CIRCLE, NETFLIX*) – Let me tell you something straight up – this song is perfect. If only the title wasn't so unnecessarily long, I have no doubt that it could easily make it to the top ten of all time for the band. I'm not just saying this – it's the truth. This is one of the best and least-discussed KISS songs you'll ever come across. What's more, this song features Paul's last exceptional vocal performance with KISS before age started to get the better of him. And if you're looking for some inspiration to take over the world, dig these lines: "I been a rebel for all my life, I never cared about regulations / I only went for the things I liked, and my guitar was my inspiration." If you feel it, you know what I'm talking about. If you don't, well, I'm sorry for you.

TOM GIGLIOTTI (*SHOUT IT OUT LOUDCAST*) – I talk about this song a LOT on SIOL and that's because it has one of the greatest KISS earworms in their entire catalog. The verse melody, along with Gene's incredible bass line, bring us into an absolutely awesome bridge and when you get to the chorus, you can't help but sing along and smile. Songs like this is why I love KISS, and I wish this had a chance at being a hit.

CHRIS JERICHO (*WRESTLER, FOZZY*) – One of my all-time favorite Paul songs. What another tremendously amazing Paul Stanley title. I love the part near the end: "I know that heaven's gonna wait! I pledge allegiance to the state!" And it's got a great opening riff and a great kind of call-and-response gang vocal. I wish they would have tried that one live. Another one where if it had come out on *Destroyer*, it would be a KISS classic.

JOEY CASSATA *(ZO2, ZROCK)* – Wow, what a chorus!! Nobody writes anthemic gang choruses like Paul Stanley. If this song had come out in the '80s it would have been a huge hit. It's one of those songs that needs to be played in an arena in front of 20,000 screaming fans!!

INTO THE VOID

TONY MUSALLAM *(RESTRAYNED)* – This is one of my favorite tracks from *Psycho Circus*. It's a throwback to classic-era Ace, complete with the space theme. To me, "Into the Void" sounds like it could have been on *Love Gun*, which is my favorite KISS album.

JOEY CASSATA *(ZO2, Z ROCK)* – This is the only true Klassic KISS song on *Psycho Circus*. Don't get me wrong, I really enjoy this record and it has some fantastic moments, like "Psycho Circus", "Raise Your Glasses", "Journey of 1,000 Years" – but those aren't the classic lineup. KISS completely missed the mark on this record by not having Ace and Peter play on the whole thing. They captured magic in a bottle on the reunion tour, but for some reason didn't think that magic would translate on to a new album. They were completely wrong. "Into the Void" has that Klassic KISS vibe that should be featured on the whole album!

RAISE YOUR GLASSES:
A Celebration of 50 Years of KISS Songs
by Celebrities, Musicians & Fans.

Ace Frehley, Joey Cassata and Steve Brown jamming
onstage at KISS Cancer Goodbye

PETER DANKELSON *(PETE'S DIARY)* – I love the guitar riff on this song – the tone in general is aggressive and sounds huge! I also love the guitar line in the chorus – it really complements the vocals in a cool, melodic way.

GARY "ACTION" JACKSON *(UGLY AMERICAN WEREWOLF IN LONDON PODCAST)* – I was interested to see what new music from the original KISS line-up would sound like in 1998. I am a sucker for deep tracks that feature someone other than the main lead singer. Ace delivers his "signature" vocals along with a rocking guitar-driven track. Definitely a highlight for me on the *Psycho Circus* album.

DARREN PALTROWITZ *(AUTHOR, How David Lee Roth Changed The World)* – Besides being "the Ace song" on *Psycho Circus*, this one holds the distinction – if legend proves true – that it is the only song on the album featuring the playing of all four original KISS members. To my ears, it is the best vocal track from Ace on a KISS album, and one of the better-written songs on *Psycho Circus*. Just as intriguing to me, however, is that the song with co-written by an outside songwriter who we've heard little about, Karl Cochran. Per research, Cochran joined Ace's solo band two years or so before KISS put the makeup back on. So was "Into The Void" a leftover solo track that Ace later repurposed? Either way, Cochran's credits also include Joe Lynn Turner, ESP (alongside Eric Singer), John Corabi, Bruce Kulick and Little Caesar's Ron Young, meaning that the guy not only worked with members of some of our bands, but also has seen some stuff. I want a Karl Cochran autobiography.

CHRIS "THE WALLET" HAICK *(GENE SIMMONS MONEYBAG SODA)* – This track is one of my favorites from *Psycho Circus*. This song couldn't work if any other of the band members sang it. It was a return to the classic and undeniable Ace guitar sound, and the vocals were made for Ace. Underrated track.

WE ARE ONE

AUSTIN MILETO *(SISTERS DOLL)* – This song has always been a huge favorite of mine since I was a kid, and is very underrated in my opinion. Beautifully written song, and an incredible performance by Gene vocally.

RAISE YOUR GLASSES:
A Celebration of 50 Years of KISS Songs
by Celebrities, Musicians & Fans.

Sisters Doll with Ace Frehley

TOMMY SOMMERS *(THREE SIDES OF THE COIN)* – In my opinion this is the best song Gene has ever written. It speaks right to the heart of everyone that is a KISS fan. Not only does it embrace the idea of being yourself and living your best life, it also makes the point to let everybody know that 'we are one', we are an army of fans that collectively love this band. This should be the closing number at the concerts as people are leaving the venue.

PETER CORY *(KISS LIVE AUCTIONS)* – So, 25 years after the release of this song that I had never heard before, Gene comes out on the KISS Kruise XI and plays this song. And KILLS it. At first, I thought he was just kind of talking, then realized it was a song and I instantly fell in love with it. Again, Gene was so pure in singing it. I wish they would have played it more on their final tours, it really speaks about the band and their fans.

MIKE BRUNN *(THE ROCK EXPERIENCE)* – I usually prefer my Demon to rock hard, but this song is just perfect. A great hook, a great message to the fans, and a great vocal. I was super-excited to see the band finally perform this live on the KISS Kruise. A great song on a mediocre album.

ALLISON HAGENDORF *(MUSIC JOURNALIST, TV HOST & PRODUCER)* – "We Are One" is a beautiful, unifying, anthemic song which celebrates an uplifting, positive side of the band. It's a bright light in their catalog for me.

Allison Hagendorf with Tommy Thayer and Eric Singer

ZEUS *(SHOUT IT OUT LOUDCAST)* – As we say on SIOL, this may not be a KISS song but it's still a good song. Gene using his 'Beatles Gene' voice and Beatles-type pop melodies and style, just like "Mr. Make Believe", "See You Tonite" and more. This song was surprisingly the second single off of *Psycho Circus* and I got to hear him sing this live on KISS Kruise X.

YOU WANTED THE BEST

WES BEECH *(THE PLASMATICS)* – Arguably the coolest song on *Psycho Circus* as it features all four original members trading vocals. For years I, like so many other KISS fans, was under the impression that the original band got together to record this album. It was a great disappointment to learn years later that that wasn't the case at all. The song starts out with a drum beat right out of glam, not played by Peter but by session drummer Kevin Valentine. The drumming is solid throughout and drives the song. Ace delivers a solo spitting out his full repertoire of licks and shows that his chops are still together. Lyrically the title is taken from the band's live introduction, and it celebrates the camaraderie among the members, but it's really just a sham as we were soon to learn. That they never performed the song live is a shame as it would have been great to hear them swapping vocal lines. The promise of a reunited band was broken, and it was the beginning of the end for the original four. Who knows what could have been had Bob Ezrin taken the production reins and maybe coaxed some songs out of Peter and Ace? We'll never know.

ZEUS *(SHOUT IT OUT LOUDCAST)* – The only KISS song to have all four original members share lead vocals. That in and of itself makes this special for me. Yes, the lyrics are corny, but all four members trading one-liners? Wow. The highlight is definitely Ace, singing (I say that loosely), "Cause it's not your place," like Bob Kraft. For all the SIOL listeners, they know what I'm talking about.

CHRIS JERICHO *(WRESTLER, FOZZY)* – I find it to be ultra-cheesy. And it's pretty funny: let's do a song where all four of us sing. I guess it's a good try. I think for them coming back and we all thought this was the reunion and they're all sitting in the studio writing this together, this was the one song where they seemed like they were having fun on it.

Tom and Zeus with Doc McGhee

MAC *(UGLY AMERICAN WEREWOLF IN LONDON PODCAST)* – KISS always takes the stage after someone announces, "You wanted the best, you got the best – the hottest band in the land/world – KISS!!" So they took that concept to give all the boys a chance to sing a couple of lines in the verses, something they never did during their original run. KISS has always chased anthems, and this is a reach. The music, riffs and guitar work fit well within everyone's wheelhouse, but the "You wanted the best and you got the best" comes off cheesy and contrived.

JOEY CASSATA *(ZO2, ZROCK)* – Not sure why this song gets shit on by so many people. I was so excited the first time I heard this song on *Psycho Circus*. Having the four original members trade vocals back and forth, basically yelling at each other is unbelievable!! I love Ace's line to Paul "You live in fairy tales, you're just a fallen star". God, I would love to hear more backstory on how this was written and the meaning behind each line.

RAISE YOUR GLASSES

HOLLY KNIGHT *(SONGWRITER)* – This song would've been great in a beer commercial! They missed the boat on that one, their management should've realized that it was a hit song. Imagine if someone had made a commercial of it: KISS, sitting in a bar (in full costume and makeup,) raising their glasses and making a toast to the likes of John McEnroe or Mark Wahlberg. Now that would've become an instant classic.

RAISE YOUR GLASSES:
A Celebration of 50 Years of KISS Songs
by Celebrities, Musicians & Fans.

Tom and Zeus with Tommy Thayer, *An Evening with Gene Simmons*, May 7, 2023

ZEUS *(SHOUT IT OUT LOUDCAST)* – This should be every high school football team's championship video montage song. Lyrics are fantastic. Kudos to the great Holly Knight and Paul Stanley. The music, the lyrics and the vocals make this the standout track on this uneven album. This song is so good it should be the title of a book.

BRENNAN MILETO *(SISTERS DOLL)* – I don't know what it is about this song, I've just always loved it. The production on this album is ridiculous, and Paul's voice is next-level. The song lyrically just gets the old heart racing; it's a very underrated KISS song in my opinion.

RAISE YOUR GLASSES:
A Celebration of 50 Years of KISS Songs
by Celebrities, Musicians & Fans.

CHRIS JERICHO *(WRESTLER, FOZZY)* – I think this is another great tune. I thought they missed the boat by not having it in a Coke commercial or a Pepsi commercial or something like that. There's a lot of those types of songs on *Psycho Circus*.

JEFF TROTT *(ART DIRECTOR)* – Long before this book was titled "Raise Your Glasses", it was and is still one of my favorite tracks on *Psycho Circus*. "Raise Your Glasses" exudes celebratory energy, urging the KISS Army to embrace their victories with unbridled enthusiasm. It's a feel-good anthem that deserves more recognition for its uplifting message. "Raise Your Glasses" is such a great tune and should be utilized at sporting events in the arenas and broadcast bumpers.

WES BEECH *(THE PLASMATICS)* – There doesn't seem to be a lot of love for the *Psycho Circus* album in KISS circles, but it's an album I've always been fond of. Of course, I was disappointed to learn that it wasn't the original group effort we were promised but there are a number of good songs on it, including this Holly Knight-penned one. The first time I heard it on a bootleg cassette I thought it was "It's My Life" as the intro is very similar. I wonder if she used that as a template for it. Paul I'm sure wouldn't want to do it as it was on Wendy's solo album, and he was probably still smarting from finding out "Thief in the Night" from *Crazy Nights* was previously recorded by her. A really good song with a big sing-along chorus, and another one of those songs that should have been more promoted. A positive message with uplifting lyrics, this could have been big at sporting events and celebrations, but it never got any traction and was ignored. Too bad as it's a feel-good song with good production.

I FINALLY FOUND MY WAY

COURTNEY CRONIN DOLD *(COMEDIAN)* – Oh Peter, you romantic you! The only thing "Psycho" about this song is that it wasn't a hit. It's the "Beth" of the 'Circus'! I realize that was the point, but I think they nailed it. This song doesn't get enough credit. It's simply beautiful, a real tear-jerker. Peter's voice alone is an instant pants-dropper to us gals. If I ever direct a douche commercial, this will be the song I use.

WES BEECH *(THE PLASMATICS)* – I finally found my way to skip this track, to me one of the weakest tracks on an album I otherwise really enjoy. That they gave this Bob Ezrin-Paul Stanley-penned dud to Peter to sing as his showcase spotlight on the album just seems wrong. Sounding like they were trying to recapture the feeling of "Beth", but this overproduced song just falls flat. The vocal performance by Peter is actually quite good as he gamely plays along, but I would have much rather heard him sing an uptempo rock song instead of this plodder, which brought down the momentum of "You Wanted The Best" and "Raise Your Glasses". It's a skip for me every time.

NICHOLAS BUCKLAND *(AUTHOR, Hottest Brand in the Land)* – Was it deliberate sabotage that Paul handed the worst song he's ever written to Peter as his "showcase" song? Without Stan Penridge, the Catman was left with a terrible schmaltzy ballad that didn't suit his voice. Not a fitting finale to his KISS career.

JASON HERNDON *(KISS MY WAX PODCAST)* – I am a fan that thinks KISS can almost do no wrong musically. There are VERY few songs in the catalog that I can honestly say that I do not like. I can name them on one hand. In reality, there are only two. And this is one of the two. What an unfortunate piece of tripe this song is.

ZEUS *(SHOUT IT OUT LOUDCAST)* – I don't understand why this song is so maligned, maybe because people perceive it to be an attempt at "Beth Part II". It's a decent ballad with a beautiful melody. Written by Paul and Bob Ezrin and sung beautifully by Peter. I think it stands well enough on its own. This song would have fit perfectly on Peter's 1978 solo album.

DREAMIN'

JOEY CASSATA *(ZO2, ZROCK)* – I am a big fan of most of the *Psycho Circus* album. This is another really strong song. Even though this was billed as the first album with the original four members, it really is much more reminiscent of an '80s KISS record. "Dreamin'" could have easily come off of *Animalize*.

Poster ad for the *Rock The Nation* tour

JASON HOOK *(FIVE FINGER DEATH PUNCH)* – Not sure if too many people give this album the appreciation that it deserves. I always liked "Dreamin'". I can't say for sure, but I'd love to know if this song was resurrected from the earlier non-makeup period.

JOEY SASSO *(THE CIRCLE, NETFLIX)* – "Dreamin'" is a track often overshadowed by the controversy surrounding this album's authenticity. Yet, amidst the chaos, this Paul Stanley gem shines as a beacon of musical brilliance, showcasing his ability to continually deliver such solid tunes that are not trying to reinvent the wheel. The song's essence is a melodic journey into passion and introspection that resonates with KISS fans. These are themes that Paul often goes back to, and when we really take this song in, the reasoning is very obvious: it works. "Dreamin'" emerges not just as a standout on a divisive album but as a hidden treasure waiting to be uncovered by KISS aficionados. I love when I see the one brave guy who stands proudly championing this song when talking about gems that few ever bring up. Have I ever actually seen that? No, I have not but I know that guy is out there somewhere, and I am standing proudly with you brother!

The song's power remains undeniable, transcending the controversy to stand tall as a testament to KISS's enduring legacy. The song carries charm and simplicity that we always love. The song deserves its moment in the spotlight, proving that amidst the tumultuous legacy of *Psycho Circus*, Paul's musical brilliance shines through brightly, captivating listeners with its infectious melody and heartfelt lyrics. So, let's set the record straight – "Dreamin'" cannot be ignored because of the turbulent era of the band that it was born into.

JEFF TROTT *(ART DIRECTOR)* – "Dreamin'" from *Psycho Circus* stands out as one of my favorite tracks on the entire album. It's a fantastic song written by Stanley and Bruce Kulick, who continues to leave his mark on *Psycho Circus* despite no longer being a part of the band. "Dreamin'" delivers powerful vocals and excellent guitar work. When Paul belts out "Things you said, fill my head, lying in a cold and empty bed, I'm only dreamin'." It's absolutely fan-fuckin'-tastic!

ALEXANDER TALKINGTON *(KISS ARMY THINGS PODCAST)* – Sometimes I wish we could secretly re-release KISS songs to the masses in today's era, but without actually saying it's KISS. This is one track that has everything pop stations would eat up: big chorus, simple message (but still deep enough to make you think it's profound), a post-second-chorus bridge, and a key change. Gotta have a key change! In all seriousness, this was a song that I used to overlook but now it has my attention every time. Bruce's involvement on this track really gives me closure on his time with band.

JOURNEY OF 1,000 YEARS

TONY MUSALLAM *(RESTRAYNED)* – I really like this song. It's very different from typical KISS songs. I like the way it builds by adding layer after layer of vocals and continues to build till the end. The orchestration at the end is interesting too.

PASQUALE VARI *(KISS ARMY NATION PODCAST)* – I know fans were not crazy about the *Psycho Circus* album, but fans must agree, the title track and "Journey of 1,000 Years" were the highlights of the album. My goodness, what a beautiful and perfect ending to the album. I love how it brought the record full circle by connecting it to the opening track.

BRAD RUSTOVEN *(SLAMFEST PODCAST)* – One word to describe this song... epic. Originally titled "Roar of the Greasepaint", this song has an amazing build to the chorus – a powerful "Or was it the roar of the crowd" vocal from Gene. During the outro, they use the melody from the title cut's guitar solo to tie the opening and closing songs together... very cool arrangement.

JASON BAKKEN *(COBRAS & FIRE PODCAST)* – *Psycho Circus* is another album that has gotten more crap as time passes and we learn more of the story. There is good stuff on here and closing the record with this song is masterful, right down to the orchestral homage to the pre-solo on the title track. I love the way it builds.

TOM HIGGINS *(KLASSIK '78)* – I am not a fan of this album at all. However, this song has something about it that "could've been" as great as the best songs on *Destroyer*. I can't quite explain what it is, but the musical and vocal dynamics on this are amazing. I think with a slightly simplified structure and an extra hook added in there somewhere, this could've been a modern classic. Much like "Unholy" has that modern classic status with fans.

RAISE YOUR GLASSES:
A Celebration of 50 Years of KISS Songs
by Celebrities, Musicians & Fans.

CHAPTER 23

"SONIC BOOM"

Released: October 6, 2009

Sonic Boom signified a significant milestone for KISS, being their first studio album with new material in over a decade. The album features a return to the classic hard rock sound that defined KISS in the '70s, capturing the band's timeless essence. *Sonic Boom* pays homage to the band's past while injecting a fresh energy into their sonic repertoire. It is also the first studio album featuring the final KISS line-up of Gene Simmons, Paul Stanley, Eric Singer and Tommy Thayer.

The opening track, "Modern Day Delilah," sets the tone with its roaring guitar riffs and anthemic chorus, reminiscent of KISS's classic hard rock era. The album continues to deliver high-octane rock with tracks like "Never Enough" and "Yes I Know (Nobody's Perfect)," showcasing the band's continuing ability to craft energetic and timeless anthems.

Sonic Boom received positive reviews for capturing the spirit of classic KISS while infusing a contemporary energy. With Sonic Boom," KISS proved that, even after decades in the music industry, they could still deliver a sonic punch that resonates with the timeless power of rock 'n' roll, and it marks a successful chapter in the band's enduring legacy.

MODERN DAY DELILAH

JOEY CASSATA *(ZO2, Z ROCK)* – I remember the first time I heard this, and I actually said out loud… "HOLY SHIT!!" This song is exactly what I wanted at the time. It wasn't '70s KISS, it wasn't '80s KISS – it was the new line-up making a great song that sounded fresh and exciting!

RAISE YOUR GLASSES:
A Celebration of 50 Years of KISS Songs by Celebrities, Musicians & Fans.

ZO2 jamming on "Love Gun" with Paul Stanley

ZEUS *(SHOUT IT OUT LOUDCAST)* – KISS, back after eleven years, with the first album featuring the last KISS lineup. This song proves that they still have it, and KISS – no matter who is in the band and who is out – will always be and sound like KISS, as long as Paul and Gene are there. This song is heavy, and the band rocks. Paul proves he still can write the best choruses. Speaking of which, as I say on SIOL all the time, if I had to bet my life on someone writing a song for me with a melody, hook and chorus that I will like, I would choose Paul Stanley without any hesitation. However, Tommy steals this song with one of my favorite guitar solos in the

KISS catalog. Speed, with touch and feel. Shame this wasn't played on the *End of the Road* tour.

JOEY SASSO (*THE CIRCLE, NETFLIX*) – Are you an honest KISS fan or do you let public opinions sway your ability to be honest about the band? To know what kind of fan you are, I only need to ask you about one song: "Modern Day Delilah." This isn't just a good "new" KISS song – it's one of their best tracks ever, and it's all thanks to the incomparable Paul Stanley. Despite what the *Sonic Boom* critics might say, this song is a masterpiece, and it's right up there with all of their classics that we expected to hear every time we saw them live. And speaking of live shows, it's a damn shame that "Say Yeah" represented this era of the band on the *End of the Road* setlist. This is the best song that this lineup has ever done, and it's criminal that it wasn't included. We know that Paul hyped up this lineup to the fans and the press, and for once, he was absolutely right. This song set the bar so high for what this lineup could accomplish, but sadly, nothing else after "Modern Day Delilah" on *Sonic Boom* ever quite lived up to it. Let's face it: "Modern Day Delilah" is not just a great KISS song, it's the last truly great KISS song that we're ever going to get. Let that sink in.

TONY MUSALLAM (*RESTRAYNED*) – This was a great way to kick off the record. "Modern Day Delilah" starts with a kick-ass, groovy riff followed by a catchy verse with call-backs to the intro riff. The pre-chorus is reminiscent of '70s and '80s KISS. The chorus is everything you'd want from a KISS song, with its catchy hook and call-and-response melody, making it a modern KISS classic.

STEVEN MICHAEL *(GROWIN' UP ROCK PODCAST)* – Killer riff out of the gate. Decent chorus. The bridge to the solo section is a bit of a weird key change, but it still works. Paul seems to struggle a bit in some of the screams, but it doesn't come off as bad. Above everything else, it's a great way to kick off the record and it rocks. I love it because I was getting new material from a legacy act.

RUSSIAN ROULETTE

STEVE WRIGHT *(PODDER THAN HELL PODCAST)* – This song just rumbles right in then goes to a sleazy feel with some really cool bass lines from Gene. Fun track. The kick up for the pre-chorus is great. Then slows some for the chorus. Great background vocals. I just love the "ah ah ah ah's" after the chorus. And yes, we do get backbone slipping on this track, which in my opinion is just fun. Paul is very prominent in the chorus. Fantastic solo from Tommy, sticking to the KISS script, which is totally fine with me. Eric Singer's drums have a great sound to them and some great drum fills. I'm into KISS for the fun, and this is a fun song!

SONNY POONI *(PODCAST ROCK CITY)* – The albums after the makeup returns in the late '90s/early 2000s get a lot of hate. If you give some of those songs a chance, they are actually pretty good. Gene has a unique way of weaving who he is into a song, and the key is… Gene can sell it. This song is written very well, the chorus is catchy, Eric creates a great groove, and Tommy does a very Ace-esque solo. Give this song another shot, it's great.

COURTNEY CRONIN DOLD *(COMEDIAN)* – This is by far one of the best songs on *Sonic Boom*. Tommy's guitar on this is so stellar, and that chorus is a sing-along hair swinger. Girls know what I mean. If they changed the title and most of the lyrics, this could have replaced "Modern Day Delilah" as the "other" song they played live from this.

ZEUS *(SHOUT IT OUT LOUDCAST)* – A fun Gene song with a catchy chorus by the band. One of many songs that Gene likes to advise you to let "your backbone slip." Tommy delivers another solid solo and outro again. But could do without the "Ah ah ah ahs."

CHRIS L. *(POD OF THUNDER)* – The second half of the one-two punch that opens *Sonic Boom* showed that Gene meant business too, just like Paul did on "Modern Day Delilah." Great vocals, great bass playing, and a mention of a slipping backbone in the lyrics that portray Mr. Simmons as every woman's fantasy. In other words, all the ingredients for a timeless Gene classic.

NEVER ENOUGH

STEVE WRIGHT *(PODDER THAN HELL PODCAST)* – This song has an old-school KISS feel to it. Great bridge before the chorus. The production is crisp, and you can hear every instrument clearly. The background vocals sound great and you can really hear Tommy in there, I like the dynamic that he adds. Check out the bridge just before the "Rock and Roll"-type solo that Tommy lays down, and the doubling in a few parts makes it that much better. Just a fun rock 'n' roll song! This is a statement for us KISS fans! It's Never Enough!

RAISE YOUR GLASSES:
A Celebration of 50 Years of KISS Songs
by Celebrities, Musicians & Fans.

TONY MUSALLAM *(RESTRAYNED)* – The verse of "Never Enough" sounds very much like Poison's "Nothin' But A Good Time". But considering that riff was based on "Rock And Roll All Nite", I guess you could say they came full circle on this one. I really like the start/stop guitars topped by Paul's hooky melodies. The gang vocal-style chorus is super-catchy and will definitely have you singing along. This is one of the better tracks on *Sonic Boom*, with a strong vocal by Paul. I would have liked to have seen KISS perform this song on tour, rather than "Say Yeah".

JOEY SASSO *(THE CIRCLE, NETFLIX)* – Undoubtedly, "Never Enough" will go down in history as the "Mr. Speed" of *Sonic Boom* years down the road. In my opinion, this song still hasn't received the recognition it deserves. We all know that some people refer to it as the "Poison rip-off song," but let's face it, it rocks! This is the track where Paul showcases some of his wisdom that comes with age and success, but he delivers it in a way that's not arrogant, but rather, enjoyable. "People waste time on their hopes and dreams / Fate is always in my hands!" – coming from a guy who was born Stanley Eisen and who wore makeup and high heels on stage in the '70s, dreaming of becoming the wildest success he could become, it's quite understandable for him to feel like he's always in control. Let's face it, he did make all his dreams come true and he spearheaded KISS forward to become the band/brand they are today, so we can't really argue with him. This song is a classic KISS track that you can simply throw on in the car and sing out loud, forgetting about the world around you. The chorus is killer, and Tommy's solo is delivered with perfect precision, never overstaying its welcome. Do you remember hating this song once? Well, I urge you to get in your car, crank the volume up, and drive while listening to it. If you aren't singing your little lungs out by the end, then there's simply no hope left for you as a KISS fan.

RAISE YOUR GLASSES:
A Celebration of 50 Years of KISS Songs
by Celebrities, Musicians & Fans.

Gene Simmons showing Tom and Zeus KISS memorabilia, *An Evening with Gene Simmons*, May 7, 2023

WES BEECH *(THE PLASMATICS)* – Personally I much prefer the L.A. Guns song of the same name. Like most of the songs from the album, it sounds like they were trying to recapture the magic from the early years of the band. This could have been a Klassik '78 track, except that it's actually KISS, or at least 50% KISS, am I right? Not a bad song, just doesn't break any new ground and almost seems lazy to me. I've never been a fan of this album, and songs like this are the reason why.

JASON BAKKEN *(COBRAS & FIRE PODCAST)* – How the fuck did they get sued for plagiarism for the song "Dreamin'" and not this blatant rip off of the Poison song "Nothin' But A Good Time"? And what does it say about where you are as an artist when you're ripping off Poison?

YES I KNOW (NOBODY'S PERFECT)

WES BEECH *(THE PLASMATICS)* – Not a fan of *Sonic Boom* or its follow-up *Monster* – but this song, even though it tries so obviously to capture that old KISS sound, stands out as a good, solid rocker. The intro immediately called to mind one of my favorite songs, "Nothin' to Lose", then it kicks in with one of Gene's more upbeat vocal performances. The guitar work by Tommy is pure Ace Frehley, and all his years of copying his style pays off on this track. And really that's my problem with the album as a whole – it's just too calculated to capture the sound and feel of the original band. Good, inspired drumming by Eric and when Gene exhorts the focus of the song to "take off her clothes", it never fails to put a smile on my face! Tommy pulls out all his Ace riffs on the solo and the song finishes on a high note. This song would have fit nicely on *Psycho Circus*, I think.

MARTIN POPOFF *(AUTHOR)* – If not for its unfortunately complicated title, "Yes I Know (Nobody's Perfect)" might have served as a smash single from *Sonic Boom*, if that sort of thing was even in the cards for KISS in 2009. It's a big bear-hug of a retro-KISS boogie rocker, and of course it's Gene that's gotta sing these, given his lascivious and raspy blues legend voice—okay, I'll draw the line at voice, because he's never sung particularly bluesy. In any event, this one just sticks out as the most connective at an emotional and nostalgic level, on an album that offers a lot of strong competition—*Psycho Circus* will never be redeemed, but I'll keep championing both *Sonic Boom* and *Monster* as long as anybody keeps listening.

ZEUS *(SHOUT IT OUT LOUDCAST)* – Gene's best song on *Sonic Boom* that's not a duet (see "Stand"). This melodic song with a catchy chorus sounds like Gene is having so much fun.   Tommy's solo is great. There's a lot of Geneisms (wait, is that a word?) An opening bass slide, an overpronounced "hot", Gene talking lyrics, "Baby it's time take off your clothes" and Gene barking orders à la Teddy Pendergrass: "Take 'em off babe!" and Gene's infamous "Oh Yeah!"

NICHOLAS BUCKLAND *(AUTHOR, Hottest Brand in the Land)* – This song could easily have worked on any of the first three albums, with its sleazy rock 'n' roll vibe. Gene's ego takes centre stage here with an unapologetic assertiveness. While most would deliver a lyric like this with tongue firmly planted in cheek, it's Gene's straight-down-the-camera, serious delivery that makes this work.

ALEXANDER TALKINGTON *(KISS ARMY THINGS PODCAST)* – The opening to this track, musically, is great! If only the lyrics were a tad more mature... "Baby it's time to take off your clothes. Take 'em off babe!" Oh Gene. That's our Demon! He never fails to put a smile on our face. Eric's tasteful drumming, especially the double cowbell prior to the chorus, makes this track even more fun! Tommy's solo is one of the more interesting and memorable on the album. But who cares, take off your clothes mama! Ow!

STAND

ZEUS *(SHOUT IT OUT LOUDCAST)* – Some people get it and some don't. This is my favorite song on *Sonic Boom*. That says a lot. A song written by Paul and Gene singing about being there for each other. I love the lyrics. It's more sophisticated than, "You can do it, Waterboy." When Paul and Gene trade lyrics on a good song it's like magic. The chorus is fantastic. Paul's vocal fills like, "When you need me!" and "Just look over your shoulder!" does make me laugh though. The verses are great, and Paul's Ezrin-like breakdown is so good. Tommy's outro is incredible, especially at the 4:25 mark. What touch and feel – another gem by Tommy that is one of my favorite guitar parts in any KISS song. I love this fucking song!

Tom and Zeus with Gene Simmons

JOEY ᛋᚨᛋᛋᛟ (*THE CIRCLE, NETFLIX*) – I will never understand the amount of hate this song gets. Yes, it may be over-the-top cheese, but let's face it, this is the cheese we all love! Gene and Paul coming together on this record to sing a corny song about friendship and brotherhood is pure gold. And here's the thing, while the song may be corny, like all things corny KISS, when I am listening to it with my headphones on while isolated, the song makes me beam with smiles of joy. To all the people who hate this tune, I have to ask, what the hell is wrong with you? We are KISS fans for crying out loud, we love this stupid shit!

CHRIS JERICHO *(WRESTLER, FOZZY)* – It's an inspiring song. It's a Paul Stanley song, 'I believe in you and life is great'. I thought the record was actually pretty good.

JOEY CASSATA *(Z02, ZROCK)* – The verses in this song are pure magic! But they lost me in the chorus. The half-time vocal delivery feels lazy and not memorable. Plus, the Paul response "When you need me!" feels forced and cheesy.

MARK CICCHINI *(THREE SIDES OF THE COIN)* – As the advertising for this LP said at the time... "This is classic KISS!!" And you know what? They were correct!! I love hearing all the guys singing throughout this uplifting, feel-good, well-written KISS anthem. Not to mention the "God Gave Rock And Roll To You"-style vocal breakdown towards the end. However, I especially love hearing Gene and Paul (à la "Shout It Out Loud") swapping the verses. I love everything about this song and this album! If you don't like *Sonic Boom*? You're wrong!! :) *Sonic Boom* IS classic KISS!!!

HOT AND COLD

JOEY CASSATA *(ZO2, Z ROCK)* – What a fantastic chorus! This song could've come right off of *Dressed to Kill*. I know it's crazy to say, but even the cowbell adds to that classic KISS sound. *Sonic Boom* is a better album than people give it credit for.

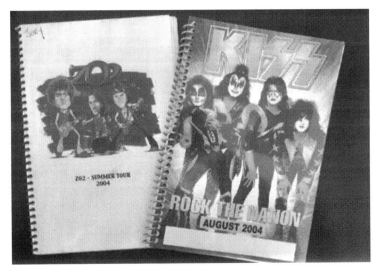

ZO2 and KISS tour itinerary books from the *Rock The Nation* tour

BRAD RUSTOVEN *(SLAMFEST PODCAST)* – A recycled song from the early '90s – sounds like a combination of '70s and '80s KISS. Killer riff and bass line during the intro. Very cool interplay between the backing vocals and Gene's interjections during the chorus. Cool breakdown section with a classic Gene line... "I've got the power and the hour / Baby feel my tower of power."

WES BEECH *(THE PLASMATICS)* – This Gene-sung tune starts out with some very banal lyrics, and you know what the next line is going to be before the words come out of his mouth. The overall feel of the song is rooted in the '60s and I think the verse bears more than a passing resemblance to The Animals' "It's My Life". Hmm, where have I heard that title before? Another cringeworthy chorus that is almost embarrassing. A lot of KISS fans like this album but it's just not for me. And Tommy's Ace-by-numbers guitar solo just pushes it too far for me. At least Bruce would infuse his personality in his solos, but here Tommy trots out every Ace cliché he can. Ugh.

COURTNEY CRONIN DOLD *(COMEDIAN)* – Yeah! More Gene idioms! I just love the part where he kicks off Tommy's solo with, "Dig this". Oh, we dig it Gene. We dig it a lot.

ZEUS *(SHOUT IT OUT LOUDCAST)* – This Gene-written song has a nice catchy chorus. How long has Gene held on to that phrase, "if it's too loud, you're too old?" There's a pretty cool bass line throughout the song, and a solid Tommy solo. A fun song.

ALL FOR THE GLORY

JOEY CASSATA *(ZO2, Z ROCK)* – I really like this song! I love that it isn't the typical "ballad for the KISS drummer" or the "old-school song about rock 'n' roll", like on *Monster*. I remember hearing this on ESPN during highlight reels when *Sonic Boom* was first released.

BRANDON FIELDS *(MINEFIELD)* – I'm 28 years old, so *Sonic Boom* was the first new KISS album I got to go out and buy. The timing was pretty coincidental as this was right around the time I became obsessed with KISS. I've always been a huge fan of Eric Singer's voice, so this track was one I was really excited for. I wasn't disappointed. The chorus features great backing vocals that are kind of reminiscent of "Nowhere to Run" in the sense that they aren't harmonies with the main vocal. Tommy Thayer did a great job of giving people what they want from a KISS guitar solo.

DAVID PEA *(KISS REPLICAS)* – I'm a sucker for songs that bring me back to my youth, and this one is right up there with any classic KISS song. Eric Singer's vocals have this rallying call, and the band sounds fantastic. It's probably my favorite song off of *Sonic Boom* and just a fun, no-nonsense tune that plays on my nostalgic strings.

JEFF TROTT *(ART DIRECTOR)* – "All for the Glory" kicks off with a powerful intro and marks the first time we hear Eric Singer on lead vocals. It's a shame they never performed it live, possibly because Paul insisted on Eric singing "Beth" for some reason. Between *Sonic Boom* and *Monster*, Tommy and Eric had four strong tracks, yet they ended up playing Peter and Ace songs instead of their own songs. "All for the Glory" is a freaking banger—a great straightforward rock song with awesome gang vocals that would have been fantastic to experience live.

ALEXANDER TALKINGTON *(KISS ARMY THINGS PODCAST)* – This song is good... but for me it doesn't REALLY kick in until the second verse. Eric's layered vocal and Tommy's accenting licks make it way more fun to hear (and sing!) But the best part about this song is the final message... "I don't run. I don't hide / Take a look, you won't see fear in my eyes / One way—MY WAY / If there's a price to pay for all that I've got, I'll give it all / I'm gonna take my shot!"

DANGER US

CHRIS L. *(POD OF THUNDER)* – Something else that surprises me with the somewhat lukewarm reaction to it from the KISS Army is *Sonic Boom*. I thought it was a triumph that achieved what the band set out to do: recreate that '70s vibe 30-plus years later. This song gets closest to sounding like a *Rock and Roll Over* bonus track, delicately drawing you in before punching you in the face like "I Want You" does. And Paul's pretty horny, which is never a bad thing (and damn admirable for a then-57-year-old man, which is the same age I am as of this writing).

JOEY CASSATA *(ZO2, Z ROCK)* – Are the lyrics cheesy? Sure, but so what!? It's KISS! This is a super-catchy, fun song that sounds like '80s KISS. Put this song on *Asylum* and everyone would have loved it!!

STEVE WRIGHT *(PODDER THAN HELL PODCAST)* – The opening guitar has kind of a sneaky feel to it, up to the kick-in. Good upper-mid-tempo song. The riff change for the latter part of the verses ramps up the intensity a notch. Some people think that "Danger you, Danger me, Danger us" is corny, but I think it's fun! The pre-chorus is good, and Tommy pulls off a ripping solo and he has more tasty leads at the end of the song. Fun KISS song, and that's what it comes down to for me... FUN!

JASON BAKKEN *(COBRAS & FIRE PODCAST)* – If you like this song you most likely prefer your steak well done. This is embarrassingly bad. Like "destroy the demo" bad. Like "let us never speak of this again" bad.

ROBERT CONTE *(AUTHOR)* – My favorite Paul track on *Sonic Boom* – the album I had wished *Psycho Circus* sounded like. Although Ace and Peter are not present, Tommy Thayer and Eric Singer's performances channel their musical spirit to resurrect the "Klassic KISS" sound. I love its story, too – two apparent type-A personalities who hook up for great, explosive, and dirty sex but might otherwise dislike each other. How many of us can identify with that carnal connection? I wished the album opened with this track and, frankly, I wished KISS performed this live instead of "Say Yeah."

I'M AN ANIMAL

JOEY CASSATA *(ZO2, Z ROCK)* – *Sonic Boom* is a pretty strong album overall. Even though it was billed as KISS going back to their classic sound, it really felt more like a nice mixture of '70s and '80s KISS. Gene's songs are pretty strong on both. "I'm An Animal" could have been on *Creatures of the Night*. It's heavy and aggressive Gene at his best.

Joey Cassata riding Gene Simmons' flying rig in Nashville

COURTNEY CRONIN DOLD *(COMEDIAN)* – YEAH ERIC! He must have needed an ice bath after this one. Was this song left on the *Animalize* cutting-room floor? It's dirty and hot, but I think it's on the wrong album. Am I wrong? Who wants to fight me?

JOEY SASSO *(THE CIRCLE, NETFLIX)* – A track often overlooked on an album that divides fans. Amidst the mixed reception, this Gene Simmons powerhouse stands as a testament to his larger-than-life persona and rock-solid songwriting. The lyric "I'm an animal and I'll blow you away / Like a fireball to your face every day" encapsulates the song's essence, a fierce declaration of primal energy and unapologetic intensity that defines Gene's musical style.

ZEUS *(SHOUT IT OUT LOUDCAST)* – A heavy Gene song with a solid pre-chorus and chorus. Tommy rips on the solo. This is Gene using his Demon voice. The song was actually played live on the *Sonic Boom* tour well over 70 times.

ROBERT CONTE *(AUTHOR)* – "Let others take the road that leads nowhere…" The Demon at his best — deep, dark, and groovy — just the way I love him! This track reminds me of classic *Rock and Roll Over/Love Gun*-era KISS, with homages to "Ladies Room" and "Almost Human." It is a rallying cry for what we know lies within us all – a beast! The original lineup could have easily recorded this song and played it. I was pissed to have missed seeing KISS perform it during the *Sonic Boom* tour, but happily settled for "Russian Roulette"!

WHEN LIGHTNING STRIKES

WES BEECH *(THE PLASMATICS)* – Hats off to Tommy for penning the best song on *Sonic Boom*. A solid rocker with an infectious cowbell that had it been sung by Ace would have garnered more play and attention, but since it's Tommy it gets buried and receives little attention. Too bad Tommy wasn't able to contribute more original songs, as it just seems he was thrown a bone here to have something to sing on this album, not unlike when Peter would get a song here and there. Tommy's more than a competent vocalist, and his guitar is tight and propels the song. Will be interesting to hear what Tommy does next musically.

ALEXANDER TALKINGTON *(KISS ARMY THINGS PODCAST)* – Tommy's autobiography. Lightning doesn't strike twice. It's very unexpected and unpredictable—just like the opportunity for a lifelong KISS fan to become the lead guitarist in KISS. "When the sky and the worlds collide" may be a new take on the classic phrase "Meet me where the ocean touches the sky." Or it could simply refer to the fact that lightning literally connects from the sky above to the world below, haha!

TOM GIGLIOTTI *(SHOUT IT OUT LOUDCAST)* – I really like Tommy's voice, and he should've been given more chances to use it. This has a great riff and a classic KISS-sounding chorus. Tommy takes a lot of heat but his songs on *Sonic Boom* and *Monster* are both awesome.

PASQUALE VARI *(KISS ARMY NATION PODCAST)* – I've always loved Tommy and what he brought to KISS in his 20-year tenure. I was glad he finally had a song on a KISS album, even though it dealt with the same old "Ace character" themes. A great song I wish Tommy had sung live instead of "Shock Me".

IZZY PRESLEY *(MUSICIAN, COMIC)* – No. Just, no.

SAY YEAH

CHRIS JERICHO *(WRESTLER, FOZZY)* – I love this song. And I know people got mad when they played it live. I think had it come out in the '70s or '80s, it would've been an all-time KISS classic. It's a KISS chanting, sing-along song. I think it's a good tune and I love the verses on it. Paul's melody is great and it's very heavy. It's probably my favorite song on the record.

RAISE YOUR GLASSES:
A Celebration of 50 Years of KISS Songs
by Celebrities, Musicians & Fans.

MIKE BRUNN *(THE ROCK EXPERIENCE)* – This is a song the band would probably say is a "current classic". Yes, it was played to death in concert for the past decade, but for a good reason. The chorus is such an easy sing-along, which makes it very memorable for those who may not be familiar with KISS's newest material. A perfect representation of the Singer / Thayer lineup and a great way to close their first studio album in over a decade!

JASON HOOK *(FIVE FINGER DEATH PUNCH)* – I have to pull something from the *Sonic Boom* record. "Say Yeah" remained a part of the live set for several years after its release. I love the pre-chorus chord change, and of course the chorus/post-chorus is catchy as hell.

MAC *(UGLY AMERICAN WEREWOLF IN LONDON PODCAST)* – KISS always wanted to recapture their anthemic glory of the '70s, but it's hard to write another "Rock And Roll All Nite". I feel like this is their attempt write a new song that the audience can shout along to and throw their hands in the air. However, as the band and fans have aged quite a bit since the '70s, this often fell short live despite their insistence to keep it in the setlist for years. Tommy does a great Ace impersonation during the solo to make it sound vintage and authentic. The slowdown is unnecessary before the big "Say Yeah", and live on the *End of the Road* tour, instead of sounding like Say YEAH!! YEAH! YEAH! YEAH!" it was more like "Say Yeah… yeah… yeah… yeah."

JEFF TROTT *(ART DIRECTOR)* – "Say Yeah" is a great song. Yeah, I said it. "Say Yeah" became the KISS punching bag, especially on the *End of the Road* tour. Did I need to hear it live, NO. Do I wish they would've played something deeper in its place? YES. But it's still a great song. It's a reminder of KISS's ability to inspire and uplift with their music. When I'm at home playing music on my home system, rather than through a phone or through ear buds, there is not a bigger banger than "Say Yeah". I look at the studio track as one of the last powerful Paul performances before he started to struggle. Turn that shit up and let me hear ya say YEAH!

ZEUS *(SHOUT IT OUT LOUDCAST)* – Yes, I know this song should not have been on the *End of the Road* setlist for 4 years. But don't let that cloud the fact that this is a great song. The echo on Paul's verses is so cool. The verses, the pre-choruses and chorus are written well and sung even better. The chorus was definitely written for a live crowd to sing the "Yeah yeah yeah" parts. The Ezrin-like breakdown is great. Once again, Paul Stanley is delivering a catchy song with an incredible chorus after all these years. I do think this is the rare KISS song that may be better as a studio track than being played live.

CHAPTER 24

"MONSTER"

Released: October 9, 2012

Monster stands as a testament to KISS's enduring legacy and commitment to their hard rock roots. The album is a celebration of classic KISS elements, featuring powerful guitar riffs, anthemic choruses, and the unmistakable stage presence that has defined the band for decades. With a straightforward hard rock sound, *Monster* showcases KISS's ability to tap into their iconic formula while infusing a contemporary energy.

Opening track "Hell or Hallelujah" kicks off the album with a burst of energy, featuring powerful guitar riffs and a driving rhythm that harkens back to classic KISS anthems. The track sets the stage for an album that captures the essence of the band's iconic sound.

"Wall of Sound" and "Long Way Down" continue the hard-hitting rock vibe, with the band delivering punchy and memorable tunes.

Monster also features "Take Me Down Below," a song reminiscent of the band's cheeky and playful side. The track pays homage to KISS's tradition of blending rock with a touch of humor and innuendo.

While *Monster* received mixed critical reviews, it was generally well-received by fans who appreciated the band's straightforward hard rock sound.

In summary, *Monster* stands as a solid addition to the KISS catalog, offering a collection of songs that celebrate the band's enduring legacy that has made them legends in the genre.

HELL OR HALLELUJAH

ZEUS *(SHOUT IT OUT LOUDCAST)* – The last opening track off of the last KISS studio album proves that KISS can still go out on top. This song is vintage Paul Stanley. What a fucking riff, with a killer pre-chorus and great chorus. Gene's "Lay down!" and "Stay down!" during the pre-chorus is great. Tommy's fills that come in on the second verse are perfect, and solo is great as well. What an incredible fast, badass opening song.

Zeus and his brother, Kerry, Halloween 1978

STEVEN MICHAEL *(GROWIN' UP ROCK PODCAST)* – I like this riff even better than "Modern Day Delilah", and I love the gang parts in the pre-chorus – "Lay down!" and "Stay down!" and they get to that chorus in less than a minute. That's good songwriting. This song rocks!

TONY MUSALLAM *(RESTRAYNED)* – This song starts with an "I Stole Your Love"-style guitar riff, hits the ground running and just plows through till the end. I like the call and response pre-chorus and chorus, both of which are very hooky. There's a part towards the guitar solo where Paul is singing the guitar part, which is a cool little earworm.

ROBERT CONTE *(AUTHOR)* – "No matter what you do, I'm runnin' through ya!" Wow, what a great opening track on *Monster*, KISS's last full studio album. Promoting the song on shows like *Late Show with David Letterman* and *Good Morning America* showed promise that the record would gain traction and attain Gold status like *Psycho Circus* did 14 years before. Alas, it was not to be. Although a well-produced second effort between Paul Stanley and Greg Collins, a generational change had taken place where even my kids remarked: "Dad, KISS is your music, not mine." Damn right, it is, and it should be yours, too (ha-ha!)

DARREN PALTROWITZ *(AUTHOR, How David Lee Roth Changed The World)* – One of KISS's final attempts at writing a single for radio. It largely reminds me of "I Stole Your Love" – yet also "Shout It Out Loud" and "Detroit Rock City" – in terms of it being an up-tempo, Paul-led, sing-along, blues-riff-based song without keyboards. The last few times I saw KISS live, the only recent song they performed live was "Say Yeah," and I would have rather heard "Hell or Hallelujah" if there had to be an obligatory post-*Psycho Circus* song within the setlist. The quality of the song reinforces, to me at least, that KISS was always capable of writing great songs that were meant to be played live.

WALL OF SOUND

STEVE WRIGHT *(PODDER THAN HELL PODCAST)* – The main riff lives up to the album title… it is a monster of a riff! Great Gene track. Some people don't like the production on this album, but I don't mind it at all. Tommy's solo kind of creeps with the tempo change, but when the main riff comes back in he really picks it up and lets rip. Heavy KISS… thank you Gene!

Tom and Zeus with Gene imposter, *Freedom To Rock* tour,
DCU Center, September 3, 2016

RAISE YOUR GLASSES:
A Celebration of 50 Years of KISS Songs
by Celebrities, Musicians & Fans.

COURTNEY CRONIN DOLD *(COMEDIAN)* – I like this song but it's another melodic pre-chorus totally ruined by the actual chorus. When the chorus starts I kind of want to soundproof the "wall" but the rest of it rocks.

TONY MUSALLAM *(RESTRAYNED)* – From the opening riff, I knew this was going to be a Gene song. But strangely enough, this feels very much like it could be an Aerosmith song. The verse is groovy and the pre-chorus is catchy. I think the chorus could have benefited from some harmony backing vocals. But overall, this is a cool Gene tune.

BRAD RUSTOVEN *(SLAMFEST PODCAST)* – Great song title, and how can you go wrong with a pick slide to start off the song? Yes, the production is compressed but there is a cool riff hidden in there. Great call-and-response lead vocal from Gene with the riff during the verses along with some great bass runs. Underlying riff is different between the first and second choruses, which I always thought was a cool arrangement.

TOM GIGLIOTTI *(SHOUT IT OUT LOUDCAST)* – The band is firing on all cylinders here – this song just pummels you right from the start. Gene sounds terrific, and the bridge into the chorus brings that KISS melody even to something this heavy. Tommy shines here with an awesome solo. A relentless deep track that proves KISS can still kick ass even in their later years.

FREAK

ZEUS *(SHOUT IT OUT LOUDCAST)* – The song was originally meant to go to Lady Gaga or a duet with her. The chorus has that typical Paul hook and awesome chorus. Is this autobiographical? Who knows, but it's a catchy tune.

BILL STARKEY *(FOUNDER, KISS ARMY)* – Many times KISS tried to produce a rallying theme ("We Are One"). But this was one of the better songs done with the current members in my opinion. It really sums up being a KISS fan. "Let them laugh 'cause I don't care / It's my cross I'm proud to bear." Most of all I can identify with the line, "I'm doin' fine – they're doin' time."

CHRIS JERICHO *(WRESTLER, FOZZY)* – Paul talking about himself and "I'm a Freak" because he considered himself to be a freak when he was a kid with the ear issue and all that.

JEFF TROTT *(ART DIRECTOR)* – Despite the criticism it sometimes faces, Paul's "Freak" is a standout on *Monster*. Its modern vibe and compelling lyrics defy boundaries, showcasing Paul's enduring challenges. If only it were given the mainstream spotlight it deserves, it could easily climb the charts in the hands of contemporary pop artists. If Katy Perry or Pink performed this song it would be a number-one hit.

RAISE YOUR GLASSES:
A Celebration of 50 Years of KISS Songs
by Celebrities, Musicians & Fans.

Tom and Zeus on KISS Kruise XI, October 29, 2022

JOEY CASSATA *(ZO2, ZROCK)* – This is a pretty decent song with a cool verse and chorus, but the pre-choruses ruin it for me. I had an old producer always tell us never use "fire" and "desire" as a lyric. It's like songwriting 101.

BACK TO THE STONE AGE

MARTIN POPOFF *(AUTHOR)* – I love the raucous garage-y nature of this one, driven hard by Eric Singer's wall of sound and *Monster*'s inspired production values. The lyric here is a little like AC/DC's "Let There Be Rock", and Gene's vocal is a little further up his usual range. Still, it's a spirited Detroit-style rocker, with a deep-dish groove and hooky transitions and parts.

ZEUS *(SHOUT IT OUT LOUDCAST)* – One of Gene's best songs from the last two KISS albums (and yes, I know that's not saying much). This is a fun song and there is nothing better than waiting for that part of the song after Tommy's excellent solo at the 2:32 mark when the music stops and Gene goes, "I like it." His scream at the 2:42 mark is amazing as well.

MIKE BRUNN *(THE ROCK EXPERIENCE)* – I won't apologize, I love *Monster* and I love this song. Gene's "Yeahhhh" scream before the final chorus raises the hairs on my arms every time I hear it. For me, this is Gene's best hard-rock song since "Unholy". Also, fun fact: this song is one of three in the entire catalog that has songwriting credits from every band member at the time.

ALEXANDER TALKINGTON *(KISS ARMY THINGS PODCAST)* – Who doesn't love old-school?? Old-school movies, music, wrestling. "I'm going back where I belong!" I love the animalistic caveman theme – the various lyrics talking about howling at the moon, praying to the sun, climbing mountains and crossing seas, finally sitting on the throne as the king... talk about a poetic summary of KISS's career.

TOM GIGLIOTTI *(SHOUT IT OUT LOUDCAST)* – This is the Gene we love. Right off the bat, we get a classic Demon wail before taking us on a trip through time. Another great bridge into an infectious gang vocal chorus that no KISS fan can deny. Tommy comes in with one of his tasty solos as Eric crushes it on the drums. KISS is doing their thing here, and I'm loving all of it. Or as Gene would say here "I LIKE IT!"

SHOUT MERCY

CHRIS L. *(POD OF THUNDER)* – *Monster* is very hit-or-miss for me (more miss than hit overall), but this song delivers. Musically, the chemistry of the Stanley-Simmons-Thayer-Singer lineup is at peak potency, and it's impossible for me to find any fault with a "hit it and quit it" story from Paul.

CHRIS CZYNSZAK *(DECIBEL GEEK PODCAST)* – I think the whole *Monster* album is a love letter to the band's early influences. "Shout Mercy" is a prime example of that. You can clearly tell that this song is a nod to Humble Pie's "I Don't Need No Doctor." Steve Marriott's influence on Paul Stanley is crystal clear, and this song is great.

MITCH LAFON *(ROCK JOURNALIST)* – This proved without a doubt that KISS could still bring pomp and circumstance. It's a fun rocker with silly lyrics that'll get your feet stomping and your fists pumping. Layer in some keyboards and the song slides seamlessly onto *Crazy Nights*. Definitely a top 40 single in 1987!

STEVE WRIGHT *(PODDER THAN HELL PODCAST)* – This track caught me instantly as a stand-out on the album. Bam, bam, bam, then a great Eric Singer drum fill launches us right into it with a great groove. Paul's vocals are right in the pocket, and who doesn't like some "Whoo hoos" with their rock 'n' roll? And we also get some Gene "Oh Yeah!s" for a bonus. Melodic start to Tommy's solo that ramps up to a shred that fits right in there. And the transition from solo back to the chorus is seamless. Great deep track.

WES BEECH *(THE PLASMATICS)* – This is what I shout after sitting through this song and album! Paul's voice is strained and almost hard to listen to on this one. Too bad, but years of screams and vocal abuse came to a head, and it shows here. Not a bad song, and I like Gene's "Oh Yeahs" thrown in. Good guitar playing, but once again the solo is marred by being too Ace-centric. Would have been nice to hear Tommy just let loose and RIP on this, but maybe all those years of doing Ace licks have got to him. All in all, one of the better songs on the album.

TOM HIGGINS *(KLASSIK '78)* – This has some classic Paul things that I always hope for. This is clearly influenced by Humble Pie's "I Don't Need No Doctor", and in the best way. I love this one. Eric has a nice swing on this song (unlike other songs on this album that desperately needed drums with some swing and swagger, but didn't get that – notably "Freak" and "All For the Love of Rock & Roll"). Some don't like the falsetto "hoo hoo" vocal bits during the verses, but I think it's classic KISS stuff. From the first KISS album onward, they used those falsetto backing vocal bits in many songs: "Firehouse", "Nothin' to Lose", "Deuce", "Got To Choose", "Black Diamond" etc. This is old school.

LONG WAY DOWN

TOMMY SOMMERS *(THREE SIDES OF THE COIN)* – This song shows you that Paul Stanley can still write an incredible rock 'n' roll song. This album seemed to be dismissed by some fans, but the ones who actually took time to listen to it seemed to really like it for a variety of the songs that are available on this. This one sticks out to me as the best track on the record. Another song I wish they would have played live.

BRANDON FIELDS *(MINEFIELD)* – This is easily my favorite track off *Monster*. This album is very underrated to me. Paul delivers a great vocal, and the verse has a great melody. Overall it's a very well-written song, especially with the punches at the end of the chorus. I'm a huge sucker for cowbell and Eric plays it the perfect amount in the chorus without overdoing it. As great as Paul is on this song, Eric and Tommy really shine; this might be my favorite combined effort of the two on the albums they played on.

STEVE WRIGHT *(PODDER THAN HELL PODCAST)* – The opening riff gives the feeling of falling down. There's a loose feel to this song, which has a different vibe to it. I like Paul's rough vocals here, and the vocal lines that are layered work. Eric's drumming with the cowbell during the bridge adds a cool element to the track. Tommy's lead fills are great. Solid deep track, another great listen. It's a shame that most of these post-reunion songs never made it to the stage.

CLAUDIO SPERA *(KISS ARMY NATION PODCAST)* – When this song was released as a single, I couldn't believe that KISS were still able to pull out something as strong and powerful. This song has an undeniable Zeppelin vibe. Eric's drumming is a true highlight. Inserting a cowbell right into the middle of the chorus is genius. The song pushes the listener to the limit, no time to breathe, just pure high-power hard rock with heavy guitars and great vocals.

ALEXANDER TALKINGTON *(KISS ARMY THINGS PODCAST)* – This is lyrically one of Paul's strongest songs. I don't think most fans have actually looked into it, even after more than a decade. "And I know this life makes fools of wise men, thieves, and kings / When we lose, we live our lives like puppets on a string." Paul's warning us—what goes around comes around. Life has a way of catching up with everyone... and it's a long way down when you fall from the top.

EAT YOUR HEART OUT

SONNY POONI *(PODCAST ROCK CITY)* – The KISS Army didn't exactly love this song when they first heard it. I actually really like the *a capella* start... and yeah, yeah, Gene used the "backbone slip" lyric again, but so what? It's a fun song and the guitar solo is great because it felt like Tommy was finally allowed to be more of himself when doing the solos.

WES BEECH *(THE PLASMATICS)* – It's too bad that *Monster* is the final KISS recording; to my ears it just tries too hard to capture the classic KISS sound of the '70s. The song itself is not bad, good snappy riff and solid bass and drums, but Gene's banal lyrics drag it down and he once again lets his "backbone slip". It's a wonder he can still walk! Tommy trots out every Ace Frehley lick he can muster, just adding to the retro sound of this track. At least Bruce would play original solos and be creative in his solos; I would have much preferred Tommy did the same. It's blatantly obvious that KISS has run out of original ideas. They are just going through the motions with this song and the rest of the album as well.

COURTNEY CRONIN DOLD *(COMEDIAN)* – Ooooh those harmonies at the top are juicy! And that guitar is flambé all day. Here goes Gene taking another common expression and removing its true meaning to be about the sexy sex he loves so much. Tommy is the star of this song. That's right, you Thayer naysayer. Eat your heart out.

ALEXANDER TALKINGTON *(KISS ARMY THINGS PODCAST)* – I gotta admit, hearing this *a capella* intro nearly brought a tear of joy to my eye the first time I heard it. I was not expecting to hear such a candid moment captured on the new (and last) KISS album, with the band doing vocal warm-ups and a countdown. I've always loved the rawness of this record. Speaking of which, Tommy delivers one of the nastiest solos in all of KISStory! It's unrelenting, ferocious... and unrelenting. We get another round of blistering licks after the final chorus that makes me wish this track didn't end!

TOM GIGLIOTTI *(SHOUT IT OUT LOUDCAST)* – Do we need the *a capella* at the intro? Probably not, but who cares, it's KISS and I love it! Gene is back to being his sleazy, slippery Demon here, and the groove of this one reminds me of some classic '70s KISS. And I'm always a sucker for a catchy gang chorus. The backing vocals after each line in the second verse are so cool and just add to the fun of this one. Songs like this remind me why I love KISS. Because a hot mess is just what I need!

THE DEVIL IS ME

JOEY CASSATA *(ZO2, Z ROCK)* – It's no secret that I don't really think *Monster* is a strong album, but this song is a good song. This sounds like old-school Gene to me. *Monster* is also the only album that really captures Gene's live bass tone. I remember the first time I was onstage with Gene during KISS's soundcheck; I couldn't believe the monstrous tone (pun intended) that he got. I realized later that night during the show that Gene's live bass tone was a big factor in that "KISS sound". Blended in with the guitars and drums it created that old-school KISS vibe that they achieved live.

ZO2 with KISS on the *Rock The Nation* tour, 2004

RAISE YOUR GLASSES:
A Celebration of 50 Years of KISS Songs by Celebrities, Musicians & Fans.

JOEY SASSO *(THE CIRCLE, NETFLIX)* – Alright, buckle up, KISS Army, 'cause we're diving deep into the demonic depths of "The Devil is Me". This track, penned by Mr. Gene Simmons, is a fiery burst of classic KISS energy that not only pays homage to Gene's iconic Demon persona, but also stands as a testament to Gene's love of his alter ego. The best lyric that encapsulates the essence of this powerhouse track has to be "I'm alive! I'm alive! I'm alive!" This repeated mantra captures the raw, unapologetic energy that Gene Simmons embodies as the Demon, reminding us of his larger-than-life presence within the band's mythology. Factually speaking, while *Monster* received mixed reviews from critics and fans alike, "The Devil is Me" emerged as a standout track that garnered praise for its throwback sound and Gene's commanding vocals.

ALEXANDER TALKINGTON *(KISS ARMY THINGS PODCAST)* – This is the kind of song that was missing from *Sonic Boom*. "I'm An Animal" was good, but this is GREAT. I believe these were mostly Paul's lyrics with Gene's title. Every member brings their A-game on this one; from Eric's quick fills and cymbal catches to Tommy's hell-fueled guitar solo.

COURTNEY CRONIN DOLD *(COMEDIAN)* – The bass is simply sinful, and the drums beat louder and harder than Satan's own black heart. Gene does his best on the Lucifer-loving lyrics, and I think Paul faked a cold that day so he didn't have to do too much on this one. Evil!

JEFF TROTT *(ART DIRECTOR)* – "The Devil is Me" is a Gene-led vocal track that delivers hard-hitting pure rock lyrics and impressive playing. Co-written by Gene, Paul and Tommy, it's one of Gene's strongest songs on the album. Despite *Monster* not being another *Destroyer*, "The Devil is Me" is a standout track. I particularly love Gene's scream of "The Devil Is Meeeeee" after the breakdown and his soft-spoken, sexy voice closing out the track—a classic Gene moment.

OUTTA THIS WORLD

MARK CICCHINI *(THREE SIDES OF THE COIN)* – Just a gem of a tune! A fun sing-along chorus on top of a not-so-subtle "Mississippi Queen" (Mountain)-influenced riff. Tommy as a lead vocalist shines, and his classic rock '70s-era solo break on this song is a total joy to listen to. You can envision the guys smiling around the vocal mic in the studio while recording the chorus! Love the phaser effect on the end chorus too. *Monster* is a great LP start to finish and this song is proof of that!

STEVE WRIGHT *(PODDER THAN HELL PODCAST)* – Varoom! This song gets moving right from the start. Excellent groove with the "Hair of the Dog"-like riff in the verses. Great call and response for the pre-chorus and chorus. And how can you not love the cowbell? Fantastic bridge leading into the solo. This solo really takes off for the second part when the main riff comes back in underneath. Tommy's vocals are strong, and you can feel the excitement in his voice for his lead vocal. For me the song really is "Outta this World"!

JEFF TROTT *(ART DIRECTOR)* – "Outta This World" stands out as one of *Monster*'s strongest tracks, propelled by Tommy Thayer's electrifying performance. It's a shame these tracks didn't get played live to represent his era. Tommy has two very solid tracks on both *Monster* and his *Sonic Boom* contribution, "When Lightning Strikes."

TONY MUSALLAM *(RESTRAYNED)* – Even though Ace was no longer in the band, KISS maintained the Spaceman themes when writing songs for Tommy Thayer. They kept it simple with this one. The verse is a fairly basic start/stop riff accented by Eric's constant cowbell hits, à la Mountain's "Mississippi Queen". The chorus is a catchy call-and-response that will keep you humming it all day long. However, I believe this would have been an even stronger song without the repetitive last 45 seconds. This is definitely one of the stronger tracks from *Monster*.

ZEUS *(SHOUT IT OUT LOUDCAST)* – Tommy Thayer is so underappreciated. The stability and professionalism he brought to KISS can never be overstated. This catchy, fun song also shows what he brings musically. The man can write a good song, sing it well and play great guitar. I wish we got to hear more Tommy tracks on KISS records. This song should have been played live along with "When Lightning Strikes".

ALL FOR THE LOVE OF ROCK & ROLL

JOE McGINNESS *(KUARANTINE, KLASSIC '78)* – This song is my favorite from the *Monster* album. The guitar riff is reminiscent of "Mr. Speed", which I love. Eric nailed the vocals. I feel like I would listen to this song even more if the album was mixed and mastered better.

RAISE YOUR GLASSES:
A Celebration of 50 Years of KISS Songs
by Celebrities, Musicians & Fans.

MIKE BRUNN *(THE ROCK EXPERIENCE)* – Written by Paul, sung by Eric Singer, this song has a throwback feel to the *Rock and Roll Over* album (*Mr. Speed* specifically). I love Eric's vocal on this, and the song is extremely catchy to me. Yes, I know that lyrically it's similar to Tuff Dart's song of the same name. Regardless, it's one of my "50 favorite" KISS songs.

PASQUALE VARI *(KISS ARMY NATION PODCAST)* – What a GREAT song sung by Eric Singer. A perfect song for him. It's a sin it was never played live except for an appearance on the KISS Kruise. This song elevated the *Monster* album for me. By far my favorite on the album.

WES BEECH *(THE PLASMATICS)* – Did I say *Carnival of Souls* was my least favorite KISS album? *Monster* may actually be the one, and this tune doesn't help matters. A mid-tempo song that just moves along, not really going anywhere. And while Eric delivers a surprisingly good vocal performance, one has to wonder why they didn't bring Peter in to do a guest vocal. That would have really elevated the song as it's right in Peter's wheelhouse. Oh well, us KISStards can dream, can't we? As a punk rocker from way back, this title was lifted from the band Tuff Darts, whose song, in my opinion, was much better.

COURTNEY CRONIN DOLD *(COMEDIAN)* – Finally, some Eric Singer lead vocals. Man is his voice sexy. This song is like *Rocky Horror Picture Show* meets classic KISS with a splash of Mc-Pop. Fitting that the last KISS studio album has another song about rock 'n' roll! It's like they're telling us, "God gave it to you, Peter got you hooked on it, now you do it all nite, and in hell. Now roll over and let me go."

KENNY BEGLEY *(KISS LIVE AUCTIONS)* – As a friend of Eric's, this song to me is him in a nutshell. He don't care about the fame and just loves to play, one of the most down-to-earth and giving people you will ever meet. He really does have a great voice, and I always wished they recorded more music together with him and Tommy in the mix. *Monster* and *Sonic Boom* are very underrated in my opinion.

TAKE ME DOWN BELOW

STEVE WRIGHT *(PODDER THAN HELL PODCAST)* – Yes! A Gene and Paul co-vocal. I have always been a huge fan of when Gene and Paul trade vocals, and this is no exception. This song has a stomp from the start, and Gene's sleazy vocal delivery; then you get the "Oh Yeah". Excellent chorus. Paul gets the second verse. I really like the "Come here baby". "I raised my flag and she dropped her dress"! Come on, how can you not love that line. This is a fun KISS song! Great build into the solo. Tommy really pulls off a ripping one. Many people rip on *Monster*, but I think it's a really fun KISS album and if it's the last one… I'm good with that! Fun KISS!

TOM GIGLIOTTI *(SHOUT IT OUT LOUDCAST)* – This song brings us back to when KISS was fun! The double entendres, the sexual innuendos and the amazing vocal trade-offs between Gene and Paul. Match that up with an awesome hooky sing-along chorus and you have arguably my favorite "new" KISS song and the standout track on *Monster*.

RAISE YOUR GLASSES:
A Celebration of 50 Years of KISS Songs by Celebrities, Musicians & Fans.

Tom and Zeus with Eric Singer

CHRIS JERICHO *(WRESTLER, FOZZY)* – This song is probably one of my favorites on the record because it was cool to have the interplay between Paul and Gene. Which is obviously something they did a lot of in the '70s and they barely did at all in the non-makeup era. I think the last time they maybe had that interplay was on "Spit". I liked that because once again, it's an element of KISS with them trading off verses. The lyrics are like "Take Me" type of fun because of this point, you have guys in their mid-60s writing juvenile Spinal Tap, Steel Panther type of lyrics. It's just pure cheese.

RAISE YOUR GLASSES:
A Celebration of 50 Years of KISS Songs
by Celebrities, Musicians & Fans.

TONY MUSALLAM *(RESTRAYNED)* – The lyrics of "Take Me Down Below" are some of the cheesiest, overly sexual words KISS have ever put to song. And you know what? It works. This is the fun, tongue-in-cheek, innuendo-filled type of song that KISS was all about in the mid-'70s.

JOEY SASSO *(THE CIRCLE, NETFLIX)* – I adore how KISS pushed the boundaries of brotherhood in "Stand", and now, on their latest album, they have come up with an absolute masterpiece in the form of their mandatory song, which screams nothing but pure cock rock! Some people have been critical of Gene and Paul's age while making this song, but honestly, that's just plain ridiculous. This song is, hands down, the best track on *Monster*, and it blows "Hell or Hallelujah" out of the water. I love how this song is sure to ruffle some feathers and make certain portions of fans go completely berserk. It's time to stop caring about age and live life on our terms, just like KISS always sang. Go ahead and take your Viagra boys, and rock on!

JASON BAKKEN *(COBRAS & FIRE PODCAST)* – Gene and Paul should have done more songs where they split lead vocals. They should have also not done this song. 60-year-old men writing songs with lyrics like: "She took my finger, here's a button to press / I raised my thang and she dropped her dress / I'll take you on a cruise you'll never forget / She said, we better move 'cause I'm already wet" is pretty cringy. Part of the issue with KISS's last two records is they tried to pretend we haven't noticed they got older. But we're talking about guys who felt their current faces were best for the avatars.

LAST CHANCE

JOEY SASSO (*THE CIRCLE, NETFLIX*) – What we have here is yet another track that might not always get its due, but trust me, it's a solid little rocker that deserves to be dusted off and cranked up on full blast. Remember my favorite lyric from the song I told you about above? That line embodies the urgency and determination that pulsates throughout the song, showcasing KISS in their full rocking glory. They are totally reveling in the moment. It's not perfect, but when it works you can really feel it. "Last Chance" often flies under the radar for many fans, overshadowed by more popular tracks on the album. That makes sense seeing as this song was never designed to be the one that goes for broke, which for me, adds to the track's cool factor by the fact that it feels very chill. However, those who give it a listen often find themselves pleasantly surprised by its infectious energy and classic KISS (Paul) charm.

ROBERT CONTE (*AUTHOR*) – Well, this title certainly sums it up, doesn't it? Did Paul, Gene, Eric, and Tommy actually "get it right" by ending the final, all-new KISS album with this song? I believe so; it's reminiscent of the band's early raw energy and would have been awesome to hear it performed live. It's Klassic KISS in principle, and a powerful coda to close out the 260 songs that make up the group's official music catalog. As a 40+-year soldier in the KISS Army, I only wish this weren't the end!

JEFF TROTT (*ART DIRECTOR*) – The grinding bass at the beginning sets the tone—freaking kick-ass. KISS always keeps you on your toes, whether dancing on the edge of a knife or even climbing barbed wire. The breakdown in this song is killer, and Tommy's solo is stellar. As *Monster* was being tracked, Paul's voice was starting to show some wear, making me wish they had recorded this song years earlier. For me, this will always be the last studio track KISS performed—none of that K-pop bullshit or "Don't Touch My Ascot". This is the true final album track recording by KISS, in my book. I know there is a bonus track, KISS police – I'm speaking about the US album tracks.

ALEXANDER TALKINGTON *(KISS ARMY THINGS PODCAST)* –
If this is the last track on KISS's last standard studio album, then I say job well done! Opening the track is a driving bass line from Gene, followed by slamming drums by Eric. Paul's lyrics and vocals are dangerous, rebellious and cut-throat. Tommy's wailing solo and the following breakdown contrast each other nicely to set up one final round of rallying! One of my favorite lyrics is, "You heard you'll be sorry, but you know that they lied."

ZEUS *(SHOUT IT OUT LOUDCAST)* – This song will always have an impact on me and I'm sure a lot of the KISS Army. "Last Chance" is the last song on the last KISS studio album. A pretty solid rock song. It's just a shame, because this proves KISS still had the capability of doing more music. Musically the band can still kill it, and man does Tommy kill it on this song, especially the solo. But as Paul sang on this track, "'Cause nobody here gets out alive!"

RAISE YOUR GLASSES:
A Celebration of 50 Years of KISS Songs by Celebrities, Musicians & Fans.

Zeus, Tom and Murph at the final KISS show,
Madison Square Garden, December 2, 2023

About the Authors

Tom Gigliotti

Tom is the co-host of the #1-ranked KISS podcast, Shout It Out Loudcast. He has spent over 25 years in law enforcement and is an avid Boston sports fan, especially his beloved New England Patriots. He enjoys collecting and listening to his ever-growing vinyl collection and watching horror movies. In his spare time, you will also find him playing with his mini-goldendoodle, Scout, and spending time with his son, Michael. The Gigliotti family lives in southern New Hampshire.

George N. Piandes (Zeus)

Zeus is a bankruptcy and real estate attorney and the co-host of the #1-ranked KISS podcast, Shout It Out Loudcast. He enjoys traveling to Greece for the summers, and coaches high-school hockey in the winters. He is an avid Boston sports fan and has been a season ticket holder for his beloved Boston Bruins since 2001. He lives in the MetroWest area of Boston with his daughter.

Joey Cassata

Joey is a drummer, actor, writer and producer. After touring the country with his band ZO2 with such acts as KISS, Poison, Alice Cooper and Twisted Sister, Joey starred in, co-wrote and co-produced the hit IFC comedy series *Z Rock*. The cast and guest stars included Gilbert Gottfried, Dee Snider, Dave Navarro, Chris Jericho, and many more. *Z Rock* became the #1-rated show in IFC history.

After *Z Rock*, Joey performed almost 600 shows with the *New York Times* critically acclaimed Broadway musical *Natasha, Pierre & The Great Comet of 1812*, starring Grammy award-winner, Josh Groban. After the release of his Amazon #1 bestselling autobiography, *Start With A Dream: A Drummer's Journey from Rock & Roll to T.V. to Broadway*, Joey then started his own production company, Satta Entertainment, and has begun writing, producing and developing several new TV projects. These include *Wrestling With Joeylicious*, starring wrestling legends Mick Foley, Jake "the Snake" Roberts, The Iron Sheik and many more. Most recently, Joey was the primary drummer on the 2024 Ace Frehley album, *10,000 Volts*.

INDEX OF CONTRIBUTORS

Made in the USA
Middletown, DE
30 August 2024

60020102R00338